SHAKESPEARE AND LOSS

SHAKESPEARE AND LOSS

THE LATE, GREAT TRAGEDIES

Sarah Beckwith

CORNELL UNIVERSITY PRESS
Ithaca and London

Copyright © 2025 by Sarah Beckwith

All rights reserved. Except for brief quotations in a review, this book, or parts thereof, must not be reproduced in any form without permission in writing from the publisher. For information, address Cornell University Press, Sage House, 512 East State Street, Ithaca, New York 14850. Visit our website at cornellpress.cornell.edu.

First published 2025 by Cornell University Press

Library of Congress Cataloging-in-Publication Data

Names: Beckwith, Sarah, 1959– author.
Title: Shakespeare and loss : the late, great tragedies / Sarah Beckwith.
Description: Ithaca [New York] : Cornell University Press, 2025. | Includes bibliographical references and index.
Identifiers: LCCN 2025009251 (print) | LCCN 2025009252 (ebook) | ISBN 9781501784484 (hardcover) | ISBN 9781501784491 (paperback) | ISBN 9781501784507 (pdf) | ISBN 9781501784514 (epub)
Subjects: LCSH: Shakespeare, William, 1564-1616– Tragedies. | Loss (Psychology) in literature.
Classification: LCC PR2983 .B43 2025 (print) | LCC PR2983 (ebook) | DDC 822.3/3—dc23/eng /20250614
LC record available at https://lccn.loc.gov/2025009251
LC ebook record available at https://lccn.loc.gov /2025009252

For Daniel Miller

Friend, blacksmith, sculptor, and reader extraordinaire

And for all the men in my life, the ones who cry and the ones who don't

Nothing is more important than the formation of fictional concepts which teach us at last to understand our own.

—Ludwig Wittgenstein, *Culture and Value*

The fate of having a self—of being human—is one in which the self is always to be found, fated to be sought, or not; recognized or not . . . this is a continuous *activity*, not something we may think of as an intellectual preoccupation. It is *placing* ourselves in the world. That you do not know beforehand what you will find is the reason the quest is an experiment or exploration.

—Stanley Cavell, *Senses of Walden*

Contents

Preface   ix

Introduction: The Art of Our
Necessities   1

1. Coming to Grief in *Hamlet*:
Trust and Testimony in Elsinore   14

2. *King Lear* and the Avoidance of Charity:
The Spirit of Truth in Love   44

3. Benefits and Bonds: Misanthropy
and Skepticism in *Timon of Athens*   69

4. Losing the Name of Action: *Macbeth*,
Remorse and Moral Agency   97

5. *Coriolanus*: Shakespeare's
Private Linguist   120

6. *Antony and Cleopatra*: Shakespeare's
Critique of Judgment   148

Notes   177
Bibliography   233
Index   251

Preface

      The image on the cover of this book is taken from a book of photographs of tears, taken through an optical microscope. The artist, Rose-Lynn Fisher, titled the tear in the cover photograph "Grief and Gratitude." She was inspired to take it when she heard of the death of a friend who had helped her in a time of pain and trouble earlier in her life. She had recently been in touch with this kind man after a distance of years.

 Each tear in Rose-Lynn Fisher's amazing book of photographs, *The Topography of Tears*, is unique.[1] Some of them are crystalline like snowflakes, some are like bits of ice lost from an iceberg, some like the rails viewed from a station platform, telegraph wires, or palm trees. They seem at once natural and artificial. There are tears of nervous exhaustion, of overwhelming, of hope and possibility, and joy; there are brief tears and the long tears of the unconsoled. One is called "Last tear I ever cry for you." Fisher's up-close tears are a map of the naturalness of responses to life's troubles, a memory and a marking of each occasion which called them forth.

 In the tragedies I write about in this book, men try—with desperation, with unnatural discipline, with a telling effort of suppression—not to cry. Sometimes they call their tears "sweat" as if they are labor. Sometimes they say they would rather break into a thousand pieces than weep. Yet tragedies elicit our tears and depend on the naturalness of pity as a form of acknowledgment of the pain of others.

 I titled this book *Shakespeare and Loss*. Over the long course of writing it, a kind of companion to *Shakespeare and the Grammar of Forgiveness*, I experienced myriad losses (of the kind all flesh is heir to). I lost a dear friend, Liz Clarke; I lost my father and he, a few years before his death, lost his capacity for speech; I lost my stepmother and stepfather; and I lost my mother-in-law. And I lost all the fellow nonhuman creatures with whom I had shared a house. I learned what Elizabeth Bishop called the art of losing, which is—though inevitable—(write it!) hard to master.

PREFACE

Grief is a response to the loss of loved ones, but other forms of loss are also important in this book. You can lose your glasses or your watch, but you can also lose your way, or your sense of personhood and self. You can clearly lose your senses, as when we might exclaim in frustration, horror, or dismay: Have you completely lost your senses? So the losses involved here are not the kinds of losses that can be restored by a stable ritual or nostalgic retrieval. I lose *my* way not yours. The losses involved in this book, as I indicate in my introduction, are losses of such things as we cannot help but know.

This book has taken me a long time to write. It was a difficult book to write. The arduousness was not the result of tricky and detailed research—that usually generates its own pleasures and satisfactions. Nor was it solely the result of life's rude interruptions, or that familiar and self-interrupting fear of having nothing to say about works that so many great writers and critics have addressed so lucidly and well. The hardness was in staying true to my responses to these devastating plays, to my reading and watching experiences, and to my growth (such as it is) in the conceptual reach of love, gratitude, and grief, as well as in the concepts of doing and acting, of giving and receiving, and of judging, that are explored in these plays. I had to think about my responses to the plays' invitations and solicitations and how to articulate them, the role of these particular words in my life with them, in short, how I loved, grieved, or encountered or evaded my responsibilities in speaking. That is what was hard.

We are notoriously living in a time when political actors and technological innovations are creating a world in which it is hard to distinguish between the fake and the real. This is not possible without an abuse of language. Shakespeare's tragedies of exile depend on the idea that their central protagonists do not mean what they say because they do not know what they are saying, or because they are blinding themselves to the implications of what they are saying (Macbeth) or refusing the commitments and cares and specificities of language in staking out positions in relation to each other (Timon). This linguistic exile is a central idea in this book. Often through a tyrannous use of language such men might fantasize that it emerges from them unilaterally as if they were authors of themselves and that public language is merely an extension of their private wills. This is always tragic because in so doing they are losing their grip on reality, which happens because they cannot mean what they say, and so they become unintelligible to themselves and others. A loss of reality happens when we become unintelligible to each other, when we cannot find our feet with each other, as Ludwig Wittgenstein says.

Sandra Laugier has brilliantly pointed out that J. L. Austin and Stanley Cavell's Austin understood that truth is not merely empirically understood as a correct or incorrect *reference*, but rather it is extended across almost every dimension of language to accommodate what is fitting, what is appropriate, and what is the right thing to say and do. This is why finding just the right words can open up a way of understanding ourselves and others. But of course we have to consent to become intelligible to others because the necessity involved in meaning what we say is a condition of intelligibility. Each of these tragedies enacts a refusal of publicness; each of them then shows us how we might recover language and the real with it.

Why do I talk of recovering the real as if it had been lost? As Austin and Wittgenstein show, the relation of language and the world is far more intimate than can be described by the word "between," as in the relationship *between* language and the world. We precisely lose the world when we use language not simply falsely, but ineptly, imprecisely, inadequately, hastily, or inappropriately. If we call someone mad when they are in fact sad, for example, then only a recognition of sadness will bring the world and the person back into focus. Falseness does not exist merely in lies but also in the sheer complexity of a situation that may be hard to discern and that does not always come into focus. When we get the right words, the *mot juste*, we feel that the world is lit up for us, so we are grateful to writers who can find the fitting words to light up our world and let its myriad aspects dawn on us. A political regime is always sick and corrupt when it corrupts language. Tragedy is often about the terrible dawning of reality on someone who had missed it and missed something in themselves. That is why failure and inadequacy are central to both Austin's and Wittgenstein's understanding of language as Cavell so memorably brought out. Shakespearean tragedy brings back life and language into a "reciprocal interiority" as Cavell defines it in *The Pursuits of Happiness*.

At the moment, we are living in a time of increasing authoritarianism in which truth is bent to accommodate the so-called strong men or is buried in a welter of misinformation, and at a time when humanistic study is under attack from without and from within. Now more than ever we need a raid on the inarticulate of Shakespeare's kind and the frameworks in which to value it.

Cavell is the great philosopher of Shakespearean tragedy. But this means not the application of his philosophy to tragedy. Rather Shakespearean tragedy allowed him to reconceptualize his understanding of skepticism. Cavell has redefined skepticism as an intellectualization, a conversion of the task of living with others into a solvable (or unsolvable) problem, and this redefinition is far-reaching and radical. His influence is all-pervasive in this book. This does not mean that his readings of these plays save me the trouble of making my own. There are several excellent accounts of Cavell's readings of Shakespeare's plays, and this does not repeat that labor. Rather Cavell's way of doing philosophy has provoked and inspired me into this act of criticism and essay in ethics.

This book is in my voice, but as I say in this book, my voice is mine as a responsibility and task not a possession. I have been in dialogue and collaboration with others all along the way, sometimes realizing only later how formative those voices were in mine.

This book has taken some time to write and I would like to thank the chairs of my department at Duke University, Len Tennenhouse, Rob Mitchell, and Charlotte Sussman, and to the deans of humanities, Gennifer Weisenfeld and Richard Powell, and latterly to William A. Johnson for allowing me to be relieved from teaching responsibilities at crucial times of this book's conception and completion (2012–2013, 2018–2019, and 2023). I also thank most profoundly the National Humanities Center for again allowing me the fantastic opportunity to initiate this book: I was the holder of the M. Abrams Fellowship in 2012–2013 and what a wonderful time to be there. The 2012–2013 fellows were an exceptionally fun crowd. My colleagues Keren Gorodeisky and Arata Hamawaki were most stimulating companions, and I enjoyed rich conversations with them that have definitely found their way into the book. Gillam and Brad and Sis made it possible for me to take some time at Nag's Head while I was completing my chapter on *King Lear*, and my progress was enabled by a powerful nor'easter that made the beach impassable! How lucky am I in such friends. The Hacienda crowd—you know who you are–brought laughter and joy at crucial moments, and to the clan of Miller (and Lloyd/Parrish) in and out of Appalachia, THANK YOU.

My colleagues at Duke have been at my side in the beleaguered and ever more crucial work of humanistic studies in and out of the classroom. I particularly wish to thank Tom Ferraro, Thomas Pfau, and Corina Stan, for believing that a life of the mind is a life worth living and for exemplifying it in their life and work. Kathy Psomiades, Charlotte Sussman, and Rob Mitchell, have been incredible colleagues from whose humane patience and practice I have learned much. David Aers has once again been at my side encouraging my progress and has been the most loyal, generous, and attentive intellectual companion as I harped on. . . . He has an unerringly judicious ear and matches that with truthful kindness and efficiency. Toril Moi and I have worked together in satisfying and productive ways in our writing, intellectual activities, and programs such as Writing is Thinking, and now, since we began a new graduate course on philosophy and literature, in our teaching. Her own brilliant and inspiring work on the revolution of ordinary language philosophy opens so many exciting pathways for thinking about the task of reading as acknowledgment and for the exercise of judgment in literary studies after Ludwig Wittgenstein.

To the actors and directors of the many riveting productions of the late tragedies I have seen over the years—thank you for continuing to take on the risky, compelling work of theater. You understand the dimensions of speech as action so practically, intimately, and integrally. You know about doing things with words as well as gestures.

I have worked out what I think about Shakespeare's plays by teaching them as well as reading and watching them. Jonathan—we thought about tragedy together and you brought the students to their feet. To my undergraduates at Duke, thank you for your great passion and enthusiasm for Shakespeare, and for testing out and exploring so much of the canon with me. Graduate students in various versions of my classes on "Tragedy and Philosophy" came on the journey of these great plays and read *The Claim of Reason* (especially the exhilarating and demanding part 4) with me. To my students in "Commitments of Speech," thank you for testing out J. L. Austin in my company and providing your trenchant and engaging insight along the way.

Then there are the colleagues and friends who created important opportunities to try out this work in progress. Thank you to all my interlocutors and gracious faculty and graduate student hosts at many inspiring occasions over the years: at Johns Hopkins University; Harvard University; University of Virginia; University of Chicago; the Center for Philosophy, Arts, and Literature at Duke University; University of Edinburgh; University of Waterloo (Stratford Campus) and the Stratford Festival Theatre, where I gave the Landy Lecture; University of North Carolina, Asheville; University of Tennessee, Chattanooga; University of Southern Florida; State University of New York, Buffalo; and University of California, Los Angeles. Michael Schoenfeldt and George Hoffman kindly invited me to Ann Arbor to test out my work on *King Lear*. Their comments and the comments of Richard Strier stayed with me for years as I completed the chapter. Paul Kottman invited me to join him to discuss Shakespeare and the Humanities at the Shakespeare Association of America along with David Schalkwyck, and I have enjoyed all of our collaborations and conversations. Julia Lupton's kind invitation to participate in the Clark Lectures at UCLA resulted in an "Acknowledgment." Thanks for the stimulus and for continuing this dialogue.

My husband, Bart Ehrman, has been understanding, kind, and loving. He has always spared the time to hear the ideas in this book taking shape. He understands the cost of living this book and the cost of living in this book. His advice is pragmatic, sane, and attuned to the reader. I am immensely grateful for his companionship and love and steadfastness on this restless writing adventure.

I have dedicated this book to my friend Daniel Miller, whose artistry and conversation are a source of great delight. And to all the men in my life who cry and who don't cry. To accept our tears as gifts is a particularly demanding and sometimes impossible task for generations of men brought up to believe that boys don't cry. The redefinition of our understanding of courage is at the heart of this book.

Over the course of writing this book, I published a group of essays exploring literary studies in the wake of ordinary language philosophy. Occasionally I have repeated sentences or ideas from these essays in this book. Readers can find those essays here: "Reading for Our Lives: A Response to Rita Felski's *The Limits of Critique*," *PMLA* 132, no. 2 (March 2017): 331–36; "Ethics, Truth and Reading," an essay on Toril Moi's *Revolution of the Ordinary*, https://nonsite.org/revolution-of-the-ordinary-literary-studies-after-wittgenstein-austin-and-cavell; "Acknowledgment" in *Entertaining the Idea: Shakespeare, Philosophy and Performance*, ed. Lowell Gallagher, James Kearney, and Julia Lupton (Toronto: University of Toronto Press, 2021); "A Vision of Language for Literary Historians," in *Wittgenstein and Literary Studies*, ed. Robert Chodat and John Gibson (Cambridge: Cambridge University Press, 2022); "Tragic Implication," in *Cavell's "Must We Mean What We Say?"* at 50, ed. Greg Chase, Juliet Floyd, and Sandra Laugier (Cambridge: Cambridge University Press, 2022); "Enter the Child: A Scene of Reading from Stanley Cavell's *The Claim of Reason*," *Philosophy and Literature* 46, no. 2 (2022): 251–62.

I also published "Hamlet's Ethics," in *Shakespeare's Hamlet: Philosophical Perspectives*, ed. Tzachi Zamir (Oxford: Oxford University Press, 2018), but there is little overlap between that essay and the chapter on Hamlet in *Shakespeare and Loss*. I published an early version of the chapter on *Macbeth* in "Losing the Name of Action: Shakespeare, *Macbeth*, and Speech as Action," in *Judgment and Action*, ed. Thomas Pfau and Vivasvan Soni (Evanston, IL: Northwestern University Press, 2017), 95–112. My analysis of *King Lear* appears in abbreviated form in "Tragic Implication." Early versions of both the *King* Lear and the Macbeth chapter have been thoroughly revised, expanded and transformed. All other chapters appear here for the first time.

I gladly owe thanks to Larry Rhu and Mike Schoenfeldt for their immensely thoughtful engagements with this book. Larry led the way with his insightful, delightful book about Cavell and Shakespeare, *Stanley Cavell's American Dream: Shakespeare, Philosophy, and Hollywood Movies* (New York: Fordham University Press, 2006). Above all, it is a deep delight to feel understood, and I thank them for their superbly helpful comments, (nearly) all of which I have carefully attended to. All the flubs, mistakes and errors, alas, are on my head! I also wish to thank Mahinder Kingra for his meticulous and generous reading and excellent shepherding of this manuscript to print, as well as the team at Cornell who helped get my work into production. Maureen O'Driscoll was a tactful and savvy copy editor, Karen Hwa and Debbie Ryan oversaw aspects of the production with admirable courtesy and efficiency. I feel very lucky in the whole team at Cornell University Press. And thank you to Rose-Lynn Fisher for permission to use "Grief and Gratitude" for the cover. I am glad my work led me to yours.

SHAKESPEARE AND LOSS

Introduction

The Art of Our Necessities

> Responsibility remains a task of responsiveness.
>
> —Stanley Cavell

In an interview, Joni Mitchell once said: "I'm a fool for love. I make the same mistake over and over." The interview quickly became philosophical. Asked about her former life with love, she laughingly said of her younger self: "I did not have a concept of love."[1] Many of us might say the same about our younger selves, at least when it comes to romantic love. Joni Mitchell was saying that although she was propelled by strong impulses and intense desires, she did not ask herself whether they counted as love. Perhaps she assumed that all her desires were loves. To see whether they counted as love, she would have had to think about her criteria for love, her history with it, including how her culture counted or discounted it, and her growth or frustration in its impasses and pathways. In thinking about what she counted as love she would have had to have thought about when and why she might use the word *love* and whether *this* counted as an instance of it. She would have had to develop her concept of love in her life with it. Her idea of love—like our own—will (and did) grow and change. Although she knew the word *love* as part of her inheritance, she was saying that she had never considered *her* criteria for loving.[2]

Such an inquiry would be "work on oneself." "Working in philosophy—like work in architecture in many respects—is really more like a working on oneself. On one's own interpretation. On one's way of seeing things," says

Ludwig Wittgenstein.³ This is a perpetual ever renewing education, a more-or-less continuous scrutiny of how we came to learn, say, to love, and what counts as an extension of loving.⁴ Is this what my culture calls love? Does it fit with my understanding? With my experience and imagination, I call out my culture but only when I take the full measure of my inheritances.

I have no more insight than anyone else into Joni Mitchell's love life beyond what she offers us in her gorgeous songs. I invoke her because I find her comment a striking example of how we habitually live with concepts in the forms of life that occasion our need for them and our use of them. Joni Mitchell's words show us that philosophy is pervasively active in our ordinary lives.

Some years ago, I read an article by Cora Diamond that gripped my imagination. It was called "Losing Your Concepts."⁵ In this seminal essay, Diamond describes the manifold ways we can lose touch with even the most basic concepts we think we know or live by. I might say, for example, that if you can defend the practice of bearing arms on a university campus, you have lost the concept of teaching and learning. Or that if you think all learning is vocational training or that teachers are "content providers," you have lost the concept of a university. To take another example, you might reproach me: "Have you lost all sense of responsibility?" or protest "aren't you obliged in this case to do what he asked?" In these instances, we can see the practical problem of what counts in each particular instance as responsibility or obligation. Or consider this. You declare you love me when you do not, and not because you are lying. Lacking self-knowledge or a fitting sense of your actual relation to me, your opacity to yourself has momentarily obscured the concept of love. Perhaps, like Joni Mitchell in her later years, you will look back at your romantic history, and as you realize what love is, a clearer self-understanding might come into view, along with a realization of the way you mistook yourself and others. This is living with concepts, in life's myriad scenes of recognition.

We might already be able to see that the idea of how we count something as something (what we call something, how we use a word) is not a question of selecting notions that fit in with a preconceived idea of the concept in question as if they are decided in advance and fixed independently of us. It is instead a complex question of our cultural inheritances, self-understanding (our ability to place ourselves in the world) and moral vision and imagination.⁶

In this book, I explore the loss of a set of key binding concepts in a group of tragic plays by Shakespeare. These particular losses define the preoccupations and form that these tragedies take and constitute them as a group. I begin with *Hamlet,* but the remaining group of plays I address come after Shakespeare's devastating discoveries of undoing in *King Lear* and include the following tragic plays: *Timon of Athens, Macbeth, Coriolanus,* and *Antony and Cleopatra.* After *Hamlet* (1600-1601) this group of plays dates from roughly 1604-1608.[7] I call them late tragedies to distinguish them from Shakespeare's earlier experimentations in the form (*Titus Andronicus, Romeo and Juliet,* and *Julius Caesar*) and because I believe *Hamlet* marks a decisive break in the trajectory of Shakespearean tragedy. I call these plays tragedies of exile for reasons I will explain.

In this group of plays, I argue that some of the most fundamental forms of understanding that seem to bind human communities become dangerously, lethally obscure. Grieving (*Hamlet*); loving (*King Lear*); giving (*Timon of Athens*); acting and doing (*Macbeth*); speaking and being human (*Coriolanus*); and marrying, conversing, and judging (*Antony and Cleopatra*) all come under scrutiny in this book as I argue they do in Shakespeare's plays. These binding concepts are interconnected and often at work in all the plays I examine, but I focus on each play's concentrated, protracted, and intense scrutiny of one concept, understanding that each is complexly, delicately, and inevitably interwoven with the others.[8]

In these late great tragedies of Shakespeare, the binding concepts in our lives come to be seen as precious, and as vital through the realization of their loss. "I cannot but remember such things were / That were most precious to me," as Macduff says in *Macbeth*.[9]

In chapter 1, I show how *Hamlet* explores a culture in which the recognition of grief, a primordial kind of loss, is stifled and distorted. To lose the forms for the expression of loss is to be deprived of a basic grammar of recognition. The play decisively ends as it puts under scrutiny one kind of heroic idiom—revenge tragedy—to explore Hamlet's vital and difficult new task of bearing witness to loss.

King Lear thinks that his language is identical to his will. He does not see that language bears a necessity of its own that is outside his control. He occludes the responses of others, and he imagines that he is the very source of all that can be given ("I gave you all").[10] Until the advent of grace in this play, he will harp on ingratitude. Lear's ceremony of flattery in the first scene of the play is a denial that others exist in his world, and when he banishes love, he banishes truth and his grip on reality, for love, as Iris Murdoch says, is disclosive of reality.[11] Love is honed in the use of words, and Lear learns what it is as a matter of painful biography.

Although *King Lear* explores the language of the social outcast more systematically than any other play, the exile from sense is where the play devastates most utterly, stripping us of all our lendings.

Timon and his wider culture (in Athens and London) have gotten into a tragic muddle about how to give and receive. *Timon of Athens* is a violent response to a radical confusion about gift and debt. Timon's passage from extravagant magnanimity to universal hatred is a path toward the loss of meaningful distinctions. His all-pervasive and exceptionless hatred makes him a skeptic in relation to language. For him now *all* words must fail, must lead to mistrust and scorn. His fully generalized distrust will defend him preemptively from all others and from the risk of any and all relations. To refuse a relationship with *all* humankind is to refuse a relationship with any human being; it is to discount even the possibility of a claim. The sheerly hyperbolic quality of Timon's hatred gets him off the hook of the need to single himself out in response to others, and so from the responsibilities entailed in such responses.

Macbeth stupefies himself to what he knows is the logic of action. His wish is to eradicate thought altogether, to remove the very possibility that the question "Why are you doing that?" could have a conceivable answer. In this self-stupefaction he conceives and disavows his murderous acts. The logic of action is recovered in the play's astonishing exploration of remorse. The obliterated other now comes into partial focus through the terrible, nightmarish realizations of remorse: "My God, What have I done?" in Lady Macbeth's nightwalking.[12]

In the most overtly political play about whose voice counts, Coriolanus tries to shape a world solely out of his assertion by structuring his relations with others on a refusal of the natural exposures of human form, human language, and human feeling. He is, I explain, a type of Wittgenstein's "private linguist," and Wittgenstein's influential fantasies about the figure of the private linguist turns out to be vital to all these tragedies of the excluding and excluded self.[13]

In the final play I examine, *Antony and Cleopatra*, Shakespeare breaks open the sovereign models of lonely masculine preeminence to provide us a new model of relationship, offering profound ways of testing Rome's coming hegemony, modeling the "marriage" between Antony and Cleopatra as a novel social and aesthetic order. In Cleopatra's late insistence that her suicide is a marriage to Antony ("Husband, I come!"), Shakespeare stakes new aesthetic ground.[14] *Antony and Cleopatra*, I argue, is Shakespeare's critique of judgment, anticipating Kant's third critique and the brilliant extension of it in the work of Stanley Cavell and Hannah Arendt.

In this unprecedented and searing run of tragedies written between 1604 and 1608, Shakespeare both begins a new form of tragedy and exhausts its form. Shakespeare's late tragedies feature protagonists who are driven out—or drive themselves out—of the social groups, the families, the friends, and the acquaintances, with whom they had kept company. Castaways from political or polite society, they seek or are banished to the edgelands of civilization, to heaths, wastelands, and enemy camps. Timon grubs for roots away from Athens; Coriolanus seeks out his bitterest enemies in Corioles; Lear rages on a desolate heathland in the company of fools and madmen.

What kinds of exile are these? I argue that the exile of these protagonists is linguistic; they are exiled from sense and intelligibility and the exile shows the loss of vital concepts of human bonding—such as loving, grieving, and giving.

Is it possible to actually lose the concept of loving, grieving, or giving in one's life? Doesn't Diamond's article describe a perfectly common understanding for anyone who works with old materials? Concepts become obsolete as certain forms of life change, develop, or fade—feudalism, for example, or courtly love, the practice of *wergild*, dueling, or private property. New concepts enter the mix—mercantilism, emancipation, revolution, industrialization, republicanism, and so on. Whole branches of intellectual history already have been devoted to that idea—surely no historicist worth her salt would dare to dispute so unexceptional a claim.[15] More intimately, provocatively, and presciently than that, Diamond describes the way in which you or I might at any point lose concepts as seemingly intrinsic to human living as gratitude, care, or grief—and not once and for all but again and again, frequently, minutely. This kind of conceptual loss does not refer only then to the kind of large-scale historical and cultural transformations that historians and literary historians chart. In the kinds of instances I examine, to recover or remember how to grieve, how to care or thank, might require work on oneself as well as a further investigation of the world we thought we knew. It might require a new form of ethical criticism, and a new understanding of the relationship of words to world.

In 1978, G. K. Hunter wrote an important yet overlooked essay, "Shakespeare's Last Tragic Heroes." His local quarry among the Shakespeare critics was a predominant habit of making *King Lear* the lead into the last plays, tracing themes of reconciliation in that play as if they were a direct line to the so-called romances, *Pericles, Cymbeline, The Winter's Tale,* and *The Tempest.* One of the many objections to this trajectory, he argues, is that it treats *Timon, Macbeth, Coriolanus,* and *Antony and Cleopatra* as if they "had sunk without trace from the Shakespearean horizon."[16] The tragedies following *Lear* are all in some senses plays of exile.

I would like to extend, even radicalize, Hunter's understanding of these plays. The protagonists of these plays are homeless not in the sense that they lack shelter. They cannot find their way home because they no longer know what home is, or what it is to be at home. They seek or are driven to find "worlds elsewhere" in terrible acts of repudiation and mad isolation. They are not simply exiled from places but from themselves and sometimes from a home in language—straining at the verge of sense, struggling for intelligibility, not knowing who they are. I will describe the kinds of exile at stake in these plays as linguistic.[17]

It is Wittgenstein's vision of language as understood by Cavell and Diamond that allows us to perceive the nature of this linguistic exile, the state of transcendental homelessness that this group of plays confronts. Diamond and Cavell's understanding of concepts is vitally dependent on their revolutionary readings of Wittgenstein. Cavell's critical reevaluation of the role of criteria in the *Philosophical Investigations* shows how concepts are, as he puts it, "of anything." Cavell begins his analysis of the *Investigations* with the idea that criteria in Wittgenstein are invoked not so much for, say, entrance qualifications or dog competitions, which have specific guidelines and rules set by experts and umpires, but rather for things such as sitting on a chair, having a toothache, reading, thinking, or pointing to something. These are things we are all in a position to know, things that need no expertise. How do we learn pain then? Well, we learn how to talk, says Wittgenstein—suggesting that our learning is not best described as a process of attaching a name to a thing, but rather as an initiation into all the complex modes of life, habits, practices, and ways of doing things that give us a world at all. "You learned the *concept* pain when you learned language" (*PI*, ¶384, Wittgenstein's italics). Wittgensteinian criteria elucidate what things are (*PI*, ¶371 and ¶373) as Wittgensteinian grammar shows us what kind of object anything is. In Cavell's revolutionary understanding of criteria in the *Investigations*, however, criteria can only tell us of the identity of something, not whether it actually exists. They are criteria for things being *so*, but not for their *being* so as Cavell so felicitously puts it.[18] (This is why skepticism is a permanently available possibility, and why criteria are fully open to skepticism). Criteria are disappointing in this respect: They cannot tell us whether that man over there is only feigning pain or actually having it, only that it is pain at issue. Criteria are doubly disappointing because they depend on our voicing them to do the work they actually do, on our counting this as something here and now in this instance, for this occasion.

In language, we make commitments, avowals, and promises to each other, and we enter agreements with each other: "Agreements we do not know and do not want to know we have entered, agreements we were always in, that were in effect before our participation in them. Our relation to our language—to the fact that we are subject to expression and comprehension, victims of meaning—is accordingly the key to our sense of our distance from our lives, of our sense of the alien, of ourselves as alien to ourselves, thus alienated."[19] We bind ourselves in our words in ways we do not know or understand, and our words bind us not simply to each other but to the world. Language "words the world" and binds us to it and not by reference alone: We are bound by the challenge and difficulty of reality even when correspondence and reference are out of play.[20] Thus, Diamond and Cavell give us a vision of language in which our adequacy to reality is central, but such adequation is now extended to the full play of language, and it is no longer restricted to reference.[21]

This group of tragedies centers on the fatedness of the protagonists' use of words.[22] A usage of a particular term entitles us to draw certain inferences; this is a question of the normativity of language, an implication that is obscured when rules are understood as imperatives or commands. This is what the learning of language comes to: We are responsible for the implications of our speech. We are responsible for those implications even when we may not know what we are saying and doing. We may not, often cannot, sometimes do not, foresee how our words will go out into the world. What Hannah Arendt said of human action is true of speech acts: They are irreversible, unpredictable, and boundless. What is done cannot be undone.[23] Like other forms of action, the effects of our speech are "irreversible"—we can recant, abjure, revoke, and retract, but we cannot unsay what we have said; unpredictable, for if we must understand what we are doing in certain explicit performatives for them to do the work they do, even in those cases where what follows is unforeseen—we know that the judge's verdict will result in a prison sentence but not how that verdict will resound in the defendant's life or those of his loved ones; they are boundless in their effects. We can begin to see some implications of implication here: inference, imputation, indication, or suggestion; implication as involvement, connection, and entanglement in bonds, as Kent puts it in Lear, "too intrince to unloose," and lastly implication in the quasi-legal sense as bearing guilt, hence responsibility.[24]

Wittgenstein claims that a philosophical problem has the form: "I don't know my way about" (PI, ¶122).[25] I have lost my direction and a sense of myself, my fundamental orientation in the world, my very understanding, even my sense of my relations with other people: Where am I? That is the sense of a bewildering homelessness. No map can help me find my way home, so how can I possibly get there? But also: Who am I? I do not know who I am anymore. This is Lear's haunting question: "Who is it that can tell me who I am?"[26] The therapeutic task of the *Investigations* is "to bring words back from their metaphysical to their everyday use" (PI, ¶116 and ¶132). The sense of lostness in the exile I call linguistic is tied to the loss of concepts that is Diamond's theme. How did these men become so lost and their cultural resources so vitiated that they forget how to grieve, to love, to act, or to speak with—rather than to—others? How do Shakespeare's plays "lead" words home, and to what end? When we are lost, when, in Wittgenstein's understanding, we cannot find our way about, it is because we are in flight from the ordinary, the conditions of necessity by which we are able to speak at all.[27] We flee into illusions of sense while evading the responsibility of meaning what we say, the necessary implications of our speech.

This is why these late tragedies border on madness and unintelligibility: The protagonists speak in a fantasy of sense, mistaking flattery for love, or evading their actions, or ignoring that others are necessary in any act of speech, or that we cannot give what we do not have. That is why they mistake both themselves and the world in the tragic collapse of such binding concepts.

But wait, someone might object, what can Wittgenstein possibly contribute to any understanding of Shakespeare as an artist who brings our ethical lives into lucid focus? Wittgenstein finds his plays "dashed off" and he was "deeply suspicious of Shakespeare's admirers." [28] Shakespeare was overpraised and for "specious reasons by a thousand professors of literature."[29] He was a "creator of language rather than a poet."[30] Moreover, apart from the *Lectures on Ethics*, Wittgenstein rarely explicitly addresses the question of ethics.[31] What an inauspicious start. But this is to look in the wrong place. Ethics are in fact all pervasive in Wittgenstein's thinking, from early to late: They shape his philosophy.

We must look rather to his vision of language than to any explicit statements he makes on either ethics or Shakespeare.

It is the understanding of language use in the wake of Austin and Wittgenstein that makes possible a different kind of ethical criticism.[32] This vision of language understands the words we speak as action, event, and expression. We are responsible for our words even if we do not know what we mean, and we are *fated* to expression, exposed in them even as we try so hard to obliterate or deny our exposure. This vision of language is perennially open to tragic implication. The work of its major practitioners (Cavell, Raimond Gaita, and Diamond) is marked by its appreciation of humanity's tragic predicaments and for its profound contestation of a midcentury moral philosophy that arguably obliterated ethics. When Stanley Cavell takes issue with the received traditions of moral philosophy in part 3 of *The Claim of Reason*, when Diamond expands on Iris Murdoch's essays on *The Sovereignty of Good*, when Raimond Gaita reflects on the tragic landscapes of his father in *Romulus My Father*, it is because they are haunted by what Gaita calls "the estrangement from morality of morally serious people," which is a consequence of the fact/value dichotomy and the hold of scientism.[33] Their Wittgensteinian vision of language shows that no particular domain of affairs—deliberation over what should be done, the vocabulary of "good" or "ought," duty and obligation—was a marked-off preserve of moral thinking. There is no particular subject matter of moral judgments—no especial range of utterances, no distinctively moral concepts set aside and marked moral. No such moral concepts are necessary for ethical thought. The problem is, after all, to recognize moral claims at all—what morally appalls me might be business as usual for you. Moral questions arise as questions of what and how we see, how we take or get things. This makes *any* use of language potentially and pervasively ethical. Ethics is simply an aspect of all our language, of what we do in speaking with each other and thus our moral sensibility pervades all our lives, and as Diamond asserts: "We are perpetually moralists."[34]

Each assertion may be a moral act, says Cavell, "intrusive or not, magnanimous or not, heartfelt or not, kind or cutting, faithful or treacherous, promising cheer or chagrin, acknowledging or denying."[35] Judgment is precisely not backed by moral law but "fronted by the character of the judger."[36] Thus, without imperatives and oughts, without an extrinsic standard of moral judgment, moral questions arise not in the decisions about a particular choice of action among others, but rather in the understanding that in the middle of your life (or at any point in it) you have lost your way and do not know how to go on. You need leading and direction out of moral chaos. You need to *find* your way. That is why Shakespeare's late tragedies are ethical inquiries and why they chart paths lost and found.

Shakespeare, Cavell suggests, is the most "responsive" of playwrights. In Wittgenstein's vision of language, our sense of responsibility is crucially tied to our responsiveness to the world and to each other; the kind of criticism I write begins with my responses to the plays in question as it invites the responses of others. So each chapter stages an encounter with the play, and the play's signal concept under examination. Like any aesthetic judgment, it must be subjective, but strive for and reach toward universal validity because I am not content to simply let it be a matter of different "opinions." This is what I see. Do you see it too? A reading can be "close" without touching on this kind of "work on oneself" at all. This book, although it is based on my readings, is neither a defense nor even an instance of close reading or of new-formalist practices of the kind that have been championed in response to the new historicist hegemony. For one thing, my readings are through and through historical in the sense that my focus is always on language *use*—an inevitably historical (although not necessarily historicist) practice. In so far as close readings or new formalism ignores use, it will continue the evacuation of linguistic agency that has been a hallmark of the structuralist and poststructuralist paradigm. It will thus lack the diagnostic skills to show the tragic implication of such evacuation that is my main topic.

Contemporary criticism sometimes escapes to theory and is dominated by what one critic has called "interpretative skepticism."[37] In other words, questions of interpretation are treated as problems that can be settled by theoretical know-how and expertise and moreover solved in advance of the experience of reading. One important implication of Wittgenstein's idea of a criterion is that no separate expert position exists when it comes to ordinary language, no final, decisive, and expert judgment.[38] The "rough ground" of reading and sense-making, as Ingeborg Lofgren puts it, is the place where our concerns with literature live.[39] In writing this book, I return to an ancient delight in the practice of reading and criticism, seeing criticism as an extension of conversation and the "making of a work of art available to just response."[40]

Wittgenstein has no *theory* of language. He does not map out in advance what falls under his concepts. The diagnostic and therapeutic work of what Toril Moi calls the "revolution of ordinary language" is retrospective.⁴¹ The need for it emerges when we are lost and when our human bonds—and our words as our bonds—are in need of repair. The work is to return us to the "rough ground" of where the concepts we need have a sense and point. The work of Shakespearean theater and the work of ordinary language philosophy, in fact, have a kinship. This is what actors and directors have found in their practice.

This mode of practice puts paying attention to details—and to language *use*—above the formulation of theories. It is no surprise that Austin and Cavell were lovers of the theater. Both practices root themselves into the intricacies and intimacies of address—who is saying what to whom, right here and right now, for what purpose, and with what intention and effect, calculable and incalculable? This is first not last word philosophy, rooted in response, relationship and connection, perpetually dissolving the lie of the sovereign self. In this practice, the first person is not separable from the second. "I" comes into the picture in a practice of interlocution.

The idea of speech as action is explored in an actor's technique used in rehearsals. I mention this idea of speech here because it is an exemplary practice, a reminder of returning the character's words to their concrete occasion of use.

Pioneered at the Joint Stock Theatre Company in the 1970s, and associated with the work of Bill Gaskill and Max Stafford Clark, this technique starts not with method but with a close parsing out of each line of dialogue, not moving inward to the psychology of the character but staying with the lines as speech acts.⁴² The idea is that actors and directors decide what any one piece of dialogue is *doing*. The verb must be transitive—so insulting, encouraging, provoking rather than musing or ruminating, and so there are now thesauruses of action verbs to aid the actor's work of "actioning." The result is clarity because playing actions has a lucidity that playing feelings does not. Actors may together change their mind about what any stretch of speech is doing, but at every point, they are natural ordinary language philosophers. Betting they can articulate what they are saying on the basis of what they are doing, they live out the full implications of Austin's idea: You will not know the meaning of something unless you know what you are doing by virtue of speaking those words. (And it is not entirely up to you to decide!) This is an excellent way of reading Shakespeare's plays as well, and it reveals the sympathy of theater with moral discourse, not in advocacy for the right action, but in enacting what Cavell has suggested is the basis of moral argument: working out the positions you take in relation to the others around you.⁴³ This technique of actioning in the theater hardly restricts the working out of a position you are prepared to take, what you might be prepared to be responsible for, to explicit performatives.

Let's try it out on the opening lines of *Hamlet*.⁴⁴ I have deliberately omitted the dramatis personae in the following citations and italicized Shakespeare's lines for clarity:

Who's there?
Nay, answer me! Stand, and unfold yourself.
Long Live the King.
Bernardo?
He.

We might "action" these lines with the following options, which clearly are not exhaustive:

Who's there? (question, demand; nervous, uncertain, or defensive/aggressive)
Nay, answer me! (counterdemand. The implication is that I won't answer your question, declare or expose myself until I know who you are—especially if the actor puts the emphasis on *me*.)
Stand, and unfold yourself! (order, command, or plea, entreaty, request; but unfold surely cannot be done in a sentence or a name. It suggests layers and covers and creases that need unraveling and invites the work of time in revelation.)
Long Live the King! (declaration of loyalty and allegiance. The revelation of identity comes not from announcing yourself but only by virtue of declaring which side you are on, suggesting a highly combative and hypervigilant frame of mind in which it may not be clear who is friend and who is foe and that this will be the most important thing to know about them, the primary way of unfolding themselves.)
Barnado? (a guess! A hopeful one in which the speaker is on the verge of relief.)
He! (the confirmation of the guess, with the ironic result that he never had to announce himself after all.)

Call it, as some have, a minirecognition scene, but only with the understanding that not a great deal has yet been revealed or recognized. The men have declared only their allegiance to the king, which is to say both everything that is currently to the point and also not much. The atmosphere of uncertainty and indeed fear shows the extent to which any discovery of who is actually there, and the very ability to declare, reveal, or unfold yourself will require certain conditions. The revelation of who you are will not be the revelation of an identity known independently of just such and other interactions but will be emergent only through them. It is misty. Approaching from different directions and from exactly where it is not clear; these men do not know the positions they are occupying in relation to each other. All that is to be discovered. This minirecognition scene can show that neither man is sovereign over his identity.[45]

The following chapters show in more detail, and across a wider tragic terrain, how human persons are bound by these and other recognitions.

Chapter 1

Coming to Grief in *Hamlet*
Trust and Testimony in Elsinore

> ignorance about those who have disappeared
> undermines the reality of the world
>
> —Zbigniew Herbert, *Mr. Cogito and the Need for Precision*

In the etymological variants of grief are human histories, maps of harm. Grief was once understood to be an action as much as a state, a verb rather than exclusively a noun. The verb *to grieve* could be used transitively.[1] "How will this grieve you / When you shall come to clearer knowledge, that / You thus have published me," says Hermione to Leontes with foresight, delicacy, and compassion when she is falsely accused of adultery and treason in *The Winter's Tale*.[2] The noun *griever* could mean one who molests or troubles another as well as one who feels distress. *Grieving* might mean causing grief as well as feeling it or showing it. With this usage, the term unites the harmed and the harmer in an action, a deed: It shows an inextricable relation. In the telling echo of grief and grievance, there is too the promise of redress. A grief then can constitute a legal cause, as when Blunt addresses Hotspur in *I Henry IV*: "The King hath sent to know / The nature of your griefs."[3] The vestigial term *grievous* survives in the English legal term *grievous bodily harm*, which should be distinguished from the less severe *actual bodily harm*. These transitive uses of grief and grieving reveal that our vulnerability and our sociability are impossible to sunder.[4]

The relationship between grief and grievance can be quick: "Let grief convert to anger" counsels Malcolm to Macduff at the news that his wife and children have been killed.[5] Grievances nurse revenge, and the relationship of wrath and grief is the central subject of Homeric and Vergilian epic, reprised in legends Greek tragedy shares with Homeric myth.

Although the term is originally Scandinavian (*groefa*), griefs are *gravis*, the Latin word indicating the connection with weight and with melancholy. To make heavy is another obsolete usage of *grieve*: As an inevitable burden, grief is bound up with being human.

Grief involves the recognition of loss; it reveals what "is precious to us" in Macduff's terms.[6] Corruptions of grieving—in avoidance, sentimentality, theatricalization, the masking of grief in wrath—are standing temptations because the recognition of loss is always a feat, an achievement of self-knowledge, and a cultural affordance.

Shakespeare explores the grammar of grief (its forms, moods, and shapes) in many idioms in his plays. He knows that "honest plain words" best "pierce the ears of grief."[7] He knows it can be "honourable," that it can "fill up a room," that it may be "patched with proverbs," that it "would have tears," that it can be smiled at if you are "Patience on a monument," and that it is best shared ("do not seek to bear your griefs yourself and leave me out"). Shakespeare knows too that it lines the joy of festive endings: "After so long grief such nativity!"[8]

It is in *Hamlet* that Shakespeare gives us a full picture of what it means to come to grief, assimilating the expressions of harming others and of feeling that harm. He explores how the blocking of the expression of grief may show that when losses cannot be recognized, a society is in danger of profound corruption, its ritual forms can be rendered a sham, and its traditional ways of joining the particular in the common can be polluted and destroyed to great consequence.

In this chapter, I explore the consequences of the inexpressibility of grief in *Hamlet* and show how Shakespeare revealed this relationship between grief and grievance in the tradition of revenge tragedy to uncover deeper recognitions and thus transformed the possibilities of English tragedy. Hamlet is a thwarted griever, rather than a revenger, and the play understands that the possibility of the recognition of loss is found in grief but not in revenge. Hamlet is at least in Ophelia's imagination a courtier, a scholar, and a soldier, and the play explores Hamlet's courtly, scholarly, and military resources for the expression of grief and thus the recognition of loss. In so doing the very nature of a human act—what Claudius has done and what Hamlet will do—is always coming under a description, always subject to conditions of intelligibility, and always under profound, transforming interrogation.

The play is thus the path to Shakespeare's late great tragic idiom in the plays *King Lear*, *Timon of Athens*, *Coriolanus*, *Macbeth*, and *Antony and Cleopatra*. It is an idiom answerable to our mutual dependencies rather than a supersession of them.

Hamlet, I argue, shows heroism in testimony rather than revenge. To show this, I explore the ritual crisis of mourning in Elsinore, focus on some of the epic and tragic contexts that the play offers in the classicizing precedents of the player's speech, and interrogate the embedding of action in the action of speech—and in particular the speech act of telling (one of this play's most dramatic innovations)—before offering a reading of the play's "last things." In so doing, I open the play's tragic trajectory to an ethical reading, but I do so only with a reconceived understanding of the relationship between linguistic and ethical competence.

"Why Seems It So Particular to Thee?"

Claudius's opening speech in act 1, scene 2, is that of a consummate politician, schooled in the art of obfuscation. The public announcement of his marriage to Gertrude so closely following the death of her former husband is tucked behind five qualifying dependent clauses:

> Though yet of Hamlet our dear brother's death
> The memory be green, and that it us befitted
> To bear our hearts in grief, and our whole kingdom
> To be contracted in one brow of woe,
> Yet so far hath discretion fought with nature
> That we with wisest sorrow think on him
> Together with remembrance of ourselves.
>
> (1.2.1–7)[9]

This acknowledged awareness of what would most fit with King Hamlet's death—that is, the brilliant flash of a nation "contracted" in woe, in which the expression of grief on faces (tensed and diminished in sorrow) is underscored by the idea of a socially unifying social compact—joins all faces together in the same expression of sorrow ("one brow"). But the passage turns on "yet" and "with wisest sorrow." The communal woe is put aside for "remembrance of ourselves." The sovereign "ourselves" obscures whether the reflexive plural pronoun refers to the whole nation; to himself and Gertrude; or, as we will later better understand, to himself. The logic of the counterpointed "yet" (still, nevertheless) strongly implies that "ourselves" refers to Claudius. The issue is whether the first-person plural is a cover for the first-person singular. A pseudo-logical "therefore" (1.2.8) creates the impression that his marriage to Gertrude is reasonable, thus following a natural logic. The counterintuitive balanced scale of "delight and dole" (1.2.13) that he purports to be weighing hints that his act is merely judicious; it hides the oxymoronic awkwardness and the offense to decorum and proper order in "mirth in funeral" and "dirge in marriage" (1.2.12). Finally, in this skillful opening flourish, Claudius assures the assembled court that they are complicit in these aberrations of ceremony. Therefore, it is not in fact inappropriate to talk of "ourselves."

We can already see that Claudius's remarks reveal a most difficult relationship between a "we" and an "I." In this court Hamlet stands alone, ostentatiously so, among all those who "have freely gone / With this affair along" (1.2.15–16), in garb and demeanor, showing his fidelity to the paternal past. The famous debate with his mother develops the fractures between what is held in common and what is particular, soldered together so calculatedly by Claudius.

In mourning, a particular death is lamented in common. "The end of funeral duties," says Richard Hooker, "is first to show that love towards the partie deceased which nature requireth; then to doe him that honour which it fit both generallie for man and particularlie for the qualite of his person."[10] Within the ceremonies, we have ample room to find that the one we lost is irreplaceable in his or her singularity, but we shed tears and wonder at such singleness together. In a funeral, an individual person is mourned. This mourning is a recognition of that unique person and a recognition of who we take ourselves to be in the singularity of death as a common fate. We experience not distaste or disagreement but rather horror, a sense that we and the dead have been violated when we see deaths not honored or recognized. Thus, a mourning rite acknowledges the dead and the grief of the chief mourners, and it also reveals a community bound by its common love. The relationship to the lost one, however, is lived out in singularity. The fact that death is an inevitable fate held in common is nothing but a commonplace if the particularity of the life lost is not *particularly* mourned. It is precisely this common-ness and the particularity that have become unmoored in act 1, scene 2, of *Hamlet*.[11]

Gertrude asks why Hamlet seeks his noble father in the dust and with an obtusely bland reassurance chides: "Thou know'st' tis common all that lives must die, / Passing through nature to eternity" (1.2.72–3).

Hamlet's response is sardonic: "Ay, madam, it is common" (1.2.74). The common as what we share—because she appears not to share his grief—is no more than a commonplace to her. "Ay, madam, it is common" can mean then, yes, it is common to die, so much is obvious, perhaps also it is common to say so; also, ay, madam it is a commonplace (implied, so what do *you* mean in pointing it out?). Gertrude, however, misunderstands his response as ratification: "If it be, / Why seems it so particular with thee?" (1.2.74-75). This prompts Hamlet's hyperbolical retreat to what he has within "which passes show" (1.2.85), a plausible retreat given that when Gertrude rejects the expressive forms of grief, "all forms, moods, shows of grief" (1.2.82), she rejects his sorrow, and she rejects him.[12] Gertrude understands Hamlet as singling himself out (making an exception of himself, also showing up the court) rather than experiencing a common fate with the particularity of his memory and his relationship with his father. In that commonplace, she is evading her position, her responses and responsibilities in grief, submerging her "I" in a generalized "We."

Claudius, too, uses the language of the common in bland and superficial ways. Because "your father lost a father, / That father lost, lost his" (1.2.89-90), he says with a chiastic flourish, so all are bound in filial obligation "to do obsequious sorrow" (1.2.92). He suggests that Hamlet is persisting in "obstinate condolement" (1.2.93), which he then goes on to describe as unmanly, impious, and most incorrect to heaven. Harping on the common again, he says, "What we know must be, and is as common / As any the most vulgar thing to sense" (1.2.98-99). The fact that something commonly happens, obviously happens, and happens to everyone does not undermine the need to feel or respond to it; for Claudius, however, what is common is not what is shared but rather is "the most vulgar thing to sense," ascribing a vulgarity to Hamlet that is all his own. He is counseling denial disguised as pious acceptance, which is an insidious moralization. Once again, he invokes the death of fathers as "a common theme" (1.2.103-4) that has been happening since the beginning of time, although it is not tactful in this case to invoke the death of the first corpse—that of Abel by Cain.

Hamlet makes visible what Claudius wants to consign to oblivion and makes apparent that Claudius thinks on the dead king "together with remembrance of ourselves" (1.2.7). For it is this remembrance of himself that has led to the murder of King Hamlet in the first place—or so we will learn later: All we know in this scene is that the ghost of King Hamlet is restlessly and nightly stalking the battlements. It is the commitment to the remembrance of himself that will lead him to suspect Hamlet, to spy on him, and later, to dispatch him to England with a death warrant on his head. What is buried with old Hamlet is an entire past, but that past is not as finished as Claudius would like it to be. In so misusing the idea of what is "common," all the particularities of Hamlet's grief are obscured. This grief is alone faithful not simply to his father but also to a better, if idealized, past. If Hamlet will accept a role as son to the new king, the court can perfectly mirror the regime's forgetfulness. He will no longer be an awkward mnemonic of his father. Hamlet senses a violation before he knows quite the extent of it and before he so much as sees his father's ghost and listens to his grievous tale.

Gertrude's moral idiocy turns out to be central: "Why seems it so particular with thee?" (1.2.75). No mourning can take place without its particularity to you or me being felt.

The relationship between the living and the dead, it is now clear, is fundamentally transformed as a result of the reformations. The living can no longer intercede for the dead in intercessory prayers for the souls in purgatory, now a "fond thing, vainly invented."[13] In the second *Book of Common Prayer*, the dead person is no longer addressed in the second person but rather is addressed in the third person, the object of the priest's words to the people, not the subject of them. "I commende thy soule to God the father almightie, and thy body to the ground" says the priest in the first prayerbook of Edward VI: The corpse is a second person, who can be addressed.[14] "Forasmuche as it hathe pleased almightie God of his great mercy to take him unto himselfe the soule of our dere brother here departed: we therefore commit his body to the ground, earth to earth, ashes to ashes, dust to dust," so says the priest to the assembled congregation about the dear departed in the second prayerbook.[15] Michael Neill, Stephen Greenblatt, Eamon Duffy, and others have helped us gain a vital sense of such radical departures in received customs, in patterns of inheritance.[16] My point builds on their careful investigations of the transformations in mourning with this important emphasis: Burial rites are, as Georg Wilhelm Friedrich Hegel said, acts of recognition.[17] Dead human bodies in mourning rites are objects of care, singled out for sorrow, the sponsors of grief, not disgust. They are, as Jay Bernstein has reiterated, "exemplary forms of social action" in that in them we are understood to be bound together and recognized as of the tribe of human.[18] As acts of recognition, mourning ceremonies are rites, rather than rights, working through our "thick" ways of acting and living together.[19] They are revocable. Cora Diamond tells the story of a group of Lebanese women beckoned over to bury their dead by the enemies who killed their husbands, only to be shot down in turn.[20] To lose a sense of violation in such instances is to lose a sense of humanity. For whom do we grieve? For whom can we care? What happens when mourning rites are theatricalized, when the shapes of true grief can no longer be recognized? What happens when they cannot seem particular to us, to you and to me? To lose these forms for the expression of loss is to lose a basic grammar of recognition. Unable to voice grief and to have it recognized as grief (rather than obstinance, eccentricity, morbidity), Hamlet has his most basic expressive resources denied. He cannot be known in forms and shapes of grief, and the court too is misrecognizing itself—its past and present circumstances—in its theatricalized ceremonies.

What, then, are the resources of Hamlet's culture for the expression of grief that, as I have argued, are inextricably bound up with questions of recognition?

Body Without Name: Some Classical Precedents for the Forms and Shapes of Grief and Anger

"Grief suggests grievance," says Stanley Cavell in his essay "Texts of Recovery (Coleridge, Wordsworth, Heidegger . . .)."[21] I have already referred to the depths of the etymological connections of grief and grievance in the history of the language. Cavell's point is that grievance fails to bring relief: "It ties us to pastness because it is a modification of vengefulness."[22] Roberto Calasso has cited Robert Frost's introduction to Edwin Arlington Robinson's 1935 collection, *King Jaspar*, in which he too parses out the connection and difference in these cognates, these homonymic words. Grief is a patient pain (this is why the pauses in revenge tragedy assume such significance); grievance can articulate pain only through vengeance.[23]

In the *Nicomachean Ethics*, Aristotle had distinguished the irascible, choleric man from the man whose bitterness constrains his spirit to nurture his wounds, finding that revenge alone will bring him pleasure and relief.[24] Commenting on the *Ethics*, Thomas Aquinas had tersely and economically stated that "anger is caused by sadness" thus articulating the relationship of anger and grief.[25] For Thomas, anger is connected to reason, nature, and justice: Anger is a rational response to injury and thus a natural good. Thomas distinguishes anger from hatred, which does not wish the good, and links it to grief. Grief and anger alike focus on "a feeling of injury."²⁶ What links grief and anger then is a sense of injury. What distinguishes them is the object of attention. Anger's target is an act or person, the perpetrator of harm, whereas grief attends to the loss consequent on the harm. "The loss, not the perpetrator remains its focus," says Martha Nussbaum.²⁷

Nussbaum usefully distinguishes anger from other reactive attitudes, such as disgust, contempt, gratitude, hatred, and envy, but it is the kinship of grief and anger that are her chief focus. It is precisely this kinship that makes anger a tempting corruption of grief, a denial of helplessness in the face of loss. Grief can be impure in other ways that obscure the painful recognition of loss and cover the conceptual link between anger and helplessness—resentment, or fear, for example. In the genre of revenge tragedy, however, the closeness of anger and grief is characteristically at issue. That genre indulges and explores a standing temptation, the masking of grief in grievance so obscuring the conceptual link between anger and helplessness.²⁸ This is why the question of *recognition* of loss is so important and wide ranging in Elsinore. To perceive this relation is one of the great achievements of *Hamlet*.

Hamlet is not so much angry as rather histrionically working himself up to it. I am not suggesting that Hamlet disguises grief in anger, but that his own loss cannot be recognized in the world of the play and that the play systematically pushes us to see the recognitive dimensions of grief. His relation to the role of revenger who characteristically disguises grief in anger is thus extremely vexed. He tries it on for size without ever fully embracing it. This is why the play takes a path through the classical precedents of Aeneas's speech to Dido, and it is also why it detours through the graveyard in understanding the specificities of loss, the forms and shapes of grief. But first the players.

Surrounded by Claudius's spies, rejected by Ophelia, haunted by his father's indeterminate spirit, hunted by necessary, contradictory, and thus impossible tasks, Hamlet greets the players with delight and relief. They offer, embody even, a different occasion for the work of memory in the studied amnesia of Claudius's court. Hamlet relies on the excellent memory of the player to remember word-perfectly the speech he can remember only in snippets, and in so doing, the player brings to life legendary stories of revenge and grief, sacrilege and lament, rooted in Homeric epic and Attic tragedy. At the end of the scene, he will suggest that the good word of players is better than a bad epitaph; they are "the abstract and brief chroniclers of the time," as he will later put it (2.2.461–62). Hamlet's incomplete memory of an affecting speech is held and preserved in the player's capacious reimagining—no wonder his excitement at the player's arrival is so pronounced.

This famous set speech places a picture of a sacrilegious murder at the dead center of a most complex classical set of precedents and at the heart of the terrible destruction of a great civilization. It is as if Hamlet wishes to test the ghost's purgatorial, yet heroic, lineage against another story "whose common theme / Is death of fathers" (1.2.103-4). Priam's death is, as Reuben Brower puts it, "a drama of fathers and sons."[29] The speech, which the player has recited once to Hamlet before, was from "Aeneas's talk to Dido, and thereabout of it especially when he speaks of Priam's slaughter" (2.2.384-85). The speech begins, twice in Hamlet's false starts, with Pyrrhus, embedded within Aeneas's tale to Dido from book 2 of Vergil's *Aeneid:* Hamlet moves from speaker to spectator as the player takes his cue and proceeds. How does the death of fathers figure in this set piece? How is this a drama of fathers and sons? How, in sounding its epic tradition and the metamorphoses of that tradition, is it also a story once again about the relation of grief and grievance?

In selecting this complex example, Hamlet is half-remembering an astonishing nexus of ideas about precisely that relation. In book 2 of Vergil's *Aeneid*, Aeneas tells the story of the fall of Troy after he sees that epochal story depicted on the walls of the temple that Dido is building for Juno in Carthage. That frieze brings him to tears, for he sees there all the battles of Ilium, and Achilles fierce in his wrath against both the sons of Atreus (Agamemnon and Menelaus) and against Priam, King of Troy. He understands that no place on earth is not full of their sorrows ("non plena laboris"): He exclaims, "sunt lacrimae rerum et mentem mortalia tangunt."[30] Fagles translates these famous lines: "Even here is a world of tears / and the burdens of mortality touch the heart."[31] I hear a Vergilian echo in the lines "unless things mortal move them not at all" (2.2.454). In these ekphrastic passages in the *Aeneid*, too, Aeneas sees Hector's body being dragged round Troy's walls by Achilles in unappeasable revenge for the death of Patroclus.[32]

In Vergil's poem, we find an astonishing reprise of Homer's *Iliad*, for the ransom of Hector's body, the scene of the great short-lived but world-shattering reconciliation of Priam and Achilles in book 24 of the *Iliad*, is referred to here as merely a sale of Hector's body ("auro corpus vendebat Achilles").[33] We are shown the spoils and the corpse of his friend, Hector, meeting his gaze and also the outstretched, supplicating, and weaponless hands of Priam ("tendentemque manus Priamum conspexit inermis").[34] It is as if the great Homeric ending of the *Iliad* had not taken place at all. Priam's hands are still outstretched, still in suspended supplication on the walls of Juno's temple. Hector's gaze holds Aeneas's gaze as if he was never laid to rest. Because it is Aeneas's tale to Dido that Hamlet remembers, it is Aeneas's tears, the "lacrimae rerum," that are also reprised, along with the unappeasable wrath of Achilles and, in this way, the player's speech half-remembers the relations of wrath and grief that are a main subject of Homer and Vergil's epics. For it is wrath that begins both poems, the *mênis* (wrath) of Achilles in the *Iliad*, the wrath of Juno in the *Aeneid* ("tantane animis caelestibus irae?").[35] Vergil wishes us to hear the echo of Homer in his depiction of Priam's death; in Aeneas's long tale of the war told to Dido, he shows that Neoptolemus / Pyrrhus deliberately and transgressively refuses his father's role in responding to Priam's supplication.[36] For Vergil, this marks a most conscious rejection of his father, Achilles's precedent: Neoptolemus taunts Priam to report his sad degeneracy in his sacrilegious murder on the altar, rejecting Achilles / Pelides compunction in the return of Hector's body and in the release of Priam back to his people in the brief twelve-day reprieve to war. It is in those days of suspended battle that Priam and the Trojans can mourn Hector.

Vergil is aware that Homer's *Iliad* begins with Achilles's wrath and with the terrifying image of men becoming carrion, food for birds and dogs, as if that anger and that violation of mourning are from the beginning bound up. In this poem of force, as Simone Weil has called it, men can become things, and the best instance of this loss of humanity is the refusal of mourning rites.[37] The ransom of the body of Hector is the precondition of the triple threnody of lament that ends the *Iliad*. His body retrieved at such risk by Priam can be lamented by the three women: Hecuba, herself about to be enslaved at Troy's fall; Andromache, Hector's wife; and, in Homeric generosity, Helen herself, the great "cause" of the war.

This ransom is above all where wrath is suspended for a grief that is shared. In book 24 of the *Iliad*, after Priam has taken the great risk of entering unarmed the enemy camp of the Greek army, he reminds Achilles of his father awaiting his return, anxious and expectant. "Remember your own father, great godlike Achilles," says Priam, "as old as I am, past the threshold of deadly old age!" Priam kisses the terrible son-killing hands of Achilles: "I put to my lips the hands of the man who killed my son." It is these very words that stir in Achilles the desire to grieve for his father: "Overpowered by memory, / both men gave way to grief."[38] In her essay on the *Iliad*, written at roughly the same time as Weil's equally remarkable essay, during the dark and difficult winter of 1940, Rachel

Bespaloff writes of Priam's speech: "This speech is quite without vehemence; self-respect gives the words the exact weight of truth." She adds, too, that "this is the only case in the *Iliad* where supplication sobers the man to whom it is addressed rather than exasperating him."[39] The two men weep together for the common grief of their loved ones, Patroclus and Hector, and for each other as men of sorrow. Achilles sees his father in Priam and sees that Priam is a father. He sees, too, that he, Achilles, is a son, and not alone a killer of sons, that Priam has a son. Before they had been only enemies, wanting only to return death for death. Now shockingly, and with full awareness of the risk he is taking, as Priam kisses Achilles's man-slaying hands, both men get the measure of filial and paternal love. The long war is halted only for a short time but the return of his son's body for mourning shows that the endless revengeful killing is held in abeyance by an extraordinary shared grief.

Vergil gives us a chilling image of Priam after his murder. He is left as a huge trunk, a headless body, a corpse without a name ("sine corpus nomine").[40] This headless, nameless corpse is a fearful rejection of the great Homeric impulse to bring back Hector's body into a space for human grief. Priam's body is left for the dogs and the birds.

In the player's speech, Pyrrhus does not taunt Priam and does not remind him to tell his father, Achilles, that he will not follow his example in responding to Priam's supplication as he does in book 2 of the *Aeneid*.[41] It is a shard of memory, a fragment from the collapse of civilization, punctuated in the pause, absent from Pyrrhus's hectic, relentless trajectory in Vergil, of Pyrrhus's sword sticking in the air over the reverend Priam's head.

It is as if this pause stands for the weight of the great precedent that Vergil elaborates so consciously as Pyrrhus scorns Achilles's example. Another infamous pause appears at the end of the *Aeneid*. Aeneas's stays his hand on the sword hilt as Turnus supplicates him, just as Priam supplicated both Achilles and Pyrrhus: "If any thought of a parent's grief can touch you, I beg you—you too had such a father in Anchises-pity Daunus's old age, and give me—or, if you prefer, my lifeless body—back to my kin."[42] In the *Aeneid*'s ambiguously terrifying ending, Aeneas sinks his blade in fury into Turnus's chest. He has seen the strap worn by young Pallas, a war trophy sported on Turnus's arm. It is that reminder of his loss that turns all into permanent red, that turns from the prospect of loss into the perpetrator of further loss, with no pause, in either case, for mourning. Tony Tanner discusses another such moment in Aeschylus's play *The Libation Bearers*, the central play of the *Oresteia*, when Orestes pauses in the murder of his mother, Clytemnestra, and asks Pylades what to do. Tanner describes this as one of the momentous moments in Western drama and describes the Shakespearean continuation of this idiom as one of great pregnancy.[43] Hamlet will later be caught in another such moment when he pauses over the praying head of Claudius (3.3.73–74).

Pyrrhus is clearly a model of revenger for Hamlet, but he is also a model of the son who refuses his father's better example of sharing grief. Before Achilles's releases Hector's body to Priam in the famous ransom, he had refused Hector's plea: "Hector, don't talk to me of pacts. / There are no oaths to be trusted between men and lions."[44] Any such pact would have to be between humans, but Achilles takes on the role of both beast and cannibal, and his desecration of Hector's body is, as Redfield notes, a reenaction of his victory over Hector, who is "an eternal object of his malice."[45] So too is Achilles's recognition of Priam's claim for the body of his son a reentry into a human world. A corpse is, as *Hamlet*'s gravedigger wittily points out, by no means a person (5.1.127–28) but instead must be granted rites of recognition, marks of honor, and not disgust.

If Claudius has provided a moralizing, inert, and obtuse maxim for Hamlet in the fact that all fathers die, the player's speech sets before Hamlet a complexly embedded example of the recognitive and powerful dimensions of grief. It is grief that is recognized here and here refused. I have shown how a layered topoi of grief and recognition also is found in the pointed Vergilian suppressions of Homeric reconciliation. The player presents a stylized, deliberately archaized and classicizing precedent of an act of outrageous impiety (the murder of Priam), as well as the response of Hecuba, at the same time the player's speech shows up the complexity of the common theme of fathers and sons.[46] In the player's recitation of the grief of Hecuba and the death of Priam, we are reminded of where the terrible death of Priam ends: a vast trunk, a headless body on a distant shore, a body without a name.

In revenge tragedy, the sharing of grief takes a particularly twisted form. In staging his death-dealing drama at the end of *The Spanish Tragedy*, for example, Hieronimo wants to force the king into a recognition of his grief; he does this by murdering his son, as his own son has been murdered:

> Speak, Portuguese, *whose loss resembles mine*
> If thou canst weep upon thy Balthazar
> 'Tis like I wailed for my Horatio [my italics].[47]

His grief is then *similar* to Hieronimo's grief. The distorted hope here is that a similar grief will help him recognize the grief he has inflicted. In Auden's great poem *The Shield of Achilles*, the poet chillingly imagines a world, a ruined postwar world in which the work of recognizing humanity in each other is at risk, where it will no longer be possible to "weep because another weeps."[48] The king in *The Spanish Tragedy* weeps in the same way as another, Hieronimo, has wept, but not *because* Hieronimo weeps. Revenge is a perversion of grief because each person can grieve like another but not because or on behalf of that other as in Auden's invocation and in Homer's poem.

Polonius impatiently interrupts the labored archaism of the speech, and we are reminded of the spectators' responses. Hamlet wants the player to "say on, come to Hecuba" (2.2.239). Hamlet's preoccupation, it quickly becomes clear, is the grief of Hecuba, as much as it is the death of Priam. Tanya Pollard has shown that versions of Hecuba gripped Shakespeare's contemporaries: Hecuba is "the period's most prominent representative of the Greek tragic tradition."[49] According to Judith Mossman, Euripides' *Hecuba*, was indeed one of the most translated and imitated Greek plays of the sixteenth century. Erasmus translated it into verse (1504); Melanchthon lectured on Hecuba in Wittenberg (1525–1526), Hamlet's home university; and Melanchthon's prose translation was published in 1540.[50] Seven annotated editions were published before 1600. Indeed, Sidney in his *Apologie for Poetry*, gave *Hecuba* as his example of a well-constructed tragedy.[51] This was the first play to be read by students in the original form and was also the first play to be widely translated into both Latin and the vernacular, as it was also the first to receive an actual performance.[52] Hecuba featured in Seneca's *Troades*, an amalgam of Euripides's plays, *The Trojan Women* and *Hecuba*, and in Ovid's *Metamorphoses* (XIII). Shakespeare also depicted Lucrece, finding the very face of distress in Hecuba's grief in the skillful painting of Priam's Troy: "Staring on Priam's wounds with her old eyes" and shaping "her sorrow to the beldam's woes."[53]

Most commentators on Hecuba have thought of Priam and Hecuba as part of an opposition between the execution of revenge (Priam) and the expression of grief at this revenge, with the role of mourning reserved for Hecuba who lost her city, her husband, her great son (Hector), and eventually all of her sons and daughters, including the terrible post-Trojan sacrifice of the son and daughter who feature in Euripides's *Hecuba*: Polyxena, sacrificed to appease the ghost of Achilles, and Polydorus who was sent to be kept safe, reliant on the *xenia* of Polymestor. Euripides's *Hecuba*, reprised in Seneca's amalgam of Euripides's two plays, *Trojan Women* and *Hecuba*, is as much about the revenge of Hecuba as about her mourning.

She is associated with grief in Seneca's rendering of the play for Hecuba's early invitation in that play is to the chorus to weep and lament for Hector, for Priam, and for Troy, while also knowing that their fates as fallen warriors will be easier to live out than the life of slaves and concubines—the lot of the Trojan women. "Strike your breasts with your hands, beat out the sounds of sorrow, and perform the funeral rites of Troy," intones Hecuba, leading the women in mourning for Troy's lost and fallen.[54] It might thus seem as if the work of revenge is reserved for Pyrrhus, just as the work of mourning and lamentation is reserved for Hecuba, the traditional division of labor in Greek tragedy and ancient culture. This certainly seems to be Hamlet's preoccupation with Hecuba in the soliloquy that follows the departure of the players. How can the player be so affected by Hecuba? What is she to him, or he to her (implying the reciprocity of response, the relation between them) that the recitation should be the cause for tears, indeed, for the perfect coherence of grief and its expression? The tears, the voice, his entire aspect, all conform to "his conceit"—that is, to the picture of woe as if it is all one, composite and integrated. The fit, the congruence of grief, and its expression are what impresses Hamlet. Hamlet can "say nothing" (2.2.504). Ann Thompson and Neil Taylor annotate this line: "Hamlet must mean 'do nothing,' since he goes on to chide himself for talking not acting."[55] This is to rewrite the words in conformity with some imagined idea of Hamlet's inaction, rather than to see that the soliloquy is preoccupied with the *stifled* expression of grief. Even Hamlet's preoccupation with what the player would "do" if he had Hamlet's motive and cue for passion is about the *expression* of grief and a fantasy of the effects of that expression and its truth on an audience. In his unacknowledged competition with Hecuba, he is concerned with how the player might express his passion if the player had Hamlet's rather than Hecuba's cues and prompts. Hamlet, for all his education, has missed what Hecuba is to him.

What has Hamlet forgotten about Hecuba and how consequential is his amnesia? Hamlet's response to the player's'Hecuba is an idea of a perfect congruence between grief and its expression. Given the profound consequences of the suppression and perversion of grief and its recognitions in this play, Hamlet's response to the player is completely understandable. So too is his subsequent investment and faith in the capacity of playing to prompt confession and reveal the truth. There is no simple opposition between "doing" and "saying." Saying is doing, as Austin taught us. In addition, we have no understanding of any human action absent how we talk about it. Hamlet's inability to express grief in his culture, his attempts to use the fragments and shards of his half-remembered humanist education, and his partially retrieved speeches and stories that are the bequest of Elsinore's heroic culture are a failed attempt to find the necessary congruence between grief and its expression. What Hamlet has forgotten is that Hecuba, like Pyrrhus in the player's speech, also links wrath to grief in the revenge idiom. In Euripides's astonishing version reprised in Ovid's version in the *Metamorphoses*, Hecuba converts grief to wrath in revenge. In book 13 of the *Metamorphoses*, her grief, rage, and blinding of Polymestor who has killed her son Polydurus turn her bestial. Hecuba howls, barks and growls when she wants to speak: She becomes a dog.[56]

Nussbaum's analysis of Euripides version of *Hecuba* is very pertinent to the investigation of wrath and grief in *Hamlet*. Polymestor traduced the most fundamental rules of hospitality (*xenia*) in killing Polydorus, Priam's only remaining son, sent to him for safekeeping. For Hecuba it is, in Nussbaum's description, the rending of a world, the "old *nomos* as a network of ties linking one person with another."[57] Polymestor destroys Polydorus and, with him, trust in those basic bonds of community. Hecuba's revenge is both "retributive" and "mimetic." [58] The child-killer must, in turn, witness his own child being killed; he must suffer the same horror he induced. Along with this, according to Nussbaum, is a claim to reveal the world as it really was all along, a world in which persuasion and instrumentality is (and in fact always was) the way of the world. Hecuba, says Nussbaum, "makes the world over in the image of the possibility of non-relation, the possibility knowledge of which destroyed her trust."[59] In this way, revenge takes over the world of value, and words become not the bonds of trust but the instruments of ends. Euripides undoes the Aeschylean binding of the polis, showing that the suspension of bonds of trust are a standing possibility. Hecuba's revenge reveals revenge's allure—offering structure and plan without vulnerability.[60]

Hamlet's amnesia about what links Pyrrhus and Hecuba shows him forgetting the relationship of wrath to grief this play so deeply excavates. Hamlet cannot perfectly remember the speech except in bits and pieces. So he cannot also recognize the unbinding consequences of the obscuring of grief, in the very literature that explores so deeply the bonds of the polis, at the center of its epic self-constructions, its *translatio imperii*.

This soliloquy also provides a notable fantasy about what the effect of his words—if he could express them perfectly—would do: He would drown the stage in tears, cleave the ear with his speech, make the guilty mad and appall the free, amaze and confound all (2.2.495-500). This is all marvelously vague, extravagantly totalizing, and all-encompassing. It produces a lot of passion but lacks point and precision. The next fantasy is that his interpolation in the play will catch the conscience of a king, and perhaps that the guilty thing might confess his sins and proclaim his malefactions.[61] It is a hope placed in theater, a hope that theater can produce the truthful speech of confession. That hope turns out to be utterly misplaced. His play exposes *him* and not just Claudius. It exposes him to Claudius and shows that his speech acts, just like any other action, cannot be controlled for the precise effect you alone want them to have. That too, as Kyd showed, was a revenger's fantasy. Hamlet has forgotten not only what Hecuba is to him but also what he is to Hecuba—that is, to see himself in relation to her, himself through her eyes. This is the only undeceived way he can understand what Hecuba is to him and thus can excavate the relationship between wrath and grief that her story exemplifies.

Nussbaum's distinctive and compelling insight about Euripides's version of *Hecuba* helps us see that what is at stake in the revenger's fantasy involves a transformation of a relationship to language. Whatever his acquaintance with Euripides, in ways Nussbaum helps us to see, Shakespeare is a Euripidean in his understanding of grief, wrath, and revenge.

The revenger has the fantasy that his act can be carved out in a world of action in ways he determines and decides; his act can be carved out of its effect on others, save the effects he wills. The revenger's act then denies his implication in the act and denies that any act is woven for its very significance and intelligibility in a world with others. His path is both violent and ignorant.

In the next two sections of this chapter, I show how people characteristically and damagingly talk with each other in Elsinore, and then I examine how the play implicates the revenger's putative act within the speech community as the inescapable horizon of intelligibility. These two sections precede an analysis of the play's scintillating ending.

Take You, As 'Twere, Some Distant Knowledge of Him

In Elsinore, people characteristically learn about each other by spying. Surveillance pervades human relations and structures Elsinorean ways of knowing.[62] Claudius wishes to remain unknown because he is a killer: The primal act on which his regime is founded is murder, usurpation, and the necessities that arise from the concealment of this basic truth. Hamlet must reveal both the murder and the cover-up so the great battle is from the start about truthful speech and its very possibility in Denmark. If Claudius must remain unknown, he nevertheless wants to know what others are thinking and doing. He can learn about Hamlet only, so he thinks, by spying on him. To this end, Hamlet's friends, Rosencrantz and Guildenstern, and his erstwhile love, Ophelia, are suborned as well as his chief counselor and queen.

Polonius reveals what words and expressions come to in this scheme of things. In act 1, scene 3, he tells Ophelia that she is not to believe Hamlet's words: His vows are merely the "implorators of unholy suits" (1.3.128) under the guise of "pious bonds" (1.3.129), spoken only with the intention to beguile and deceive. With utmost scorn and a conviction hard to gainsay if you are his (fragile) daughter, Polonius tells her that Hamlet's words to her, his "tenders" (1.3.98) are "Springes to catch woodcocks" (1.3.114).[63] Polonius converts the tenderness (tentativeness, hope, unguarded openness) to a commercial or legal offer. In his untender words, Hamlet's expressions can only cover over an unworthy intent (Polonius thinks it is lust). Hamlet has indeed tendered his love to Ophelia: In his poor sonnets, he writes: "Doubt truth to be a liar / But never doubt I love" (2.2.116–17). The very awkwardness and amateur craftsmanship of the sonnets indicate their authenticity. When he rejects Ophelia, he also destroys her trust in his former words, and in the words of any man: "You should not have believed me" (3.1.116) makes her the gull that Polonius merely thinks she is. We are left with "believe none of us" (3.1.129), which is not livable.[64] This sentiment echoes what her brother and her father have already told her. There are now no masculine exceptions to the regime of suspicion as far as Ophelia is concerned. (Does this knowledge kill her?) Polonius's general idea, call it the paranoid style in Elsinore, is that "best safety lies in fear" as Laertes says to Ophelia. (1.3.42).

Polonius has specifically undermined Ophelia's natural credence in the words of her lover. Indeed, on the only occasion in which she answers her father back, she does so twice to insist that Hamlet has shown his love "in honourable fashion" (1.3.110) and "hath given countenance to his speech, my lord / With almost all the holy vows of heaven" (1.3.112–13). One can hear in that "almost" how subtly and pervasively Polonius has already infected her. Ophelia has believed not only his vows but also his words. In trustful conversation one does not need royal words to commitment, such as vows and promises, to be believed.

It is fully natural to Polonius, merely the height of good strategy, to find out about people by spying: He prefers to know about his son through means the scene with Reynaldo makes clear: "Take you, as 'twere, some distant knowledge of him" (2.1.13), says Polonius. That distance is central: Polonius can learn about Laertes without being known to him, and without being in communication with him at all. For Polonius this is a *surer* way to know: Such "evidence" is more reliable and certain than the trustful ways in which we might more naturally take someone *at their word*. Indeed, Reynaldo is to give his own thoughts no tongue (a common piece of advice from Polonius); his words are "baits" to trap the "carp of truth" (2.1.60), that is, by indirections finding out directions.

In taking this tack, which is also paradigmatic of Claudius's diseased state, Polonius shows up a central philosophical picture of human relations in which we opt for a more certain knowledge than we think we can derive from accepting each other's "mere" words. The knowledge gained by taking someone's say out of the picture is judged to be more secure than if we were to trust to or rely on their imperfect testimony. What I require is information about you, and it is more secure and more reliable that anything you might have to say if it cannot be independently verified.[65] This model is a picture of skepticism as knowing others in ways that bypass their specific relation to us. Claudius describes how he and Polonius will spy on Hamlet as he talks with Ophelia as "seeing unseen" (3.1.32). Thus, Rosencrantz and Guildenstern spy on Hamlet; Polonius spies on Laertes, Hamlet, and Ophelia. Human expressions have been treated as evidence, and the spy has avoided the risk of exposure.

It is easy to forget this is an odd, and sometimes perverse, way of thinking about exchange with others. Its naturalness in Elsinore is an indication that human communication as such has been distorted, and profoundly so. Everyone in this play learns about each other more or less obliquely. This is a vitiation of our usual ways of understanding. Mistrust and suspicion are seen as natural in Elsinore, and this is unnatural. It is as if the surer way of finding out what someone is thinking or feeling is to obliterate his or her expression, to distrust the commitments he or she is enacting in talking.[66] In talking, a speaker is not invariably—or only under special circumstances—presenting his or her words as evidence. Richard Moran shows the effects of substituting epistemic access for avowal in respect to a speech act, such as a promise, the kinds of vows and promises, for example, that Hamlet makes to Ophelia: "For the speaker to offer a promise as evidence must mean she must be offering it at, at best, as defeasible evidence, with respect to which the promisee is on his own. And to do so is contrary to the point of making a promise, which is binding assurance."[67]

The evidential view, Moran suggests, reveals a fundamental disharmony between speaker and audience. To tell someone something is to aim at, to bank on, being believed. (Ophelia is acting with the usual, normative kind of trust in which we go on with each other in the exchange of words.) What Moran calls the evidential stance decouples the speaker's responsibility in speaking from its reception in his audience: It is the difference between "now I have spoken, make of it what you will," and "Take it from me." It is the difference between, in another of Moran's examples, accepting an apology in which this means putting away resentment and taking the apology as *evidence* of a certain state of mind, and making of it what one wills.[68] Radical distrust, of the kind that is ubiquitous in *Hamlet*, is a form of other minds' skepticism, and this turns out to be lethal.

In the *Philosophical Investigations*, Wittgenstein leads us to understand that trust is the indispensable and normative background in and by which we come to know others. This is hard to see because trust is assumed not on the basis of reason or past experience but instead as the invisible background to talking and acting. Trust becomes visible only as mistrust. Jay Bernstein has suggested that the difficulty in accepting the centrality and normativity of trust comes from how elusive it is, because when it is operating ideally, it is invisible. It is likely to appear paradoxical to philosophies that are based on speculative reason.[69]

Polonius's pseudo-philosophy is Hobbesian: "He that performeth first has no assurance the other will perform after; because the bonds of words are too weak to bridle man's ambition, avarice, anger, and other Passions without the feare of some coercive power."[70] Trust is impossible to understand as anything other than credulity or gullibility in this picture as in Hecuba's dreadful understanding in Euripides' imagination. The Wittgensteinian philosopher Peter Winch has suggested that the concept of "being bound" is impossible in Hobbesian psychology.[71]

In such a Hobbesian world, the project of knowing others and oneself through acknowledgment, which involves the kind of relationship abjured in the evidential model, becomes more or less impossible. The default condition of communication cannot be mistrust—the idea that, on the whole, people are just as likely not to tell the truth as to tell it. The liar, after all, relies on the norm of truth-telling in his or her audience, and his or her abuse of truth is also an abuse of trust. To understand this is also to understand that a commitment to truth means not merely correspondence between one's statements and reality, but also the truth of one's *relationship* to the audience or interlocutor.[72]

Claudius's theatricalization of grief, as well as Polonius's generalized mistrust of words as traps, show that they are skeptics in relation to language. This is part of what is rotten in Denmark.[73] Attempting to see without being seen, the distant knowledge of the other turns out to be, when not simply wrong, catastrophically destructive. It is so because the naturalness of expression (the language of feeling) has become degraded and the possibilities of knowing and being known within it have been compromised severely. The vitiation of the languages for grief and loss are part of a more pervasive impairment of words as bonds of trust, and its relation to love and care.

Telling

For the revenger, the act projects an isolated event, imagined in his fantasy to be shaped solely to meet the ends he both desires and determines. But the very nature of the act Hamlet is enjoined to do is in this play inseparable from the way it is enjoined, understood, communicated, and bound up in acts of witnessing and testimony, and thus in trust. For that reason, I explore the complexity of the speech act of telling in the play, a speech act that has the benefit of also being "indicative of the necessities in a wider range of language games."[74] I have shown that the telling of grief becomes impossible in this play, and this makes the articulation and identification of loss impossible in consequential ways.[75] But the play scrutinizes acts of telling as a whole in ways that do differentiate it from any other form of contemporary revenge tragedy. Indeed, the radical innovation of *Hamlet* is to return us over and over again to the community of speakers in which any act takes shape. It is the indispensable, inescapable imbrication in a community of speakers that entails that no act is self-standing or subject to the definition of the actor alone. The play decisively refuses the revenger's fantasy, which turns out to be a fantasy about the capacity to carve out an action according to your own definition.

Hamlet goes out of its way to reveal the complexities of the act enjoined, the difficulties of discerning it from the testimony of speakers. It provides us with an astonishing ending that renders the very nature of the acts Hamlet performed inseparable from and dependent on the responses and articulations of those around him.

In *Philosophical Investigations*, Wittgenstein says we regard it as too much a matter of course that one can tell anything to anyone.[76] In his article, "Captivating Pictures," Steven G. Affeldt, building on some remarks of Stanley Cavell in *The Claim of Reason*, parses out some of the necessary conditions of the speech act of telling.[77] I go over his careful reasoning with examples from *Hamlet*.

"Buzz, buzz," says Hamlet when Polonius announces that the players have come to Elsinore (2.2.330). His mockery implies that this is old news; he knows it already. In such circumstances, Polonius is not telling him anything at all. In the chilling sequence in which Hamlet has finally confronted the ghost of his father, Hamlet mutters about arrant knaves being villains in Denmark. The point, as Horatio notes, is tautological. Horatio's response invariably gets a laugh when this scene is staged: "There needs no ghost, my lord, come from the grave / To tell us this" (1.5.123–24). Hamlet is telling Horatio nothing at all, just as Polonius is telling Hamlet nothing. One is making sure to withhold what he has to tell, and the other's news is simply stale.

But even if the teller has something to tell, he cannot tell it unless the other is in a position to receive it, and specifically from the teller. A basic condition of telling is that you are believed; if not, your words will count for nothing. This is a question of the position that the teller and the recipient take themselves to hold in relation to each other. Take the characteristic riposte: Why should I take that coming from you? If you give me a piece of advice that you have by no means adhered to yourself, I may fail to respect your authority to speak to me on the subject. Ophelia gives a mild reproach to Laertes along these lines when he warns her off Lord Hamlet, heedless of his journey along the primrose path (1.3.45–49). In the surveillance society of Elsinore, as I have suggested, the idea of believing particular people is dispensed with, and this is a fundamental discounting.

When you tell someone something, you make it clear what relation you stand in to them; you want their acknowledgment, their response, and thus you show not only the light in which you hold them but also how you imagine they stand in relation to you. It is impossible to engage in the act of telling without such revelations taking place.

It is vital that in Hamlet (unlike say, Kyd's play, which is framed by Don Andrea's ghost and the figure of Revenge) we learn about the secret act on which the entire regime of Claudius is founded from a tale told by a ghost whose provenance is unclear, and who will tell his tale alone to young Hamlet. Young Hamlet in turn cannot tell that tale to anyone else. Everything about the act of telling makes us alert to the tricky conditions of possibility and address in a community of speakers. It is not just that we do not know definitively where the ghost comes from but that he will speak only to Hamlet.

We initially hear about his father's ghost entirely through testimony—from the testimony of Marcellus and Barnardo—before he makes his entrance. Even then, he will not speak, although enjoined to do so: He will not speak to Horatio. When he does speak to Hamlet, he has become not an "it" but a second person, singling out Hamlet just as Hamlet singles him out in exchange. The exchange is theirs alone. Furthermore, after he has this dreadful knowledge from the ghost, Hamlet cannot tell anyone about it for this king is a most plausible monarch, and Hamlet is unlikely to be credited. Hamlet becomes burdened not only by his impossible "task" but also by his inability to share his grief. After pondering the player's speech he bewails the fact that he "can say nothing" (2.5.504). The players on the contrary "cannot keep council-they'll tell all" (3.2.135); and he hopes his play will prompt Claudius's confession, so that his "occulted" guilt will not have to be told by Hamlet but rather will issue from his own mouth (3.2.76). Hamlet, of course, spends a great deal of time making sure he cannot be understood to say anything at all.

In his article on telling, Affeldt says that the everyday action of telling involves "projecting the grounds of intelligibility": "One can, perhaps, *say* anything at all to another, or at least at another. However, one can only *tell* another something if the other is able to comprehend what is told, and that will be inseparably connected with understanding *you* and understanding your telling when and as you do."[78]

The usefulness of putting it this way comes from the standing possibility that we will be unintelligible to each other, that our ability to tell each other anything at all is itself a fragile and breakable relation. Once again, it is the desire for recognition at play in the most basic of speech acts. This is precisely what Shakespeare is alert to in this astonishingly transitional play. He has taken a genre that predicates itself on a singular piece of scripting: The playwright and the revenger are alike in their instrumentalizing of words, scripting roles for others to play, carving out their act according only to the consequences they intend. Shakespeare, on the contrary, has shown that even the most simple of speech acts concerns claims to acknowledgement and to recognition.

When Polonius devastatingly says to Ophelia, after they have set her up as a stooge with Hamlet in act 3, scene 1 that "you need not tell us what Lord Hamlet said- / We heard it all," he discounts her utterly (3.1.178-79). In so doing, he reveals how the culture of surveillance is a culture of discounting anyone's say in the matter at hand.

Hamlet's concern is always significantly more with the finding of truth than with the revenge of his father. His play is an attempt to elicit a confession from Claudius. He attempts likewise to "confess" his mother. Confession in this understanding is truthful speech, the opposite of a lie, which seeks possession of language. At the same time, Hamlet must act in such a way that he "tells nothing," because to reveal himself is to expose himself, even as he is mesmerized by players who, as chroniclers of the time, "tell all."

All of these instances show the extent to which the play is concerned with the idea of testimony as the knowledge acquired through a speaker's telling, a most fundamental and routine way in which we routinely act in our dealing with each other. Above all, in ways I will shortly examine, Hamlet's final act is utterly dependent on Horatio's telling for its most basic significance. Absent Horatio's telling, the audience on stage and off would not understand what he had done. But we must go through the graveyard, as Hamlet does, to arrive at the last scene of the play.

In the Graveyard: Ends and Endings

Hamlet is at a most important crossroads in the interconnection between ethics and tragedy. Drawing on the idea that speech enacts—minutely and at every point—a relationship between people that shifts at every turn, and for which we are accountable, *Hamlet* shifts the very terrain of tragedy and our understanding of tragic action. "Why seems it so particular with thee?" turns out to be one of the play's most central questions. I close this chapter by showing how this question plays out in the last stunning scenes of the play.

In Elsinore, it is impossible to express grief, for that would reveal the truth of the usurping king's relation to the past. In revenge, the relationship between grief and grievance is nurtured but in such a way as the relationship between them is obscured further still. For this reason, Shakespeare has so scrupulously marked the dense classical precedents of this story, for the crisis in grieving is a crisis in the heroic culture. Hamlet has for too long been seen according to an utterly deracinated moral theory, one privileging choice over attention.[79] The ethical dimensions of the play have been lost as questions of "choice" usurp and mask our ethical attention and thus the very object of the play's scrutiny. It is only when we see the profound examination of the concept of action undertaken in *Hamlet* in relationship to the genre of revenge tragedy and its epic precedents in Vergil that the radical nature of the play comes to light.

The relationship between the commonalty of death and the necessity of understanding its particularity (why it seems so particular with thee) is utterly reoriented in the last scenes, chiefly through Hamlet's encounter with the skull of Yorick and with the corpse of Ophelia, both of whom are intimately particular to him, bound up with him in a singular biography. Indeed, the trajectory of act 5, scene 1 for Hamlet is to single out the known dead from the vast generalities, the massed and disintegrating bodies who can be recast according to Hamlet's imagination. As Hamlet and Horatio enter the graveyard, they see the witty and tuneful gravedigger displacing all kinds of old skulls as he makes room for a new coffin. The question of whose grave this "belongs to is" thus playfully deferred for their death-talk. Hamlet speculates about the identity of the first two skulls unceremoniously flung on the stage. The first skull might be Cain, the first murderer, or perhaps a politician, perhaps a courtier. Hamlet assigns words to the skull, casting him in a morbid drama: "Good morrow, sweet lord, how dost thou, sweet lord?" (5.1.77–78) As Hamlet ponders the fine revolution of death that brings his imagined courtier to the chapless, knocked about, worm-ridden state he is now in, a second skull lands next to him, as so much spray off the gravedigger's shovel. Once again Hamlet conjures up miniplays: perhaps the skull was once a lawyer, involved in complex land conveyancing, and he goes on to imagine the concrete details of lawyerly work, imagining a set of purposes now suspended or made pointless by the end to which he comes: "Is this the fine of his fines [F], . . . to have his fine pate full of fine dirt?" (5.1.104–5). Hamlet has surpassed himself in making four puns with the use of *fine*. A fine is a legal document by which entailed property is changed to freehold possession; it is fine as in elegant and praiseworthy; it is fine as in thin and refined, and it is *fin*—an end—evoking the deepest pun in the play: the one on endings and ends, end as telos or purpose, and end as death, the cessation of life. Hamlet now decides to engage in conversation with the gravedigger rather than simply watch over his work. For how long has he been making graves? The gravedigger's answer dates his current employment to the twin events of old King Hamlet's duel with Fortinbras and to Hamlet's very birth. It is as if the jester's death has shadowed his own. How long, Hamlet asks him, does it take for a man's body to begin rotting and disintegrating? As the gravedigger gives his expertise on the subject—a tanner's body outlasts that of others—he selects an exemplary skull, a skull he dates to be precisely twenty-three years old. At this point, Hamlet wants to know: "Whose was it?" (5.1.165). He does not, however, expect to know the one-time inhabiter of the skull. The anonymous bones now tossed up from a sea of death, the countless and innumerable prior generations suddenly give way to one with a minute and particular history, a history that turns out to have been an intimate part of his own. This was a man Hamlet knew. "Alas, poor Yorick. I knew him, Horatio" (5.1.174). It is shocking. No longer part of a history of truisms and platitudes, such as "all that lives must die," no longer an evasive harping on the common theme of deaths of fathers but instead an encounter—raw and surprising—with one whom he once had an intimate relationship. It pertains to him. He cannot cast this skull as a courtier, doctor, or lawyer; he cannot ascribe him any mordantly witty words that come into his head, but instead he must contemplate a man whose life was once so particularly entwined with his own. It "abhors" his imagination and pushes him out of satirical distance into horror and repugnance.[80] His mind moves quickly away from these particularities again, as he imagines even the most mighty of military commanders coming to just such a foul-smelling and ignoble end, and more, stopping a bunghole. He has recast Yorick as Alexander, and then he has imagined Alexander himself as a piece of loam to stop a beer barrel.

This wordplay is interrupted by the "maim'd rites" (5.1.207) of a funeral cortege. Once again, death's great and common generalities are interrupted by a particularly known and loved person. When he asks for whom he is digging the grave, the gravedigger tells him he is digging a grave for a woman. We know it is Ophelia's grave, but Hamlet does not. That knowledge is deferred for several more lines as Hamlet deflects his intimacy with Yorick into further speculation about Alexander and the bunghole. Once again he experiences a transformation from a sense of the common generality of death, to the stark realization of a particular dead person who is profoundly intertwined with his history. Hamlet identifies Laertes as he declaims the churlish priests about the "maim'd rites" given to his suicidal sister. It is in this way that Hamlet realizes that it is Ophelia who is dead, one who has been "particular to him." Exactly how particular we are about to learn in Hamlet's astonishing declaration: "This is I, / Hamlet the Dane" (5.1.246-47), as he too steps into the new grave. He says he will fight with Laertes forever on "this theme" (5.1.255). We have learned that the queen wished Hamlet to marry Ophelia, so Polonius's advice to Ophelia has been pointless, her enforced return of Hamlet's "remembrances to her" wasteful and cruelly redundant. Gertrude now asks on what theme he wishes to fight Laertes, and he bursts out: "I loved Ophelia" (5.1.258). In singling her out, he singles himself out as a lover—one who loved, and was perhaps loved, although thwarted in that love. It is a world of possibility lost, and now only realized through that loss.[81] It is as such an affirmation of a world worthy to be lived in, worthy to be loved.

In a memorable production at Stratford in 2013, Ophelia's body was left on stage for the entirety of the rest of the play.[82] The periphery of the stage was made of earth, which gradually encroached on the boards framing her burial site with its loamy, advancing dust, the promised oblivion of death. It was, I think, a deeply appropriate image of Ophelia's centrality in the play, for it is alone in her exquisitely sad and broken fragments that anyone at all is appropriately mourned: "And will 'a not come again?" (4.5.182). It is Ophelia who blesses her father buried "huggermugger": "God a' mercy on his soul. / And of all Christian souls" (4.5.191-92). We might be reminded that Hamlet is torn between his fascination with the death of Priam and the grief of Hecuba.

Hamlet's astonishing declaration in Ophelia's grave—"I loved Ophelia"— "takes us beyond the questions of what we ought to do to what it is good to be, and then even beyond that, and related to that, to what can command our fullest love."[83] I do not think we knew that he loved Ophelia. His world was not one conducive to the expression of love, and his poor love, Ophelia, is bullied into rejecting him on the falsest grounds and on altogether wrong assumptions. Ophelia's madness, her drowning, is the truest indication of the price of such stupidity, and it is given to her, as I and many other critics have suggested, to offer the most fitting funeral rites of the entire play.

In declaring his love, he declares himself: "It is I, Hamlet the Dane." He discloses himself as a lover, a lover of Ophelia, but not of Ophelia alone, because the declaration is also an affirmation of a world in which love is possible, an affirmation of a world that can command our love.

The possibilities now opened up by this way of thinking help us make sense of the ending of the play. After the graveyard scene, Hamlet and Horatio engage in two extraordinary conversations. It is worth observing that we are learning about Hamlet not through his soliloquies (he stops soliloquizing after 4.4: "How all occasions do inform against me") but through his interactions with others.[84] His antic disposition and his histrionic trying on of roles has obscured our understanding of him as a courtier, soldier, and scholar. We can now learn about him through his engagements with others around him for he is no longer hiding. In these conversations, he tells Horatio of the events on board the ship—both his discovery of his death warrant in Rosencrantz and Guildenstern's keeping, and his substitution of theirs for his as well as the utterly fortuitous capture by pirates that allow him a safe voyage home. All this he says he did "Rashly— / And praised be rashness for it" (5.2.6-7). His deep plots have palled, and it is through unplanned and responsive action that he fortuitously has saved his own life. Hamlet ascribes these events to a providence shaping our ends. This coheres with Lionel Abel's sense that our exits—in that famous dramatic metaphor, their timing, the way they happen—are not fully under our control and that this is one of the great insights of the graveyard scene.[85]

When Horatio advises Hamlet not to engage in the duel with Laertes, my students often call Hamlet's response fatalistic: "We defy augury. There is special providence in the fall of a sparrow. If it be, 'tis not to come. If it be not to come, it will be now. If it be not now, yet it will come. The readiness is all, since no man of aught he leaves knows what is't to leave betimes" (5.2.197-201).

But it is only from the point of view of the naked human will that these words can be seen in a fatalistic light. Hamlet is saying that his end will come, and this is not so much fatalistic as true. His end is inevitable; but he cannot know or predict how it will come about. An acceptance of one's necessary ignorance in a contingent world is not the same as fatalism. What he knows now is what he does not and cannot know. He accepts the inexorable contingency of the world and what happens in it. The attitude of the will has undergone a thorough-going transformation. He is not concertedly willing, plotting, or designing the end of the king, but he is ready to face whatever comes his way, including his own death. We are no longer on the terrain of the oughts of action but in the category of *response*. Hamlet, at this point, is not going to plot or plan but rather will be ready for whatever may come, while not anticipating or knowing what that is or what it will be. Such an attitude might involve a trust in one's own resources. More important, it involves relinquishing any fantasies of will rough-hewing our own ends or the ends of others. Of course, the complex pun on ends involves its meaning as both purpose (the teleology or end of action, the purpose toward which it tends) and also the ending of life (one's own life, or the other's life on whom revenge sets its violent and histrionic designs). In this astonishing finale, the play concludes with a great sense of the mystery of the life beyond, the undiscovered country. Hamlet ends midsentence with his enigmatic phrase: "The rest is silence" (5.2.342). He wants and needs Horatio to explain the circumstances and causes of the carnage around him so that what he has done can be properly understood. We observe a great sense of a continuation of life that does not totally end in our deaths. Charles Taylor puts it this way: "The point of things is not exhausted by life, the fullness of life, even the goodness of life"; this might be "an affirmation that there is something beyond death on which life draws."[86] Hamlet is open now to this possibility and it has changed him. He is converted.

For what does Hamlet do at the end of the play? Under one description we could say this: He duels with Laertes bravely. He wins the first two bouts with Laertes. The queen drinks to his health against the king's advice. (Very much depends on how Gertrude plays this line.) In the third bout, they exchange daggers in the scuffle and they both hit each other; but because Hamlet now mistakenly has Laertes' poisoned dagger, Laertes is poisoned by his own dagger in Hamlet's hand. The queen announces to Hamlet that she is poisoned and lets him know that the king has envenomed the drink. Laertes tells Hamlet that he is poisoned by the rapier, and he tells Hamlet that the king is to blame for both the poisoned cup and the poisoned rapier. It is now and only now that Hamlet stabs the king with the poisoned dagger and forces him to drink the remaining poison from the chalice.

Let us pause to consider the fast-moving action and reaction in the last scene: What has Hamlet done? His act could superficially be described as an act of revenge. Critics of Hamlet's delay can also breathe a sigh of relief to say, "Mission accomplished!" This action, however, might just as easily be described as an act of self-defense or revenge of the mistaken death of the queen, who has gone out of her way to save Hamlet's life and not the king's face. His truth is out; it is public, and for that reason, Hamlet has killed the king not in a private act of vengeance but as a tyrant who has usurped his brother's throne and wife and has perverted the course of justice in such a way that it is obvious to all that the entire court and kingdom have been living lies. Another way of describing this is the following: He has succeeded in dealing with Claudius without becoming like him, without, that is, becoming evil.[87] He has also overcome the specter of his former self—the hatred expressed in the fifth and sixth soliloquies. He has not undertaken an act of secret murder, which would have been his act had he killed the king in prayer. We might also say that he has, despite the horrors of murderous lust that seem to have subsumed for him all possibilities of human erotic affection, succeeded in both loving and declaring his love. He has succeeded in seeing that both a human and a divine love are possible. We can still think him with Horatio, as a "sweet Prince" (5.2.343) and join the prayer that flights of angels may sing him to his rest.

In a superb book on Hamlet, Nigel Alexander has said that it is thus also Hamlet's triumph that he has rescued the mourned dead from the oblivion, those whose memory has been submerged, made invisible through Claudius's "remembrance of himself." In this project, both memory and understanding are subsumed in will. Hamlet's dramaturgy theatrically restores the past and brings it to bear on the present. Alexander says that the "entire play acts as a theatre of memory which stamps upon the mind of the audience an impression of Hamlet's consciousness."[88] Thus, even in the awareness of the great disintegrating anonymity of death, in the company of the sardonic gravediggers, ready to face the odds stacked against him, the prince can know that no matter the universality, the commonness of ends, of death, how we play our particular part is all important. The commonness of our fate absolves us of no responsibility for figuring out our role in it.

Only under the most superficial description is Hamlet's act what his father's ghost envisaged. We might also say of Hamlet's act at the end of the play that it is his act, and not his father's. This is a remarkable achievement of identity—that is, to play his role and not the role his father's ghost has given to him. He wants and needs his act to be described aright because he knows that it could fall under many descriptions.

Consider what the witnesses of the last scene confront and how they might describe it. To those witnessing the duel, and seeing Hamlet pour poison down the king's throat and thrust him with the poisoned rapier, his actions might seem those of a murderous madman, a regicide. They have seen Gertrude die announcing she is poisoned, but they do not know who poisoned her. Although they might hear

Laertes pronounce the reason for his imminent death and Gertrude's, the king is still calling for defense and thinking with remembrance of himself. Hamlet announces that there are things he could tell us, but he is dying and hence not able to tell them. Those in a position to tell, Laertes and Gertrude, are dead. Hamlet will not be believed. All depends on Horatio to report the situation aright if the onstage audience members are to understand what has passed before their eyes. Nothing can be comprehensible to them outside a pattern of significance that now only Horatio can trace, and only if he is to be counted as authoritative in the story.

It is astonishing how very much in the middle of things Hamlet is when he dies. Whether or not we think that Hamlet's last sentence is grammatically incomplete, broken off by death, he ends with the enigmatic "the rest is silence" (5.2.342). What is affirmed is not an isolate heroism but the deep dependence on others for the story of his life, in Horatio's hands and not under his control, delegated to us in an act of trust. To the end, our dependence on each other in grief and in love is affirmed, our testimony of grief and sorrow in showing what we care about.

Chapter 2

King Lear and the Avoidance of Charity
The Spirit of Truth in Love

> For trouthe it is that all Charite is love; but it is not trouthe that al love is charite.
>
> —Thomas Lupset, *A Treatise of Charity*

King Lear is a play about the grammar of love; its role in the value of our lives; its fatal misconstrual, deformation, and obscuring; and the conditions necessary to recover its binding ties. To explore love's grammar, we look at how the word love is used by the lovers in the play, measuring it against our own use of the word, for there is no love without the language of love.[1] On what occasions is this the right, the most fitting, word? When are we called on to speak it? When does that word, fittingly used, bring the world and ourselves into focus? We recall our history with love and its language, our growth—and our failures—in its idioms.[2] We confront our culture's criteria with our words and our life, and we confront our words and our life with the words our culture imagines for us.[3] We look at its connections with a family of interconnected concepts involved in the weave of our lives with love: These might include care, justice, truth, patience, faith, hope, charity.[4] The weave of words with love is so dense in our lives and in this play, so impossible to extract from our forms of life—try to imagine a life without love, any form of love—that my focus in this chapter can only be on love and charity, with some reference to truth and justice. *King Lear* holds before us a "schematism of love," as Eli Friedlander has said, "as if it were holding it in the balance with other fundamental concepts of human existence."[5]

Stanley Cavell has claimed that it is love that King Lear avoids in Shakespeare's astonishing, harrowing play.[6] What can Cordelia do (what can she say) in the face of Lear's question: "Which of you shall we say doth love us most?" (1.1.51).[7] Her first words are an aside: "Love, and be silent" (1.1.62).[8] Cordelia cannot speak her love. *Cannot*, not will not. It is a grammatical, not a psychological, point.[9]

Stanley Cavell calls his great essay on the play "*King Lear* and the Avoidance of Love."[10] I have called this chapter "Shakespeare and the Avoidance of Charity," because it is charity that brings out the implication of love in justice and truth most forcefully. The play extends the avoiding and near voiding of love into an excoriating examination of the theatricalization of charity. It demonstrates the catastrophic workings of that avoidance. It is a play that takes us to new forms of pity and fear and into a new form of tragedy—the tragedy of responsibility.

King Lear begins with a hurtling precipitousness. By the end of the first scene, in a shattering, disrupted ceremony, we have a truthful, loyal servant banished, a daughter brutally discarded and dismissed, the kingdom divided into two, flattery rewarded, and a new hastily improvised plan for Lear's retirement, all effected with remorseless speed. One way of thinking about this scene is as a casting out of love. Seen in this way, the implications of the first scene drive the logic of the play in its entirety. The reach of such a claim is understood only insofar as we understand love not solely as a feeling but as a relation. Augustine expresses that relation by saying: "Love is not loved unless it is *already* [my italics] loving something; for where nothing is loved, there is no love."[11] Love is a bond expressed in relations of charity, before any choosing of the will. The word *charity* is present in the most mundane words of visitation articles and parish and gild records; it is the topic of relations of peace in all manner of human groupings.[12] There, as in the homiletic tradition, *caritas* is a bond, a relation loosed by all things that vitiate it.[13] Love is also a practice of virtue, bound up with how we care and what we care about.[14] For Augustine, it is the form of the virtues. In *City of God*, he says: "A brief and true definition of virtue is 'rightly ordered love.' "[15] To confine the grammar of love to the emotion of loving would hardly show what is *tragic* in this play. Only if love's disclosive relation to justice, care, and truth is brought out can we understand Lear's outcasting, where that gerund works both transitively and intransitively, when it is Lear who casts out and is cast out. Love in this play is a virtue that tends us and turns us to the good *when we recognize it*.[16] Aquinas understood charity as inextricably bound up with justice, and with friendship with God. For Aquinas working in the Augustinian tradition, love of neighbor, God, and self were indissolubly bound up with each other. This is also why the trajectory of the first scene is not alone psychological.[17] When love's power to disclose reality, to show justice, is banished, nothing is left to stand in the way of the violent, instrumentalized, and predatory love of Goneril, Regan, and Edmund.

Love, and Be Silent: The Banishment and Silencing of Love

King Lear begins with a number of speech acts whose effects resonate throughout the play: They are speech acts of bequeathment, disclaiming, disowning, banishment, cursing, and exile. Lear wishes to speak as if there is no gap between his sentences and his power (1.1.171). From that fantasy stems his undoing of reality in speaking, for he speaks as if no others can have a say that he himself has not scripted.

Lear begins, for example, expressing his "darker purpose" with a set of imperatives: "Know we have divided.... Tell me, my daughters" (1.1.35–36; 1.1.48). We might pause over these speech acts. Can you tell someone to "know something?" You can say, "Let it be known," but not "I order you to know." You can *tell* your subjects that you have divided your kingdom, but you cannot tell them what they will know about this division. The gap between his sentence and his power is already there, but it is not a gap Lear knows. He is blind to further necessary implications of speech. By redrawing the spatial boundaries of the kingdom, he is by fiat obliterating the usual path and past of inheritance, which properly depends on his death, and ignoring all future contingencies, ignoring, one might say, the very fact of contingency.[18] He understands his fiat in spatial but not in temporal terms. If spatial and not temporal, his speech act can occlude time's unfolding, and the "impropriety of action," the idea, that is, that his action is not his property.[19] The drawing on the map is an illusion of his will and sovereignty, his autonomy and self-sufficiency, his misrecognition of his needs. It is a picture of sovereign agency: one that imagines the care of others only in relation to their care of him.[20] The idea that he can retain the name and the addition of a king without the trappings of kingship, without those conventions of ceremony, crown, land, property, and relations of obeisance, fealty, and allegiance owed to the office of king, is a fatal confusion of his person and his role, although, of course, his place in a ceremonious world of obeisance and allegiance might lead him to misunderstand that difference. Giving away the kingdom without its trappings is a misunderstanding of his position, a confusion of office and person, and therefore of his responsibilities. His speech enacts fantasies of power, ones that nevertheless are momentarily underwritten by the mirroring, yea-saying, and "obedience" of those around him who sustain the fantasy of a sovereign will. Kenneth Graham suggests that "for the Lear who presides so majestically over his court, formality is reality," and although it might be his last royal act, his word for now still goes as law.[21] Shakespeare thus economically stages how the gap between Lear's sentence and his power widen to an impossible breach. It is all will, divorced from the responsibilities entailed by speech as action.

Lear orders his daughters to tell him who loves him most, but he does so in the form of a question. By asking "Which of you shall we say doth love us most?" (1.1.51) he reserves for himself the sole right to determine ("shall we say") who loves him most. It is an invitation to winning and losing, to a rivalrous competition that obliterates the love for which he appears to have asked. Can we say he does not know what he is doing? Cavell says he is avoiding love and requesting flattery. That is what his speech acts amount to because under these circumstances he *cannot* be requesting love.[22] Under these conditions, as Cordelia so rightly sees, love cannot be spoken without becoming something else—flattery, emotional extortion, competition, rivalry, deceit, or bribery. To say how much she loves him on this occasion would be to rival her sisters, to flatter her father, to take part in a cynical show of obedience in exchange for land and status, converting her words into play acts and rendering them hollow. What Cordelia tells us in her first aside—a form of words both overheard and underheard, as Cavell points out—is that she does love her father, but that her love cannot be voiced, she cannot speak it. Her resounding "Nothing, my Lord" (1.1.87) reveals the problem with his command/request and shows its incoherences. Her stark "nothing," in its unadorned bluntness and granite simplicity, shows fidelity to the value of words.[23] Her words also expose Lear's request, in Cavell's argument, as an avoidance of love's knowledge and love's exposure, for love is mutual where flattery is not. Neither party to the address is revealed in flattery; for this reason, it is a mutually serviceable lie.[24] The flattered is not so much revealed as concealed in flattery, and the flatterer too also does not reveal herself in the proclaimed "love." As Simone Weil says, one distinction between love and flattery is that love "needs reality," whereas flattery is careless of it.[25] The play will explore the devastating consequences of the silencing of love, and the concomitant mistaking of reality. Lear may not have known what he was doing, but he will come to know what he has done. The play will remorselessly track down the consequences of speech acts. Anthony Cascardi has usefully said: "The power of Shakespeare's work rests on his ability to envision characters who live out the fate of their words relentlessly, without compromise or escape, or who suffer disastrously from their failure to do so."[26] It is part of its great innovation to have so pressingly investigated the nonsovereign nature of human action in speech and thus to explore the ethics of address in the exchange of words, in acts of speech.

Lear seeks to overcome the conditions of the bequeathal of a kingdom (his death) and the separate contingencies of the freedom of response of others. Both constitute denials of finitude and the separateness of others. In imagining that he is the source of all that can be given—he asserts, "I gave you all" (2.2.439)—he fantasizes an overcoming of his own given-ness, and what must be in place before he can so much as speak or love. In imagining that he can ask for flattery and call it love, that he can shake off *all* cares and still be cared for, he negates the very relations that sustain him.

Lear's universe at the beginning of the play is thus defined by his imagination that language is a mere extension of his will. He does not see that language bears its own necessity, the necessity of sense, because he occludes the response of others.[27] Until the advent of grace in the figure of his daughter, he will harp on ingratitude. Lear's ceremony of flattery is a denial that there are others in the world. When he banishes love along with the truthful figures Kent and Cordelia, so too he banishes truth and his grip on reality, for love, as Iris Murdoch has told us, is disclosive of reality.[28] Love is not so much an experience or psychological feeling in this regard as it is a concept, honed in the use of words. Lear learns what it is as a matter of painful biography. Because it is a matter of such biography—that which must be lived through and felt—and not externally taught, it is not moralizable.

To draw out the full implications of what Cavell means by an act of speech, it is necessary to differentiate his inheritance of J. L. Austin from the way he is conventionally received in literary studies. Only then can the full ethical force of speech as action, and Shakespeare's radicalization of the idea of action in tragedy, emerge.

In his title essay in *Must We Mean What We Say?*, Cavell argues that a usage of a particular term entitles us to draw certain inferences. This is a question of the normativity of language, an implication that is obscured when rules are understood as imperatives or commands.[29] This is what the learning of language comes to: We are responsible for the implications of our speech. We are responsible for those implications even when we may not know what we are saying and doing. We may not, often we cannot, sometimes we do not, foresee how our words will go out into the world. What Hannah Arendt says of human action, that it is boundless, unpredictable, and irreversible—what is done not being capable of being undone—is true of speech acts.[30] Like other forms of action, the effects of our speech are irreversible—we can recant, abjure, revoke, and retract, but we cannot unsay what we have said. They are unpredictable because, for example, we know that the judge's verdict will result in a prison sentence but not how that verdict will resound in the defendant's life or those of his loved ones. They are boundless in their effects, for one speech act can begin a proliferating chain reaction which cannot be limited or defined in advance. We can begin to see some of the implications of implication: inference, imputation, indication, or suggestion; implication as involvement, connection, and entanglement in bonds "too intrince t' unloose" as Kent puts it (2.2.73) and, last, implication in the quasi-legal sense as bearing guilt, and hence responsibility.[31]

Cavell's inheritance of Austin is brilliantly distinctive. It follows a different path from the way it came to be developed in the field known as performance studies. Austin has been taken up by many critics, but in a sense that is often opposed to the spirit of his writings. For Austin did not think that some language was performative. He thought rather that we do not understand an utterance unless we understand the point of what someone is saying: what they are doing in and with their words. The semantic words will not register a meaning absent the point of saying these words in these particular situations, which explains the kinship between theater and ordinary language philosophy. For Cavell, one might say, theater is a form of ordinary language philosophy. It requires us to ask: Why do Edgar, Goneril, or Coriolanus say just this just now, in response to what, and inciting what response? On what do they stake their authority for saying what they say? Is that authority contested, interrupted, countermanded, or exposed as fraudulent and ill-founded? Is it assumed, insisted upon, arrogated, or risked? In pursuing these questions we will not only be doing what good criticism requires—making the work available to just response—but also imagining precisely, concretely, the simple yet difficult fact that words are said and meant by particular people in particular situations.[32] Theater can thus aid in the consequential flight from particularity, from the world-denying and self-forgetful elimination of the contexts in which words have a use.

Austin helps us to see that if we pay attention to what we do by virtue of our words, we are always talking in relation to the positions we are prepared to assume in relation to each other. You tell me at great length about the rules of baseball, but as I was the local sports reporter for at least ten years and know the team well, I may find you patronizing. Your mother tells you not to drink, but this morning she had a terrible hangover. Even so simple an act as telling someone something is bound up in all kinds of complex ways with our authority in relation to each other. In each of these exchanges, our position in relation to each other shifts—shifts with my waning sense of your authority as I spot your well-meaning hypocrisy, or my simple boredom, or my discomfort with your unyielding condescension. In his essay "Three Ways of Spilling Ink," whose manuscript title was "responsibility", Austin says: "Questions of whether a person was responsible for this or that are *prior* to questions of freedom."[33] Austin's work opens us up to the responsibilities of our responsiveness to each other and the contexts we find ourselves in, and so to an inevitable ethics of speech.

Austin's method for investigating a concept, for doing what he calls "linguistic phenomenology" is to ask, "What should we say when?" (to ask on what occasions do we use certain words and not others) and to parse out the differences and distinctions made in the history of our language.[34] Cavell explains that when we ask that Austinian question (What should we say when?), it is a question about the first-person plural. Sometimes I might be just plain wrong, and it might be indeed a question of evidence at stake. If I am mistaken about what we do, however, that is "liable, where it is not comic, to be tragic."[35] We, as native speakers, are the authority for what we say. These systematic agreements in judgments display accord in our practices and apprenticeship in learning word and world both together and inseparably. To be wrong about what we say and do is to mistake the very conditions and consequences of speech; it is to exile ourselves from the shared and necessary conditions of our existence. To be wrong is not to be put right "with a more favorable position of observation or a fuller mastery of the recognition of objects: it requires a new look at oneself and a fuller realization of what one is doing or feeling."[36]

Cavell argues that conceiving our words as speech acts opens them up to all the problems to which human action is heir—what he calls the pathos of the necessity of action. We might talk about speech *acts*: what we do in and by virtue of speaking. But Cavell also says that speech acts are heir to the pathos of the necessity of sense (hence Cordelia *cannot*, not will not, voice her love in the opening scene), and this entails that his work will be a brilliant extension and reworking of Aristotle's idea of tragedy as an imitation of action.[37]

Cordelia says that she loves her father according to her bond—no more, no less. But this does not entail a diminishment, shackle, or constraint. It is a recognition of a relation she is already in, deeper than a covenant or agreement, for the child does not covenant with her father. Her birth is accident or gift; in any case not willed. The bond with her father is there: It may be accepted or denied, acknowledged or disowned. When Lear attempts to dissolve that bond, the bond of father to child, "disclaiming all (his) paternal care" (1.1.114), disowning the claims to pity and relief of even a neighbor (1.1.120), making her his "sometime" daughter, he denies bonds that precede formal allegiance and agreement (1.1.121). When Austin explores what our words do (what we mean by them), he is indicating the exorbitance of the idea that our word is our bond and that our bonds are not disclosed in particular acts of speech alone but in all we do and say. Niklas Forsberg puts it this way: "The responsibility to mean, to learn, to know, and to love and be loved is a kind of responsibility that never exceeds or surpasses the fact that our word is our bond."[38] This is an ethics in and of speech.

It is not then, I am suggesting, that Cordelia will not express her love because she is stubborn, willful, or clumsy. It is that it is love that she yearns to give Lear, and she cannot speak it under these conditions. For under these conditions, it could emerge only as oily and glib flattery of her father, as competitive rivalry of her more seemingly compliant and clever sisters. We already see emerging from Cavell's analysis of this first scene of the tragedy the conditions of felicity to the speaking of love. Not just anything will count as the voicing of love. Even when the word love is used, the concept may be lost when people do not mean what they say.

It is part of Shakespeare's astonishing insight in this opening scene to perceive that when love is cast out in this way, then so too is truth: "Thy youngest daughter does not love thee least" (1.1.153). We will return to the idea that love is disclosive of reality.

Love and Charity

Biron's magnificent comic speech at the end of the eaves-dropping scene in *Love's Labor's Lost* ends on a high note of self-delight and self-justification:

> It is religion to be thus forsworn;
> For charity itself fulfils the law,
> And who can sever love from charity?
>
> (4.3.337-339)

Mashing together some allusions to Romans 13.8 and Romans 13.10, Biron wittily vindicates the courtiers forswearing of their noble, ascetic aspirations.[39] He shows them how to lose their oaths to find themselves. Biron's delicious equivocation, all in the aid of releasing his companions from their unself-knowing oaths to abjure women, justifies their love as charity. His rationalizing quibble turns on a distinction that had some cultural weight. In Sir Thomas More's compendious debate with William Tyndale, *Dialogue Against Heresies*, continued in the even more expansive *A Confutation of Tyndale's Answer*, More is infuriated by Tyndale's consistent translation of the Vulgate's caritas as love.[40] Where the Vulgate had translated agape as charity, Tyndale preferred to translate it as love. What is at stake in this difference? To More's ear, the idea of charity is fundamentally bound up with the pax, the peace of the mass. Charity is not something given as a donation dispensed in one action, as in Blake's devastating poem "The Human Abstract."[41] Charity is rather something you are *in*. The two different prepositions—giving charity *to* someone and being *in* charity with someone—entail different understandings between those involved in such charitable relations. To be *in* charity is to be implicated in mutual relations. The preposition "to" exposes the separation and one-way traffic of charity. "In" implies relation and mutual participation.[42] It implies bonds that are not subject to negotiation.[43] These relations are fundamentally expressed in the medieval mass and later in Cranmer's *Book of Common Prayer*.[44] You must not come to the table out of charity with your neighbor, for that would be to take the eucharist to your damnation.[45] Those out of charity are to seek out the parish priest to be reconciled with their neighbor. "Therefore, I pray thee prince of pees / That thou wilt make, as thou may best / My hert to be in peece and rest / And redy to love all maner of men," as *The Lay Folk's Mass Book* says.[46] Charity, for More, bears on the relation not alone between a human soul and God, but between neighbor and neighbor, self and soul, and self and God as an indissoluble aspect of each other. If you leave out the neighbor, then love is between soul and God alone. It is a private and not a social love. For the soul that seeks its direction alone from God absent the neighbor has ceased to encompass mutual imbrication and mutual dependence and also has ceased to find it obvious that there can be no such thing as a private relation with God. More's argument with Tyndale rests on how the word charity is commonly used: "charyte signyfyeth in engleysh mennys eres / not every common lore / but a good vertuous and well-ordred love."[47] To his ears, Tyndale's "love" is innovative. It severs the long scriptural tradition whereby agape was rendered as caritas; it severs the communal bond of love and peace associated with the church as the body of Christ; and finally it utterly obscures the association of love with the trinity of theological virtues. Faith was prior to love, but it was incomprehensible without both hope and love.[48] Tyndale, claimed More, "put the indifferent word love in the place of the undowted good worde cheryte."[49] Like Thomas Lupset, More thinks that "though charyte be always loue, yet is not ye wote well love always charyte."[50] Why put the "indifferent word love in the place of the undowted good word cheryte"?[51] Charity carries the Augustinian associations of rightly ordered love: It is, in short, good love.[52]

I have argued, following Stanley Cavell, that love is banished in the first scene with devastating consequences, and I have insisted that this is a grammatical and not a psychological point. For love is disclosive of reality, as Iris Murdoch has claimed.[53] A world in which the honest expression of love is impossible is a world of predation, calculation, and appetite. If love discloses the reality of someone, if it is bound up in and with acknowledgment, then the play extends the grammar of acknowledgment into every imagined social relation and traces out the avoidance of charity as well as the avoidance of love.

The exploration of the avoidance of charity is most evident in the figure of Poor Tom, but it emerges forcefully and pervasively throughout the Gloucester subplot. For the dispossession of Lear and the exile of charity is from the beginning bound up with the terrifying extension of the Cornwalls' jurisdiction. The coming of the Cornwalls to Gloucester's household, where fully fourteen of the play's twenty-six scenes of the play take place, and their assumption of complete power over Gloucester's home, is a gradual, remorseless evacuation of all and any form of charitable love.

The outcasting of the play begins in Lear's banishment of Kent and Cordelia but continues in earnest in Gloucester's household. Before Lear is barred from Gloucester's household—for his own good, so he can taste his folly—before charity is prohibited by the Duke of Cornwall and his wife, their jurisdiction and its terrifying implications are established. Kent is stocked, a punishment reserved for rogues and vagabonds, and the doors are barred to Lear following the pitiful and painful negotiation to keep at least some of his followers. Finally, the home is turned into a torture chamber, where the Cornwalls reveal their lust for domination and where power is nakedly exercised because it can be: "Though well we may not pass upon his life / Without the form of justice, yet our power / Shall do a courtesy to our wrath, which men / May blame but not control" (3.7.24-28).

"When I desired their leave that I might pity him," says Gloucester, "they took from me the use of mine own house; charged me on pain of perpetual displeasure neither to speak of him, entreat for him, or any way sustain him" (3.3.1-5). A world in which leave must be asked for the natural and necessary expression of pity is a world in which some bodies may be whimsically instrumentalized for others; it is a world of domination and violence, a world that leads to torture more terrible than death.

The vocabulary of love extends to charity in the Gloucester subplot, as love's exile is acted out.[54] After Regan's cruel housekeeping—"This house is little; the old man and's people / Cannot be well bestowed" (2.2.474-75)—charity must hide. Gloucester fatally asks his son to cover for him with the duke when he decides to help the king, "that my charity be not of him perceived" (3.3.15). He appears to have been transformed out of listlessness and moral stupidity by the depravity of the Cornwalls' unceremonious takeover of his house. He seeks out Lear against the injunction of the Cornwalls. To Edmund, Gloucester's charity is merely evidence of a putative betrayal that serves his purposes, grist to the mill of his desire, at any cost, to top "Legitimate Edgar" (1.2.16), to become the Earl of Gloucester in his father and his brother's place.

Lear is cast out, debarred from the home.

The Outcast: Charity and Poverty

So we arrive at the strange society of outcasts on the heath: a madman, a fool, and a beggar. Those daring to help them—Kent and Gloucester—are or will be outcast, too. Cavell spells out the centrality of the question of acknowledgment to the figure and idea of the outcast: "So far as we think that the human being is naturally a political being, we cannot think that some human beings are naturally outcasts. So if there are outcasts, we must have, or harbour, *sub specie civilitatis*, some explanation of their condition."[55]

The condition of the outcast is one that fundamentally entails the idea of recognition at its heart. A relationship exists between the outcaster and the outcast, but this is disavowed. The kinds of explanations called for by the outcast may encompass the following ideas, all rehearsed in *King Lear*. The condition of the outcast is deserved. This is Goneril and Regan's position: "The injuries that they themselves procure / Must be their schoolmasters" (2.2.494–5). Or perhaps the outcast is simply unfortunate—his situation lies at the gates of chance. Each of these positions is a denial of the responsibility of the one who casts out. A further fantasy is rehearsed about the outcast. The outcasts are mysteriously in league with each other, a secret confederacy known to each other but opaque to the rest of the world, and in need of decipherment.

Poor Tom is the most obvious instance of the play's complex and comprehensive extension of love to charity and thus with the techniques by which charity as well as love are evaded and avoided. Edgar chooses the disguise of an outcast that complexly exemplifies a theatricalization of charity. The country he says, "gives me proof and precedent / Of Bedlam beggars" (2.2.184–85) who "sometime with lunatic bans, sometimes with prayers / Enforce their charity" (2.2.190–91). His disguise as Poor Tom bets on the double invisibility of "the basest and most poorest shape" (2.2.178). He will not be recognized as the Earl of Gloucester's erstwhile son because he will disguise himself as a bedlam beggar, but to be a beggar is precisely to be unseen, avoided, and unrecognized as a fellow man. Edgar relies on his culture's fear of beggars. In her book *The Fear of Beggars*, Kelly Johnson says: "Although abstractly most people recognize that all of us are in some respects dependent upon each other, the sight of a stranger asking for help outside the public order of rights and the private affection of the family shakes us up."[56] The figure of the Bedlam beggar adopted by Edgar is, I argue, a theatricalization of charity.

If we assume that poverty is merely an assumed role, we will not feel obliged to respond to it. This attitude is nurtured and conjured, fed by the proliferation of literature about the vagrant. It merges straight out of an inventive, long-lived literature of cony-catching, a literature that began with the epistemological drive to distinguish the deserving from the undeserving poor. The literature that spawns the bedlam beggar and the Abraham man is a literature of discovery and exposure. It translates the so-called canting underworld with its dense confederacies and imagined opaque conspiracies and lays it bare to the judicial eye. Such confederacies are to be taxonomized, discovered, and revealed in their cozenage; their language is translated so that it is now transparent to the ruling classes. The poor are pretending, and their pretense must be displayed to avoid being the cony whose charity is enforced. For example, Harman, in *A Caveat for Common Cursitors*, exposes the ruse of a "dummerer," one who acts dumb so as to be more pitiful: "The most part of these will never speak, unless they have extreme punishment, but will gape, and with a marvellous force will hold down their tongues doubled, groaning for your charity, and holding up their hands full piteously, so that with their deep dissimulation they will get much."⁵⁷

Harman's tract builds on other cony-catching pamphlets, and his purpose it to detect the counterfeit more easily: "I have repaired and rigged the ship of knowledge, and have hoist up the sails of good fortune, that she may safely pass through about and through all parts of this noble realm."⁵⁸ Harman reveals then that the project of this literature is epistemological: It displaces acknowledgment for knowledge. The relation to the poor man is one in which knowing precisely blocks the natural response of pity. Indeed, what you learn about him in these helpful materials, obviates the need for any other response apart from avoidance and self-protection. In Poor Tom's disguise in the Gloucester subplot then, the avoidance of love, of charity, is not merely a personal oversight on the part of the man who was king—"O, I have ta-en / Too little care of this" (3.4.32-33)—but rather a systematic and rigorous display of the conditions of the avoidance of charity as an aspect of love. The "Abram man" is a figure straight out of this literature. The marks on their flesh are self-made "with a sharp awl pricking or razing the skin to such a figure or print as they best fancy." Thomas Dekker's *O per se O* (1612) compounds this tradition: "All that they beg being either lure or bouse [money or drink]." His gestures are "antic," "ridiculous," "counterfeit," a "puppet play" culminating in "Good dame, give poor tom one cup of the best drink-well and wisely."⁵⁹ Beggars are charlatans or under suspicion of being so. Linda Woodbridge has shown decisively that the pictures of penury and beggary derived from this "underworld" or "canting" literature feeds the legislation that compounds poverty and vagrancy.⁶⁰

When Lear responds to his daughters' cold calculation of his needs for maintenance, with this outburst: "O, reason not the need! Our basest beggars / Are in the poorest thing superfluous" (2.2.453-54), he is in a long lineage of inquiry about the question of need. It is a spontaneous outburst showing his acknowledgment that need cannot be calculated, as the horrors of now being spoken for by these daughters dawns on him. In examining Langland's complex exploration of the figure of Need in his great allegorical poem *Piers Plowman*, for example, Kate Crassons has shown the costs and longevity of a mode of depiction that renders the question of need a problem of knowledge rather than a problem of response. Poverty, she suggests, and Langland shows, requires recognition. It privileges the category of human response. Langland is responding to the complexity of poverty in his culture, which was innovative for establishing an ambitious system for documenting and identifying the poor in the legislation of 1376 and 1388. The Commons Petition Against Vagrants (1376) and the subsequent Cambridge Statute of Labourers (1388) established a scheme for documenting and identifying mobile workers. It combined—as later poor laws were to do for a considerable period of time—both a regulation of work and a regulation of poverty, attempting to make possible the discrimination of the deserving and the undeserving poor. Crassons insightfully says that "the single feat of asking someone for some identification was meant to replace other more challenging forms of human response that required people to exercise moral judgment by acknowledging need, dismissing its real presence, or refusing to scrutinize what they thought ultimately unknowable."[61] Langland brilliantly insists, as does Lear, on the opacity of need: It cannot be reasoned in the way such legislation presumes. Indeed, Paul Slack, one of the leading historians of Elizabethan and Jacobean poverty legislation has said that the system "made paupers and delinquents by labelling them."[62]

When Shakespeare wrote *King Lear*, the mobile workers of the land lacked political recognition. In a land where laws dealing with poverty and laws mandating labor had for two centuries worked hand in glove, the poor lived out the bitter ironies of a culture that had often—through poor harvests, marginal existence, and enclosure—driven them off the land. Poor law legislation attempted to discriminate between the deserving poor—too old or impotent to work—and those mobile laborers who were deemed to be vagrant or roguish. They were whipped and sent back to their parish to work. The unsettled poor lacked recognition for they inhabited a society in which identity was still defined by place. The unsettled were sent back to their parishes, and the mobile poor were consciously separated from vagrants as a punishable offence only in 1662 with the Settlement Acts, when a provision was made for the return, without punishment, of migrants likely to be chargeable to the parish. The poverty and vagrancy laws made poverty an epistemological issue. Donors were obliged and encouraged to discern the difference between the deserving and undeserving poor, with the confidence that such an act was so much as possible. It was, in fact, proscribed to give to the undeserving, and so telling them from the real poor was essential, if impossible. The difficulties of acknowledgment are covered over with the technologies of knowledge, and charity's links to gratuity and generosity, to fellowship and neighborliness, are severed. Edgar talks of "enforcing charity"(2.2.191) as if charity must be coerced and acquired by threat, thus again vitiating it.

In the Sam Mendes's 2014 National Theater production of *King Lear*, the stage was populated by eight or nine actors playing a community of vagrants. They are cleared out of the way for the ceremonial entrance of the king, a striking gesture of ridding the king and court of their presence. Yet in Lear's great address—"Poor naked wretches, whereso'er you are" (3.4.28)—he envisages not the labeling and taxonomy of poverty but an imaginative sense that we ourselves might be such naked wretches. Homeless (houseless?) as he now is, he calls on "poor naked wretches" wherever they are, looped and ragged, their very bodies utterly open, houseless to the world: "How shall your houseless heads and unfed sides, / Your looped and windowless raggedness, defend you / From such seasons as these?" (3.4.30-31). The awareness of exposure and defenseless vulnerability is now linked to his own lack of care. If he persists in seeing Poor Tom, who enters as if on cue as a very instance of the "naked wretch," as an image of himself, "Didst thou given all to thy two daughters?" (3.4.48), and as the very philosophical picture of an unaccommodated man, and if he wishes in his failing senses to show himself as "unaccommodated" as Poor Tom, he nevertheless takes shelter in his company. It is the beginning of care, and it stirs in him an idea of profound injustice in which he has played a part. This implicates him with the claims of others even in his incipient madness.

"How have you known the miseries of your father?" Albany asks Edgar (5.3.179). "By nursing them, my Lord," Edgar replies (5.3.180). This is not quite true, for we may say, as Edgar shortly says of himself, that he has known but not acknowledged the miseries of his father. He has sought to cure them and "Never—O fault revealed myself unto him? / Until some half-hour past, when I was armed" (5.3.191-92). For to acknowledge his father's miseries would have been to reveal himself not as a hero, not as the fair unknown of romance who will perfectly reconcile gentility with true gentleness, but as the one disowned, abandoned, and dispossessed.

It is Cordelia who knows the miseries of her father by nursing them. Before we can arrive at that scene of care and love, we need to continue to understand the play's relentless and searing investigation of love's banishment in Cornwall's jurisdiction.

Jean Améry, in his astonishing exploration of his torture at the hands of the Gestapo said: "Whoever has succumbed to torture can no longer feel at home in the world."⁶³ What links the outcasts on the heath with the terrible scene of Gloucester's blinding is the connection of careless love to transcendental shelterlessness. These men are not "houseless" (3.4.30) but homeless. When Améry says he cannot find a home again, he does not mean he will not once again find shelter. He means that his fundamental trust in the world is a condition from which he is forever exiled; he is transcendentally, not empirically, lost.

Torture, Devastation

Simone Weil may have had *King Lear* in mind when she posed the following question in her essay "Human Personality": "What is it, exactly, that prevents me from putting that man's eyes out, if I am allowed to do so and it takes my fancy?" We might think immediately of Cornwall's power doing "courtesy" to his wrath. She answers: "What would stay it is the knowledge that if someone were to put out his eyes, his soul would be lacerated by the thought that harm was being done to him." For at the bottom of every human being from earliest infancy until the tomb, she claims, "there is something that goes on indomitably expecting in the teeth of all experience of crimes committed, suffered and witnessed, that good and not evil will be done to him."⁶⁴ Cora Diamond has linked Weil's exploration to the grammar of love by saying that "the awareness of the other being that impedes doing injustice is a kind of love, or loving attention."⁶⁵ This, I suspect, is the reason that Shakespeare confronted us with the most terrible scene in British theater: act 3, scene 7, the unprecedentedly harrowing scene of torture.⁶⁶ In this scene, as Cavell points out, it is Gloucester's calling out of his hope that "I shall see / The winged vengeance overtake such children" (3.7.64–5) that precisely prompts Cornwall's act of blinding. What he wishes to eradicate is thus not just Gloucester's poor eyes, but the very idea that justice will be, will *ever* be, seen to be done. Weil's essay is an argument with a moral theory based on rights, which separates justice from "love, pity, and tenderness," from the naturalness of our responses.⁶⁷

"Bind fast his corky arms" (3.7.28). On the Duke of Cornwall's orders, Gloucester is first made helpless. Gloucester's bound impotence is an essential prologue to torture. For it is our natural expectation that if we suffer, we will be succored. It is against this background of the thought that aid will come to us that we grasp the connection between pain and help, between suffering and succor. Gloucester cries out in his pain, and that pain is incorrigibly plain and present to us but chillingly absent as a reason for action.⁶⁸ The binding of Gloucester's "corky arms" prepares him for the severing of suffering from the expectation of aid. This is a radical dispossession. Gloucester began by reminding the Duke of Cornwall and Regan that they are his guests, but the rules of hospitality, whereby even a stranger might be welcomed, do not apply here. Gloucester is unneighbored and deprived of every consolation. The son he calls on to avenge this "horrid act," he is told, is the one who betrayed him (3.7.86). Stripped of his very agency, he is also stripped, radically, of his trust in the world, that primordial trust linked to the expectation of good.

In the weave of our lives with love, trust is primordial and primary, woven into our earliest dependence and care, and allowing us to inhabit our dependence and vulnerability, without having to face the full extent of our helplessness. It is these relations in Améry's and Jay Bernstein's accounts that show how systematic the destruction of trust is in torture and how radical the dispossession. For what Gloucester is left with—what drives him to despair and suicide—is that he counts for no one and that the undoing of his person, not the pursuit of information, "Be simple answered for we know the truth" (3.7.43), is Cornwall's point and obscene passion. In destroying his trust in the world, Cornwall has severed the natural and normative relation between love and trust as well as the deepest bond between self and other.

If this analysis rings true for this devastating and prescient scene of harm, Shakespeare has staged the undoing of personhood not just in the dispossession of Poor Tom or the dispossession of Lear's wits in his confusion and madness but also in the devastation of Gloucester's person through the undoing of who he has taken himself to be, through his forced disowning of his self.⁶⁹ Only through a sense of the normativity of trust can the links between love and justice be parsed out, as in this scene of devastation.

Love, Grace, and Forgiveness: The Responsibility of Response

Lear's encounter with Cordelia in act 4, scene 7 is an exquisite extension of the grammar of love in this play. Through the minute responses of Cordelia and her father, love's reach becomes intimately exposed and extended in its claims and responsibilities. This is as true for Cordelia as it is for her father. The great scene of recognition (4.7) is also a *real-ization*, an awakening to reality and to the intimacy of love with truth. The lover has to be *in* his or her words to express love. She has to mean what she says for her love to be loving. This expression of love simultaneously involves a kind of presence to the self and to the other.

In this famous encounter between Lear and his banished daughter, the question of acknowledgment is first flagged between Kent and Cordelia by way of prologue. Cordelia greets Kent in gratitude of his care and goodness: "O thou good Kent, how shall I live and work / To match thy goodness?" (4.7.1–2) Kent's answer is that "to be acknowledged" is "o'erpaid" (4.7.4) As if in response to this question, Cordelia requests that he discard his disguise and resume his appearance as the Earl of Kent, that he be present as himself, but in return Kent asks her not to "know" him until "time and I think meet" (4.7.10–11). The great sadness is there is no meet or suitable time in this play for Kent to be acknowledged, at least by Lear, although much depends on Lear's greeting: "You're welcome hither" (5.3.287), which he says to Kent in the play's harrowing last scene after he has revealed that he was "your servant Kent" (5.3.281). Although Cordelia can privately acknowledge Kent, it appears that Kent does not want to be recognized by anyone else, perhaps on the understanding that his services to Lear are for now better served in disguise. So the acknowledgements between Kent and Cordelia remain private, and are not extended into a wider world. They remain hidden and to that extent, still in retreat. The relief in the meeting of these two, faithful lovers all, is a large relief for them and for us, too: "To be "acknowledg'd is "o'erpaid" (4.7.4).

As the Doctor and the Gentleman enter, Cordelia's first question is to ask how "the King" does (4.7.12). Told that he is still sleeping, she first addresses the gods in a prayer for his cure. The prayer acknowledges his damaged and bereft state—he is a "child-changed" father—changed by his children or changed into a state of childishness. Her prayer also expresses a faith in harmony that precedes chaos, for she pays witness in her prayer to his "untuned" senses, as if the natural state is accord, attunement (4.7.16). Before he is fully awake, she kisses him, a kiss we might remember when he asks us to look, look there at her lips in the play's devastating end, for it is a kiss of repair and reverence. The shocking confrontation with his face—"Was this a face / To be exposed against the warring winds?" (4.7.31–2)—and with his lostness—"poor perdu" (4.7.35)—registers his worthiness for care and her astonishment at her sisters' carelessness. Her words bear a full understanding of the extremes of his exposure, and perhaps in the face of this, there is a momentary balking, a hesitation before the encounter, and she asks the Doctor to speak with him. He replies that it is fittest for her to do so. It is fittest because the breach between these two, between father and daughter must be addressed. The delicate but utterly precise propriety of the scene calls out for *this* meeting. It must be risked, gone through, if these two are to be in relation.

Every fact about their meeting is risky: that they are there now at all, marked out for capture, with enemy encamped around; that Lear may not be intelligible; that he may not share the same world as Cordelia; and that she might once again be turned away because of his deep shame, the old and the newly found. The results of this fitting encounter cannot be foreknown or guaranteed; their bond will have to be felt out word by word. She at last addresses him as her "royal lord" and "majesty," granting him the reverence and dignity due to a king but—surely—due to an old man, too (4.7.44). Is this an address? For he is still asleep. They allow him the time to get his bearings, they wait on him, and they attend to him: "He's scarce awake. Let him alone awhile" (4.7.52).

Cordelia's response to his casting out is this striking phrase: "Mine enemy's dog / Though he had bit me, should have stood that night / Against my fire" (4.7.36-38).[70] It is striking given the state of charity in Britain that Edgar's guise and disguise has shown. Cordelia would have sheltered even the vicious dog of one who wished her harm. Cordelia's love is not confined to any single object; her love of her father extends to the creatures in the world, even to their noncomprehending harm of her. Her exclamation shows that love of the world accompanies the open-hearted love of others, extending its gratuitous good from the single objects of its care and attention. Her response to Lear seeks no justification or reasons; it is purely instinctive and responsive.

Lear does not know where he is—in heaven, hell, or, if on earth, in France or England. Nor does he know how he comes to be clothed in the garments he is wearing, or where he spent the previous night. He worries whether he is in possession of his wits. All this comes a bit later. For now, slowly awakening, he will say words that indicate that he thinks he might be dead. If he is dead, she seems to him like one from heaven, a soul in bliss, as he is in hell bound on a wheel of fire. The quarto gives Cordelia's next line as "Sir, know me." Is this a plea, an entreaty, or a request? It cannot be an order or a command for she has already shown, by addressing him as majesty, that the obeisance is owed to him and not to her. The folio changes this to the more fitting: "Sir, do you know me?" (4.7.48). This is a question to which the answer is not yet clear, and yet it is the most important question of the play. The scene will delicately and beautifully illuminate what it means to know someone, to acknowledge someone, and it will insist that such acknowledgments are always mutual. Lear will hesitatingly and slowly find his way toward his daughter only by acknowledging that he is fond and old. Earlier in the play, Regan had invited just such a confession: "Sir, you are old: / Nature in you stands on the very verge / Of her confine" (2.2.335–36), a cruel accusation to which Lear bitterly responds: "Dear daughter, I confess that I am old; / Age is unnecessary" (2.2.342). To another daughter, feeling his way into speech, Lear belatedly responds to her question "Sir, do you know me" with "I know not what to say" (4.7.54). He cannot swear that even his hands are part of a composite body. He is "not assured" of his condition, alive or dead, a spirit or a human (4.7.56). He pricks himself with a pin to see if he is flesh and blood: Any true response to Cordelia's question must come from the acknowledgment of his flesh and blood, his folly, his vanity as part of the history of actions that are not and were not his alone to define or own. Cordelia kneels and asks his blessing. She seeks his benediction, his good speech, over her. He, too, will seek to kneel as if to seek the same, the good in speaking. The rest is all benediction, all blessing, and they share each other's lines: "*Cordelia:* You must not kneel. *Lear:* Pray do not mock" (4.7.58).[71] It is as if all the lines are still an attempt to answer her question: "Sir, do you know me?" These are everyday, ordinary words. To acknowledge her as his daughter is to acknowledge his disowning, his banishment, of her.

Then he risks the expression of what he thinks he does know: "I know you do not love me" (4.7.73). It is all he can venture for he cannot yet envisage a love whose fidelity would survive such a cruel banishment. She has cause not to love him. He is expecting and he is owed a love according to his deserts. Her answer to this is profound: "No cause, no cause" (4.7.75). What is she doing here? She is not so much forgiving him as suggesting that she is not operating in an economy of guilt or punishment in any world of desert or deservings. Cause has the sense of reason and the legal understanding of cause as a matter you are entitled to take to law. (We have of course seen all legal structure utterly collapse in this play: Who can arraign me? is Goneril's challenge (5.3.157). Lear can arraign only a joint stool in his heartbreaking search for justice.)

Is there any *cause* in nature that makes these hard hearts? This has been Lear's devastating, unanswerable question. To his reply that Cordelia has a reason not to love him, her answer is that reasons and causes do not come into it. To his desire for punishment at her hands—"If you have poison for me, I will drink it" (4.7.72)—she offers a different ground, a groundless ground. "No cause" is the ground of grace. Tony Tanner has beautifully said of this scene: "Hearts are causes. . . . Is there any cause in nature that makes these gentle hearts?"[72] Emilia's response, as he reminds us, is the best: "They are not ever gentle for the cause, but gentle for they're gentle."[73] Cordelia also reveals that love is not funded by causes; they come after the fact of loving, to justify and enhance the unanticipated, unsummoned gift of love.

In the first scene of the play, in the plea to her father before France, she had asked that her father make it clear that what deprived her of her father's grace and favor was a want of the glib and oily art that separates the speaker from her true purpose in speaking. "What I well intend," she says, "I'll do't before I speak" (1.1.227-28). She understands that empty words of love evacuate the concept of love, and betray both her father and herself. In this scene, she does not *speak* of love at all. But she reveals it in her every care for his dignity and attention to his frailty and awareness of his shame, although such shame does not diminish her love for him. Perhaps her own love has extended beyond the bond of childhood, the bond of marriage, to an exorbitant love that cannot know what claims might be made on it, and whose words are the more delicate for that harrowing experience of suffering another's devastation. Love encompasses but spreads far beyond duty returned, obedience owed, and honor due.

In Mendes's rendering of this scene in the 2014 production, Simon Russell Beale as Lear gave a long pause between forget and forgive. *Cordelia:* "Will't please your highness walk?" *Lear:* "You must bear with me. / Pray you now forget and forgive, I am old and foolish" (4.7.82-84).[74] Bearing with each other is the only thing this play offers in the end. It may not seem to be much, but it is everything.[75] The long pause between forget and forgive—the first time I ever heard these lines spoken in this way, offer a complete reversal of the way I usually read and heard them. Forget and forgive deliberately reverses the more conventional forgive and forget, forgetting, coming conventionally after forgiving. Now, however, forgive is the slowly realized afterthought, painfully added on, coming after the desire for oblivion and serving as an antidote.

Grace is groundless and gratuitous. It is unprecedented and given, and it is not generated by the structures of the will. The Reformation, with its deep encounter with the thought of Augustine and Saint Paul, sees that the recognition of sin is retrospective and so deepened the Christian appreciation of grace. We can only bear the recognition of our sinfulness in the light of the grace of God (*simul justus et peccator*). Grace does not come after a recognition of sinfulness but rather is that recognition in the light of the good it has absented from view.[76] If Cordelia's love is divine, like Christ's love, it is because it is known only in the acknowledgment of it.[77]

We know Cordelia dies, that her death is unbearable for Lear, that he dies perhaps imagining that she is not yet dead, and that even that consolation—if that is what it is—is an illusion. The work of grace in this play is neither a theodicy nor a justification of the ways of God to man, but rather a pattern of response to bear with. What happens in this scene can be described as the advent of grace as love and forgiveness, and now, Shakespearean tragedy seems unimaginable outside this glimpse of graced awareness. Lear's dawning awareness of Cordelia is not generated by his will and is no longer confined by his deserts. Lear is faithful, for the rest of his life and the rest of the play, to the space held open by Cordelia's loving loyalty and by his awakened ability to attend and see it for love.

The kind of love Cordelia offers brings truth not consolation. That is why we can talk about realization—in which case realization is a recognition of a reality, and a making something real.

In registering the weight of her love, Cordelia said that it was more ponderous than her tongue and that she could not heave her heart into her mouth because of it. It is as if she understands the gravity and the grace of words as bonds. It was Augustine who beautifully said, "My weight is my love."[78] This is Lear's cue when he comes in bearing Cordelia in his arms. Nicholas Rowe was the first editor to add the word *dead* to the stage direction: "Enter Lear with Cordelia dead in his arms."[79] It is a demand of physical stamina that every older actor has to undertake; and it is an existential task for the character, Lear, to bear the weight of her shortened life and the desperate hope of deferring her death. This is the burden of a finite love, to have its preciousness so singularly and distinctly embodied. With Lear we all want to say: "Stay a little" (5.3.269).

In his invitation to bring our words home, as if we have been exiled from our flight from what we mean by them, Ludwig Wittgenstein enjoined us to "look and see."⁸⁰ *King Lear* ends with the old, frail king, now incapable of distraction, looking at Cordelia, in particular at her lips, "Look on her: Look, her lips, / Look there, Look there!" (5.3.309-10). In some stage versions of *King Lear*, Lear gazes at the air around him as if Cordelia's soul has departed with her last breath, as if he is seeing it. In others, Lear is caught in the illusion that she is alive, as if the old romance form from which Shakespeare had so carefully excavated and inverted the Lear story is back as a romance: She is alive! Paul Fiddes, however, has suggested that Lear is doing what he says, asking us to look at Cordelia and see her for her wonder, her life, her very being.⁸¹ For what we know from Lear is that love (and trust and pity) are forms of recognition and that we are sustained only through love's relation to care. For creatures revealed and exposed in our dependencies, for creatures so intrinsically, so intrinsicately, bonded to each other, the loss and the preciousness cannot be separated.

The play restores us to love's hard realities and the forms of our lives with love. Why do I talk about the banishment of love when there seems to be a plenitude of it among the characters Goneril, Regan, and Edmund, and in other relationships of allegiance? And why "restoration"? The same word is, after all, used by the play's evil lovers. At the end of the play, Edmund can say, extraordinarily, "Yet Edmund was beloved" (5.3.237), when he realizes that, "The one the other poisoned for my sake, / And after slew herself" (5.3.238-39). This late understanding of being beloved might even sponsor the good he means to do immediately afterward: "Do you want to discern the character of a person's love?" asks Augustine: "Notice where it leads."⁸² The love between Goneril, Regan, and Edmund is rivalrous, however, and continues the competition in love introduced in the first scene and the illusion of its quantification. Edmund imagines that to be loved by more than one woman is to be loved more; the love of Goneril and Regan is mutually death-dealing. Absent a vision of a sharing that precedes it, absent an understanding of the priority of being in relations of primordial love, Goneril and Edmund's unhandsome and predatory grasping, their compelled appetite, and their instrumental use of others show the word to be reliant on its prior use. But this use distorts the concept, for example, severing the links with truth, charity, and justice and with the "loved" one's separate gratuitous worth. It has ceased to mean anything like a bond in which rivalry is suspended or inapplicable, or as John Burnaby puts it, not "monopolizable."⁸³ The exploration of love's grammar is then in order precisely because the lovers in the play are stretching the concept, subordinating it to the isolated, choosing will, while also using the same word. In subtle ways, the kinds of loss involved in such a narrowing down of the concept of love might be hard to see.

When representation is the chief focus of criticism, and adequation to reality is seen solely in terms of reference, then other (moral and ethical) ways of thinking about reality drop out. Then we will ignore what Diamond calls the "difficulty of reality" as a moral question and the difficult task of seeing, say, the reality of another person.[84] In the vision of language of ordinary language philosophy, we do not lose contact with reality, and with ourselves and others, when we represent something that does not exist. Rather, we lose contact with reality when we lose our grip on *sense*, because language and reality are internally connected.[85] When we cannot make sense or cannot understand the sense others are making, when we cannot see the point of what they are saying, then we lose our grip on our reality and the reality of others.[86]

Peter Winch has expressed this idea when he says: "Reality is not what gives language sense. What is real and what is unreal shows itself *in* the sense that language has."[87] Becoming real, seeing what is real (which may have all along been right in front of us), appreciating the reality of others in our lives is a moral and ethical task. Our everyday language reflects precisely this understanding of reality, not only its fragility and evanescence but also the relief that comes from clarity and insight, the way we come into focus for each other when we see the point of our words on any particular occasion. It is the sense of reality evoked in such phrases as "I barely existed for him" or "When I actually met with her, I realized that my version of her was fundamentally distorted by my sense of resentment and envy, and I was able to appreciate different things about her," that create a sense of the difficulty of reality for us as it emerges in everyday ways in our relationships with each other. The ways in which reality is caught up in our speech acts is thus never general and is never secured by anything outside our relations with each other. Forsberg puts the point very well when he says: "If words are not merely the names of things—though they can be that too—but more importantly interconnected to how a particular life is led, then, the matter of 'meaning' means listening to the sense of our words and to one's other. To lead by listening is to know and understand how a word and the speaking person belong to a particular context of use or form of life."[88]

Perhaps current criticism focuses on a too-narrowly circumscribed region of language—representation—and mistakes it for the whole of language. Perhaps it ignores how we are implicated in our speech acts other than by being represented. *King Lear*, with its extension of tragic action to the actions of our words, might bring this perspicuously into view, showing us the very shapes of love and how its intrinsic connections with hope, faith, patience, trust, and truth unravel to such devastating effect.

Chapter 3

Benefits and Bonds
Misanthropy and Skepticism in Timon of Athens

beneficium sine altero non est

—Seneca, *De Beneficiis*

If I owe for everything I own, I do not have what I think I have. It is not mine. The Apostle Paul asks: "What hast thou, that thou hast not received?" (1 Cor. 4:7)[1] In this idiom, owing all that you "own" is not debt but grace. In the first instance, I owe money. In the second, I owe thanks in giving and receiving. One is debt; the other is gift. A society that gets in a muddle about these kinds of debts is liable to become graceless.

Timon of Athens, that elemental, austere, and starkly emblematic play, is an exploration of these two modes of dispossession and the primal horrors evoked when giving and receiving go awry. In its exploration of ingratitude and the responses it provokes, the play helps us to think about giving, receiving, gifts, debt, and bonds as what we owe to each other in ethical relation.[2]

Timon of Athens is a play about the *depths* of human bonds. It addresses the ways we are tied to each other in relations of obligation, claim, and responsibility. The bonds at stake, as I shall show, are bonds of recognition. Those bonds are subject to fatally divergent understandings in the play, and sometimes too in the criticism about the play. Are we bonded to each other only in the language of contract, explicit promises, vowing? Or, if our word is our bond, do all our words link and tie us exorbitantly, minutely, and precisely at each and every moment in ways we sometimes fail to see?[3]

It is hard to stay on one's feet in the face of Timon's blast of "No!" to life. The play is famously, fundamentally aversive: We see hatred, anger, revenge, resentment, cynicism, betrayal, and disgust, all in extremis.[4] It is as if the play tests our most fundamental capacities for attachment, including to the play and to its eponymous hero/antihero. If he hates all humankind, he hates us too. The very force of Timon's powerfully articulate hatred keeps him linked with us (hatred is a bond; indifference, not hatred, is the opposite of love).

Its central protagonist, Timon, has been betrayed in his tacit yet fundamental expectations of reciprocity, his expectation that others might do for him what he has done for them.[5] The unspoken (unthought?) assumption of give and take in a world of universal brotherhood is only revealed in its betrayal, after the fact, and retrospectively. The brothers turn out to be "mouth-friends": The pseudo friends coin money from Timon but come up empty when asked for a return of his benefaction. Timon will later characterize the entire cosmic and natural world as one of universal thievery; advantage and exploitation are no longer exceptional but are the world's way of working. Out of his rage, out of his sense of violated trust, he bitterly, hyperbolically, primally curses one and all. He wishes every bond of love, duty, and obligation—and all that supports and sustains those bonds—to be undone, corroded and confounded. He comes to believe, along with his later interpreter Karl Marx, that the poisonous yellow gold of money is the most astonishing solvent of all.[6] It undoes bonds that, in Kent's important and felicitous phrasing in *King Lear*, we might have thought were "too intrínce" to "unloose."[7] Whether these bonds are "too intrince to unloose" will be a continuing question in this chapter.

The play is repulsive and difficult. It is repulsive not only because it focuses so relentlessly and thrillingly on the aversive emotions but also because it appears to deprive its audience of any understanding to repair its fractured bonds, or even to approach the excoriating ressentiment, preemptive hatred, and utter suspicion of the man, Timon, whose sense of moral injury is unassuageable.

The difficulties of the play are notorious. Is it unfinished?[8] There were certainly no records of performance. It is included in the first folio only by accident: John Heminge and Henry Condell put it in the folio when *Troilus and Cressida* was pulled from its original position between *Romeo and Juliet* and *Julius Caesar* because of problems with copyright.

Timon filled the gap but left eight blank pages because it is a shorter play than *Troilus*. It is arguable that the joint authors (Thomas Middleton and William Shakespeare) have different pictures or visions of social relations such that the satirical and the tragic impulses of the play pull against each other.[9] Tragic effect usually banks on our sense of value, that we can find something precious in the very act and fact of loss. What might have been must pull at us. Things happened this way. This need not have been so, but because it is so, the consequences unfold necessarily. Satire, although it may offer us an unblinkingly clear view of our moral failings, lacks this sense of necessity. In satire we are disgraceful but reformable. Satire encourages our moral judgment and usually gives us good reasons to be judgmental, whereas it is characteristic of Shakespeare's late tragedies that our responses *are* our form of recognition. Moral judgment works precisely through those responses, thereby exploring the responsibilities of response.[10] Satiric energies tend to be prospective, rather than retrospective like tragedy's energies. These questions about genre register the kinds of claims the play makes on us, and our difficulty in response.[11] The play's challenges illuminate the question of ethics and tragedy at the heart of this book. Timon's misanthropy is exposed as a refusal of moral relation. Shakespeare and Middleton's inheritance of a discourse of benefits, and good deeds, indicates what is at stake in a grammar of giving and receiving and the recognitions implicated in such a grammar.

Words Are Rascals Since Bonds Disgraced Them

The word *bond* in Shakespeare is multifaceted and dense. I give a few brief instances across the Shakespeare canon to suggest the tensions and pressures on the concept of binding.[12] We come across it, for example, in a jocular pun of the fool Feste in *Twelfth Night*, in which he says to Viola: "Words are very rascals since bonds disgraced them" (3.1.18). Feste's words pun on bonds as written contracts, and he seems to mean we cannot trust words (they are rascals) because the agreements between men and women are now based on written contracts rather than on their word.[13] He might also mean that people have broken their bond so often that words can no longer be trusted: It is men and women, through their words, who are no longer trustworthy. Either way or both, his words indicate that trust is at issue in the most fundamental ways in which we have a world with each other in so far as "our word is our bond." Anthony Nuttall calls it "a remark of breath-taking cleverness, since 'disgraced' probably includes, as a subaudition, 'disgraced', that is, 'removed from the element of grace and gratitude.'"[14] If we forgo our words in bonds of trust, we have in some vital way foregone ourselves for we make commitments in our speech acts in which we are necessarily implicated.

In *The Merchant of Venice*, we are reminded of that terrible bond secured by a pound of flesh: "Do you confess the bond?" asks Portia.[15] Cordelia declares, in ways shattering to her father and vital to the play, that she loves her father according to her bond, no more nor less. In *King Lear*, as I argued in chapter 2, Cordelia's words struggle against the flattery that evacuates and empties out the essential relation between love and justice. Her words are impossible to understand if we reduce the idea of bond to contract. Cordelia keeps faith with language because it is impossible to utter words of love in the flattery competition Lear has established. When Posthumous is lying in chains (in bonds), imprisoned by the Romans at the end of *Cymbeline*, he prays to die to "cancel these cold bonds" (5.4.28).[16] It is not simply his material chains of imprisonment but his life that he wishes canceled, paid in a poor exchange for Imogen's life. Posthumous's words are literal: He is in chains (bonds) at this point, but his words rely on a fundamental theological understanding of the whole of life as gifted, and therefore ontologically owed to God.

Even in these brief examples from Shakespeare's witty comedies, problem plays, tragedies, and tragicomedies, it is possible to see that an exploration of bonds is pervasive across Shakespeare's work. The language of bonds sounds out a domain of bondage that may, on different occasions, encompass legal, penal, verbal, theological, and ethical implications as well as explorations of kinship. Any inquiry into the language of bonds might take us into familial, legal, linguistic, and theological territory.[17]

If the word pervades Shakespeare's plays, it is also rich in semantic meaning in his culture, under pressure from various forms of covenantal theology, from new forms of indenture and service, from modes of credit and redefinitions of usurious relations in an increasingly market-oriented economy.[18] What bonds can be disgraced or canceled? How are we bonded to each other? How is that bond connected to what we owe each other, and the ways in which we belong together?

Bonds allow us to recognize each other as human and define the ethical and tragic landscape of *Timon* and its adjacent plays. For whatever date we determine for *Timon*, according to one of its editors, it "belongs to the most magnificently productive phase of Shakespeare's tragic writing."[19] In plays such as *King Lear*, *Coriolanus*, and the later play *The Winter's Tale*, Shakespeare appears to explore figures who imagine that language is their possession or property, and thus that its power originates with them in isolation. Such first-person fantasies tragically de-realize the other: Other voices are ignored, stifled, and not acknowledged. Because acknowledgment is mutual, this is always a self-blindness. Coriolanus, also from the ancient world (although here Roman rather than Athenian), thus seeks to be "author of himself," knowing no other kin, as I will go on to explore in chapter 5. King Lear and Gloucester too try to disown their children (unchilding themselves), as if those bonds are dissolvable, and unilaterally to boot. The play, as I have indicated, explores with great profundity what it means to ruin and devastate each other, the depth at which we live out our human bonds with each other through recognition and acknowledgment, and therefore what kinds of claims we have on each other that we can so disown and ruin each other.

A bond is what joins, links, or ties together. The bonds between people are constitutive, the second person coming before the first person, the you before the I, such that it is in the primary address of you to me that I learn I am capable of being a first person.[20] We are bound by these recognitive modes of address, bound by recognition, and bound by our capacities to understand and misunderstand, long before any more technical or restricted meaning comes into play.[21] The kinship of bond with the Latinate term ligature show the roots of obligation, enacted also in the contractual language of agreement (of indenture, credit, and law). The kinship with band (from Middle English) as not only hoop, join, bandage, strap, truss, and tie but also as mark (as in the stripe on a bird) indicates the way binding language singles and marks us out for each other. When is a bond too tight a tie? When is it a shackle, a tether, manacle, or fetter, in short, a constraint? How can a word function as a bond? If our word is our bond, how does that make us answerable to, and implicated in, each other?

I suggest that grasping the nature and extent of bonds in *Timon* will help us see (in more than one sense) the depth at which Shakespeare works when it comes to bonds. Insofar as we share an overly contractarian view of language, we too will miss that depth.

I start by discussing how Timon imagines bonds and how his interlocutors appear to understand them. I then consider whether these understandings are problematic and why. (I take it to be axiomatic that we must involve the self-understanding of those engaged in these bondings.) Next, I explore the grammar of giving and gratitude in the Senecan tradition, and the phenomenology of trust in the play, before turning to the steward's important relation with Timon in the context of the servant's ethical fellowship. Last, I explore the fantasy of an end to all human exchange, including language. At this point, we will be in a better position to explore Shakespearean tragedy as an ethical practice.

The Problem with Timon's Bonds

Timon frees Ventidius of his financial debt and thereby frees him from prison (1.1.97–112); he funds his servant Lucillus with enough money so that he can make a love match, which the bride's father otherwise will not countenance (1.1.113–58). The recipients of his gifts understand themselves to be "bound to him" by virtue of his actions.[22] Timon, however, tends to refuse the language of thanks, the gratitude appropriate to any gift. When Ventidius tells him "in grateful virtue, I am bound / To your free heart, I do return those talents, / Doubled with thanks and service" (1.2.5–7), Timon replies: "Honest Ventidius, you do mistake my love: / I gave it freely ever, and there's none / Can truly say he gives if he receives (1.2.10–11). Timon is refusing any return, seeing it as repayment, which would make his gift a loan. He is also unwilling to receive even thanks—for this, too, is what Ventidius offers him, his "talents, / Doubled with *thanks*, and service." He makes even the expression of gratitude, a virtue of recognition, very difficult.

Timon's bonds are confusing. He defends the gratuity of the gift with the pure logic of Derrida or the gospel of Luke 6:34 ("If ye lend to them of whome ye hope to receive, what thanks shall ye have?"), thus making room for generosity and preserving the gift's freedom. But there is something very tricky in his giving.[23] His gifts are entirely one way; he cannot conceive of himself as a recipient. Even Marcel Mauss's agonistic theory of gift-giving, which discuss the potlatch and the "big giving men", the men who give more than they receive, discussed three obligations of a gift: to give, to accept, and to reciprocate.[24] The latter two are absent in Timon's practice and imagination. Mauss is only echoing a much older examination of the gift from Seneca's *De Beneficiis*, a known source for *Timon*, which I will be examining in more detail. The gift, according to Seneca, is what binds a society: It is based on the reciprocal obligation to give, to receive, and to return. That is why the three Graces dance with hands interlinked because the circle needs to be unbroken for the gifts to return upon themselves.[25] Timon is incapable of understanding himself as receiving as well as giving; he will accept no givers in the world except for himself. Even before his self-imposed exile and isolation in the second half of the play, Timon is a solipsist, a twisted version—or commentary on—Aristotle's magnanimous man. His understanding of friendship is fantastical as is his version of a sovereign self.[26]

In his book on generosity, Romand Coles has said that "insofar as the condition of the power of giving involves receivers, the giving ground is pierced with contingencies of possibility and danger that erode pretentions to independent sovereignty."[27] Timon gives without receiving and is thus refusing bonds of reciprocity. It also becomes apparent that he has in fact misrecognized his generosity. He is giving what is not his to give.[28] In this way, he has fundamentally misconstrued both himself and his relation to others, but he has done so in a culture in which insincerity, flattery, and hypocrisy have become part of the very fabric of donation, as Apemantus churlishly realizes. It becomes clear soon enough that with every gift he gives, he incurs a further debt. His gifts are not an instance of his freedom, but rather its forfeiture, sounding an ambiguity in liberality.

It becomes clear—not immediately, but quite quickly—that it is by virtue of ignoring and dismissing his steward, Flavius, who has on many occasions and at the cost of numerous rebuffs, pointed out the nature of his debts to him, that he has been able to imagine himself as a giver in the first place.[29] His misrecognition of himself as giver is based on a refusal to listen to his steward, who with many of the other servants in the play, understands the true nature of fellowship. Timon's version of friendship is a fantasy, a kind of universal brotherhood of plentiful rich overlords who will fund each other's excesses. It is hard to make sense of his claim in response to Lord 1 that he might wish himself poorer so that he might "come nearer" to his friends (1.2.99). In retrospect, it is possible to see that he has simply imagined that all the wealth of his rich friends is at his disposal or that he has blanked out the possibility of being unable to fund his lavish gifts. On this fantasy, he can build his picture of himself as a generous man: "Why, I have often wished myself poorer that I might come nearer to you. We are born to do benefits, and what better or properer can we call our own than the riches of our friends? O, what a precious comfort is to have so many brothers commanding each other's fortunes" (1.2.101–103). But it becomes apparent that these "brothers" see Timon's gifts in fully commercial ways: To give something to Timon is to have it return "sevenfold above itself," breeding the giver a return "exceeding all use of quittance" (1.1.285-87), where use, as the Arden editors note, may be both interest and "usual practice."³⁰ "If I want gold, steal but a beggar's dog / And give it to Timon, why, the dog coins gold"—as one senator puts it (2.1.6). A gift from the Lords to Timon is an excellent investment.

Bonds in this play are tied up with complex forms of obligation (that word itself hinting at how we are tied to each other). The first time the language of bonding is invoked, as I remarked, is when the recipients of Timon's gifts declare themselves bound to him (1.1.107; 1.1.147; 1.2.5). But the bonds emerge as remarkably actual and material as the play progresses. Timon is handed writs, bonds, and promissory notes all with implacable, nonnegotiable due dates: "Take the bonds along with you, / And have the dates in" (2.1.35), says one of the senators who has lent Timon money and who now needs the liquidity because his own credit is failing. Timon is outraged and amazed, experiencing these wholly legitimate writs as extreme, utterly unanticipated affronts: "How goes the world, that I am thus encountered / With clamourous demands of broken bonds / And the detention of long-since-due dates / Against my honour?" (2.2.38-40). Unattractively, he reproaches his steward and blames him for the state of his affairs (2.2.124-127). If you had told me before I might have curbed my expense! We watch Timon slowly realize that he has nothing: What remains after the forfeiture and selling of Timon's land will not "stop the mouth / Of present dues" (2.2.147-48). Flavius's metaphor hints at cannibalism; the dues are insatiable and will consume him. His next words show the vulnerable fragility of a world that Timon had thought was secure: "O my good lord, the world is but a word; / Were it all yours to give it in breath, / How quickly were it gone" (2.2.152-3). "The world is but a word"—that's how we have a world at all, given with our words as light or substantial as they are. (We will return to this in more detail.)

The protracted and painfully extended scenes in act 3 show the senators and fraternal brotherhood of the super-rich squirming out of the claim that Timon is making on them. The "mouth-friends" in this scene are held firmly under the shocked scrutiny of those who serve—and observe—them. "Is't possible the world should so much differ / And we alive that lived?" asks Flaminius (3.2.45-46) who has been casually brushed aside by Lucillus when asked for funds with the complacent expectation of his complicity: "Good boy, wink at me, and say thou sawst me not" (3.1.43-44). The satire is all too recognizable: "I love and honour him / But must not break my back to heal his finger," says one of the senators blithely evacuating the words "love" and "honour" of significance, while helping themselves to their received and usual meanings (2.1.24-25). In Flavius's brilliant description: "They answer in a joint and corporate voice / That now they are at fall, want treasure, cannot / Do what they would, are sorry" (2.2.204-206). Flavius exposes their fantastic excuses, revealing the collapse of any fantasy of friendship. Why should they now give money on "bare friendship without security"? (3.1.41-42). The words "love," "honour," and "friendship" are as empty as the empty box Flaminius has asked the friend to fill (3.1.17).

This passage can be parsed out in various ways. Timon was utterly deceived in his wealth and was giving what was not his to give. (He has misunderstood what was his.) He has thought of himself as Aristotle's magnanimous man; but he is actually participating in a fully usurious economy.[31] Fortune shined on him, but he accrued a great mass of dependents so imaged in the depiction of the poet at the very beginning of the play, and sycophancy and profit from his gifts have obscured his indebtedness to others. Timon is forced to see what he owes (rather than what he owns). The bonds brought to him function more like contracts. In that case, they are limited, entered voluntarily and freely (rather than being unchosen), subject to a set of articulated norms, legally sanctioned if transgressed, "a promise that law will enforce," in the words of Regina Schwartz.[32] This is to distinguish them from bonds of friendship, love, and charity. Charity is something you are in—rather than something you give, as I explored in chapter 2. It is a relation in which you are implicated, a position you are in in relation to others, rather than something you exclusively donate. Bonds of kinship, of love, are indeterminate, unspecifiable in advance, and exorbitant. They are often unchosen bonds we are in, as child, parent, or lover. A child does not contract to be born; a lover "falls in love" and has no *reasons* for her joy; a parent receives a child in a mysterious unknowingness. All these relations are capable of being experienced as gifts in a secular as well as a theological idiom, for lives lived in the key of gratitude. Notably, no children appear in *Timon*, as if nature's gifts cannot be acknowledged, and hardly any women are featured—all are borrowers and lenders; masters, servants, messengers, statesmen, and warriors. If we experience ourselves as given, however, we are already and always receivers and responders; we are already in relation with each other.

If Timon has simply been unaware that his bonds were actually contracts, then he is easily castigated as no more than a fool. But this is moralistic. It neither recognizes nor addresses Timon's primal rage; nor can it envisage his desire to revenge himself on the world in toto and without exception, or his all-purpose cursing, his sheer commitment to future hate.

A closer look at one of Shakespeare's intertexts, *De Beneficiis*, and some of its later insightful commentors will help us understand the centrality of noncontractual bonds, the moral not legal relations so entailed, the pivotal role of the steward and his model of service, and the way in which the depth of the bonds at stake expose the kind of betrayal of trust from which Timon speaks. It is these interlinked strands of the play that show its dramatic moral philosophy, counterpointed with any overtly philosophical position taken up by the plays' cynical and churlish philosophers.

"We Are Born to Do Benefits": The Vocabulary of Beneficium

"We are born to do benefits," says Timon (1.2.99–100). What, then, are benefits? Seneca's treatise *De Beneficiis*, addressed to his friend, Aebutius Liberalis, sometime between 56 CE and 64 CE, during Nero's imperial rule, was the most influential and far-reaching consideration of benefits, available in more than three hundred manuscripts.[33] Widely copied from the late eleventh century onward, when print superseded manuscript as the main mode of transmission, it was translated by intellectuals and humanists such as Erasmus (1515), Marc Antoine Muret (1585), Justus Lipsius (1605), and Arthur Golding (1578) and Thomas Lodge (1614).[34] It was a treatise known to Shakespeare, a treatise that might well underly the contemplation of ingratitude that unites *King Lear*, *Coriolanus*, and *Timon*.[35] Seneca's treatise can help us understand the moral philosophy at work in the Greco-Roman world of benefits in the play, for *Timon* is of Athens. It is not necessary to make an argument about "sources" to see that Seneca's treatise about benefits—with its striking picture of ingratitude as a monstrous disorder, destructive of the most fundamental social ties and bonds—illuminates Shakespeare and Middleton's bold experimental play.

The problem of how to translate this archaic word strikes us immediately. Is *beneficium* a good turn, a favor, a good deed, or a well-intentioned act?[36] What is good about it? How is the *bene* recognized? Miriam Griffin and Brad Inwood keep the Latinate word *benefit* in their translation because the term carries crucial and useful distinctions lost in the alternatives.[37] A *good turn* is too casual (although this term is favored by Golding); a *favor* is too close to bribery and preference; a *good deed* comes close but loses the telling historical difference; and a *well-intentioned act* nicely emphasizes the intention vital to Seneca's account but is too diffuse.

Seneca's philosophical concern is precisely to highlight the good intention and gratuity of benefit, preserving it from other words that might suggest bribes, loans, or transactions either legally obligated or commercial and pecuniary.[38] For Seneca, to contemplate a benefit is to explore a fundamental grammar of giving and receiving for people who have either lost or never mastered the practice. People do not know how to give, receive, or reciprocate gifts in imperial Rome (1.1.1). They are ignorant as to the very nature and concept of benefits. Benefits, he says are "bestowed badly" and "owed badly" (1.1.1). Seneca offers us numerous examples of such gracelessness: tactical evasion of requests; gifts ruined by arrogance or scorekeeping; lack of care; gifts framed by coercion and haughtiness; gifts forgotten; gifts confused with bribes, loans, and favors; and gifts received in ignorance of the good intentions of the giver. Do not send wine to a drunkard, he helpfully recommends, or medicine to the hypochondriac (1.11.6). Do not give someone something your recipient already has in abundance (1.12.3); do not be churlishly hesitant in giving (2.1.2); do not use your gift to single out the recipient or to enhance your good deed with good words. Do not give gifts that might humiliate the receiver, even if you are a prince (2.7.8). Do not give gifts as subtle or pointed criticism of the receivers' vices or bad habits. Seneca gives sane and practical advice.

For Seneca, the stakes are high because the giving, receiving, and reciprocating of benefits is a practice that, more than any other, binds together human society: "quae maxime humanam societatem alligat" (1.4.2). Seneca's treatise covers the chief aspects of benefits—giving, receiving, and returning—to understand the moral, not legal, obligations entailed in the relations established through benefits. The donor must give freely (1.4.3) with a good intention that must be recognized as such for the gift to count as a gift (1.4.5). The gift lies not in the thing itself or in its monetary value (1.5.2), but in the good intentions of the giver (1.5.6).[39] The donor must forget that he has given the moment his gift is made, but the receiver must both recognize the good intentions of the donor in so giving and remember that good deed. His proper receiving of the gift is distinguished from his ability to reciprocate and these facts—the forgetfulness of the donor (2.17.7), the remembrance of the recipient—preserve both generosity and gratitude. For a persistent inability to *receive* is at the heart of the ingratitude that erodes the gift's gratuity.[40] Seneca is concerned throughout his treatise with the character of appropriate or fitting response. He dwells on the souring of human relations that occurs from corruptions and traducements of gift, gratitude, and thanks.

Seneca contemplates such vital questions as whether one can give a gift to oneself (one cannot), whether a gift can be given accidentally (it cannot), or whether a son can give to a father or a slave to a master (he can).[41] The gift comes from the man as a man, "a bare man" outside of his duties and offices, and in this sense, importantly, there is no office of giving (3.18.20).[42] Benefits, in fact, refute solipsism, for the gift is not possible without others.[43] Indeed "no none can give except to another person; no one owes except to another person, no one returns except to another person. What on each occasion requires two people cannot take place within one person" (5.9.4).[44]

The benefit is not an obligation: The gift must be freely given to count as such, and this means that it establishes neither legal nor financial obligations or exchanges, but rather moral relationships.[45] This becomes clear when Seneca addresses the question of why ingratitude, if it is so terrible and destructive of human relations, should go unpunished. Were ingratitude subject to legal sanction, the gratuity of the act is vitiated: Men would receive and return benefits only "gratefully" because they would be punished otherwise. A benefit is honorable because of the risk of losing: Legal sanctions would ruin "two of the finest things in human life, the grateful person and the benefit itself" (3.7.1). Seneca's entire account makes space for gratitude: gratitude as response to benefaction, to generosity, and as a crucial acknowledgment of it, not owed but freely given, and made distinct from the return or reciprocation of a gift.[46] The good intentions of the giver must be recognized for it to count as a benefit, and in this respect, the relations involved are moral relationships bound by recognition. Among what is recognized is the goodness of the deed. The benefit is a test case for trust: to put trust in souls not seals (3.15.3). Seneca worried that benefits were misrecognized; he understood the gravity of such misrecognitions. *De Beneficiis* was of use to Shakespeare as he dramatized the horrors of ingratitude, for it is only by virtue of seeing the terrible personal and social costs of ingratitude that one might understand how such a social order might be bound together by such fragile recognitions.

Benefits are, on this account, the chief factor in tying human societies together: "quae maxime humanorum societatem alligat" (1.4.2).

It is precisely because these benefits are the very bonds and ligatures of a society that a gift should never be given carelessly, or coercively; and benefits should be given with judgment. A gift should not just be given to anyone indiscriminately; it should single out the recipient as special to him or her. Seneca insists that the way the gift is given is a significant aspect of the gift: "It matters not what is done or what is given, but with what attitude, since the benefit consists not in what was done or given but rather in the intention of the giver or agent" (2.6.1.). A benefit is an act of virtue: "It is utterly shameful to confer one for any other reason than to see it conferred" (4.3.1).

Seneca's account is almost unrecognizable from the "pure gift" in twentieth-century theories of the gift from Marcel Mauss to Jacques Derrida.[47] For one thing, it is not a scandal in Seneca's account that receiving and returning are part of benefits.[48] Seneca's separating these two acts is in itself significant: It is this very separation that preserves the benefit's grace, for it makes appropriate room for gratitude. Gift theory has been rather singularly focused on the gift giver and her impossible purity. In Derrida's influential, rigorous, and emphatically purist conception of the gift, the very whiff of reciprocity cancels out the gift as given: "For there to be a gift, there must be no reciprocity, return, exchange, countergift, or debt. If the other gives me back or owes me or has to give back what I give him or her, there will not have been a gift."[49] Seneca might have responded as he did to his own interlocutors: "No benefit is so complete that an envious gaze cannot pick it apart; but none is so limited that a generous interpretation will not enhance its impact. If you look at benefits with a negative attitude you can always find grounds for complaint" (2.28.4). Gift theory has sometimes been caught then between cynicism and "a fideistic leap to the impossibility of generosity, giving, love, friendship, and so on."[50] What gets left out is the ordinary naturalness of gratitude and thanks in the acceptance of a gift, whose status as gift is not negated by any ingratitude by which it may be received. The etymology of benefits, as John Barclay has shown, tells us that Greek bequeaths us the same word for charity as it does for thanks (*charis*).[51] The expression of gratitude in thanks is part of an ethical relationship in the recognition of the benefit, the good deed: part of the realm of ethics, not etiquette, part of practical relations, not mere sentiment.[52]

Judged by Seneca's lights, Timon is right to understand the monstrousness of ingratitude and the suffering it induces. But he might have learned from a judicious reading of Seneca that you cannot give what you do not have; that to give indiscriminately and extravagantly is to be blind to the needs of the recipient and to avoid the thoughtful singling out that is in the nature of the gift's good intention; he might have learned that you need to be able to receive as well as to give. The denial of reciprocity—a reciprocity honored in thanks and services and not alone in material return—is ungracious and does not acknowledge the other. The gift is not possible without others (and the recognition of others I add): "beneficium sine altero non est" (5.10.1). It requires a second person (5.10.4) and is an intrinsically social act (5.11.5). Seneca's work might even be seen as a repudiation of Aristotle's magnanimous man whom Timon mirrors. Aristotle's magnanimous man confers benefits but is ashamed to receive them. But for Seneca, "he who is unwilling to owe is ungrateful" (4.40.3).[53]

Trust and Betrayal

Seneca helps us to understand the differences between moral and legal bonds, a distinction central to *Timon of Athens*. If contracts, not bonds, are broken, we would be mystified by Timon's desire to revenge himself so entirely on the world, his all-purpose cursing, his emphatic refusal of all exceptions to his misanthropy. Timon might be severely disappointed if his friends broke a contract. He might feel let down; they were, after all, unreliable. He might even be angry and filled by a sense of injustice. But he would not rage or hate; he would not be entirely consumed in obsessional and biting disgust and utter contempt, his implacable hostility fueled by his sense of helplessness, the impossibility of redress. His untrammeled resentment and all-consuming detestation are a response to a much deeper sense of betrayal. It is not broken contracts but broken trust that explains Timon's outraged, bitter, exorbitant *cri de coeur* and fuels his unending invective. Timon's sense of the torn fabric of his world is a horrifying realization of the gossamer threads by which any social order hangs. Trust, says Annette Baier "comes in webs, not in single strands, and disrupting one strand often rips apart whole webs."[54]

In *Timon*, trust is revealed as an ethical relation. This is the primordial trust that, as Ludwig Wittgenstein says, comes before doubt.[55] Prereflective and primal, it is not an act of the will, nor is it informed by reason. It begins in unchosen relations and continues as an unspoken and invisible capacity to talk and be with others, to walk down a street in a city of strangers, to believe what people say to you unless you have a specific reason to doubt (trust and truth being thereby connected). It is, as Knud Ejler Løgstrup points out, "given," but not "of our own making."[56] It is taken for granted, wholly under the radar of our attention except when it makes itself known as mistrust, that is, when trust is broken. It shows the depths at which human bonds operate. Yet it is a perfectly ordinary part of our interactions with each other. I address you and I am accountable to you for what I say. You address me and you are accountable to me; my trust in you entails my assumption of your responsibility to me. But this is an open-ended assertion in that I do not trust you between Mondays and Fridays, or between 9 a.m. and 12 p.m., nor do I trust you in just this one instance: I trust *you* rather than trust that you will do this one thing I asked you to do (in which case I rely on you rather than trust in you). Trust allows us to give and take each other's words.

Trust is grammatically related to truth, for in general—unless for a good reason—we mean what we say. Of course, trust is related to justice and the good, for we trust in the good, and it is also related to, and posthumously revealed by, betrayal.[57]

Broken bonds, not broken contracts, push Timon into a tragic register, moving out of satire or comedy where he—and types like him—are gulls or fools. In the world of city comedy, it is usually possible to have been cleverer than we turn out to be, to have seen through the untrustworthiness of others, and thus in a sense, we might have avoided our humiliation. But *Timon* offers no such recourse. Mistrust, not trust, has need of reasons. In Shakespeare and Middleton's play, Timon's broken trust reveals his gifts to friends, not returning to him in that graceful dance, as retrospectively something more like daylight robbery, profiteering, or rapacious exploitation.[58]

Timon's hatred resulting from his sense of betrayal, is all inclusive, and thus a defense against self-knowledge and relation. His cursing, his hyperbolically totalizing detestation of everyone and everything is, I am suggesting, a useful shield against the kinds of dependencies and vulnerabilities that run wholly beneath any contracts we might make with each other. Timon's rage cannot be understood in the thin language of contract. A contract, as I suggested earlier, is limited, entered into willingly but with a certain set of conditions of fulfillment, and with a distinct terminus.[59] Timon's rage can be explained only by the kind of betrayal that runs between people in what Avishai Margalit has called "thick relations," thus my fellow Jew, my mother, my friend, and my husband, but not my lawyer or my psychiatrist. When we are betrayed in these relations by abandonment, infidelity, or rejection, we are more likely to feel rage, despair, and utter shock, and perhaps those who are in these thick relations with us, those who have betrayed, abandoned us, or sold us down the river, might be expected to feel remorse, or guilt. "Can thick relations of belonging be terminated?" asks Margalit. He gives this example: "After leafing through one's Stasi file one can say, 'My ex-son-in-law betrayed me to gain promotion in the party.' But one cannot make literal sense by saying, 'My ex-son betrayed me to get promotion in the party.'" . . . One can turn from a son-in-law to an ex-son-in-law, but one cannot turn from a son into an ex-son: once a son, always a son." He might be able to terminate his relationship *with* his son, but not his relation *to* him. In *Timon* trust is revealed as an ethical relation, and so is betrayal.[60]

At his great inverted feast for his mouth-friends, his trencher-friends, in which he feeds them nothing but lukewarm water (perhaps an echo of Revelation 3.15-6), he gives his anti-grace, the second in the play (3.7.68-83). His guests are nothing to him, and so he calls on nothing in them to be blessed. It is an antiblessing, an antithanks, an attempt to negate the very idea of welcome and hospitality. From the moment of his realization of betrayal he adopts invective, and the inverted language of prayer, welcoming the violent cutting and tearing of bonds of trust that line every social, civic and familial relation: "Matrons turn incontinent / Obedience, fail in children; slaves and fools / Pluck the grave wrinkled senate from the bench / And minister in their steads . . . Bankrupts hold fast; Rather than render back, out with your knives / And cut your trusters throats!" (4.1.3-6, 4.1.8-10).[61] It is trust that underlies "peace, justice and truth, / Domestic awe, night-rest and neighborhood, / Instructions, manners, mysteries and trades, / Degrees, observances, customs, and laws" (4.1.15-20). He could, I sense, go on and on in an endless list, with hardly a pause for breath, brooking no interruption, no disruption of his forceful detailing of all the relations that can be ruptured and ruined. Trust is the fabric of relation: Pull one thread and all those adjacent threads pucker and crumple. His manic and proliferating itemization, piling up possibilities, shows him in a task of negative realization. The point, however, is that once distinguished, they must all be "confounded," mixed up together so that they cannot be told apart. The point is "confusion" (4.1.21). Let it live.

Before I return to the purposes and effects of Timon's exceptionless misanthropy and its relation to our word as our bond, I want to extend my analysis of Seneca into his scholastic afterlife, because it is here that

BENEFITS AND BONDS   85

we see the extraordinary, central role played by the play's numerous servants. These materials can help us examine the play's continuing probing of moral relation.

Can a Servant Give Anything to His Master?

The play offers us an astonishing, unprecedented cast of twelve servants—some named individually, and some named after their masters.[62] Flavius, differentiated as the steward, is pivotal in both halves of the play. The go-betweens and messengers from the rich, oblivious, and self-interested masters of Athens' patrician class are invisible except as functionaries to their masters. Their point of view not only discloses and exposes their master's rapacious self-regard and the patricians' moral impoverishment but also offers gentler, kinder affinities and social and ethical possibilities.

Three strangers are brought in precisely to offer their views on the creditors refusal to reciprocate Timon's benefaction: "Religion groans" (3.2.78) at "the monstrousness of man":

> When he looks out in an ungrateful shape—
> He does deny him, in respect of his,
> What charitable men afford to beggars.
>
> (3.2.75-79)

But it is the servants of the play, bonded in service to their masters, who clearly see their masters' profound limitations. One of Timon's servants roundly castigates Lucius's "politic love" (3.4.35); Flaminius throws back the coins given to him by Lucullus, who has told him it is "no time to lend money, especially on bare friendship without security" (3.1.42-4), exclaiming that this is a disease of a friend. When the servants of Isodore and Varro meet to collect dues from Timon, Caphis's pun—"Would we were all discharged"—can be taken to express a hope that their dues be paid, but it can just as easily indicate a reluctance to perform the duty of collection assigned to them (2.2.14).

After Timon's household has been left destitute and he has left in a flurry, forgetful altogether of his dependents, a touching scene unfolds among the community of servants. Although they now must be out of the bonds of service (hence vagabonds), their "hearts" still wear Timon's livery (4.2.17). Their loyal society will continue to serve in shared sorrow (4.2.19). "We are fellows still"; "Good fellows all", "Let's yet be fellows" (4.217, 22,25): These words suggest a commitment based on a shared history. "We have seen better days" (4.2.28) reflects a shared experience as "broken implements of a ruined house" (4.2.16), informing a commitment to future fellowship. The experience of ruin intensifies their links with each other.[63]

Flavius shares money, a responsibility altogether neglected by Timon: "Nay, put out all your hands-not one word more, / Thus part we rich in sorrow, parting poor" (4.2.28–29). The open hands are not stretched out in a performative "dream of friendship" (4.2.34) but rather express a common need. Then, as the stage direction instructs, they embrace, sharing love and sorrow.

This is a model of giving as sharing. Their fellowship will remain as part of a shared history and thus will create a new bond, based on their grief and loss and the fact of sharing it. They are fellow fellows betrayed by their master's oblivious "dream of friendship" to destitution; they are broken but capable of repair, offering the possibility of a more graceful community.

This scene immediately succeeds Timon's terrible inverse prayer for universal hatred, which ends with a plea: "Grant as Timon grows his hate may grow / To the whole race of mankind, high and low!" (4.1.39–40). Different models of loving and living are right under Timon's nose, if only he could see them, offering a striking example of loyalty, outside the bonds of service: "Yet do our hearts wear Timon's livery" (4.2. 17). Flavius addresses them as "my fellows" (4.2.2); the second servant calls Timon "our companion" (4.2.9): To share is not simply to "divide," divvy up, and apportion, but rather to participate and to partake in something common. We are offered an illuminating and powerful form of affinity.

Seneca pays some attention to the relationship between masters and servants. In book 3 of *De Beneficiis*, Seneca embarks on a revelatory discussion about whether a slave can confer a benefit. Seneca's treatise—and later scholastic commentaries on it—can help us see the moral rather than legal relations under analysis. They reveal what the narrower version of bonds as contracts misses, and they help us see how central those who serve prove to be in the play, and the implications of Timon's failures of acknowledgment.

Seneca is arguing with those who think that if a slave cannot hold back a benefit, he cannot give one (3.18.1). On this account, a slave's legal situation is such that "nothing he provides gives him a claim on his superior" (3.18.1). He has nothing to give; because everything he is and does is owed as a condition of service. From this point of view, a servant's "services," his duties, simply exclude the concept of benefit, and a servant cannot do a good deed for his master. Seneca understands that complying with this logic would render every social subordinate unable to do good turns or favors. Seneca argues passionately to the contrary.

A slave can benefit his master because it is not his legal status that is important but rather "his state of mind (3.18.2). To deny the slave that capacity to do a good turn, to be able to give to his master, is to fail to see the autonomy of his mind and to deny his capacity to freely give something he is not obligated to do (3.21.1). The entire discussion is a vital test case for the free agency of the giver: "Why should the social role degrade the deed, instead of the deed ennobling the social role of the agent?" (3.28.1)

Seneca is struggling with the question of the duties and legal obligations that attach to the roles we occupy in relation to each other. But for Seneca the free state of mind is central in the act of giving. In his defense of the gratuity of giving, he separates out gift from loan or bribe, or a merely rivalrous grandiosity designed to outdo or humiliate the receiver. What we owe to each other by virtue of our roles needs to be separated from what we owe and give to each other as human beings and this distinction preserves our gracious acts. Anyone who denies that a slave can benefit his master is "just ignorant of the rights he has as a human being" (ignarus iuris humani; 3.18.2) and is guilty of a refusal to recognize virtue. Seneca is at his most inspirational when he says: "Virtue shuts the door to no one. It is open to everyone and lets us all in, invites us in: the freeborn, ex-slaves, slaves, kings, and exiles" (3.18.3).

When Thomas Aquinas read Seneca, he had fully absorbed the implications of such distinctions. In the second part of the second part of the *Summa Theologica*, in his discussion of thankfulness, he cites Seneca declaring that when a slave "does more than a slave is bound to do, it is a favor; for as soon as he does anything from a motive of friendship, if indeed that be his motive, it is no longer called a service."[64] Although Seneca's influence is pervasive in these sections, Aquinas approaches master-slave relations in a slightly different manner. His concern is not so much whether a slave can give to a master, but whether thanks are owed to the slave for what he gives. They are. This is part of Aquinas's exploration of gratitude as a part of justice. Aquinas makes an elegant Latin pun underscoring Seneca's point: "enim beneficium magis in affectu consistit quam in effectu" (for a benefit/favor consists more in feeling than in deed).[65]

For Seneca and Aquinas write from the virtue tradition: What is at stake is precisely the "bene" in "beneficium," what is good in the deed.

It is precisely where the servant or steward surpasses what is owed that the gratuity of gift is seen. Aquinas relates the giving of thanks and the repayment of a favor as belonging to three virtues—justice, gratitude, and friendship.[66] When it concerns the virtue of gratitude, he is unequivocal: "It has the character of a moral debt."[67] Finally, Aquinas says that the debt of gratitude is linked to love: It flows from charity. The more it is paid, the more it is due, citing Romans 13:8.

Thomas treats ingratitude in his discussion of the virtue of justice and under the heading of *religio*, which concerns what people owe God (*ST* 2-2, 81, 4). Gratitude, he says, is an aspect of justice, but it is paid freely and not because of legal obligation.

In the fourteenth century, as Andrew Galloway has shown, interest emerged in gratitude as mercantilism began to trouble canonists and theologians. *Gratitudo* is, in fact, a scholastic coinage from *gratia*, and the powerful middle English word *kynde* is recruited to translate *gratus*, with *unkynde* as *ingratus*.[68] The refusal of reciprocity in Timon's giving and in the Lords' rejection of his claims is not only *ingratus*, but *unkynde*, that is, a refusal of kinship. So the dimensions of gratitude take up both a theology of grace as well as a moral ontology of human being.

No wonder then that one of the strangers says in the face of the Lords' ingratitude: "Religion groans at it" (3.2.78), activating precisely those forms of binding and rebinding (re-*ligare*) of joining and fracture the "bond in men" (1.148).[69]

A Failure of Acknowledgment: The Rhetoric of "All"

Flavius is just one of the many visitors who disrupt Timon's attempt at isolation. All of Athens appears to seek him out. Alcibiades and his train of women approach. The churlish philosopher seeks out the man who "affects his manners" (4.3.198); then there is a visitation of thieves, upstaged in their ministry, at least one of whom is reformed by virtue of Timon's more cosmic and thorough-going vision of banditry. Flavius visits him before the return of the poet and painter; finally, the senators return. I focus on the scene with Flavius because it is Flavius who highlights Timon's commitment to misanthropy without exception, and thus to Timon's hyperbolic skepticism.

Flavius's scene with Timon moves out of the flyting, competitive emulation, and vindication, the rebuff and repulses, that set the tone for Timon's inverted hospitality with his nonguests. It offers a vital and touching glimpse of kind fellowship. That mere glimpse threatens—for just a moment—to stop in its tracks Timon's hurtling momentum of hatred, his abhorrent efforts to unbind himself from all the others of the world.

We now see Timon not as the vituperative subject but as the pitiful object of Flavius's compassionate regard as he views Timon without yet being seen by him. Flavius's words recall Christ's commandment to love your enemies (Matt 5:44): "How rarely does it meet with this time's guise, / When man was wished to love his enemies."[70] We are hearing love sounded, and it is almost shocking. There has been more language of estimating and prizing than loving. The word is used: "You mistake my love" (1.2.9), says Timon, when Ventidius tries to repay him. One senator declares he loves and honors Timon—but only as he is about to shaft him with bills and due dates (2.1.23). There is "small love among these sweet knaves" as Apemantus says (1.1.255).

Flavius decides to present his "honest grief" and service to Timon (4.3.464). The word *present* happily carries the sense of offer, attend upon, make a gift of, and make known, and the scene draws on all these facets of acknowledgment. To present yourself is to offer yourself, to give yourself up to another. Thus, in the possibility of rebuff, it is to be *in* your words, to reveal yourself in them, and to mean them. Flavius wishes to offer to serve Timon, whole-heartedly "with my life" (4.3.465).

His affectionate greeting "my dearest master" is greeted with rejection and disavowal: "Away!" (4.3.466). Flavius asks if Timon has forgotten him: Timon's reply is that he has forgotten all men, and so this includes Flavius in arrogant choplogic. He is right, however, that he cannot differentiate Flavius from other men. So Flavius introduces himself as "an honest and poor servant" of his, referring to the past history they share. Timon stops at the term "honest" (4.3.472) and claims honest men were never around him. It might seem as if Timon is thinking about his putative rich fraternity, but because he talks about the "knaves" he kept, he must be referring to those who served him. "I know thee not" (4.3.471) is brutal. It is as brutal in its way, as Prince Hal to Falstaff: "I know thee not, old man," and perhaps, in its oblivious cruelty, even more so.[71] Flavius's loving persistence is remarkable; he carries on waiting on him, presenting himself to him, wishing to be known, but also so that Timon can own his history and see himself true. What he cannot help presenting now are his tears, involuntary witness of his love and grief: "What dost thou weep?" (4.3.476).

Once again, Timon's misanthropy is deflective: Because you cry, you must be a woman, and therefore technically excluded, because flinty mankind never cries. Even when pity is right under his nose, he avoids it in his wider abstraction: "Pity's sleeping" (4.3.480).

Flavius's tears are the warrant of his care for his master, but as he begs for acknowledgment—"I beg of you to know me" (4.3.482)—and asks Timon to accept his grief and allow him to serve still, it becomes clear that Timon cannot connect the man before him with the past as he conveniently remembers it.[72] He pauses enough to question himself—"Had I a steward / So true, so just and now so comfortable?" (4.3.486)—and is halted enough to look at Flavius: "Let me behold thy face" (4.3.488). This man is indeed "born of woman"—and he asks Flavius to forgive his "general and exceptless rashness" (4.3.490). Exceptless appears to be a Shakespearean coinage and hits the scene's logic. The universal and all-encompassing hatred cannot be total if there are exceptions. He must be "exceptless," convinced of the total depravity of all humankind, to fund a misanthropy that can brook no distinctions or qualifications. He proclaims, "one honest man" (4.3.493)—but please, gods, do not send more! What is the tone of "No more I pray, and he's a steward" (4.3.493)? Is it wonder and gratitude that there might be such a man? Is it more like Sir Toby Belch's sense of stewardship in his withering words to Malvolio ("Art any more than a steward?") or the Cornwalls' terrible question, "A peasant stand up thus?"[73] Does Timon's scornful patrician condescension imply that stewards do not count? If he is honest only he can count as honest because the avowal cannot be allowed to compromise his misanthropy.

Whatever momentary glimpse of true service and honesty there is, suspicion and doubt quickly contaminate it. Is his kindness "usuring" (4.3.504)? Does it expect return? Is it merely mercenary? For Flavius, "doubt and suspect" (4.3.507) come too late and are directed against the wrong actors. With his momentary allowance that Flavius is honest, Timon tries to give him treasure on the condition that he lives apart and hates all, curses all, and shows charity to none, in other words, he withdraws or seeks to overcome the very conditions of a *gift*.[74]

What then has Timon failed to remember when he does not recognize Flavius? We learn from *King Lear* that all failures of recognition are failures of self-recognition. Three things need to be stressed. The first is that in not recognizing Flavius, he refuses a knowledge of himself as the man who rebuffed the truths Flavius offered him. It is from Flavius that we know that Timon is severely in debt, that he owes for everything he gives, and that he has made this known on several occasions to Timon and has been rebuffed. So his failure to acknowledge Flavius on this occasion is a more conscious and emphatic reprisal of his earlier failure. Flavius is indeed the only man honest enough to tell him the truth, and so his failure to acknowledge where he stands in relation to Flavius is also a failure to acknowledge where he stands in relation to all other men in the play. Flavius tells him that his suspicion and doubt come too late and indeed are directed toward the wrong man. Timon is just another one of Shakespeare's magnanimous men who cannot recognize love: "That which I show heaven knows is merely love" (4.3.520).

Second, in rebuffing Flavius again, he also rebuffs the only true friendship offered in the play, but it is one that necessarily involves seeing Flavius as a fellow fellow, the model for which, as we have seen, is the fellowship of servants in act 4, scene 2.

Third, Timon cannot recognize the "bene" in a beneficium, when it is right under his nose, right before him in Flavius's offer of service. Timon's final words to Flavius are "Let me never see thee" (4.3.531), which are a refusal not only of seeing him, and thus risking recognizing him, but also of being seen, being recognized, and having his unmitigated hatred compromised by Flavius's redemption.

This failed recognition scene shows us Timon's refusal as a rejection of Flavius's single claim on Timon. Simply put, Timon can no longer be wedded to his hatred if he allows Flavius's claim on him—that is, if he not only acknowledges that Flavius was his honest steward (hence he was his oblivious Lord) but also acknowledges *him* and his capacity for grief and love (hence Timon is himself honestly served and truthfully loved). Flavius shows the significance and cost of this universality with no exemption.

The extravagant "all" is the characteristic mark of Timon's misanthropic rhetoric. "Henceforth hated be / Of Timon man and all humanity" (3.7.103–104), he declaims, "and grant as Timon grows his hate may grow / To the whole race of mankind, high and low!" (4.1.39–40). If one man is a flatterer, then "so are they all" (4.3.15–16), "all's obloquy (4.3.17), and "all feasts, societies and throngs of men," he disdains (4.3.21). Timon's all-encompassing philosophy of disdain, his contempt for every social relation, shows the point in disdaining all distinction, confounding every single claim in universal repulsion.

Timon's "all" deals death. "It is vain" (5.2.1) to speak with him, says Flavius, because there is no point in speaking if all is confounded, if you cannot enact the differences and distinctions of speech.[75] Timon responds, "Speak, and be hanged!" at Flavius's invitation to speak, as the senators approach during the last visitation to Timon's fecund and sociable wilderness. You will be hanged if you speak; I will speak and then I will kill myself; if you speak, you can go and hang yourself (an invitation he repeats late in the scene). Quite what he says is indeterminate, except that in each option there is an association of speaking with dying. Let words—true and false ones—"blister" and "cauterize" to the "root 'o' th' tongue" (5.2.17–18). To speak at all is to die of self-consumption, to consume oneself with speaking (5.2.19). Timon has lost all conviction in speech. For speech to be intelligible action, there must be a point in it, and a point to it. The very project of speech as intelligible action has collapsed. The word of others can no longer be taken: They are not oathable (4.3.136). He thus can no longer give his word.

Nothing is left to speak but an epitaph. When the senators approach, Timon is writing his: "I was writing of my epitaph" (5.2.70). Timon's last words are a crux: Is it "Let four words go by, and language end," as the folio has it? If so, then which are the four words? (He continues to speak for more than four!) Or, is it, as Rowe emends, "Let sour words go by, and language end" (5.2.105)? The logical end in either case is the end of language—an end to speaking, talking, and communing; an end to the necessities of speech.

It is part of the play's unquenchable artistic generosity, even in this most harsh and gravid play, that it offers this extravagant, despite-itself gift: Timon's bequeathing of himself is regenerative. For he tells the senators that his "everlasting mansion" (his grave) will lie "upon the beached verge of the salt flood, / Who once a day with his embossed froth / The turbulent surge shall cover" (5.3.100–113). The gravestone will speak: It will be an oracle. The nature that has kept on offering itself to Timon so abundantly in his "wasteland" will now—at that limen where sea meets shore, where the ground gives way to a different element—diurnally cover and recover his grave. It is a kind of self-abandonment of which he has hitherto been incapable. In giving himself to death, he speaks in epitaph—and he goes on speaking, for his words are reprised both by the soldier who visits and takes a wax imprinting of them and finally by Alcibiades at the play's end. To speak is to give words and take them—to pledge ourselves.

The logic of the hyperbolic "all" is not local to Timon; it is part of the play's investigation of the political economy of speech. "Let not thy sword skip one" (4.3.110), he says to Alcibiades, and the "exceptless" rhetoric is sounded again in Alcibiades's parleying with the senators as Athens faces a total destruction at the play's end. Timon's lethal misanthropy is rhetorical, and it consumes him to death: Alcibiades's payback is ruthlessly military, and he is credited with the power to annihilate Athens. The survival of Athens, however, depends on abandoning the "all," in relinquishing the habit of "confounding" that funds Timon's misanthropic skepticism.

One of the senators pleads with Alcibiades to spare some of the city: "We were not all unkind, nor all deserve / The common stroke of war" (5.5.21–22). Another senator urges that Alcibiades distinguishes between the guilty and innocent (5.5.23–24) and repeats: "All have not offended" (5.3.35). Their offer is that Alcibiades "decimate" the city—kill one person out of ten, an indiscriminate and arbitrary path but at least not killing every single citizen: "Kill not all together" (5.5.44). "Use the wars," they urge, "as thy redress" and "not as our confusion" (5.5.52). This "confusion," to my ear, reprises the Timonian rhetoric of mixing it altogether, disdaining distinction again.

Alcibiades accedes to this; he offers his glove and pledges that the senators shall choose the offenders who will be publicly tried according to the city's laws. He invites them to "descend" (from the ramparts of the city) and "keep your words" (5.5.65). The safety of the city, the enaction of its laws, and the future prospects of Athenian *civitas* will depend on the giving and taking of words in trust.

News of Timon's death interrupts the scene, and Alcibiades reads his epitaph: "Here lie I, Timon, who alive all living men did hate" (5.5.70). There it is again—that emphatic, exceptionless "all"—Timon's baleful words in his mouth, sounding out a bitterness and animosity with no reprieve, falling on all alike. Does this allow him to begin to make just those distinctions Timon did not care to make? Timon "abhorred'st us in our human griefs"; and he scorned "our droplets . . . which from niggard nature fall." (We might recall that particular turning away from the weeping Flavius.) But "rich conceit" taught Timon to make Neptune "weep for aye / On thy low grave" (5.5.77). Your rich imagination taught you to build right there, where tears are nature's donation. Or—the imagination is not entirely his—it comes to him, and it is given to him. By planting his grave next to the sea, the whole sea will always weep for him. The epitaph is redeemed by what abundantly surrounds it, the sea's vast yet daily rhythms, drawn out and returned, by energies that dwarf and resituate the fat, relentless ego. Alcibiades's conceit about the grave by the sea leads him to the idea of weeping for faults forgiven, to the olive branch, and to the breeding of the peace with which the plays ends (5.5.80).

Our Word Is Our Bond: Moral Relation

Timon of Athens has revealed that the political economy of money in the play is just a part of its meditation on the political economy of speech. We credit someone when we believe them: We count something as worth saying when we say it and when we speak; we say what counts for us. Counting, recounting, and accounting, as claiming, reclaiming, and acclaiming, are part of our speech and show that speech is essentially owed.[76]

In his brilliant and underread third section of *The Claim of Reason* on morality, Cavell investigates the rationality of moral claims. The point of moral argument is not to reach agreement but to establish what we are prepared to take responsibility for, the extent of our cares and commitments. Cavell's redescription of skepticism is, through and through, an ethical project, provoking us to confront ourselves and others, to determine where we stand in relation to each other, to find and be answerable to the responsibilities of our responses.[77] Cavell developed this understanding in relation to J. L. Austin's work, charting that underworked domain of his teacher's insight: passionate utterance. His work can be regarded as the work inaugurated and prepared for in part 3 of *The Claim of Reason*.

When Cavell began again with Austin in his late work, feeling the perlocutionary to have been neglected, he opened up the analysis of what we do when we speak to both passion and morals. Cavell painstakingly and precisely makes analogies with the conditions of illocutionary speech that Austin had outlined in *How to Do Things with Words*. For those speech acts to do the work they do, a whole set of conditions must be in place: There must be an accepted conventional procedure, and the particular person and circumstances must be appropriate; the procedure must be correctly executed. But in the perlocutionary utterance, there are no conventional procedures and effects—the speaker is on his own in relation to them—and appropriateness is decided and is at issue in each case.[78] In each exchange of words, one person, being moved to speak, singles out another and demands a response here and now. At stake is not correct procedure but moral relationship. In passionate utterance, our authority is not given by virtue of a particular role and its attendant rituals and conventions—such as the office of judge or priest—but rather is worked through in our everyday and more or less ceaseless claims and answerabilities. This is the domain not of what we ought to say, and not of speech regulated by rule or ritual, but rather "what we must or dare not say, or have it at heart to say, or are too confused or too tame or wild or terrorized to say or think to say."[79] It is in our passionate utterances that we expose and reveal ourselves, and show how we stand toward each other. We single ourselves out and are singled out.[80] When Austin said our word was our bond, he understood all our words as speech acts, doing things that ritual makes explicit, but that puts us in relations quite outside the conventions he sought (but failed) to hive off as illocutions. Any word of mine commits me and marks me out in relation to you in a specific way. The bonding cannot be reserved alone for explicit binding performatives, as in I promise, I swear, I vow, but it is part of a routine and fundamental way in which we offer and take each other's words. We naturally have trust in each other's words; such trust is implicit in every speech act. It is distrust that makes trust only retrospectively come into view. Although the promise is singled out for philosophers as foundational, it is my word, no particular word, but all my words, that are my bond, as I unremarkably, take your words to be too. For Cavell, however, Austin did not take the threat and truth of skepticism seriously enough. He failed to take seriously the idea that insincerity is often unfathomable. Criteria can tell you only what something is, but not whether or not it exists (criteria tell us what something is, not that it is).

This analysis helps us to see that misanthropy is a reprieve. Timon's characteristic "all" relieves him from all this singling out, and being singled out, from the distinctions necessitated by speech. It also means he will be spared the self-knowledge and the knowledge of others that emerge from this relation to our words. That is why Flavius's loving approach to Timon in his wilderness is such a challenging call, even a temptation to Timon. Cavell helps us see that Timon's failure is moral; his misanthropic skepticism is a cover the play blows.

If we are creatures who can only come to an understanding of ourselves through others, if, we are second persons, before first persons, then our dependency on others is virtually limitless, as are our capacities to deny that vulnerability. Both capacities are at stake in tragedy and in our attempts to define it. After brilliantly surveying the myriad attempts to define the form of tragedy, a misguided enterprise from the start, Terry Eagleton says that in everyday language, the word *tragedy* means something like "very sad." The truth, he suggests "is that no definition of tragedy more elaborate than very sad has ever worked." Very sad, however, is to my mind sufficient. For it asks that any play we call tragic depicts us as the kind of beings who can ruin and devastate each other, who can be capable of experiencing and naming such ruin as violation, yet in the tragic retelling of such ruin can be sustained by each other in response. In this way, to respond to tragedy is to be hopeful, because only hope takes despair seriously enough, hope being a form of love.

Timon is a fallible human being, not a gullible fool. Shakespeare prizes him from his comic, Lucianic tradition to see if he can be tragically inherited. Nevertheless, Timon's commitment to the "all" can mean that he cannot single out what is precious in that which is lost. Timon's despair negates the hope that might cure it. So he stands in the way of tragic hope, both his own and ours. To this extent, his hatred also stands in the way of the loving, mournful, hopeful retelling that renders even the saddest stories of suffering capable of being spoken about and thus participating in the possibility of moral repair.

Chapter 4

Losing the Name of Action
Macbeth, *Remorse,* and Moral Agency

> Comprehension of good and evil is given in the running of the blood.
>
> —Czeslaw Milosz

For a while in the literary academy, the word *human* never appeared without its little strait jacket of scare quotes, as if those would save us from the fear of saying it. It has been the dogma of the academy for quite some time that talk of the human *automatically* invited universalism or essentialism, that it was *automatically* exclusionary and implied an arrogant presumption of the place of humanity in the world and in nature.[1] The savage institutional, economic, social, and political structures and habits that sustained such arrogance are rightly to be eschewed. I do not underestimate the long, unfinished labor of contesting an insular yet viciously successful hegemony.

It is perhaps no wonder that we are troubled so much for the word for our kind, the human. For we live in a society that seems incapable of knowing what a human life is worth. John Berger suggests that this is because it cannot afford to: "If it did, it would either have to dismiss this knowledge and with it dismiss all pretenses to democracy and so become totalitarian: or it would have to take account of this knowledge and revolutionize itself. Either way it would be transformed."[2] Then perhaps our scare quotes are an inchoate hedging, helping us avoid our aspirations to be human, which is a task, not a given.[3] In that task we live, as Stanley Cavell is fond of saying, between acknowledgment and avoidance.

But who were we trying to scare away with those scare quotes? The scare quotes—a marked feature of literary theory in the height of its poststructuralist grip—were supposed to put us at an ironic distance from the word protected by the little punctuation marks. The first usage of scare quotes dates to 1960.[4] The *Oxford English Dictionary* describes scare quotes as "quotation marks used to foreground a particular word or phrase, esp. with the intention of disassociating the user from the expression or from the implied connotation it carries."[5] Scare quotes then are not a piece of grammar but rather a rhetorical maneuver to suggest that the very usage of the word is a problem without this ironic distancing.

When I say, "legitimate rape," I want to put it in scare quotes because I do not share Todd Akin's dangerous lunacy.[6] In that instance, I am showing that I am using Akin's language and not mine. The quotation marks are in this instance citational. The distancing seems fully appropriate. But from whose usage, whose particular usage, am I distancing myself when I use the scare quotes for human? Those who did this so habitually might say: "Well, I am distancing myself from those who are assuming that the white Western liberal subject speaks for the human; I am showing that I understand this to be a usurpation." Only these two examples are not analogous. Akin's term "legitimate rape" shows that he does not understand what rape is. In contrast, the person distancing himself from the putative haughty humanist or the unwitting sexist or racist is relying on a shared understanding of the human when he thinks he is guarding against only one usage of that term. In that sense, he has not quite done what he thinks he has done. The human is not the haughty humanist's term in the way that "legitimate rape" was in Akin's crazy solecism. He in fact depended on the shared understanding of the term and then used the scare quotes to try to highlight a reduced usage of it. In this sense, Akin's scare quotes are not citational at all. So whom is the scare quoter distancing himself from? What is *he* scared of? And who is he scaring off?[7]

The rejection of *all* talk of the human has left the humanities pathetically enfeebled and almost defenseless against the combined but formidable onslaught of the corporate university, the business model of education, and the consequential abandonment of the common reader. Such a total rejection of the human has radically undermined any sense of what we hold in common in the fragile task of taking on the responsibilities and burdens of humanity in a world we share.[8]

Shakespeare offers us a way to talk about the human—not as he "invented" it, and not as either a metaphysically grounded or biological entity distinguished as such by the protocols of science, and not as a definition that excludes nonrational creatures, but as a form of life to which we are fated.[9] He understood the "importance of being human," as Cora Diamond has put it, in our most basic and our most sophisticated linguistic and ethical competencies.[10] In particular, his tragedies are involved in an exploration of how it is internal to being human to wish to escape from this condition, and the cravings, ruses, compulsions, the costs, and consequences of this avoidance.

The invocation of Shakespeare is no panacea; it is no guarantee against these corrosions absent a patient description of how we take on the exposure and risk of human form, human expressiveness individually. In this chapter, I explore the idea of a "common humanity" and its home in mutual responsiveness, recognition, and the responsibility, repudiation, and rejection of the human in our dealings with each other in *Macbeth*. In particular, I pursue the idea of pity and remorse as a "form of conviction" in *Macbeth*, which brings into focus the terrible deeds the play stages.[11] I am particularly interested in the way that the Scottish play, when approached in a certain spirit, helps us both sharpen and deepen our understanding of, and indeed *through*, remorse.

The word *deed* is mentioned in *Macbeth* more than in any other play except *Richard III*. The play explores murder: as imagined, as committed. It envisages a contaminating and disastrous infection of evil that overtakes the murderers, involving them in a kind of decreation, yet it holds them in the hard and lucid light of pity. Macbeth's thinking goes fundamentally, catastrophically astray: The play chillingly shows us how it is possible to commit terrible evil. It also shows us how remorse brings back into shocking view the nature of the deed, the doer, and the ones—all the individual ones—so unutterably and wantonly destroyed.[12] The interconnections the play forges (of human action, remorse, moral agency, and evil) do not work through arguments, but they are nevertheless conceptual; they help us get a grip on questions of human action that are all too liable to become philosophically dry, narrow, and attenuated.[13] The play's subtle and pervasive focus on "deed" shows moral agency in a tragic idiom, both terrifyingly obscured and recovered.

Shakespeare cherishes the human, and this is nowhere more obvious than in his profound analysis of the process of dehumanization. (I will ask again at the end of this chapter whether this is the right name for what is happening to Macbeth, but I will let this stand for now).

Losing the Name of Action

We can smell trouble at the beginning of act 1, scene 7, when Macbeth refers in his soliloquy to the imminent murder of Duncan as "it." He surrounds his "it" by a conditional "if" and, more, a subjunctive "were": "If it were done" (1.7.1).[14] It is as if he imagines the future precipitously as the past, moreover a past in which a deed has been done with no apparent doer. In a few short words, he has removed himself from the picture. Against the contorted rhythm of Macbeth's obfuscations, Shakespeare sounds the beat of the deed: done, done, done, three times in one and a half lines. And then he adds another conditional "If," followed by a string of complex evasions: Now the murder is an "assassination," and he is imagining a world in which deeds have no consequences.[15] Because this cannot be the world of human action Macbeth is denaturing himself, imagining he is more or less than human, and exiling himself from the shared meanings on which his words depend.

In her brilliant book, *The Human Condition*, Hannah Arendt discussed action as necessarily irreversible, unpredictable, and boundless. To do and to suffer are opposite sides of the same coin, she claims, and an act begins a story whose consequences are "boundless" and "unpredictable" and caught up in the reactions and responses of others. The meaning of an act is retrospective, and it "can reveal itself only when it has ended," if then.[16] That a deed once performed cannot be taken back is what tragedy focuses on: the irreversibility of action. So now in the nasty compactness of "surcease" (another evasion) and "success," Macbeth tries to short-circuit the very logic of action (1.7.4). He is imagining a deed, "this blow" (1.7.4), that would be entirely sufficient to itself, bringing with it purely the consequences he desires. So the deed would be his alone to define, carved out of the world of the responses of others.[17] And now Macbeth talks on emphasizing *here*: "that but this blow / Might be the be-all and end-all here" (1.7.4–5).[18] The stunning coinage of "be-all and end-all" is a fantastical attempt to dislodge the inexorable temporal bond, the fully natural succession of act and consequence. That this is a crazy, cock-eyed impossibility is shown in the unstoppable spill over to the next line: "but here, upon this bank and shoal of time" (1.7.6). Macbeth is tutoring himself in the denial of his agency, in the avoidance of the very nature of the deed he is about to commit, and what that deed makes him. In separating his agency from the deed, in denying the nature of the deed he is committing, he is traducing the very nature of human action.

For Macbeth is denying some basic facts of human nature, facts not fixed by custom or convention, facts so obvious they might go unnoticed: "such as, for example, the fact that the realization of human intention requires action, that action requires movement, that movement involves consequences we had not intended, that our knowledge (and ignorance) of ourselves and of others depends upon the way our minds are expressed (and distorted) in word and deed and passion; that actions have histories."[19]

A pronounced turn in this extraordinary soliloquy comes with the mind-stopping "But" in line 7: "But in these cases, / We still have judgment here" (1.7.7). "Even-handed justice" understands that we put to our own lips the chalice we poison with our evil deed. Macbeth enumerates the relations of trust he is in with Duncan—he is his kinsman, subject, and host. In this soliloquy, we see Macbeth at once both grammatically obscuring his future deed, evading a logic he knows, while also acknowledging the extent of the violation he contemplates. Tony Tanner points out that *Macbeth* embarks on the opposite trajectory of the tragic protagonist: His is a rushed and urgent dash from self-knowledge.[20]

When we next see Macbeth speaking alone, we see him apparently in the grip of an apparition. Is the dagger he sees before him a "fatal vision" that is "sensible / To feeling" (2.1.36–37), or is it a dagger of the mind? Whatever it is the dagger is a "thou," given personality, intimacy even; it is a *thing* that appears to solicit him and that he addresses as if it has agency. It is marshaling him along a path he is already traveling: "thou marshall'st me the way that I was going" (2.1.42). He does not need a marshal then to usher him on the path he was already traveling, but it is another self-canceling thought. The marshal is a companion, a guide, and it takes the edge off his agency, his responsibility to imagine himself directed in this way. He has just earlier instructed his servant to ask Lady Macbeth to strike a bell when his drink is ready. Now as Macbeth attempts to "screw his courage to the sticking place" (1.7.61) by summoning up Senecan images of horror, imminent rape, witchcraft, and depravity, the bell rings. Macbeth, I want to say, is turning his action into behavior: "I go, and it is done: the bell invites me" (2.1.62). Once again, he elides his agency in the act, imagining that he is drawn by the visionary dagger, instructed by the whole of nature, and finally summoned by the bell that invites him to heaven or hell. James Calderwood has brilliantly said of these lines: "The whole speech marvelously illustrates the workings of a self-protective consciousness as it projects its inner impulses to create a behaviouristic world to whose stimuli it can then respond."[21]

This slip from action to behavior is important. For in representing his action as a response to a set of stimuli—the bell, the natural world, the dagger—he begins to think of them as *causal*. In so doing, he abandons the entire domain of responsibility, which is internally connected to human action, in which talk is properly of reasons, not causes.[22] For we do not know what action has been done without understanding the intentions with which it was done, without an answer, potential or actual, to the question: "Why did you do that?" It is for this reason that Alisdair MacIntyre, building on Elizabeth Anscombe's work, has said that "the concept of an intelligible action is a more fundamental concept than that of an action as such."[23]

In the first part of the second part (*Prima Secundae*) of his great *Summa Theologiae*, Thomas Aquinas contemplates human actions "proper to man as man." "Those actions are properly called human which proceed from a deliberate will. And if any other actions are found in man, they are called actions *of a man*, but not properly *human* actions, since they are not proper to a man as man" (1-2, q. 1, a. 1).[24] For Aquinas human actions simply are moral actions: In the human realm of deliberation, they are moral.[25] An action, according to Anscombe in her modern classic *Intentions*, is purposive: It is one that can be most naturally addressed by an answer to the question: "Why are you doing that?"[26] Notice that the claim is by no means that the intention controls the meaning of the action—as an editor, translator, and friend of Ludwig Wittgenstein's, Anscombe was hardly likely to make that blunder. Human action would be rather different were that to be the case: Intention is intrinsically linked to a sense of responsibility.[27] What follows from Aquinas's deeply Aristotelian understanding of action is that we are the deed's creature. What Macbeth is blinding himself to is the shaping role of the agent's deeds in forming and building his character. In denying the natural logic of man and woman and deed, Macbeth is denying his humanity.

The dagger marshals him, as if in a dream. Soon he will be melodramatically conjuring himself as Tarquin and pleading with the very earth not to respond to him. The path to murder in this play is to obscure responsiveness to the world and the world to you. Macbeth requires the earth's deafness—"Hear not my steps which way they walk" (2.1.57)—and the world's darkness—"Let not light see my black and deep desires" (1.4.51)—as a presage to his act. As he seeks the world's blindness and indifference, as he covets the darkness that he imagines will render his deeds invisible, the physical integrity of his person cracks up. His eye will wink at his hand (1.4.53). The invisibility to himself, which he covets, call it soul-blindness, will result not merely in a blackening out of self—"to know my deed 'twere best not know myself" (2.2.74)—but an intense isolation and self-deadening. It is a presage of the deadening that will come at the end of the play. There, surcease and success have reached a different accommodation; there, the succession of days, "tomorrow and tomorrow and tomorrow" (5.5.18), annihilates novelty. The evil man's world is a solipsistic world. He can "take things from others, but he can receive nothing from them."[28]

Were Macbeth able to do what he desires—to extricate his murder from all consequences save that of his own succession to the crown, to define the exact limits and contours of the act unilaterally—it would not be human action. In Shakespeare's understanding, he has to deny and avoid his humanity to perform actions that logically must have the consequences of human actions. Macbeth is beginning to have merely the illusion of sense, which is why his nihilism is the logical end point; he has stopped making any sense at all and has stupefied himself.

How does Macbeth stupefy himself? We witness this process immediately after as well as before the murder. When Macbeth describes how he could not say "Amen" when he overhears the prayers of the grooms as if they had seen him with his "hangman's hands" (2.2.28), Lady Macbeth responds: "These deeds must not be thought / After these ways; so, it will make us mad" (2.2.34-35). Macbeth, being afraid "to think what (he) ha(s) done," must not think at all. (2.2.53). When he hears that Macduff has "fled to England," he wishes entirely to eradicate any gap that might exist between the conception and execution of a deed, such that "The very firstlings of my heart shall be / The firstlings of my hand. . . . Be it thought and done" (4.1.146-47). His wish is to eradicate thought altogether, to remove the very possibility that there could be a conceivable answer to the question: "Why are you doing that?" He renders himself thoughtless: This is the "sweet oblivious antidote" (5.3.43) that he ministers to himself.[29]

Closely allied to his willful thoughtlessness, his self-stupefaction, is his desire for isolation. "We will keep ourself / Til suppertime alone" (3.1.42-43). "How now, my lord, why do you keep alone?" (3.2.9), asks Lady Macbeth, who has encouraged his oblivion, his thoughtlessness: "Things without all remedy/Should be without regard" (3.2.11-12). "What's done, is done" (3.2.13) and is hopeless to reassure, which is echoed in the harrowing, "what's done cannot be undone" now sounded as if from hell (5.1.67). "What's done," what's effected (done) is not finished (done) but only the presage to further murderous deeds in a relentless pursuit of an end to the "torture of the mind" (3.2.22). For now, Macbeth tells her that "there shall be done / A deed of dreadful note" (3.2.43-44). (Again, his use of the passive tense averts his agency in the murders he has ordered.) To her inquiries about what is to "be done," he asks not for her consultation, but for her applause after the fact: "Be innocent of the knowledge, dearest chuck / Til though applaud the deed" (3.2.46-47). In his next address, "Come, seeling night," I imagine him turning away from his wife: I imagine her on stage but no longer in his presence, so that in the penultimate line of the scene, his "hold thee still" might signal her attempt to move away from him in a silence in which the horror of their acts and her sense of his profound aloneness, and of her new irrelevance to him, is beginning to dawn. Then his "go with me" has to force a common exit at the very point at which they are no longer going anywhere together. Lady Macbeth is reduced to being a retrospective cheerleader for nameless, authorless deeds, deeds he will not and cannot now share. To share them—in prospect or retrospect—might be to name them. (And how, innocent of the knowledge, *could* she applaud the deed? Macbeth is removing any possibility of judgment and understanding from her ability to discern his action.) Once again, we see the separation of reason from will, the denaturing of action, and the concomitant destruction of intimacy and community. Wishing not to know his deed or himself, he can scarcely afford the risk of human company, the risk of being known by anyone else.[30] "Blood will have blood" (3.4.120) he says. He has now conceived himself as wading in a river of blood so deep that to continue across is *all the same* as to return, negating the point of action to a bloody and terrible sameness, to whose horror he is nonetheless deadened (3.4.134-35).[31] His deeds "must be acted ere they may be scanned" (3.4.138).

How, it might be asked, do I reconcile my idea of Macbeth's self-stupefaction with his clear articulation of the trust he is violating? He knows that Duncan is his kinsman, his king, and his guest, that Duncan is a monarch of virtue, clear and pure in the execution of his office. He knows there will be judgment on him at the end of time; he knows that divine justice will "blow the horrid deed in every eye" (1.7.24). Such knowledge can only be disowned. But how?

Macbeth shows that suppressing or avoiding the capacity for *articulating* what we are doing gradually fuels self-deception. The play is a brilliant portrait of self-deception precisely because it shows the importance of naming actions. This "dead butcher" is an entirely unfitting portrait of the regicide for this very reason.[32] This understanding of self-deception assumes that to become explicitly conscious of our actions requires the development of the skill of articulating (saying) what we are doing or experiencing. Herbert Fingarette calls this "spelling out some feature of the world we are engaged in."[33] In avoiding these articulations, we avoid conscious awareness of what we are doing; we also avoid becoming conscious of our own avoidance. Macbeth is in possession of the criteria of right and wrong, but he avoids applying them (spelling it out). "This supernatural soliciting / Cannot be ill; cannot be good" is an example of the refusal of the application of criteria (1.3.132–33). It echoes the illusion of sense in "Fair is foul, and foul is fair" (1.1.9), and it shows why and how the weird sisters (imperfect speakers) work on his linguistic consciousness in ways that he only retrospectively understands.

The obscuring and self-darkening of Macbeth's mind is shown in his disowning of the criteria he already has; he avoids articulating what he is doing and naming his actions.[34] This is another reason for gratitude to Shakespeare's moral powers of articulation. Shakespeare has not lost the concept of action. How else can he keep its contours so firmly, so relentlessly before us? And how might they be recovered?

In this play, what is good, what is precious, what is of inestimable value is prior: It can be decreated, but it cannot altogether be destroyed.[35] Macbeth might be understood as negating his knowledge of the good in the hopeless task of eradicating his agency; if, however, he seeks to outrun reason, "the pauser," the evil he does is importantly causeless.[36] His attempt to pass off "vaulting ambition" as the spur to action is entirely unconvincing. Even his wife radically qualifies his ambition: He is not without it (1.5.18), but she doubts he has the "illness" (evil) that might make his ambition effective.[37] When Macbeth images his "vaulting ambition," he invokes it as a "spur" he needs as a rider on a horse, but in this somewhat confused metaphor, horse and rider "oer-leap" and fall (1.7.26–28). This seems like a man who needs the "sides of his intent" pricked; it is a kind of desperate hunting for a reason for an act he knows is utterly beyond the reach of justification. Dante understood this in the *Inferno:* We have lost the way; in the midst of our lives, we have missed the true path and we do not know how we lost it. [38] So did Primo Levi: "Hier ist kein warum" (Here there is no why), says a guard to Levi as he grabs an icicle to soothe his parched lips.[39] The play entertains the idea that we enter hell not as a place of punishment but as "the condition to which the soul reduces itself by a stubborn determination to evil, and in which it suffers the torments of its own perversions."[40] There is no glamour or self-sufficiency to the evil envisaged here.

Indeed, what makes best sense of Macbeth's act and the immediate and consequent eradication of a world that can be loved and valued, the relentless, dreary path to the poor player's empty sound and fury that signify nothing, is Augustine's picture of the evil will as "defective," as fundamentally causeless. An evil will begins a nihilation. Evil is not, says Augustine, "a matter of efficiency, but of deficiency: the evil will itself is not effective, but defective."[41] He continues: "To try to discover the causes of such defection—deficient not efficient causes—is like trying to see darkness or to hear silence." We are aware of darkness and silence by absence of perception. When we know things not by perception but rather by absence, we know them "in a sense," but "not-knowing, so that they are not-knowing by being known—if that is a possible or intelligible statement."[42] Charles Matthewes suggests that Augustine's argument that evil is a "privatio boni," a privation of a prior and real good "discerns a crucial clue for the ontological truth about evil, namely, that evil action is in itself not action at all."[43] This is another way in which Macbeth "loses the name of action."

Lady Macbeth's Cry

The recovery of the concept of deed and doer in the world of human action may come through remorse, whose characteristic voice is: "My God, what have I done?" It is Lady Macbeth's terrible cry, uttered while sleepwalking (which I can only now and forever hear in the shattering, soul-searching, soul-touching cry of Judi Dench).[44]

Lady Macbeth has conjured the stopping up of "th'access and passage to remorse" (1.5.44) so that the compunctious visitings of nature cannot shake her murderous purpose (1.5.43).[45] But we can only feel remorse over what has the power to haunt us, and Lady Macbeth will feel her remorse once the access and passage to it is unstopped, in the unremitting horror of her awakening yet somnambulant memory. There she will feel, as Emily Dickinson says in her brilliant poem, "Remorse": "A Presence of Departed Acts— / At window—and at Door—."[46] It is in remorse that the doer recognizes the one wronged in all his or her particularity, in the recognition of what she has done. Remorse is to be distinguished from shame in that the focus is unerringly concentrated on the reality of the one wronged, not in his or her *general* humanity but in precisely her or his uniqueness and irreplaceability. In remorse, one recognizes what one has become simultaneously with the particular reality of the other. This remorse is to be distinguished from regret because regret can be used for actions performed by others: Remorse is personal. You cannot feel it on my behalf, nor I on yours. Remorse makes central the agent in a way that mere regret does not. One regrets what happened: One feels remorse for what one has done. It is therefore internally connected to my actions as mine, which is internally connected to *my* responsibility in what I have done, a responsibility bound up with responsiveness to another. Raimond Gaita puts it this way: "A certain sense of her victim's individuality is internal to a murderer's understanding of the moral significance of what she did." "That," he says, "is part of what it is to be aware of the reality of another human being."[47] Gaita is not saying that we feel remorse *because* we see that something is wrong. He is saying that our natural dispositions to remorse and to pity are one of the determinants of our concept of remorse and of what a human being is. Gaita makes the analogy to what he calls Wittgenstein's astonishingly radical remark that "pity is a form of conviction that someone is in pain."[48] Pity, he suggests, is not a psychological state but, as he puts it, "*normative* [my italics] for the description of the forms of our indifference to the suffering of others."[49] We know pity not epistemically but through our most basic *responses* in healing, binding, wounding, hurting, comforting, and crying, and in the fact that we look into someone's face when binding his wounds. In *Philosophical Investigations*, Wittgenstein says, "if someone has a pain in his hand, then the *hand* does not say so (unless it writes it), and one does not comport the hand, but the sufferer: one looks into his eyes."[50] In remorse, says, Gaita, in a parodic and piercing depiction of how remorse is characterized in Kantian traditions of moral philosophy, "He is not haunted by his principles; he is not haunted by the moral law; he is not haunted by the fact that he did what he ought not to have done . . .: he is haunted by the particular human being he has murdered."[51] Again, *haunted* is the right word. In Lady Macbeth's night-walking scene, the passages to remorse are utterly unstopped. She is haunted nightly by the old man who had so much blood in him, by the Thane of Fife's wife. She is haunted by *them*. It is a picture of the human not in general but *this* particular one, in his or her sole preciousness.

How is she haunted by her deeds? How then does her remorse bring in the reality of the other? It cannot quite be said that hers is a conscience awakening to what she has done. She is, after all, sleepwalking, yet her somnambulism shows the truth in her torment, and the difficulties that stand in the way of a consciously truthful acknowledgment, terrible as that might be. She is in hell, rather than purgatory, which offers us a despairing and permanent re-doing of the act, only now the words she says, "a little water clears us of this deed" (2.2.67), are ironized by the carelessness with which she said them then, with their irreversibility and their boundless echo in her poor tormented soul. "What's done cannot be undone" is an undiminished, unassuageable torment.[52] In that thought, she can only now undo herself. For that undoing, announced by the off-stage cry of women, there can be no time: "She should have died hereafter" (5.5.17).[53]

Remorse is one of the ways in which the concept of human action is recovered for it is in remorse that, bitingly, agonizingly, the contours of this terrible deed, the very significance of the act performed, reemerge in the particular harm done.[54] Gaita has said that remorse is a "disciplined remembrance of the moral significance of what we did."[55] So the doer, the deed, and the one harmed come into focus all together, inextricably and mutually. Like Macbeth, Lady Macbeth has consistently evaded the fact of murder and regicide in her language: "He that's coming / Must be provided for" (1.5.66-67) is a terrible, barely submerged vision of the hospitable accommodations usually made for a guest, and a guest moreover of royal stature, but it too is fundamentally evasive and avoidant.[56] Like Macbeth, she too conjures the night to blind herself and God himself to the nature of her action (1.5.50–54). Haunted by the old man, the Thane of Fife's wife, and by Banquo, she haunts her own life, too. Gaita says this: "The terrible recognition of what we have become is the necessary condition of the recognition of the evil we have done."[57] Remorse brings a terrible understanding of yourself and your action and, with it, a searing sense of the reality of another person in the harm you have done them. It involves a self no longer carving out its self-definition, a project of its will, but rather an understanding that your actions are involved with the life of others, subject to their say in them, and an understanding that those actions define you. You are, inevitably, the deed's creature, the deed is not your creature.

There is no time to mourn Lady Macbeth, for Macbeth has abolished time. This is what happens when the "ignorant present" is disdained for the "future in the instant" (1.5.57–58).[58] He assimilated himself to a timeless will, a will that has anesthetized its reasons and rationales and has replaced them with causes it experiences as compulsions, extrinsic to his will. To refuse remorse, as Rowan Williams has said, is to "refuse to think what it is to be a subject changing according to processes and interactions outside my own will."⁵⁹ Macbeth shows us that picture of the will as murderous. The stopping and unstopping of remorse are Shakespeare's way of retrieving the very concept of human action from a murderous will (Macbeth's) and from a *picture* of the will that is deadly and bound up with violence.⁶⁰

Losing Our Concepts

In charting the internal relations between the concepts of action, evil, and remorse in *Macbeth*, as well as the danger of losing the name of human action; in recovering it again in the disciplined remembrance of past deeds, in which remembrances the doer perceives himself painfully as the evil doer he has become by virtue of his deeds; and in charting the play's contours in these respects, I wish to allude to the notion of conceptual amnesia. This chapter's title, "Losing the Name of Action," comes, of course, from *Hamlet*. It comes at the end of the most famous soliloquy of all in that play, "To be or not to be."⁶¹ We might describe at least part of this soliloquy as Hamlet trying to force himself to be more like Macbeth, as he entertains the idea that conscience makes cowards of us, turning awry enterprises of great pith and moment so that they lose the name of action (so that they are impossible to act on, so that they cannot properly be called actions). That play too is an astonishing exploration of action—who authors an act or seeks to do so, how action escapes intention, how death supersedes all revenging plots in the face of which, finally, only readiness is all. I have borrowed the phrase "losing the name of action" for the title of this chapter to suggest the work of conceptual amnesia. This idea is central to Thomas Pfau's book *Minding the Modern*, and it may also be said to have its roots in Iris Murdoch's pithy and brilliant essay "Against Dryness." It is also beautifully elaborated in the work of Cora Diamond, and especially in her important essay "Losing Your Concepts," which, as I mentioned in my introduction, is a powerful inspiration for this book.⁶² In "Against Dryness," Murdoch says: "We have suffered a general loss of concepts, the loss of a moral and political vocabulary.... We no longer see man against a background of values, of realities, which transcend him. We picture man as a brave naked will surrounded by an easily comprehended empirical world."⁶³

Both Diamond and Niklas Forsberg distinguish the ways in which concepts can be lost. They can be lost historically—things change in such a way that we no longer understand certain ways of life; they can be lost philosophically, as Wittgenstein argues when, for example, he shows how our conceptions of inner life have been radically misconstrued.[64] For Murdoch, conceptual loss involves *our* loss of conceptual realities, ones that derive from a conflict between ourselves and the pictures of the good life we strive to emulate. We strive to become the naked choosing wills pictured in our moral philosophy.[65] Murdoch wanted us to see that moral agency and our reasons for action were not properly conceived solely in terms of choice, that often choice is irrelevant (because someone cannot conceive a choice in which others might so conceive it, or because the very formulation of something as a choice is already morally degrading).[66] Furthermore, as Forsberg has shown, the conception of human freedom as choice, the picture of the naked will in a supermarket of options, strips us of our reality and makes our attempts at self-understanding merely "regional."[67] The picture of the human as a naked will makes it hard to see, and easy to forget the intricacy of the connections between conceptions of action, remorse, evil, and the central way in which our modes of describing and misdescribing what we do are bound up with our self-understanding.

The phrase "losing the name of action" names Macbeth's conceptual amnesia. Macbeth has worked hard to stupefy himself, to dull himself to the concept of action. By imagining deeds without succession (a deep pun in the play), he is both denaturing the shared sense of what an action comes to, its reality, and at the same time, he is losing his self-understanding in one and the same thought. (We tend to lose an understanding of the world and an understanding of ourselves together.) If he were to know his deed it were best then, not to know himself: Right there is an acknowledgment of the horror of regicide and murder. But he cannot know his deed without knowing himself, that is, without understanding what his action entails. Shakespeare shows us the very process of conceptual amnesia in Macbeth's mind, just as he shows how he loses his grip on self, world, and action.

My brief exploration of remorse in relation to *Macbeth* has shown that it, too, is internally connected to questions of the nature of a deed in the light of the doer and the one harmed. With the concept of remorse, then, comes the concept of evil. When concepts of the will are desiccated, so too are concepts of evil. "Is there something in our experience that can . . . teach us what evil is? There is, I believe. It is remorse."[68] Macbeth has been called "Shakespeare's most profound and mature vision of evil."[69]

In his brilliant chapter "Evil Done and Evil Suffered," in *Good and Evil: An Absolute Conception*, Gaita suggests that moral philosophy has separated out evil done from evil suffered. He shows us how problematic certain conceptions of evil are in moral philosophy by virtue of a powerful thought experiment, the kind of experiment that Murdoch might have had in mind in her essay "Against Dryness," in which she contemplates the shortfalls of contemporary moral philosophy in her time. Gaita takes the example of the kind used by consequentialists: What if you could save ten people by shooting one? He claims that those who think that it is obvious that one should be shot to save ten have no sense of evil done or evil suffered. He imagines the response of someone who is saved by shooting one among the ten. I will give a short excerpt from his rich account:

> If he dies, then I will live, because he died, and because there are nine others with me. Each of the nine others will be able to say the same. Yet when he is dead, will I be able to console myself by saying that he died for one tenth of me? Though you think you must kill him not for me or for any of the others taken individually but for all of us taken together, when he is dead, each of us must accept the fact that insofar as he was murdered for our sake, he died for us singly and undividedly. Each of us is implicated in the evil of his murder.
>
> There are ten of us but we do not make "a ten." . . . If you must count let it be like this: one, one, one . . ., and when there is no more "one" to be said, content yourself with that and resist the temptation to say, "And they total ten whereas there is only one over there.[70]

Gaita is trying to get at the failure to perceive the individuality of each man in the utilitarian counting, at the artificial separation of evil done and evil suffered, at the focus of morality on the question of "what ought to be done" exclusively, and at the moral idiocy of choice in certain examples. He sees these thought experiments as disregarding "the ways in which people for the sake of whom we do evil are morally implicated in what we do."[71] "My example," he suggests, "shows that the most important philosophical question is not 'What ought to be done?' The most important question is how to characterise the situation and to capture the evil in it."[72] Gaita's superbly perceptive writing has enabled us to *see* the situation posed by the consequentialists in a different light. The situation now comes under a new description and renders absurd the strict parameters as it is conceived in the moral philosopher's dilemma, parameters that entirely dissolve reality. For in imagining and protecting the surveying eye/I, viewing a range of options in a world of possibilities, the real dimensions of self and world are vanishing from view.[73] Gaita's point—and it is surely Shakespeare's point, too, in *Macbeth*—is that what we do, our actions, come under myriad descriptions, and these descriptions define us because they articulate the positions we are prepared to take and what we hold ourselves responsible for.[74] Gaita consistently helps us to see the inadequacies of the idea that moral agency involves a world of facts and attitudes we might take toward them. As Lars Hertzberg has said in a lucid commentary on Gaita's work: "As I read him, he considers the question of what I take to be the case and the way I respond to it to be inseparable aspects of the situation."[75] This is how vision, not choice, is a central dimension of moral agency, and it is why the way we see the world is as revelatory of us as of the world we see, respond to, and describe in everyday life and in fiction.[76] In remorse, the deed, the doer, and what is done are realized together in a biting, retrospective recognition. That is why seeing the shape of evil and the shape of love are coterminous, and that is also why remorse is an encounter with "the reality of the ethical."[77]

The play, as a whole, does not share in the nihilism it exposes in its central protagonist, but rather it sees that pointlessness, that signification of precisely nothing, that tale only of sound, fury, and idiocy, as the logical end of the extinction of action. This is achieved precisely not in a moralistic way but through our pity in what Macbeth has become.[78] Interpretations of the play that see some generalized existential statement about the emptiness of life in Macbeth's "tomorrow and tomorrow and tomorrow" have failed to motivate the words in Macbeth's mouth. Why is he saying precisely this right now? The immediate cue is his wife's death in the midst of a forthcoming battle, in which there is no time at all to mourn her or even register her loss: She should have died at a better time. Macbeth's imagination always leaps over the present to find the future in the instant and to imagine another time that is not this one. He imagines through the relentlessly growing pile of corpses his own "perfection." Each imagined death—Banquo, Fleance, Macduff, Macduff's children (fill in the blanks, the structure is the same)—is an obstacle to him being "perfect" and "safe." "To be thus is nothing, but to be safely thus," he muses (3.1.47). The death of Banquo and his son Fleance, for example, will make him "perfect" (3.1.109). When he hears the news that Fleance has escaped he says, "I had else been perfect" (3.4.19). Each person is there only as an obstacle to the perfect (complete, entire) accomplishment of his wishes. But the mounting deaths cannot get him what he wants, which is to *live as if he had not killed* them all with the crown joyfully and triumphantly on his head. What he wants is an illusion: The telos of his actions is not possible. "Tomorrow and tomorrow and tomorrow" is the life drained of significance, but it is drained of that significance by him, his moral identity utterly shorn. Tomorrow cannot be separated from the history of todays that have led to it.

Under some dominant ideas of action, we imagine that feeling pity for someone would mean that we are slackening our sense of what it is they have actually done, perhaps because we can think of holding someone responsible only in terms of blame. But *Macbeth* helps us to see that it might precisely be by virtue of our pity that we might hold Macbeth responsible for all that he has done and that we might also pity the creature he has become. Our pity might be part of the very fabric of our moral imagination.[79]

What we need, Murdoch suggests, against simplistic ideas of freedom of the will, and the will's agency in action, is a "renewed sense of the difficulty and complexity of the moral life and the opacity of persons."[80] She finds literature to be a good home for the exploration of concepts, where vision is enlarged.[81] Seeing what is "most precious to us" is a task I see at the heart of Shakespeare's late tragedies. There what is precious is realized only through a recognition of loss.

The Thane of Fife Had a Wife: What Is Most Precious to Me

I take the phrase "most precious to me" from Macduff's response to Malcolm when he has received the news of his wife and children's death (4.3.226). I want to dwell on this response to show how the play continually refines and holds open to view not how to choose between different actions—"what ought to be done?" (cry like a woman or fight like a man?)—but rather to reveal a sense, a vision (in Murdoch's terms) of what is precious to us. Macduff's response helps us see that moral judgment is about the *apprehension* of a world apt for valuing, rather than a choice between different values.[82] To explore Macduff's response, we need to appreciate what it is a response to.

In Michael Boyd's 2012 Royal Shakespeare Company production of *Macbeth* at Stratford-upon-Avon, the moral center of the play is the murder of Lady Macduff's children at the castle in Fife.[83] This scene was sometimes cut in eighteenth- and nineteenth-century productions. It has also often been produced historically in a highly sentimental fashion (the boy is too sweet and banal understandings of femininity—weak not wise—get in the way of Lady Macduff's clear-sighted understanding of her betrayal, isolation, and abandonment), which corrupts the lucidity with which the scene was written. We encounter the courage of a young boy standing in for his father toward a wife and mother, abandoned by her great warrior husband who will redeem the land. Only no such redemption is yet at hand. This is what it is to live in the Scotland of *Macbeth*. We know that *Macbeth*'s Scotland is a land ruled by and through fear. Fear pervades the atmosphere of the play from the inception of the murder. There is the fear of discovery, of course: "I am afraid they have awaked," says Lady Macbeth of the grooms as she awaits her husband (2.2.10). "I am afraid to think of what I have done," says Macbeth, when he realizes he needs to return to the scene of the crime with the daggers that he has mistakenly carried with him (2.2.53). For a while, Macbeth will find that every noise "appals" him (2.2.59). Feeling fear, Macbeth becomes the major instigator of fear in others: Malcolm and Donalbain flee immediately. Macduff also departs from Scotland. Macbeth "fears" the existence of Banquo and his sons as those who will wrench "unlineally" the throne from his occupation (3.1.55). Macbeth must "scorch the snake" and kill it to assuage his fear and sleeplessness (3.2.18-20). But he fears everyone: He keeps a "servant fee'd" in every house and exists in the tyrant's dire world of trustlessness and panic, both fearing and engendering fear (3.4.131). The terrible scene in Fife minutely shows fear's voracious infectiousness and terror, spreading from the tyrant to encompass the whole country, destroying trust.

The exchange with Ross and Lady Macduff at the beginning of this scene is vital. In the preceding scene, we saw Macbeth in dismay at the news of Macduff's flight, declaring that he will "surprise" Macduff's castle in Fife and seize his lands, and "give to th'edge of the sword / His wife, his babes and all unfortunate souls / That trace him in his line" (4.1.149-52). The firstlings of his heart will be the firstlings of his hand, in a relentless outpacing of thought—"be it thought and done" (4.1.146-48).

In the next scene, we move to Fife, and Lady Macduff is being brought the news from Ross that Macduff has fled the land. Her first question is to ask what had her husband done that he should flee? She thinks his flight is madness, that he has become a traitor (to her and his children) by virtue of his fears: "When our actions do not / Our fears do make us traitors" (4.2.2–3). To this Ross tries out the idea that she does not know whether it was wisdom or fear. Lady Macduff replies that it cannot be wisdom to "leave his wife; to leave his babes, / His mansions, and his titles in a place / From whence himself does fly?" (4.2.6–8). For her, this is a sign that he cannot love them, for even the wren fights against the owl to protect the young ones in her nest: "All is the fear, nothing is the love" (4.2.12). This is a description apt for the denaturing of Scotland. Ross offers again the thought that Macduff is "noble, wise, and judicious", and "best knows / The fits of the season" (4.2.16–17). But he admits that the times are cruel "when we are traitors / And do not know ourselves, yet know not what we fear, / But float upon a wild and violent sea / Each way and none" (4.2.20–22). Not enough credence is usually given to Lady Macduff's apprehension of what wisdom might come to, against the initially bland, superficial, and false consolations of Ross. And then Ross, too, leaves. A messenger comes in warning her to flee. But he too departs. It is left to her son to be the man. And he is, in this striking staging, the best man in the play, his actions and vision the least corrupted, his heart the purest. The scene anatomizes the effect of fear and how liable it is to make us traitors even when we do not know what we fear, floating "each way" and therefore "none", that is to say, with no way or direction. To draw out the depth of Macduff's response to their slaughter, this scene needs to be free of condescension and needs to be as clear-sighted as Lady Macduff is within it.

Macduff's response to the slaughter of his entire family and household insists on the responsibility of responsiveness.[84] In Polly Findlay's remarkably quick-moving production at the Barbican in 2018, Edward Bennett as Macduff holds an agonizingly long pause after Ross has delivered the news that his castle has been surprised and his wife and children "savagely slaughtered" (4.3.206). This long silence prompts and motivates Malcolm's outburst "Merciful heaven. . . . Give sorrow words" (4.3. 208–10). Bennett maintains the great weight of bewilderment and grief in his slow repetitions: "My children too? . . . My wife killed too? . . . All my pretty ones? . . . did you say all? . . . All? . . . All my pretty chickens, and their dam / At one fell swoop?" (4.3.212, 4.3.214, 4.3.218–20). The slow trajectory of Bennett's performance in the rapid, hurtling movement of the play, the play in which Macbeth has sought to obliterate time is startlingly effective. He is told by Malcolm that he must dispute it like a man.[85] To Malcolm's morally feeble, instrumental words, "Be comforted. / Let's make us medicines of our great revenge" (4.3.217), he finds it enough to comment: "He has no children" (4.3.219), a line I take here to be about Malcolm rather than Macbeth. And then:

> I shall do so
> But I must also feel it as a man:
> I cannot but remember such things were
> That were most precious to me.
>
> (4.3.224)

All Malcolm can think of is turning Macduff into the instrument of revenge against Macbeth, converting grief to anger (4.3.231–32). Macduff is reminded of all that is precious in the world, the remembrance of which, the recovery of which, is what he thought he was fighting for, although he now realizes that he might have forgotten this. Macbeth has destroyed what is precious to him; he has destroyed what he cares about and values, and so it is what is precious, what is valued that is enlarged and put before us to care about. The horror felt in Macduff's response is intrinsically linked to his sense of what is precious, just as violation is linked to the intrinsically and irreplaceably valuable. As Diamond has said, there is no "grammar of value in general." We see value as alive in a human life when we see what responsiveness to that value might be, and what failures in such responsiveness comes to.[86] The horror now deadened in Macbeth is utterly alive in Macduff's response. The pause stops the hurtling speed of the play, its drive to thoughtlessness in the actions of Macbeth. Macbeth will eventually know that he has destroyed the things he can no longer look to have—honor, love, and troops of friends (5.3.24–25).

Macbeth puts before us an anatomy of evil whose contours can come clear only because of remorse, and the subsequent revelation of the shape of harm. In so doing, it shows us what is at stake in the concept of human action, but also what gets lost by dry versions of what it is that human beings do, dry versions of the so-called dilemmas before them.[87] When deracinated pictures of the will in modern moral philosophy are sovereign, they will miss the kind of violence and danger revealed in this play; they will be blind to the very analysis of deracination it depicts in the mind of its central murderer.

The Responsibility of Responsiveness

Being human is aspiring to being human, says Cavell: "Since it is not aspiring to being the only human, it is an aspiration on behalf of others as well."[88] The concept of the human, human action, remorse, and pity are thus *internally* related.

The chapter epigraph is from Czeslaw Milosz's poem, "One More Day." After the first line "Comprehension of good and evil is given in the running of the blood," the poem continues:

> In a child's nestling close to its mother, she is security and warmth,
> In night fears when we are small, in dread of the beast's fangs and
>   in the terror of dark rooms,
> In youthful infatuations where childhood delight finds completion.

Milosz wants to draw our attention to the natural patterns of response without which our moral notions would be incomprehensible. "Should we discredit the idea for its modest origins?" he asks. The poem lovingly mulls over the naturalness of these responses. The security a child finds is related to the warmth of her mother's body, just as her fears may be a response to the unknown and fancied darkness of a devouring space, like Jane Eyre in the red room. Or ponder, suggests Milosz, our unreasoned desires toward the people to whose beauty we respond, or to the fabulous gratuity of birdsong, the presence of light, and the architecture of a tree. In Milosz's poem, this responsiveness is related to our moral sense: We learn that "good is an ally of being," as "the mirror of evil is nothing" ... According to the nature of our bodies, of our language." Our natural responsiveness helps to form and forge the fabric of relationships through which we acknowledge one another as proper objects of care and concern.[89]

In the continuation of the speech analyzed earlier in this chapter ("If 'twere done when 'tis done"), Macbeth introduces a most astonishing image of Pity as a "naked newborn babe." Imagining an inescapable doomsday judgment, he envisages a heavenly response to Duncan's "taking-off." At the day of judgment, Duncan's virtues will plead for him, and "pity, like a naked new born babe, / Striding the blast, or heaven's cherubin, horsed / Upon the sightless couriers of the air, / Shall blow the deed in every eye, / That tears shall drown the wind" (1.7.21–25). Pity is the babe who will witness and judge because it is the naturalness of pity and its irreducible claim on us that is in "the running of the blood." Pity is naked, and newborn, a wholly dependent creature, inviting and making needful our loving concern for its survival. Pity as the newborn babe reminds us of the helpless beginnings we share; the babe, however, is our implacable judge. It "blows the deed in every eye": The tears of the pitying drown the wind.[90]

Pity is, as Wittgenstein puts it, a "form of conviction," a form of acknowledgment of another's suffering, and our feelings of pity have a normative claim on us. It is the lack of pity for suffering that demands explanation. That is why, after Macbeth's invocation of the babe, Macbeth announces to his wife that "we will proceed no further in this business" (1.7.31). It is also why Lady Macbeth has to so distort and twist the concept of manhood and courage and the appropriate objects of fear as in the fully obvious idea that it is proper to fear harm to a baby but not to use harm to a child as exemplary of *her* courage.

Macbeth has not rendered himself inhuman. But only a human being can behave inhumanly. This is why being human is not a given. "Being human is the power to grant being human."[91] "What gives us *so much as the idea* that human beings think, can feel?"[92] Nothing, because it is not an idea. "I am not of the opinion that he has a soul."[93] Our responsibilities are intrinsically, internally bound up with our responsiveness to each other.[94]

Before we reject the human, before we imagine we are posthuman, we should know what it means to cherish and acknowledge our humanity.

We sometimes call on each other to treat each other as human beings. We seem to need reminders. We say, for example, that the way she humiliated him was inhuman, or that the rapist sat on her to tie up his shoelaces after he raped her as if she was interchangeable with a log or a bench. Is there any other way to treat each other except as human?[95] Surely we—and not the rapist either—do not need reminders of the difference between a log and a woman?[96] Such phrases are rather a call to justice, a plea that she will fall into the realm of justice as a stone or a log does not. They are a shamed acknowledgment that it is precisely in the realm of the human that people treat each other with a cruelty likely to madden us if we contemplate it too surely.

It is perhaps too comforting a thought to imagine that tragedy is about our finiteness, about what we cannot know or do. If we see it that way, we can avoid our irreducible, inevitable responsibility in adopting an attitude toward each other's souls. If we follow Cavell's logic, of the embeddedness of knowledge in acknowledgment and response, then the idea of our finitude as limit might come as a relief from the perpetual burden of having to read each other, and having to express ourselves, of having to draw the connections we draw between body and soul.

Shakespeare's moral achievement in *Macbeth* is to bring into view our irreducible role in seeing each other as human, as a task, not a given. Criticism is making a work of art available to just response.[97] If we justly respond to Shakespearean tragedy, can it help the humanities, help us, be humane?

Chapter 5

Coriolanus
Shakespeare's Private Linguist

When blows made me stay, I fled from words.

—Coriolanus

Is it possible to escape being bound by what we say? The clearest dramatic and political expression of this fantasy of unboundedness is Shakespeare's *Coriolanus*. The clearest philosophical expression is Ludwig Wittgenstein's private linguist, a figure who appears in the *Philosophical Investigations*.

Wittgenstein's examination of the would-be private linguist in the *Philosophical Investigations* illuminates Caius Martius's flight from words.[1] It also affords us a new understanding of how *Coriolanus* is a political play. In addition, it diagnoses with unprecedented clarity the relation of speaking and human being.

The dating and ordering of the Shakespeare canon is a tricky business. *Coriolanus* is likely to be the last tragedy in the canon (if we exclude *Cymbeline*) that comes under that rubric in the folio, but *Cymbeline* is more sensibly called a tragicomedy.[2] So *Coriolanus* ends the long run of plays of exile I have explored thus far. It confronts presciently and directly the disdain of the good of human articulacy, and the radical attenuation of it, and helps us understand the way that these tragedies form a dramatic group.

In this chapter I begin with the act of asking in *Coriolanus*, a speech act that exemplifies mutual dependence, before exploring Wittgenstein's private language fantasy. I show how exploration of this common temptation, taken as a fantasy of overcoming the conditions of speaking, and thoroughly exposed in Caius Martius's extreme ways of interacting with others, can provide a new understanding of how the play is political. Finally, I turn to the play's climactic final scenes that awaken new forms of responsiveness and responsibility in the play's protagonist and, in the process, reveal the ethical stakes of Shakespeare's late dramaturgy.

The Man Who Would Not Ask

Do you know people who refuse to ask, say, for directions? They do not want to appear lost. A woman who was once my neighbor had a fall and smashed her hip. She did not use the phone beside her to ask for help because it was nighttime, and she did not want to disturb anyone. She would rather have died than ask for help. Still, we ask for help: We ask for consent, for advice, for clarification, or for trouble. We ask, in various ways, depending on our need or sense of entitlement, for money. Men used to say that women asked for "it," and to say that of them was a way of diminishing or humiliating them. There are things you cannot ask for, like love (King Lear does not know this). If you ask for money or food from a stranger in the wrong place, you might well be forcibly moved on, your request denied.

There are multiple ways of asking. I demand that you write that letter, and you might think I am imperious. You question me closely as to my whereabouts. Then I am a suspect, or perhaps you are simply jealous. Policemen interrogate; beggars beg. One can petition, supplicate, crave, entreat, invite, inquire, plead, query. One can be a suitor, a petitioner, but not, generally speaking, an asker. There is no office of asking.[3] When I ask, I reveal myself to be in need of something, and I acknowledge you to be the person who might give me money, a helping hand, a piece of information you know, and I do not. I show myself to stand in a certain relation to you and to think of you in a particular way. In short, I am in need of you. Such are the ways in which we depend on each other habitually and in everyday ways. Imagine a world in which no one ever asked for anything. It would not be a human world. Asking makes a claim; it requires a response even if that response is a rebuff or a refusal. Asking shows us that we need each other and that can be hard.

In Shakespeare's grimly brilliant, remorselessly inquiring play, *Coriolanus*, Coriolanus hates to ask. His fundamental antipathy to asking is bound up with his desires and claims to be "alone," to act *as if* he were the very author of himself (5.3.36).[4] He does not much like being asked either, and the play is structured around scenes of asking. This structure appears to be a means to explore, as its central problem, the recognition and denial of creatures in forms of dependency. Indeed, the climactic scene of the play stages the moment when Coriolanus's mother, wife, and child—his kin—ask mercy of him for themselves and for the city of Rome. It is at the beginning of this extraordinary scene that Coriolanus declares:

> Let the Volsces
> Plough Rome and harrow Italy, I'll never
> Be such a gosling to obey instinct, but stand
> As if a man were author of himself
> And knew no other kin.
>
> (5.3.33–37)

These scenes are a profound reflection on mutual dependency and need, on the specific costs of the rejection of pity, and on the society that founds itself on such rejections. The play explores what it means to be kind to others and thus participate in kindred with them. Asking is related to the things (*res*) that are shared, in common (*publica*), and the tragic costs of denying this kinship.

Consider some of the following scenes of asking in *Coriolanus*. We hear of Coriolanus before we meet him and understand that in the eyes of the citizens, he is a "very dog to the commonalty" (1.1.26). He certainly asks questions in the first scene, but he is entirely uninterested in the answers. Consider his question as he greets the mutinous and starving citizens whose reason for protest is the withholding of grain: "What's the matter? you dissentious rogues / That, rubbing the poor itch of your opinion, / Make yourselves scabs?" (1.1.159–61). This question does not even grant the citizens the capacity for articulate or articulable speech, and it is answered by Menenius, not by the citizens. It is a question that evinces such scorn as to be almost unanswerable. Ask nicely (i.e., respectfully), as your mother may have told you, if you really want an answer. What the citizens say, in his view, is not legitimate; it is more like a flea bite, a disreputable sensation, a bodily reflex that needs no considered answer because it is not so much as speech. His second question is an insult and accusation: "What would you have, you curs, / That like not peace nor war?" (1.1.163–64). Caius Martius will not put himself in the position of needing or wanting anything from people so ignorant, wayward, and changeable: "With every minute you do change a mind, / And call him noble that was now your hate" (1.1.177–78). The issue is one of trust: "Trust ye?" (1.1.176). Such people cannot be trusted to have opinions: He does not grant them a view on the world or a voice in that world. It is no surprise to learn that he considers the extension of a franchise to "their vulgar wisdoms" (1.1.210) as thoroughly impolitic. From the very opening of the play then, the question of having a voice at all, of mutual acknowledgment, and of political legitimacy are deeply intertwined.[5]

His great victory at Corioles has secured his military but not his political might. This in the form of a consulship is the "one thing wanting" (2.1.195) by his mother. He reluctantly agrees to stand for consul at her urgent and instructive cajoling. He asks that the usual custom of displaying battle wounds to entreat their voices/votes in support of his consulship be foregone. He has won fame by his sword not his word, but he is expected to "ask kindly" (2.3.74) the voices or votes of the commonalty to be made consul. Having won his fame by the sword, not his word, he seeks to avoid a position of vulnerability and, above all, the supplication he must make to the citizens for their votes and voices. But the citizens under the influence of Sicinius and Brutus, Rome's new tribunes, will gloss his "request" as rather a mock than a proper petition, and Coriolanus fulfills Sicinius's confidant sense that "He will require them / As if he did contemn what he requested / Should be in them to give" (2.2.155–57).[6] What is your price, asks Coriolanus, and the citizen answers merely to "ask it kindly."

The citizen's specification is simple but momentous. The requirement of asking kindly entails that he must ask them as if he actually wants what they can give him, that he, in short, acknowledge and recognize that they are in a position to give him something as simple as their affirmation. This is what is involved in asking: To ask kindly is to recognize a humanity he holds in common with the one being asked, that he is of their kind, that they are of his kind, and that they are of one kind. It is not surprising that Coriolanus should blanch at putting "on the gown," standing naked, and entreating the people "for (his) wound's sake" for their suffrage (2.2.136–37). He has won a great military victory, whereas they have not risked their skins; he deserves (alone) and on these grounds to be a participant in the political process (in the senate) without having to ask. In his view, the asking is incoherent for he does not grant them the capacity to confer on him what should be his already. Why ask what they are not (in his eyes) in a position to grant? It is precisely this refusal to recognize them that will lead to his condemnation and banishment. This is one reason Plutarch describes him as "churlishe, uncivill and altogether unfit for any man's conversation."[7] Asking kindly does not simply mean asking politely, asking as opposed to insulting, rebuffing, disdaining, mocking. Asking means expressing kinship. It is a revelation of the fundamental shared nature without which there can be no grounds of intelligibility.[8] To ask at all is to posit a "we" in mutuality. Coriolanus impossibly wishes to make a world solely out of his assertion. Even more radically, he imagines that his deeds will speak for themselves as if no community is needed to voice or name those deeds in praise or supplication.[9]

The play *Coriolanus* is structured around these astonishing acts of asking: one that so crucially and utterly backfires on Coriolanus's inability to recognize himself as one of a kind with the citizens of Rome; and another in which his mother, wife, and child seek recognition of their kinship, with him as son, husband, and father. The next crises of the play have to do with how Coriolanus, now banished and set on devastating Rome in revenge for his dismissal, is to be asked for mercy. This precipitates the play's most central "unnatural" scene in act 5, scene 3.

That climactic supplication scene, to which I will return, is carefully anticipated by the play's precise and telling focus on the grammar of asking. The play features a protracted elaboration of who is in a position to ask Coriolanus to spare Rome: Who can coherently, intelligibly, ask Coriolanus to save Rome and imagine that he could accede? In act 4, scene 6, after the banishment or self-exile of Coriolanus, an extended conversation unfolds about who can petition Coriolanus to save the city he now seeks to destroy. "We are all undone," says Menenius, "unless / The noble man have mercy" (4.6.110–11). Cominius's response is entirely to the point: "Who shall ask it?" (4.6.112). Who indeed? The tribunes are the ones who have orchestrated the banishment of Coriolanus: They cannot ask him "for shame" (4.6.113). To receive a request for mercy from them is barely credible. Even the tribunes who threatened Coriolanus with death and have banished him from Rome can hardly ask him to save a city in which he is not recognized as a citizen. The request would have no chance of being received as legitimate. Simply nothing they could say here would make any sense at all. There are no grounds of intelligibility from which to project such a question.[10] Cominius likewise cannot ask because he has already tried and come away unanswered. Coriolanus's response to Cominius was that his petition was "bare" (thread-bare? bare-faced?) given that the city had punished him (5.1.20). At the plea to spare his "private friends," Coriolanus replies that he would not stay "to pick them in a pile / Of noisome musty chaff" (5.1.25-26). Menenius decides that he is the only one in a position to ask and that he can venture out to plead on the basis of his long friendship with Coriolanus. He bets on the longevity and strength of this relationship in the hope that his appeal will call out an answering response from Coriolanus. Brutus, too, banks on an answering kindness in Coriolanus: "You know the very road into his kindness / And cannot lose your way" (5.1.58-59). Menenius, however, finds it difficult even to gain access to Coriolanus. He is treated with utter disdain by the first watch. How can Menenius, *or any Roman*, be in any position to ask for anything from the man they have evicted from their city? Aufidius's watchmen, refusing him his audience with Martius, voice this clearly: "Can you, when you have pushed out your gates the very defender of them, and in a violent popular ignorance given your enemy your shield, think to front his revenges with the easy groans of old women, the virginal palms of your daughters, or with the palsied intercession of such a decayed dotard as you seem to be?" (5.2.40-46).[11] When Menenius eventually sees Coriolanus, he addresses him as father to son: "O my son, my son" (5.2.70). He presents him with his tears: "I was hardly moved to come to thee but, being assured none but myself could move thee, I have been blown out of our gates with sighs and conjure thee to pardon Rome and thy petitionary countrymen" (5.2.72-75). Speaking on his behalf and on the behalf of his countrymen, he stakes himself in his words. Coriolanus's response is brutal and short: "Away!" (5.2.79). He refuses to hear another word. At this point, we are set for the "unnatural scene" for there is now only his family to plead for the city. Again, in this scene—to which I shall return—it is through the grammar of asking that Coriolanus and his mother are fundamentally exposed to each other. Coriolanus attempts to stop Volumnia from asking:

> I beseech you, peace!
> Or, if you'd ask, remember this before:
> The thing I have forsworn to grant may never
> Be held by you denials.
>
> (5.3.78-81)

You can't *call* my refusal to you a denial of you, he desperately and hopelessly claims. There's the rub: Coriolanus cannot unilaterally redefine what his denial of her request comes to. Her insistence on asking, on asking kindly, will force him to confront the cold-bloodedness of his rebuff: "Yet we will ask / That, if you fail in our request, the blame / May hang upon your hardness. Therefore hear us" (5.3.89-91). They are asking for mercy. The granting of it breaks (and makes) Coriolanus, showing the tragic cost of his denial of humanity, and the costs of the acculturation in such denials that Rome demands of its warriors.

Wittgenstein and Private Language

In his analysis of the preceding scene, Stanley Fish has offered this striking and prescient observation: "There is finally only one rule: the word is from Coriolanus and it is the law: it acknowledges no other authority, it recognizes no obligations that it does not stipulate . . . it hears no appeals; it is inexorable. . . . It follows, then, that when Coriolanus stands against it, he is destroyed. It is his own word that convicts him, and it is able to convict him because he has pledged his loyalty to it and to nothing else."[12] In the chapter title, I suggest that Coriolanus is Shakespeare's "private linguist," and I want now to explore the implications and, I hope, the interpretative promise of this assertion. (My differences with Fish's understanding of what he calls "speech act theory" will emerge in what follows.)

One of the many thought-experiments in which Wittgenstein asks us to participate in the great workbook called the *Philosophical Investigations* is the one in which we are asked to imagine a language that might be known to one person alone: "But is it conceivable that there be a language in which a person could write down or give voice to his inner experiences—his feelings, moods, and so on—for his own use?—Well, can't we do so in our ordinary language?—But that is not what I mean. The words of this language are to refer to what only the speaker can know—to his immediate, private sensations. So another person cannot understand the language."[13] A series of remarks follow in which Wittgenstein attempts to imagine precisely such a language. These sections of the *Investigations* have come to be known as Wittgenstein's "private language argument," and it is thought that the point of the argument is to demonstrate that any thoughts we might entertain as we try to imagine this private language come to nothing and thus founder on their incoherence. To get this idea going, Wittgenstein asks us to imagine that I wish to keep a diary about "the recurrence of a certain sensation" (*PI*, ¶ 258). I write down an "s" whenever I have a sensation, but I have only my memory of the sensation to go on. The "s" is unusable in a language because no criteria of correctness are available to establish any degree of consistency in the way it is deployed, my memory of the sensation being far too fickle and unreliable a guide. Wittgenstein asserts: "One would like to say: whatever is going to seem correct to me is correct. And that only means that here we can't talk about 'correct'" (*PI*, ¶258). On this reading, Wittgenstein is *arguing* the *thesis* that there can be no such thing as a private language: He is *arguing* that language is a shared phenomenon through and through. The ramifications of this argument are both intricate and far-ranging because they fundamentally challenge not only the picture of language, self, and body at the heart of both Cartesianism and solipsism but also an entire tradition that makes epistemology and particular pictures of knowledge and self-knowledge the starting point of philosophy in sorting out our relation to the world.[14]

Wittgenstein nowhere uses the term *argument* to discuss his would-be private linguist. He invites us to see if it is possible to conceive of a language known to one person alone and motivates this fantasy through a number of ways to try it out. That it is a fantasy rather than an argument is central to Stanley Cavell's reading of these passages in *The Claim of Reason*.[15] It is not possible to argue anyone out of a fantasy, but a fantasy may be expressed, recognized, and occasionally released. This is Wittgensteinian therapy. One particular view of language underwrites the private language fantasy: It is the idea that words might be connected to their objects without *my* intervention. The private linguist would like, as it were, to baptize the objects in his or her mind internally, rendering the mediation of others unnecessary. In such a picture, language does not have to be shared, nor do we need to be exposed in it. What the private linguist fantasizes in Cavell's extraordinary reading is the elimination of human expressiveness, of our fatedness to expression.[16] Cavell suggests that the upshot of the question about whether we can imagine a private language turns out to be "that we cannot imagine this, or rather that there is nothing of the sort to imagine, or rather that when we as it were try to imagine this we are imagining something other than we think." Each attempt does not seem to satisfy the fantasy of privacy that the interlocutor craves. It is as if what he wanted was to overcome the idea of expressiveness because at each point in the fantasy "a moment arises in which, to get on with the fantasy, the idea, or fact, of the *expressiveness* of voicing or writing down my experience has to be overcome." The fantasy of a private language is about a need to deny the extent to which language is public and shared and this turns out to be a fantasy or fear of "inexpressiveness." According to

Cavell, "The wish underlying this fantasy covers a wish that underlies skepticism, a wish for the connection between my claims of knowledge and the objects upon which they fall to occur without my intervention, apart from my agreements."[17]

The moral of the private language fantasy turns out to be the dependence of reference on expression.[18] If we *cannot* be known, then we will no longer have to make ourselves known to others, to take on the burden, responsibility, and exposure of speech; to risk our incoherence, inarticulateness, and the pain of not being understood. If others too *cannot* make themselves known to us, then we are relieved of the responsibility of the claims they might, that they ineluctably do make, on us.

Why would we want to deny the depth to which language is shared? Sharing a language to the depths that we do, and in the ways we do, makes us deeply vulnerable to each other. We would rather not suffer such exposure. This powerful reading supplies us with the idea that the desire to fantasize a fully private language is a desire to escape the condition of being human and the naturalness of the claims of others upon us; it is a denial of our humanity. So the burdens and resources of speech are the burdens and resources of human form. Sandra Laugier goes so far as to suggest that subjectivity is reinvented as *voice*. The private language fantasy imagines that the disconnection of self-knowledge from the requirements of communication will not lead to the loss of identity.[19] I can say, and know, who I am without others.

Coriolanus is a would-be private linguist because he will not suffer the exposure of being legible to others. His deeds should speak for themselves—as if any deed could be understood without a community of speakers in which such deeds are intelligible. The private language fantasy gets at Coriolanus's impossible refusal of the role of others in his life, their say in him, his inevitable need of them if only in his glory; it gets at the terrifyingly lethal nature of that denial; it shows that the denial of the depth to which we share language is also a denial of finitude and his humanity; it explains Coriolanus's aspirations to be more than human. The idea that language is shared—and to a depth utterly underestimated in standard and more contractual visions of language—is cause for neither weary emphasis, the condescension of correctness, or argument. It is rather an occasion for both fear and wonder, which is enacted in our myriad embarrassments and exposures and in our futile attempts to master our legibility and our fantasies that we are either fundamentally unknowable, or perfectly knowable without the aid of others. The private language fantasy is lived in Coriolanus's willful, violent, and indefatigable extremism, and in his attempt at invulnerability, which is to say inhumanity. The fantasy is visible in the other late great tragedies and more mundanely in the psychic elimination of others that funds this desire.[20]

It might at first seem entirely counterintuitive to claim that Coriolanus, of all people, is a would-be private linguist. After all, no hero of Shakespearean tragedy is reputed to have less inner life, less psychic complexity than Coriolanus. He is a man of action and lives in a city of swords not words. He is a killing machine; self-designedly and deliberately thoughtless. Although the word *alone* is one of his favorites, we never see him alone. "We'll hear naught from Rome in private" (5.3.93), he says, and indeed he hears nothing in private and says nothing in private save the brief lines in act 4, scene 3, as he approaches Antium, a city in which he made widows, and a few lines later meditating on the depth of his hatred toward friends fast sworn. The setting of the play is, as Robert Miola, Paul Cantor, and Gail Kern Paster have argued, relentlessly public and carefully delineated.[21] Cavell's analysis of Wittgenstein's remarks might help us see that Coriolanus craves metaphysical not empirical privacy. He would like to evade his exposure in word and expression, and this is a standing skeptical temptation. The impoverishment of his inner life is related to the impoverishment of his political life because to grow in self-knowledge is at the same time to find and form the knowledge of the membership of the community you inhabit.[22] The fact is that Coriolanus has an impoverished inner life but not because he is a fully public creature. He has an impoverished inner life because he has an impoverished public and political life. Self-knowledge, as Wittgenstein makes clear in the *Investigations*, does not come about through the solitary introspection of the minds internal *objects*, but rather by seeing oneself in a variety of situations with others. If your world is made up of your assertions, then you are unlikely to be able to learn anything from others, and you are unlikely to ever be able to receive a view on yourself from them. (Conversely, if, as Shakespeare portrays the citizens, you readily submerge and drown your voice in the voice of others, you will also never discover who you are or of what you are capable.) Linguistic competence and ethical competence go hand in hand. Before he is banished and exiled from the city of Rome, he has exiled himself from the city of words: "I fled from words," (2.2.70).

Cavell's understanding of the private language fantasy allows us to see what is implacable and consistent in Coriolanus: His every action and gesture—whether through swords (force) or words—is an attempt to construct the very world out of his assertion, and such an attempt is tragic. Coriolanus is a would-be private linguist in just this sense: He structures all relations with others on a refusal of the fully natural exposures of human form, human language, and human feeling.

Counting and Being Counted: Voices and Votes

Recall how the plays opens: "Before we proceed any further, hear me speak," the first citizen cries out (1.1.1). The word *proceed* is nicely ambiguous as to whether the action they take will be part of a formal process or not. Does it mean before we initiate our action or before we rule on this collectively?[23] The same word is taken up a few lines later—"Would you proceed especially against Caius Martius?" (1.1.24), so it quickly emerges that this "proceeding" is to be an (informal, extra judicial) execution. The first citizen invites or incites the group to kill Martius: "Let us kill him" (1.1.9). It is Martius who informs Menenius that another group of citizens off stage have pursued another course of action: They have "vented their complainings" at the Capitol, the seat of Rome's government, and been granted "Five tribunes to defend their vulgar wisdoms, / Of their own choice" (1.1.210-1).[24] So there seem to be two ways of proceeding at issue: force (and I will say more about this later) and political recognition. These two ways are at issue for the length of the play.[25]

The play begins in the first-person plural. This is how political claims are entered. The "we" comes before the "I."[26] It is a claim made by a speaker among speakers who speaks as if for others—not in the assumption of a preexistent collectivity, but in search of one.[27] The basic condition of speech and action is, as Hannah Arendt says, human plurality.[28] A speaker arrogates to him- or herself the right to speak, the authority lying in the claim, which can be recognized or refused. Instead of being merely distinct, claims Arendt, people distinguish themselves not as physical objects but *as men* through word and deed.[29] "This appearance," she claims, "rests on initiative, but it is an initiative from which no human being can refrain and *still be human* [my italics]."[30] In so speaking, one inevitably speaks for others as well as for oneself because to speak for oneself politically "is to speak with others with whom you consent to association, and it is to consent to be spoken for by them—not as a parent speaks for you, i.e. instead of you, but as someone in mutuality speaks for you, i.e. speaks your mind."[31]

It is commonly remarked that *Coriolanus* is a political play; and that claim is sometimes entered as "it is his *most* [my italics] political play."[32] The play most obviously concerns the political community of Rome in a crucial stage of formation.[33] In Livy's history of Rome, *Ab Urbe Condita*, with which Shakespeare is intimately familiar, the later success of Rome is owed precisely to the successful management of the relation between patricians and plebeians, and Livy's view of Rome's management of the plebeians is favorable.[34] That careful management, according to Livy, is what has brought Rome to perfection, ensuring its future stability and acting as a curb on patrician insolence. Machiavelli concurs in his *Discourses on Livy*.[35] Critics have pointed out the role *Coriolanus* plays not only in responding to the demands of the commons as a result of the food riots but also in working through both Ciceronian and Tacitean versions of republicanism in Rome's history.[36] The play is political in these obvious senses: It examines conflicts over who is to constitute the polis and how the people are to be represented in government.

But the *play* is more extensively and more properly an examination of the very conditions of political life. The happy confluence of the play's vocabulary of voices and votes can help us, because the word *voice* designates vote, and thus extends the political machinery of counting and discounting to accommodate not the mere acclamation of seventeenth-century parliamentary process, for example, but rather the question of how we count for each other.[37]

The word *voice* appears multiple times in *Coriolanus*. One of *Coriolanus*'s editors has counted fifty-four uses of the word *voice* in the Shakespeare canon, thirty-six of which are in *Coriolanus* (and twenty-seven in act 2, scene 3, alone).[38] The kinship of voices and votes shows that being counted is not only a political process but also a fundamental aspect of speaking—showing what counts for you and whether what you say counts for anyone else.

The citizens do not count for Martius and so their votes are not worth counting, their voices are not worth being heard. In Coriolanus's prepolitical society, in his prepolitical head, force is always available in cases in which the citizens are not quiescent (even to the point of accepting famine as their lot). Martius's "we" does not have to be bound together by consent (con-*sentir*); force is a ready option, violence being precisely the failure of politics.

The first citizen speaks, but we cannot know in advance who is the *we* constituted by his act of speaking. The community is not the foundation of my voice but rather my voice and yours and others is what determines the community. But this does not mean we decide what that community is as in a Fishean interpretative community.[39] The moral of Wittgenstein's private language fantasy was precisely to take us out of the sacred inner recesses of our minds, out of the striving for connection with an unattainable world we cannot reach, and orient us toward the activities we share, the interconnections between speech and action, and the background in place for a stretch of speech to be possible, to the conditions for mutual intelligibility.[40] Wittgenstein asks us to consider the countless things we do with words and takes us beyond an exclusive focus on naming, stating, or referring.[41] He puts weight on our agency in speech, glossing our agreement *in* rather than about judgments (*PI*, ¶241). Cavell, in his interpretation of Wittgenstein, recalls two aspects of judgment in predication and proclamation. Counting something as something, determining what it is (what it is called) depends on our calling it, proclaiming it, and counting it under a concept at all. Cavell, suggests that talking, claiming, calling, and counting are the major modes in which we word the world.[42] In a bravura passage in *The Claim of Reason*, he invokes J. L. Austin's idea that the distinctions in our language show the differences we have found worth making, as well as Wittgenstein's "surveyable representation" (*übersichtliche Darstellung*) of our use of words (*PI*, ¶122): "If to the pairs telling and counting, and counting and claiming, and claiming and acclaiming or clamoring, hence proclaiming and announcing, and denouncing and renouncing, and counting and recounting, or recounting and accounting, we add the notions of calling to account or accusing, hence excusing and explaining, and add computing and hence reputing and imputing; what we seem to be headed for is an idea that what can comprehensively be said is what is found to be worth saying."[43]

It is getting at the interdependency of voice and world that is important. Laugier says that "in Cavell and in Wittgenstein the community cannot exist except in its being constituted by the claims of individuals and the recognition of the claim of the other."[44]

Coriolanus explores with uncanny prescience and unnerving brilliance the relationship between speaking as a fellow human being and as a political community. A polis is a group of people searching for agreement, and an intimate link exists between the human capacities for speech and for political life.[45]

Recall that Cavell had revealed that speakers inhabit the *same* relation to Wittgensteinian criteria: There is no higher court of appeal, no decisive expertise except for the community of speakers. "Every surmise and every tested conviction depend(s) upon the same structure or background of necessities and agreements that judgments of value explicitly do."[46] The criteria Wittgenstein appeal to are ours, and when I speak, that is, voice my criteria, I do so as a representative human. It is the category of the human that is as much at issue in this penetrating play as the capacities of the citizen. You can at any point refute me and say I cannot speak for you in this instance—but then my authority has been restricted with respect to you, rather than my claim disconfirmed. Who can speak for whom is a pressing and more or less continuous issue in *Coriolanus*, and the play intricately and notoriously relates voicing to voting. If Coriolanus comprehensively discounts the citizens, and is consequentially banished by them, how do they count in this play?

They are given numbers, rather than names. This is the case with some of the other dramatis personae: senators, messengers, soldiers, conspirators, and servants are numbered not named. The citizens are always numbered—except when they speak as "All"—acquiring the number that identifies them by the order in which they speak in each scene. Thus, they are individuated but not uniquely, hence numbers, not names.[47] This is the way they are both counted (as heads) and discounted, because it is alone their ratification, their acclamation of Coriolanus in the ceremony of the wounds that "counts." Indeed, in the scenes in which Coriolanus seeks for their voices for his election to the Senate, they approach him in twos and threes as they have been instructed. But they are equally discounted. For although the *dramatis personae* accords them the status of citizens, and although they are counted and differentiated by number, the play provides us with numerous ways in which they are viewed as a mass, an undifferentiated mob, a crowd in which their individual voices are merged with each other, thoroughly consolidated and coalesced. There is a remarkable plethora of names for them collectively, and they are detested as an anonymous, surging group, the source of threat. What are they called?

In the play's stage directions, they are sometimes called "citizens"—that is, members of a polis (even if initially unenfranchised)—and they are also "plebeians," "a rabble of plebeians," "a troop of citizens," "the commons," and even a "munity." For the play's ruling classes, they are variously "the commonalty," poor suitors, but also the rats of Rome (1.1243), dissentious rogues (1.1.159), curs (1.1.163), camels

(2.1.245), geese (1.1.167), quartered slaves, fragments (1.1.217), dry stubble (2.1.252), multiplying spawn (2.2.76), needless vouches, Hob and Dick (2.3.114), the mutable rank-scented meinie (3.1.68), measles (3.1.80), the minnows (3.1.90), and woolen vessels (3.2.10). They do not speak—they "vent." Their sound is not speech but either the calls of an animal, or so much vacuous hot air and breath but not intelligible action. They are only ever regarded—perhaps most of all by the tribunes who purport to speak for them—as manipulable, and thus instrumental.

In the play's progress, although the citizens have gained the representation of the tribunes, they lose their voices. It is not just Coriolanus's outrageous hauteur that makes of their voices, animal sounds, or hot air; nor is it due to the utter disdain and sleazy strategies of the tribunes whose contempt matches if not exceeds Coriolanus's own and is more disreputable for being so hypocritically displayed; but rather it is the characteristic pattern of the play to amalgamate their voices as one. The voice "all" arrived at by the crowd is no longer the sum of many. It has lost any sense of the commitments of speaking, the burden of articulate expression. One is submerged in all, and "all" banish Coriolanus but do so in such a way that none can feel singly responsible. It is the ethics of the undifferentiated mob who are shown to go back on their word or rewrite it with alarming ease at the promptings and manipulation of others.

Force

I argue that we are offered two modes of proceeding at the start of this play: force and political recognition. In both, the question of being human is at stake. Volumnia glories obscenely in the force of her son, but also greedily wishes her son to be recognized in the Senate and not alone in the glory of the battlefield.

I deliberately sound the word *force* because Simone Weil's diagnosis of it in her searing essay on the *Iliad* reveals that the same issues of recognizing a fellow human being are at work on the battlefield as we have seen they are in the polis. These concepts are vital to see how the concept of human being is recovered in the climactic scene in act 5.

Coriolanus is the warrior who *cannot* be a politician. In refusing to exhibit his wounds, a custom deemed necessary in Shakespeare, although not in Plutarch, he continues to refuse not only the exposure of his body but also the exposure of his speech (because to speak is to reveal yourself to others). The kinship of speaking and politics is again pressed upon us.

Volumnia gives him a lesson in how to ask the commoners for their acclamation:

> Go to them, with this bonnet in thy hand,
> And thus far having stretched it—here be with them—
> Thy knee bussing the stones, for in such business
> Action is eloquence.
>
> (3.2.74–77)

Coriolanus, she reminds him, has told her that "Honor and policy, like unsevered friends / I'th'war do grow together" (3.2.43–44). It is not dishonorable to be politic for you yourself have claimed that in war policy can be honorable. She's putting words into his mouth. This is implacably not the view of Coriolanus, for whom swords and words are utterly opposed. He flees from words, and pictures himself in battle-glee as a sword: "Make you a sword of me?" (1.6.76). Whether Coriolanus can be assimilated into the polis is one of the play's questions. First, he is banished by the tribunes and the plebeians, then set on war with his own people, and finally sacrificed for the safety and peace of Rome.[48] Is valor the chiefest virtue, as Cominius claims, echoing Plutarch's question (2.2.82–83)?[49] If it is, can it be politically assimilated and managed in the form of public life called politics?

If Coriolanus is Shakespeare's most *political* play, it is also his most relentless in its attention to the counterpolitical and lethal force of war. War is not extrinsic to Rome. The play begins after all, as we have seen, with a riot or an insurrection—call it an incipient internal war. One group agrees on the assassination of Coriolanus: "No more talking on' t. Let it be done!" (1.1.11).

In her book *On Violence*, Hannah Arendt shows power and violence to be opposites. Violence can destroy power (the capacity to act in concert); it cannot create it.[50] This is a useful way of understanding the polis (actual and incipient) in *Coriolanus*, as we have seen. Coriolanus derives his entire identity from war, that is to say, from military and not political power. Military power is "the social organization of lethal violence," as Michael Mann, one of its most comprehensive students, has defined it.[51] This lethal violence is woven into the Roman culture of the play, and the play is unprecedented in offering us a picture of the form of life of war into which Martius is initiated.

Rome was an empire before it was called one. It is a culture almost never not at war; militarism defined it. The lust for spoil was an intrinsic feature of Roman war because no separate realm (such as trade or mercantilism) ensured the acquisition of wealth. Political aspirations were central to the warrior caste, and power could be consolidated through means of war, as Tacitus, writing during the days of the empire so pointedly noted in the *Agricola*: "They have plundered the world, stripping naked the land in their hunger . . . when in their wake nothing remains but a desert, they call that peace." So much is evident from a careful reading of Tacitus, but how do men become initiated into war? In *Coriolanus*, we are given a portrait of the warrior as a young boy. The military man does not arrive fully fledged as "the thing of blood" (2.2.107). What pain-behavior has Coriolanus learned as a boy? With what joy and exultation did Volumnia greet his cuts, his wounds (physical and psychic), with what vehemence did she turn away from tears or grief, and with what scorn? What did Coriolanus learn in learning to speak, say, about pain, his pains and those of others? This is the form of life of war, of pain in Rome. In so portraying Martius's apprenticeship in the glory of killing, the play displays honor as a mode of hegemony, obscuring war's chilling reason for being—killing. In this process, the intoxication of force is primary and helps us to see that the question of the recognition of human being works across the fields of lethal war *and* "peaceful" speech.

In her memorable and profoundly illuminating essay on the *Iliad*, written in the immediate aftermath of a global war, Weil declares that the "true hero, the true subject, the center of the *Iliad* is force." Weil characterizes force as "that which makes a thing of whoever submits to it." Force can turn a human being into a stone: A suppliant pleading for his life at the victor's knees may simply not be present to the victor, may have no presence as a human being. Lethal force turns a human being into a thing-like corpse. If force annihilates, it also intoxicates those who think they possess it. The weak and the strong imagine each other as different species: victors and vanquished. The application of force is double-sided—"those who use it and those who endure it are turned to stone." No one possesses force. Fate merely loans force to the victors; they too will perish of it.[52]

This is apt for *Coriolanus*. The mighty warrior is imagined as an "engine" (5.4.15); a sword, this by himself, in joy (1.6.76); a wolf (2.1.7); a sea (2.2.96); a god, "a thing / Made by some other deity than Nature" (4.6.94-95); and perhaps, most chillingly, a "a thing of blood, whose every motion / Was timed with dying cries" (2.2.105-6). He is "a creeping thing" (5.4.12-14) pupating from man to dragon. He is a "thing made for Alexander" in Menenius's words (5.4.22). Even Aufidius calls him a "noble *thing*." When Volumnia declares that Death, "in's nervy arm doth lie / Which being advanced, declines, and then men die," she is gripped by the intoxicating fantasy that Coriolanus possesses (rather than merely loans) a force that will also tear him down. Volumnia terrifyingly invokes the poem Weil examines in her riposte to Virgilia, who alone understands that the invocation of Coriolanus's bloody brow betokens a wound, not a badge of honor. "The breasts of Hecuba," Volumnia retaliates:

> When she did suckle Hector looked not lovelier
> Than Hector's forehead when it spit forth blood
> At Grecian sword condemning.[53]
>
> (1.3.42-44)

Leni Reifenstahl could not have expressed it better. The flesh (breasts) that succor and nurture are less beautiful, less admirable than the explosive expulsion of her son Hector's deathly blood. Hector's blood is lovely and generative. It is a harsh reversal of death and birth, maternity and its repudiation repellently pushed together. Weil's analysis of force in this poem illuminates lethal violence in *Coriolanus*, its intoxicating allure masking the fact that force is only borrowed in this poem. The warrior Coriolanus carries noise before and tears behind him (2.1.154). In Cominius's speech before the Senate, Martius is described in tones of awe and admiration as "run(ing) reeking o'er the lives of men, as if / 'Twere a perpetual spoil" (2.2.117-18).[54]

Weil observes that Andromache prepares a warm bath for Hector at the very instant when he is on the battlefield, beaten down by Achilles, because of green-eyed Athena. She notes that the *Iliad* gives us strikingly moving scenes of the contrasting world of Trojan civilization— "the far away, precarious, touching world of peace, of the family, the world in which each man counts more than anything else to those around him." The *Iliad*, she says, "takes place far from hot baths."

And so does the action of *Coriolanus*. Virgilia alone offers a tiny glimpse of domestic life, but she maintains a stubborn silence for much of the play as if such a form of life is not speakable. Coriolanus's intoxication with war and force is no personal idiosyncrasy but the very prototype of Roman-ness, of the "autarkic selfhood" nurtured by Rome.[55] The man Volumnia (conditionally, narcissistically) worships makes widows who do not share the same world with her for she can feel for them no grief.[56]

Weil helps us to see that force blinds both those who think they possess it as well as those who are mown down by it. What is at stake for her in *Iliad* and for us in *Coriolanus* is the standing possibility of the thingification and dehumanization of others, the refusal to see kinship especially in war, but also in peace. Not for him to hear words that might cut through force, the address of the fallen to those who fell them: "I am the enemy you killed, my friend."[57] Weil brilliantly helps us see that we are bound together in acknowledgment and so the lethal dangers of the avoidance of a shared humanity.

Holds Her by the Hand, Silent

Had Shakespeare read Seneca's essay "On Mercy"? "Of all the virtues in truth none befits the human being more, since none is more humane."[58] After his petition to spare Rome has been rebuffed, and as if to continue Seneca's thought, Menenius says to Sicinius that there is no more milk of mercy in Coriolanus than there is in a male tiger (5.4.28–29). Yet the play will decisively offer us mercy as a candidate for virtue over valor. Until the climactic scene of petition, Coriolanus has been able to imagine that he is more or less-than human.[59]

Coriolanus, claims Leah Whittingdon, "exists for the sake of one scene, the crucial, riveting scene of supplication."[60] It is the final part of the play's investigation of the grammar of asking, and an uncompromisingly public exposure of Martius's evading, and then accepting, the truth that he cannot live as if he is author of himself. Everything in the scene is choreographed toward the moment that Martius had so ardently hoped to avoid, the moment of inevitable, now undeniable realization—deferred and suspended for so long—that Caius Martius is neither a God, nor a beast or machine, but a human being. How does this scene make a drama of *that*? What can such a realization come to? Because it is blazingly obvious that he is a human being, the scene can only stage the dissolution of his evasion of that surd fact and the hopes he—and others—had placed in it. Martius's momentous acceptance that he is human is then the business of this scene and the costs of the denial and belated acceptance of his fate as a human being constitute the tragedy that Shakespeare alone made of the sources of a familiar Roman story. But his acceptance that he is "not / Of stronger earth than others," that he is not autochthonous, but the flesh of other flesh, is "mortal to him" (5.3.189). He knows he will not be spared in the peace he brokers. Being human is being mortal: such knowledge will hardly spare us from, still less prepare us for, the fate of dying. Martius, however, has very little time or space for a life that might be enhanced as well as threatened by this realization.

We might say of this extraordinary scene what Rachel Bespaloff said about the famous scene of supplication between Priam and Achilles in the *Iliad:* In an "exceptional deviation" from the laws of violence in that poem, "supplication sobers the man to whom it is addressed instead of exasperating him."[61]

Two vital actions in this scene are pivotal in accommodating Martius to the vulnerability of his shared humanity. I choose the word *vulnerability* with care, sounding its Latin root in *vulnus* (wound).[62] Martius has refused to show his wounds to the citizens, and it is a Shakespearean innovation that he foregoes the customary procedure of affirmation. Those wounds show the form of his denial: Treated by himself, his mother, and Menenius as the insignia of his victories, and thus phantasmically turned into their opposite, marks of victory and not vulnerability, he will not countenance the citizens their conventional say in his path to the consulship. His mother and Menenius glory in his wounds, their number, their extent. Every "gash" was "an enemy's grave" rather than a place from which life might bleed out (2.1.151–2). These wounds can be paraded in triumph, but not exposed. Above all, Martius will not countenance others speaking for his wounds. We are offered that grotesque image, continuing the language of the body politic, in which the commoners are to put their mouths into them, that is, speak from and for the wounds: "If he show us his wounds and tell us his deeds, we are to put our tongues into those wounds and speak for them" (2.3.6–7). Martius will not endure the condition of speaking, which means being spoken for.

Kissing and holding hands are the two vital actions on which the scene turns. The kiss he shares with his wife and the act of holding hands with his mother in the famous stage direction are fundamentally acts of reciprocity. Where in kissing and holding hands does one body end and the other begin? There in those most nervous places each touches and is also touched with mouth or hand. After the kiss, after holding his mother's hand, how can Martius stand his solipsism with conviction? It is here undone.

First the kiss. Shakespeare has once again transformed Plutarch. In Plutarch's *The Life of Caius Martius Coriolanus,* Martius advances to meet the supplicants; in *Coriolanus*, Martius must await their coming, must wait upon them. The scene puts at stake the responsibility he might find in his response to them. In Plutarch, he first kisses his mother and embraces her "a pretie while"; tears fall immediately from his eyes.[63] There is no kiss with Virgilia. In Shakespeare's version, it is Virgilia who speaks first, a dramatic breaking of her graceful silence, and a claiming of her "lord and husband" (5.3.38). Martius thus speaks with his wife first before he speaks with his mother, and asks her to forgive his "tyranny," but not to appeal to him to "forgive our Romans" (5.3.43-44). He is trying to hold off a full acknowledgment that his actions are lethal to his family as well as all other Romans. Editors usually add the stage direction "[They kiss]" that they surmise from Martius words: "O, a kiss / Long as my exile, sweet as my revenge!" (5.3.44-45). The long "O" implies that the kiss is not made equivalent to exile and revenge, as some critics have argued, but rather counterbalances it.[64] The kiss is long; it is sweet. Different editors quibble over who kisses who first. Of his editors, Brian Parker, has Virgilia kiss him first. Peter Holland thinks Bevington's similar stage direction to be "more than anything the text requires."[65] Bliss simply adds the stage direction "[They kiss]" before Martius's exclamatory "O!" Who makes the first move is sometimes important.[66] But a kiss is mutual (and if forced, it is not a kiss). It is an open-mouthed acceptance of another, and like a handholding, one is intimately and inevitably both being touched and touching. Caius Martius has lived his life, as Weil says of the protagonists in *The Iliad* "far from hot baths," far from anything that resembles the conversation of Anthony with his Cleopatra, far from anything resembling the domestic life with which Virgilia is altogether associated (for she will not venture out of the house until Coriolanus returns safely from the wars).[67]

One definitive gesture of the scene is the kneeling, the formal gesture of supplicants, that Martius finds so terrible a reversal of filial relations, a world upside down that appalls him completely. The acts of kneeling by his mother, wife, and son punctuate the scene: These gestures are crucial inclinations as they bend toward each other: His mother bows (5.3.30) and kneels to Martius a few lines after he has kneeled to her and been blessed. Some editors and directors have Caius raise his mother up, asking "Your knees to me?" (5.3.58). The young Martius is invited to kneel by Volumnia a few lines later, and after Volumnia's very long speech, she motions all the supplicants to kneel: "Down! An end, / This is the last" (5.3.170-71). At agonizing moments, it seems that Martius will not respond. An uncanny stillness falls in this loud and noisy play. Volumnia at last directs them all to rise and to go, their mission rebuffed, their city and lives now unprotected from the ravaging to come. Volumnia understands Martius's silence as a fundamental undoing of the bonds that tie them. She understands that he will not acknowledge them as his kin: "This fellow had a Volscian to his mother, / His wife is in Corioles and his child / Like him by chance" (5.3.178-80). She will not lead the suppliants out until he formally dismisses them as she thinks in heart he has done already: "Yet give us our dispatch" (5.3.180).

I imagine that it is as she turns to go that he "holds her by the hand, silent," as the stage direction instructs. Jarrett Walker, in a fine analysis of this scene, has suggested that this is the only stage direction in the first folio that puts a stop to all speech and action.[68] Directors and actors use their discretion here, but some prolong and distend the moment, making it almost unbearably pregnant with tension and possibility. The silence is held (stopped and contained) by the actors on stage: In the auditorium, you might hear a pin drop as Volumnia's hand is contained, retained, sustained, and detained by Caius Martius (detain, contain, and so on are all derivative of the Latin roots in *tenere*, to hold). What is being held and carried here?

The stage direction diverges significantly again from Plutarch. First, according to Plutarch's sequence, Martius says: "O, mother what have you done to me?" He holds her hand and then continues: "Oh, mother, you have wonne a happy victory for your countrie, but mortall and unhappy for your sonne." There is no hold, no pause. In the play's extravagant, daring pause, we can imagine all that might be passing through Martius's mind; we might see it on the actor's face. Consider these options: The pause leaves space for the unsurmountable admission that he cannot forgo those he loves, that he must hold them, and that he must protect them; the defeated but stark realization that he will die, and thus his mother's victory will be a hollow triumph bringing the death of her son, (he holds this thought for her because she has not yet grasped it); the longing to simply stop as when we might say, Hold up! Hold everything! The pause contains the cost of holding everything dear; the knowledge that now he is at last holding his own with his mother, that is, he is separate from her, even *in loco parentis* for her unwitting self; the cost of upholding this dawning truth before it dawns on her, the realization that it will dawn on her; all this and more might be contained and held in the silence.[69] Second, in Plutarch, the gesture is not a holding of hands but rather an act of detention, a more unhandsome grasping and clasping. Coriolanus is described as "holding her *hard* by the right hand."[70] The play appropriately excises the hardness in Plutarch's version. And this lack of hardness, this softness even seems crucial.[71]

Consider what people do with their hands in the world of the play. In Volumnia's awful mimicry of Martius in battle, she acts out his "mail'd hand" wiping his "bloody brow" (1.3.37) Aufidius's passionate enmity for Martius is expressed in the desire to "wash my fierce hands in's heart" (1.10.27) but he also "sanctifies himself with's hand" (4.5.198). In the explosive conflict after Martius's contemptuous "petitioning" of the citizens, there is much laying on and seizing: "Lay hands upon him / And bear him to the rock" (3.1.222-23). When he has gone over to the Voscians, Martius's "speechless hand" dismisses Cominius (5.1.67). Hands are part of the play's synecdochal language of body parts and fragments, so Menenius, punning on the idea of handicraft, can say to the tribunes: "You have made fair hands / You and your crafts!" (4.6.120-21). We are as likely to see a fist as an open hand, as when Aufidius feverishly imagines the two warriors "fisting each other's throats" (4.5.127). On his banishment, Coriolanus will say to Menenius: "Give me thy hand," (4.2.58). But this is a rare instance in a play in which hands are far more likely to grasp, seize, clutch, or be gripped than held. Hands then are more likely to be closed than open; they enforce rather than offer and invite. In the final supplication scene, young Martius's hand is held by his grandmother, and all their hands are held together in their ardent gesture of petition, supplicating his mercy.[72]

In the primal act of holding hands, unless you pull your hand away, you are both holding and being held. That is why shaking hands is a sign of trust, and hand-fasting a form of pledging. It implies commitments felt through the flesh, carrying the promise of fidelity. It might be hard to let someone down after you have held hands with them. You feel their warmth and their sentience; you feel that you are kin. That is the kinship I imagine Martius *feels*.[73]

The whole scene is predicated on Martius response, and it is this primitive, visceral response to his mother in the handholding that brings the responsibility he now assumes for her and for his family and, by extension, for Rome. Cavell has suggested that Martius's words that end the silence can be read as its interpretation. If so, his words express his foreknowledge with the relentless clarity of truth. It is a truth that he will accept: "Let it come" (5.3.189). The patience, the awaiting that the scene has necessitated, the scene's insistence on the sheer power of response in its actors and its audience, is carried on in the final scene, for there Coriolanus *suffers* his death, he lets it come to him. Etymologically, patience is suffering, not doing. Coriolanus "forgets his part" in prideful isolation. The voluble Volumnia is silent for the rest of the play, compounding the realizations made through the silent handholding.[74]

A Tear Is an Intellectual Thing

I want now, and finally, to speak about the tears of Caius Martius. For Shakespeare's late tragedies have designs on our capacity for pity as they renovate tragic form. When Wittgenstein explores the response of pity in the *Philosophical Investigations*—"How am I filled with pity *for this human being*?"—he is suggesting that there is something imperatival, a call, a claim, a demand made on me by virtue of you being human, that response to other human beings is instinctive.[75] It is not that he is pointing to metaphysical or biological facts about the human; he is pointing to the idea that we are fated to our human forms.[76] We are not talking about a scientific fact of human nature but a givenness of our condition that we must either grant (accept as our form of life, as the form of life that it is) or deny (avoid). The condition of humanity and the extent to which it is admitted as common is something of central importance in *Coriolanus*.[77]

But first, a tale of two fathers: A few years before he died, my father had a massive left-sided stroke. He lost control over the right side of his body; he lost the ability to speak. When I visited him in the stroke unit shortly after the experience, he was lying in his hospital bed. His eyes were closed so he did not see me. He was almost motionless. He was crying—weeping not sobbing; tears fell silently and steadily from his eyes. It was the first and only time I ever saw him cry.

A friend's father died of cancer. He had held off the pain medication to be lucid with his family during his final days. He beat his thigh in pain; he said, "Mama told me not to cry." These stories of the tears of old men fill me with sadness, the sadness of their losses, past and to come, the sadness that the natural route to such sorrows was so private, so forbidden.

Late in his magnificent book about ethics and the practice of medicine, *A Fortunate Man: The Story of a Country Doctor*, John Berger tells us that when the eponymous country doctor, John Sassall, was unaware of his presence, he saw Sassall weep. He goes on to say that a man or woman sobbing recalls a child, yet in an unsettling way. This, he suggests, is partly because contemporary mid-twentieth-century social conventions discourage a man from crying but allow children their tears. This, however, does not account for why and how we might be unsettled. A sobbing man comes to resemble a child in the falling away of an adult's bearing. His movements come to seem as primitive as a child's. The hands clench and paw, the body falls in on itself fetally, and all seems focused on the mouth "as though the mouth were simultaneously the place of pain and the only way by which consolation might be taken in." We are unsettled, suggests Berger, because the man sobbing at once conjures the child to mind, such anguish bringing him to that state of childish helplessness, and at the same time, blocks off the child's expectation of recovery and the route to it. The man does not cry as the child does, to protest, but rather cries only to himself. Berger says: "It may even be that by crying again like a child he somehow believes that he will regain the ability to recover like a child. Yet that is impossible."[78] These comments seem to me to bear on the man-child Martius.[79]

As usual, Shakespeare gives us his stage directions through the words and responses of his dramatis personae. It is clear that the climactic supplication I just examined in the previous section of this chapter elicits his tears. In Gregory Doran's 2011 production for the Royal Shakespeare Company, Sope Dirisu as Martius takes up the cue. After the almost unbearably long silence and restraint of the famous stage direction, he grasps his mother's face, holding her to him and releases his tears, as if they are shaken out of him as he utters the words: "O, mother, mother! / What have you done?" Those long, round, open-mouthed, and repeated sounds, the largest vowel and most extended note in the wooden O, precede and succeed the desperate vocative. It is as if the full knowledge of this relationship as *his* can only be exclaimed, *expressed*, hurled, and howled in this distraught cry: "O, mother, *my* mother, O!" and in his uncontrollable tears.

In the aftermath of this outburst and of his assent to his mother's supplication for peace, he appeals to Aufidius and asks, "Were you in my stead, would you have heard / A mother less? Or granted less, Aufidius?" He is no longer the man who would not ask. The repetition of Aufidius's name betrays some anxiety: He is no longer boasting of standing alone but is appealing to what he hopes they have in common. Would you not have done the same? Would not any man? Caius Martius Coriolanus has never set himself up as any man. Aufidius grants laconically that "he was moved withal" (5.3.193). Now Martius alludes to his own tears: "It is no little thing to make / Mine eyes to sweat compassion" (5.3.195-96) as if his tears can be acknowledged only as hard physical labor, as earned through exertion. His tears are sweat; he worked to produce them. It is a futile and transparent attempt to make his tears subject to his will. They are instead called forth in a primitive and involuntary response. Plutarch shows how unable he is to control his tears, although he begins rather than ends the climactic supplication scene with them. He shows immediately what Shakespeare dramatically defers: "And nature so wrought with him, that the teares fell from his eyes, and he coulde not keepe him selfe from making much of them, but yeelded to the affection of his bloode, as if he had been violently carried away with the furie of a most swift running streame."[80] In Plutarch, as in Doran's production, Martius's tears are profuse, the victory of his body and heart over his will and over his long and brutal apprenticeship in Rome's hardness, the spontaneous and reflexive signs of his bonds with his family and the world he imagined he had banished.

These tears, and the cost of living them, such a vital part of the "unnatural scene" witnessed by all on and off stage, will now be the chief weapon of Aufidius's revenge and reclaiming of his former fortune (5.3.201-2). Aufidius, the first conspirator tells us, is not welcomed home but Martius is returning "splitting the air with noise" (5.6.50-51). Aufidius must manipulate Martius as well as the commoners who now so uncritically support him if he is to gain the upper hand he has never had over his ally and foe. In the last scene at Antium, Aufidius's slurs touch exactly the most vulnerable point as he knows they will. First, he calls Coriolanus a "traitor"; then he deprives him of the name "Coriolanus," derived as a kind of rebirth in the primal scene of his singular victory over Corioles. Then, reproaching him for calling on the god of war whose name he also holds, Aufidius taunts him as a "boy of tears" (5.6.104). This is bitter. The tears he wept were kind; his pity was not overwhelmed by his wrath. Now they are degraded as "certain drops of salt," (5.6.95), a refusal to acknowledge what they—and the long silence preceding them—express. Aufidius comprehensively rewrites the scene he admits moved him. His words are a schoolboy taunt. Martius's tears are denounced as "woman's rheum" (5.6.45). Caius Martius Coriolanus is a mother's boy: In what world can this be an acknowledgment of a truth and not a smear? He has thrown away Volscian victory over Rome for a "nurse's tears" (5.6.99). The scoff puts him back at the very breast from which his mother so savagely weaned him. Aufidius reconstitutes the homosociality through the gibes and jeers: "The pages blushed at him" and "men of heart" wondered at it together (5.6.101–2). Caius Martius is newly isolated, but not as the inviolate victor, forging a name in the fire of burning Rome.

"Boy" hits home. Martius repeats the word, tries to throw it back three times, and it is not quite his last word in the play. "Alone I did it! Boy!" (5.6.117). Some editors, for example, Peter Holland in his fine Arden edition, place "boy" in inverted commas, taking up the characteristic way Martius has of scornfully mouthing and throwing back (now like missiles) the words of others. He subjects them to his voicing, and they come back transformed. This is plausible, perhaps even likely, but it should not blind us to other options. Perhaps he is hurling this insult to Aufidius. *He's* the boy here! (Are we in the schoolyard? Has it come to this?) Or, and I prefer this, could it be a full-throated almost gleeful owning that he is a man-child, that is a man who was once a child, rather than a man who emerged fully fledged fantastically (thus inhumanly). "Boy" then retains the memory of his acknowledgment of his boyhood not only as his inextricable bond with his mother but also as a cry against what Rome does to those it trains to kill.

This is true to Berger's great insight and describes with accuracy the complexity of our response to his tears. To see the man as *reduced* to a boy in *Coriolanus* in both scenes is a disavowal and a refusal to acknowledge whatever discomfort his tears cause.[81] They are the tears of a *man*. They are tears he must, like Macduff, feel as a man. For is it compassion he has sweated? How can he disown that? He does not.

These considerations are hardly anachronistic. Chapman defends Achilles's tears in *Iliad* against the idea that a hero as great and renowned as Achilles should not cry like a woman or a child.[82] Chapman, according to Jessica Wolfe, refutes Scaliger's mocking of Achilles for "crying in front of his mother." Christ weeps and so does Aeneas and Alexander the Great. Tears can be a sign of courage and hardiness; they also can be "teares of manliness and magnanimitie." The implications are that tears cannot impugn epic's greatest soldier as they might lesser men. Shakespeare's inflection is entirely different, and it is no accident that the play offers us an economical and bleak portrait of his childhood in his mother's famous depiction (1.3.16) and in Cominius's daunting depiction of his adolescent rite of passage into war (2.2.85). Martius's childhood shows that he has been apprenticed in the form of life of force. This does not exonerate him, although it might indict Rome and the Roman matron who has lived by those values. As we have seen Volumnia's "victory" hollows out and even ravages the putative triumph of Rome.

Martius's taunting of Aufidius leads not to a new pugilistic encounter with him. His words are more like a dare to kill him. He invites the Voscians to "cut him to pieces, Volsces, men and lads" (5.6.113) in a dismemberment he suffers rather than resists. His desire is not to overcome Aufidius or to enjoin in battle with the Volscians, but rather to appeal to the truth of history: "If you have writ your annals true, tis there / That, like an eagle in a dovecote, I / Fluttered your Volscians in Corioles" (5.6.15-17) reclaiming his singularity and his name. The play concertedly changes Plutarch to show the citizens not standing by but remembering his butchery of their daughters, sons, cousins, and fathers, prompting their single-minded and chilling cry: "Kill, kill, kill, kill, kill him!" (5.6.131). That cry opened the play, but the effects of Martius's actions have been deferred until now.

Force was never Martius's to possess. But neither was language. His career as a private linguist, as much as his trajectory as a warrior, is mortal to him. Coriolanus is Rome's terrible mirror. It cannot countenance what it sees. Can we?

Chapter 6

Antony and Cleopatra
Shakespeare's Critique of Judgment

> For love is strong as death
>
> —Song of Solomon

Cicero detested her.[1] To Horace she is a "fatale monstrum."[2] Vergil can only expostulate: "That outrage, that Egyptian wife!"[3] To the classical men of the Augustan age who were her contemporaries—poets, rhetors, and historians—Cleopatra evinces horror, scorn, and disgust. Does she provide them with a welcome opportunity for the enjoyment of their outrage? The pleasures of moralism are deep, and the corruption of moral seriousness is hard to see by those who purify themselves through its means. When they "behold" her, they "see" a most dangerous enemy of Rome.

Philo frames the two lovers in the opening scene of *Antony and Cleopatra* for Demetrius and for the audience, and the censoriousness, the moralized blame that passes for judgment seems perfectly in keeping with this climate and tradition of Augustan depiction.[4] I am tempted to say that Augustan fear is passing itself off as disdain. The play begins, in censure and negation, with Philo's "Nay," which is later reprised in Dolabella's softer "Gentle madam, no."[5]

It was Cleopatra's misfortune to come under the moralized judgment of some of the most skillfully articulate men of letters in Augustan Rome. Caesar sought to do no less than frame her in a parade through his triumphal arch after the Battle of Actium. Her spectacular and brave suicide thwarted the triumphal theater of Roman honor.[6]

Shakespeare's final scene, his version of Cleopatra's suicide offers an alternative theater, at once an apotheosis, a marriage, and a death that shows love, play, and indefatigable purpose, as well as a vitality so magnificent and creative, so daring and intimate, that it makes it paltry to be Caesar. Above all, Cleopatra judges what kind of life is worth living and expresses what she holds dear in her death, dying because she lives by those values. For this reason, the final scene claims our unabashed admiration for her scintillating invention and courage. What kind of *claim* she makes is central to Shakespeare's "critique of judgment." Her suicide is "a noble act" in a play that tests nobleness: "The nobleness of life / Is to do *thus*."[7] Cleopatra's staging of her death contests Octavian's understanding of nobleness as dominion and refutes and refuses Octavius's desire to fix her forever as the token of his glory. In the process, the play offers us a vastly enlarged vision of moral imagination, one that implicates its spectators and achieves its effects through the responses it summons.[8]

Shakespeare stops in its tracks a long-established tradition of moralized judgment of the two great lovers. He offers us the most extended dramatic examination of the texture and difficulty of mutual love and its relation to conversation before Ibsen. What we see, for all Philo's emblematic pointing and Caesar's framing, is not obvious: What we see is a measure of who we are as spectators. Our responses and reactions implicate us and are also the source of self-knowledge. The pleasures of moralism keep intact a sense of superiority and righteousness because they break the link between judgment and self-knowledge, between responsiveness and responsibility (that being one of the chief satisfactions of moralism). By the end of the play, we will discern the difference between morality and moralism.[9] *Antony and Cleopatra* asks us to contemplate a far more revolutionary, implicative, and extensive understanding of judgment, one that is bound up with the radical claims it makes on our imaginative capacities in Cleopatra's daring and life-enhancing end. What do we value and care about? And why? How do our judgments link us to the world and to each other? How must they engage and concern our self-knowledge, and how do they challenge a dominant modern picture about judgment that holds us captive?

In this chapter, I examine a concept central to humanistic and aesthetic education and to this radically original play: judgment, moreover a judgment not reducible to blame or even to a moral *act* of judgment but judgment considered as the inevitable, fallible, pervasive, and always particular way in which we make a claim on others, count what is important to us, and respond to each other and to the world, and that in affording us that world may also enlarge it.[10] In the first instance, I show how judgment becomes a "problem" in some important twentieth-century criticism of the play, and second, I show how it parts company with a more everyday sense of "perspective" under the pressures of philosophy, leaving the ordinary sense of the word behind. I also show that the difference between rules and criteria, as it emerges in the Kantian directions taken by both Hannah Arendt and Stanley Cavell, both working on judgment in the early 1960s, helps us put back the selves and voices, cares and commitments (hence capacity for self-knowledge) evaded or overcome in modern theories of judgment and criticism. In my reading of *Antony and Cleopatra*, I show that love, marriage, and conversation are central to the audacity and challenge of this play and that the claims it makes on us, while constituting an astonishing defense of drama and the work of imagination, are not confined to the sphere of aesthetics.

Crisis! Danby, Adelman, and Judgment

I look at two of the most agile, learned, and influential treatments of judgment in *Antony and Cleopatra:* These two essays admirably point out vital dimensions of the play. They also bring us to an impasse, as they reveal a *crisis* of judgment that is not local to their treatment of the plays but that shows what judgment has become under conditions of modernity.

John Danby called *Antony and Cleopatra* Shakespeare's "critique of judgment" in an indispensable essay written in 1949.[11] "*Antony and Cleopatra:* A Shakespearean Adjustment" was first published in the Leavisite journal *Scrutiny*, and it later appears in Danby's essay collection as well as in many subsequent anthologies.[12] Although judgment is a longstanding Shakespearean preoccupation, in *Antony and Cleopatra*, Danby claims, it is not only a prominent theme but also the central dialectical way of looking. The play is a "Shakespearean adjustment," linked with *King Lear* and *Coriolanus*, anticipating the radical break in style in Shakespeare's late romances. The question of value was central in *Troilus and Cressida*, and *legal* judgment was profoundly under scrutiny in *The Merchant of Venice* and *Measure for Measure*, but even in *King Lear*, Goneril and Reagan are, claims Danby, "reliable judges" of their father's condition. (Lear's deeply unwise actions, the riotous behavior of his troupe of knights, for example, anchor their judgments, although they do not justify their actions as a result).

Antony and Cleopatra makes a break with its predecessors in the canon in that it offers a dizzying variety of irreconcilable perspectives, but no one particular viewpoint is granted lasting authority, hence stability, or finality. Nearly all the dramatis personae of the play endlessly judge, assess, describe, and comment on each other—more so than in any other Shakespeare play. What others say about the characters, what they say about themselves, and what they do are all notoriously hard to square with each other. The play's style, says Danby, is dialectical. It mixes contrarieties, works by means of a "rapid impressionism," and a "careful lapidary enrichment," intermixing past and present and time and space. Everything is framed by "perspective" and comes from a point of view constantly qualified, gainsayed, or even undone. This is, in Danby's assessment, a discreating society whose sheer glamor cannot obscure the fact that the world of *Antony and Cleopatra* rots itself with a motion and restlessness that puts us all at sea, with no firm ground of judgment to find our feet.[13]

I cannot reproduce all the details of Danby's elegant and compelling analysis but the key points, accounting for the essay's later influence rests chiefly here: (1) no comment can be taken at face value—it may at any minute be contradicted or subverted by the play's ironic movement; (2) there is no possibility of "final assessment"; but (3) characters make "continuous and insistent claim(s) on the spectator for judgment." We cannot and in short, should not, choose between Rome and Egypt as a long precedent of critical tradition advises. It is in this sense that *Antony and Cleopatra* is Shakespeare's "critique of judgment." Shakespeare's splendid trickery with our "normal standards and powers of judgment" creates a universe in which several standards of judgment apply but with no prospect of resolution: this is Shakespeare's dialectic and his "adjustment." The play's universe is morally ambiguous; ambivalence is its fabric and principle of operation.[14]

Janet Adelman, in her marvelous book-length essay *The Common Liar*, is one of the most rigorous and insightful inheritors of the Danby tradition of finding "moral ambivalence" to be at the heart of the play's concerns. Judgment is a "dilemma." The whole play can be seen as a "series of attempts on the part of the characters to understand and judge each other and themselves."[15] We "are forced to participate in the act of judgment," that is, we are invited to judge at almost every turn, but the judgment "depends on where one stands," and this seems to tell us as much about the judge and his perspective as it does about the accused." We see both "the validity and the limitations of all perspectives," and this "movement of perspectives" is the characteristic climate of *Antony and Cleopatra*.[16] The uncertainty that pervades the world of *Antony and Cleopatra* both in love relations and in affairs of state renders fidelity to any particular set of values pointless. Like the vagabond flag on the stream, the fluidity, variety, multiplicity, and transformation of judgment threatens to hollow out any sense of purpose, point, or direction.[17]

Danby and Adelman have articulated judgment at crisis point. They argue that Shakespeare depicts a world in which no indefeasible judgment is possible—because (within this logic) it cannot be final or determinative; judgment must be suspended or deferred in ambiguity and ambivalence. Shakespeare both identifies and inhabits that crisis and not merely in the play's chronic hesitation between Rome and Egypt, Roman measure or Egypt's "o'erflowing" of rule long noted by former critics. The play invites us to judge all the time but undermines our confidence in every judgment we might come to. "We are forced to judge," says Barbara J. Bono, "and shown the folly of judgment at the same time."[18]

Danby and Adelman claim that *Antony and Cleopatra* both diagnoses and lives this crisis of judgment. Their insight is valuable not merely as brilliant illuminations of the play at hand but also because they speak to the pervasive crisis of judgment we inhabit. We get out of the way of our judgments lest they are "merely" subjective; we grant exclusive authority to the ungainsayable methods of science even when our questions and concerns are quite beyond its remit. Vivasvan Soni has compellingly argued that in modernity, the very concept of judgment becomes unintelligible, the practice has been concealed, and our very faculties of judgment face a danger of atrophy.[19] Absent for decades from literary studies, often confused with moralism or aestheticism, and seen as an epistemological rather than as an ethical concern, this fundamental concept has become obscure to humanistic inquiry.[20]

How has the concept become unintelligible? How has the practice itself been concealed? Soni sees the avoidance of judgment in a scientism that assumes that judgments can be empirically determined (this is measurement not judgment) and in the assumption that subjective judgments will lead to relativism (myriad "opinions" or personal "tastes") or a chronic deferment of judging. Our options seem to be decisionism or a celebration of indeterminacy, and both of these are forms of avoidance.

We go on judging of course, because we cannot *not*—this indeed is the crisis. Either external grounds for judgment are then not "ours" or no grounds are firm enough to be sure of our calls. In our daily lives, we constantly discern, assess the situations we find ourselves in, and deem each other hasty, worthy, ready, funny, despicable, lazy, and so on more or less continuously. In my daily life, I hardly restrict myself to judging a person as right or wrong, correct or incorrect. I am more likely to find you, say, variously tin-eared, insensitive, tactless, fair-minded, harsh, sanctimonious, cowardly, bold, inaccurate, in retreat, brilliant, or joyful. These opinions are among the myriad and more or less continuous ways we hold each other in view. If judgment lines our every thought and deed, if our judgments are pervasive and inevitable, if we live by means of them, then judgment is not the problem, only our avoidance of it. Fallible and vulnerable though our judgments might be, unavoidable as they in fact are, they seem to have become a "problem."[21] What picture of perspective is at work that this should be the case?

If judgments are assimilated to rules; if our concepts are understood as rules by which we count something as something, having it fall under a concept, then the absence of common and agreed standards will be devastating and will lead to irresolvable conflict.

Perspective and Its Fortunes, or Where Is Your Sense of Perspective?

In "The Dialectic of Perspective," the philosopher James Conant contrasts an earlier concept of perspective—an intrinsic art of judgment—with the much more confined and limited reduction in range it later assumes. Modern critics, such as Danby and Adelman, have been gripped by a picture of perspective that makes the subjective a problem, something that needs to be overcome to understand what anything truly is. According to Conant, this philosophical view has lost touch with the ordinary use of the word *perspective*.[22] In the ordinary or literal use of the term, several factors are at play. We can and do, for example, freely alter our perspective. That perspective both *affords* us a view of an object and is specifiable within "a matrix of alternative perspectives."[23] Those multiple perspectives share a common object or set of objects and together, mutually, they in turn allow us to correct for distortions and *together* help us to achieve *a relation* to the object of view. This picture of perspective, Conant points out, resting on an idea in the practice and theory of Renaissance painting "invites an internal relation between objective and subjective moments in a perceptual encounter between a perceiving subject and the objects of his perception."[24] Objectivity and subjectivity are mutually related. This sense of perspective as changeable, granting us access to the world, in conversation with and corrigible by many other perspectives to establish a common object together is almost unrecognizable when judgment is understood to be in crisis. For now, it seems as if a point of view that had hitherto afforded us a view is seen as confined to a single perspective, moreover one we cannot freely alter. What the subject sees now seems *dictated* by that perspective, and the perspective is not shared or tested against competing ones. In fact, it is not clear how or where it stands in relation to other perspectives and no common object is afforded by such multiplicity. Our perspectives separate us from others and from the genuine knowledge of each other or the world: These perspectives must be suppressed, overcome, or avoided. When judgments come from us, they are "merely" subjective. Thus, in the introduction to the Arden, 3rd ser., John Wilders says that Cleopatra's final vision of Antony bestriding the ocean can be seen as magnificent or delusional, but it "is also subjective (as is everyone's opinion in this play)."[25] Judgment has become opinion. This version of perspective is epistemically isolated and all encompassing, and in it, we must remain apart from the world not within it.

Notice how judgment has become epistemological and no longer seen in ethical or existential terms. In the process, we are separated from and shut out from the world. We must ascribe to heteronomous standards whose objectivity can be secured only by keeping our "opinions" out of it, or we can delay and defer judgment by inhabiting a moral ambiguity and ambivalence that can be celebrated or deplored. Both "solutions" sever judgment from responsibility: The one overturns judgment to an external authority, and the other simply defers it. If, however, as Vivasvan Soni has argued, "judgment is the groundless and inherently risky process by which we shape our lives and assume responsibility for our existential choices," judgment cannot be avoided, only responsibility for it.[26]

When Danby called *Antony and Cleopatra* Shakespeare's "critique of judgment," he was playfully alluding to Kant's third critique, *Critique of the Power of Judgment*.[27] The Kantian allusion is not developed in Danby's essay, but Kant's far-reaching insights in this critique have been developed with striking originality by both Hannah Arendt and Stanley Cavell in the early 1960s.[28] Although Kant's claims were made in relation to aesthetic judgment, Arendt and Cavell saw how Kant's insight could be extended both to political judgment (Arendt's concern) and to an entire ethical and existential understanding of language.[29] Their work makes available a way of animating Danby's playful but unexplored allusion, as it might help us retrieve a concept of judgment.

When Kant discussed aesthetic judgment in the *Critique of the Power of Judgment*, he isolated and developed with great rigor the peculiar rationality of aesthetic judgments, the kinds of reason we enter into when we call something beautiful. He calls aesthetic judgments reflective, and he distinguishes them from determinative judgments in which a particular is subsumed under a universal, counted under an already established concept or rule. When we feel something is beautiful and call it so (because aesthetic judgments call for expression and require articulation), our judgment is necessarily subjective, passing through our experience.[30] Our judgment is importantly free; if it fell under a preexistent concept of beauty, it would be neither free nor essentially my judgment. At the same time, the claim of beauty has "subjective universality": When I call something beautiful, I demand everyone's assent. Aesthetic judgment is utterly distinct from opinion and from what is simply agreeable or pleasing.[31] Kant's language is strong: I demand assent when I make an aesthetic claim, I rebuke anyone who claims otherwise and deny the validity of their taste. We do not count on assent to our judgment, but it is part of the logic of aesthetic judgment, as Kant reveals it, that we do demand it. Kant says an aesthetic claim is without a concept. Were it to "fall under" a preexisting concept, it would have a different kind of necessity. An aesthetic judgment has the grammar of a claim and is as vulnerable as a claim is. A claim cannot prove its relevance. The grammar of claim is central to the Kantian idea of aesthetic judgment—to impute my judgment to my psychology or our sociology is to lose this idea of a claim, and the peculiar kind of agreement it projects and posits.

If you claim that Cleopatra is a tawdry has-been, a wayward embarrassment on stage, and you simply cannot understand what anyone sees in this play, let alone this particular production, our relationship might be at least temporarily strained. I might not be able to talk to you for a while, until we have found a way round this, even if you articulate your reasons compellingly. Our judgments raise questions, such as "do you see what I see?" "This is how I look at it." "Can't you *see* that?" They are questions of a vision we share or do not share, and we do not feel we can be indifferent, as if we can let each other alone in a retreat to opinion or different tastes.

The role of Kantian aesthetic judgment is fundamental in Stanley Cavell's writings. One commentator has suggested that "from the outset Cavell has proclaimed an intimacy, at times amounting to a virtual identity, between the *logic* of aesthetic claiming (the logic appropriate to our claims, evaluative and interpretative, about works of art and, by extension, the logic of those works, their claiming) and the *logic* peculiar to ordinary language philosophy ('what we say when' and 'what we mean when we say it')."[32] The logic that is claimed for aesthetic judgments works across the whole of our use of language. This is how Cavell develops Ludwig Wittgenstein's exploration of rules in the *Philosophical Investigations* using Kantian insight. Wittgenstein's exploration of rules in the *Philosophical Investigations* is an investigation about words and concepts and how we acquire them.

The radical innovation of Cavell's insight developed in the first two essays in *Must We Mean What We Say?* and the first chapter of *The Claim of Reason* turns on his understanding that what governs our judgments was not rules (platonically preexisting our encounters) but criteria emerging from our shared forms of life. Cavell explores Wittgenstein's extensive consideration of rules and how we follow them, obey them, are guided by them, and grasp them to conclude that our speaking together and the concepts we arrive at together are not "everywhere bounded by rules" or universals.[33] Criteria replace rules for Cavell. Moreover, the criteria by which we count something as something, call it anything, are not the criteria of experts, such as those who can adjudicate the difference between swifts and swallows or golden doodles and labradoodles. We grant authority to ornithologists and twitchers or to dog breeders or those in the know at the Westminster Dog Show to those kinds of distinctions. Wittgenstein wants us to think about the criteria for being in pain, for having a toothache (whether incisor or molar), for sitting on a chair (whether Chippindale or Bauhaus), in short for the kinds of things we cannot fail to know and for which we are all in the same boat, not one of us in possession of surer knowledge than any other. Cavell leads us away from the Augustinian picture of language by which we label things in the world to a vision of language in which we are initiated into forms of life, learning word and world together.

Two relevant differences emerge in this picture of criteria and judgment. Cavell repeatedly calls attention to the fact that, for anything to count as anything, we have to deploy criteria, and we have to count something as something on any particular occasion. Borrowing from Kant on aesthetic judgment, Cavell calls this (incessant) voicing of criteria speaking with a "universal voice." The claim is on everyone else, but I have to voice it, and in this sense, it is my counting, telling, calling, and speaking through which criteria alone count. Cavell's aim was to bring the human voice back into philosophy, something that this picture of rules rules out. So, using criteria is showing what counts for us, what we care about and value. Cavell's felicitous phrase refers us to "the importance of importance" in this way of thinking.[34] To tell anything—to count and recount it is to say what matters—"recounting what is important, taking up the details of where importance lies, is the task Cavell assigns to philosophy."[35] The question of value is intrinsically linked to questions of voice, and hence to self-knowledge, and Cavell understands ordinary language philosophy as a quest for self-knowledge. To explore our concepts, our criteria, we ask when and how and for what reason do *I* count something as something?

Furthermore, Cavell's emphasis on the elicitation of criteria rather than rules puts our relations with each other back into the picture. The implication is that the attraction of rules outside of these relations is precisely to escape the contingency and fragility of these relations, in search of something more firm and reliable. As Richard Eldridge says, "in staking and testing oneself as an articulator of criteria, one is at the same time staking and testing one's relationship with others."[36]

The idea that our judgments are merely subjective preferences dies hard. For surely rules can only be trusted, their impartiality and principled nature secured, if they are fixed independently of our responses. The world of value must be separated from the world of fact. In the humanities, we think we have overcome these tired antinomies, even when we have barely begun to confront them.[37]

In this picture, we cannot isolate certain specific acts as carrying the weight of judgment. This is not to deny that certain specifiable speech acts by particular people in particular situations carry that authority: The umpire rules; the judge gives a verdict. In these instances, certain precedents are followed and certain agreed standards apply. But we have already established—and this is the fruit of Danby and Adelman's insight—that no such judgments are available in this play. We are all in as good, or bad, a position as any other to judge.

If Cavell's reading of Wittgenstein, unlike the epistemologized understanding of perspective examined by Conant, gives us the notion that our judgments "word the world," bring the word and world into alignment through our use of words, then our ways of talking can shrink or enlarge the world and can contract and constrict our relations or enlarge our perspectives.

Cavell's Kantian reading of Wittgenstein illuminates the question of judgment in *Antony and Cleopatra*. It helps us move beyond the "problem" or crisis of judgment to grasp the logic of the aesthetic and imaginative claims the play makes on us, especially in its last staging of Cleopatra's death and in her unprecedented dramatic claim that her death is a marriage and that Antony is her husband. I next show both how the vast geographic and global reach of the play reveals a diminished planet, and the nature of the claims Cleopatra makes for her relationship with Antony, and why the logic of those claims is aesthetic.

Wording the World: Modes of Talking

This invocation of the world is a notoriously striking feature of *Antony and Cleopatra*. Global dominion is at stake in this crucial period of transition of republic to empire: Who will be the "universal landlord" (3.13.76)? The world is a geographic and political entity inhabited by all the play's players who live in the forcefield of the world's "pillars," those who supposedly uphold it (1.1.12). Rome and Egypt, the fertile Nile and Alexandria's pastimes, are richly conjured, the play's famous antinomies. Other whole countries are casually traded and divided between the big men: "You have made us offer / Of Sicily, Sardinia," says Pompey (2.6.34-35). Antony does give crowns and crownets—"Lower Syria, Cyprus, Lydia"—to the "absolute Queen," Cleopatra (3.6.9-11). Shakespeare lifts wholesale from Plutarch the kings and regions Antony assembles to give his "empire to a whore": Cappadoccia, Arabia, Mede, and Lycaonia (3.6.70). The world in *Antony and Cleopatra* is both vast and particularized. We are given specific locales for Fulvia's death (Sycion, northwest of Corinth), for example, or for Pompey's gathering force (Misena). Ventidius is deputized to take care of Parthia (2.4). The geographic settings are numerous and vaster than anything yet envisaged in previous plays. The worldly semantics also invite us to think about how the world comes into view, which is a feature of that invitation to perspective and vision we have just examined: Do you live in the *same* world as me? "The world of the happy is quite another than that of the world of the unhappy" said Wittgenstein in the *Tractatus-Logico-Philosophicus*.[38] The world of lovers might be different from the world of the unloved and unloving. How do we have a world at all, and is our world shareable? How can it be both vast and paltry, worth conquering, but worth losing altogether? How is the world "worded," imagined, and projected in *Antony and Cleopatra*?

The world in *Antony and Cleopatra* is grandiosely vast: Its rulers are vaunted as quasi-divine. The whole world must witness their love: Antony invites "the world to weet" the "mutual pair" (1.1.40); after Antony's death, Cleopatra dreams that Antony's reared arm crested the world (5.2.81-2); Antony claims he quartered the world with his sword (4.14.58-59). But this exalted world is diminishing. The three triple pillars—Caesar, Lepidus, and Antony—do not so much share the world as compete for it. With the elimination of Lepidus who never stood a chance in the story, there are now only a "pair of chaps, no more" (3.5.13). The world is finally consolidated under the universal landlordship of Caesar, where all are his tenants. If we think of the world as afforded by the richness of the perspectives we bring to bear on it, however, this vast ranging empire is not so much growing as shrinking. To Cleopatra, after the loss of Antony, the world becomes merely "dull," with nothing "left remarkable / Beneath the visiting moon" (4.15.64, 68-69) and Caesar becomes "paltry" (5.2.2) For Antony, one single tear of Cleopatra's weighs and wins in the balance of "all that is won or lost" (3.11.69-70). Rome shrinks the world as it dominates it; it becomes uninhabitable for those of larger vision. This is established chiefly through modes of talking in the play.

Cleopatra brilliantly captures Roman talk in her mimicry of it in the first scene. The mood is imperative, a world of "mandate" and "dismission" (1.1.23, 1.1.27). "Do this, or this, / Take in that kingdom and enfranchise that. / Perform't or else we damn thee" (1.1.22-24). Cleopatra ventriloquizes Caesar's commanding voice as she empties it of significance. Caesar's favorite address of commands and orders attempts to limit the range of response to obedience and disobedience. He likes to set out the script beforehand: "Do not exceed / The prescript of this scroll" (3.8.4-5). He counts open-ended play and festivity as unproductive "waste": Antony "wastes / The lamps of night in revel" (1.4.4-5). Every occasion of talking is strategic with an end he has determined. The response of others is mostly irrelevant except in so far as it coheres with his predetermined end. All talk that does not have an end in mind (an end he defines) is in vain. His world is the new world that will emerge from his victory: The world of empire, and Rome's victors will be framed in his triumph. In a world divided between conqueror and conquered, the responses of the conquered are only relevant in so far as they figure forth their conquered state. Although vast in geographic scope, although huge in power and might, the world under Caesar's conditions is a diminished and degraded world, a meaner and a poorer one. This world has little room for the voices of others in their integrity and individuality. The perspectives—multiple, corrigible, affording us a common world—are profoundly reduced and degraded.

But what of the world in Antony and Cleopatra's talk? Something of the grandiosity, overreach, melodrama, magnitude, and glamour of Antony and Cleopatra's claims on us are expressed in the play's heightened style. The play is marked by astonishing metrical subtlety and variety—short sentences, pleonasms, ecphonesis, and lines that overflow their measure with feminine endings, lines with inverted word order, and lines that are notably and frequently interrupted by the speaker or by others. Madeleine Doran has elaborated on one of the play's most persistent tropes: hyperbole.[39] Several outstanding analyses of the play's incomparable style have explored this most poetic of plays in which the creativity of language is so sustained and so subtly explored.[40] By contrast, I wish to investigate the pair's practice of conversation and its role in the play. For conversation between the two is both the medium of their acknowledgment of each other and the means of transformation. It is the quality of talk between Antony and Cleopatra that marks such an unprecedented departure from the dramatic tradition with its neoclassical preponderance of soliloquies and declamations. As one of its editors observed, *Antony and Cleopatra* is "in many ways a quiet play, conversational rather than declamatory."[41]

Milton put conversation before procreation in God's ordaining of marriage.[42] Marriage was to be a comfort for the "evil of solitary life," and God implies "the apt and cheerful conversation of man with woman."[43] Why should conversation be a model for marriage? What is being suggested? How does Shakespeare imagine the conversation between Antony and Cleopatra such that it finally carries the weight of their opposition to Roman rule?

This is one more extension of Danby's light allusion to *Antony and Cleopatra* as Shakespeare's "critique of judgment." In his book *Pursuits of Happiness*, Cavell posits a new genre, the Hollywood remarriage comedy of the 1930s and 1940s, which he claims begins with Shakespeare's *The Winter's Tale*.[44] He sees the last scene of *Antony and Cleopatra*, too, as matching *The Winter's Tale* in presenting us with a new ceremony of marriage.[45] Unlike the romantic comedies in which the truth of a young girl's desire wins out against an older generation of patriarchs, such that the play reconciles love and marriage in its ending, the older couples in remarriage comedy begin married. The question of the play is what constitutes their union, and it is not the state, or the church, or the social order that in the premise of this new genre has lost its power over the authentication of marriage. What binds or sanctifies in marriage? Shakespeare inaugurates remarriage comedy, but it reappears in the medium of film, with the invention of the talkies, because the marriage to which we grant our consent is worked through in conversation and by means of it: "In thus questioning the legitimacy of marriage, the question of the legitimacy of the society is simultaneously raised, even allegorized."[46] Remarriage is Cavell's word for the ongoing consent that legitimizes itself in the mutual acknowledgment of the couple. It is, as one critic has put it, a vision "for a society based on speaking to and for each other."[47] In *Contesting Tears: The Hollywood Melodrama of the Unknown Woman*, Cavell regards his reformulation of what legitimates marriage in the remarriage comedies, "marrying as declaring you are already married," as a kind of comic purloining of Kant's aesthetics. It is, as he puts it, "pleasure in one another without a concept," beginning from no prior definition or rule of church or state, or by the fact of children, but emerging to find new words, and new worlds.[48]

In the opening scene, when Cleopatra asks for an accounting of Antony's love for her, Antony replies there is beggary in the love that can be reckoned, taking telling, and counting love as measuring it. We already have been told—it is the first thing we are told—that Antony's love "oe'rflows the measure" (1.1.2). To be able to tell Cleopatra his love would mean "finding out" new heaven and new earth," claims Antony (1.1.17). Much has been made of the image from the Book of Revelation, but I want to stress the "finding out." It will be the work of the play to show the cost of love's reckoning, and it is something that must be found out. Antony and Cleopatra must find a language for their love and find themselves out in it too. The "new heaven, new earth" must be discovered beyond Roman rule and in despite of it. Being "without a concept," their conversation / marriage can be discovered and sustained only through conversation. A key word in thinking about the marriages in Shakespeare's play is thus conversation. The bond, not being assumed, is to be refound, reestablished multiple times. This turns out to be one of the patterns of the play.

"Husband, I Come!"

This chapter opens with Vergil's heated remonstrance: Cleopatra is "that woman, that Egyptian wife." But *coniunx* can mean both "wife" and "woman," and the distinction is particularly important in this play. North's Plutarch harps on it, and in Shakespeare's play, it is structural to the play's design and for our understanding of Cleopatra's death as a claim to marriage: "*Husband*, I come!? / Now to that name my courage prove my title!" (5.2.286–87). The titles of wife and husband are not conferred by the Roman state or any other external authority, such as temple or church, but they derive from the logic of the claims and courage of the mutual pair to a kind of love that demands recognition.

Although other neoclassical versions of the story fudge the legal status of Cleopatra's relationship with Antony, Shakespeare's version turns on it. In Shakespeare's play, Antony *is* married but not to Cleopatra. First of all, he is married to Fulvia and consequently to Octavia. Antony's second marriage to Octavia is a bond with Octavius. Octavia's consent barely figures in it. Shakespeare deliberately stages this as if it is Octavius and Antony who are to be married by mimicking the marriage service over a line break. Agrippa proposes marriage "to hold you in perpetual amity" (2.2.132), "to make you brothers," and "to knit your hearts / With an unslipping knot" (2.2.132–3), language usually reserved for the bond of love between the two parties of the marriage. This idea is pointedly and subtly reinforced when Agrippa says, "Take Antony," and just shy of the momentary pause of the line break, we might almost imagine that it is Caesar who Antony is marrying before the next line specifies Octavia (2.2.134–35). But if Octavia's say in the marriage is of no account, this is the marriage that is authorized in a last-ditch attempt to bind the hoops of the world together. Antony is bound to Octavius by means of his sister, and although we know that Octavia's position is untenable, her task impossible, the marriage has the full backing of the Roman state, indeed the empire, through its great progenitors.

In his essay on the play, "Love and Art in *Antony and Cleopatra*," Robert Ornstein declares that Cleopatra wants to be a Roman wife.[49] But this cannot be right. Cleopatra does not want to be a Roman wife, the model for which is Octavia. She does not want the sanctification of the Roman state. Rather she claims legitimacy for her brilliant mutual being with Antony—she claims he is her husband solely by virtue of their relationship, justified through their open-ended love. Its legitimacy derives from their mutual delight and continues by means of it. The glorious declaration "Husband, I come!" has the form of a claim. The play turns on the point from which the legitimacy of marriage is derived: from the law or out of the fabric of their love. I will return to the logic of Cleopatra's claim as it is developed in the play's climactic last scene.

In North's Plutarch, Cleopatra's advisers belabor the difference in the way Octavia's relationship is recognized at the point in the narrative at which Octavia has come to meet Antony in Athens in the midst of the Parthian wars. Cleopatra's advisers hope to persuade Antony not to go to Octavia. "For Octavia" they say, "that was maryed unto him as it were of necessitie, bicause her brother Caesars affayres so required it: hath the honor to be called Antonius lawefull spowse and wife." But "Cleopatra, being borne a Queene of so many thowsands of men, is onely named

Anthius Leman, and yet that she disdayned not to be so called, if it might please him that she might enjoy his company, and live with him: but if he once leave her, that then it is unpossible that she might live."⁵⁰ The very necessity of the marriage—for legitimacy, for political alliance, for the great homosocial and world-saving bond between Caesar and Antony—is precisely what undermines its integrity. Cleopatra will suffer the shame of illegitimacy with honor because her relationship with Antony rests on love, not necessity. No external support, such as a brother's anger, a brother's army, the Roman state, the judgment of sensible political men, or the general polity underwrites the love between them. In Shakespeare's play, this is what lends the lovers their characteristic style of testing, suspicions of betrayal, jealousies, and grandiosity of expression for their relationship cannot be secured by legal means or external ratification. Their love proclaims itself as exemplary when "such a mutual pair / And such a twain can do't" (1.1.38-39). They made, as Plutarch says, "an order between them, which they called Amimetobion as much as to say, no life comparable and matcheable with it."⁵¹ The volatility, insecurity, and utter grandeur, the inventiveness and daring of their relationship, as well as its self-conscious showiness, instability, astonishing vulnerability and occasional degradation are all encompassed in the idea of their marriage as a claim on their readers and audiences, a claim explicitly reserved for Cleopatra's last scene.

This idea of marriage as a claim of recognition is peculiar to Shakespeare: It is his unique idea, and this is why he reserves the word *husband* for Cleopatra's death scene, after Antony is already dead. In the neoclassical versions Bullough collects, the name husband is quite casually thrown around. Cinthio has Cleopatra claim that Heaven "has made me Antony's wife." Garnier calls them husband and wife; so much later does Dryden. Samuel Daniel omits the question.⁵²

In this tremendously busy play with its constant traffic of messengers concerned with the urgencies of war and empire, in the midst of a world replete with orders, commands, negotiations and strategies, in a play of some four hundred entrances and exits, a play of multiple small scenes, and manifold locations, ranging from Rome and Alexandria to Athens and the Greek sea coast, it might seem odd to claim that the conversation between Antony and Cleopatra is one of the play's chief media and subjects. Where is the time for such converse? The pair are simply not seen alone; an audience is always on stage for their talk, and the lovers are acutely aware that they appear in the world and that the world is their witness. They speak together in only ten of the play's rapidly succeeding forty-two scenes.⁵³ For long stretches of the play they are apart. They do not appear together at all in act 2. Act 5 is Cleopatra's alone: Antony appears there only in her visionary imagination. This leaves only a few scenes in which we see them talking together: the opening scene framed by Demetrius and Philo (act 1, scene 1) and very soon afterward (act 1, scene 3) in which Antony explains to Cleopatra that he must leave for Rome, a scene already marked by an imminent separation. In act 3, they share brief exchanges on the battle to come, and in act 3, scene 11, in the aftermath of the debacle at sea, a scene of devastating intensity stages the most intimate and searing conversation of them all. The exquisitely tender scene in which Cleopatra helps Antony arm himself (act 4, scene 4) is followed by Antony's rage (act 4, scene 12), which cuts off the possibility of conversation more or less entirely. Finally, after all the physical comedy and exertion that enables their final encounter in the monument, in one short scene Antony manages to give Cleopatra advice about how to manage Caesar, advice she constantly interrupts, may not trust, and does not take. Clearly, how they exist in each other's imaginations is vital to establish their love. Nevertheless, it is in the astonishing dramatic economy of their conversation that their love is honed and refined, and it is here that they—and we—recognize their love and its claims. Despite the continuous audience for their conversation, one of the achievements of their talk is an astonishingly raw intimacy unprecedented on the English stage.⁵⁴

Shakespeare might have found a clue in Plutarch's admiration and appreciation for Cleopatra's wit and learning for he says that "so sweete was her companie and conversacion, that a man could not possible be taken."⁵⁵

One gloss on conversation and marriage is provided by Enobarbus. Octavia, Antony's new intended, is of a "holy, cold, and still conversation" (2.6.125), says Enobarbus. Menas's conventional response affirms the Octavian model: "Who would not have his wife so?" (2.6.126). Enobarbus's reply—"Not he that himself is not so" (2.6.127)—might have in mind a woman worthy of a different kind of devotion, one blessed by holy priests when she is "riggish" (2.2.249-50). Antony, says Enobarbus "will use his affection where it is" (2.6.132). Michael Neill, in his edition of the play, glosses this nicely as Antony "will use his passions where they are really engaged."⁵⁶

From the beginning, their conversation is persistently interrupted by Rome, and Rome designs the end of it, for Caesar demands that Cleopatra gives up Antony. Their points of union are fragile, tender, and sparse, a point often underplayed in productions that belittle Cleopatra's charms in a crudely overplayed or lurid sexuality, missing the exposure of a precious and precarious intimacy, an intimacy fundamentally beset by Rome.[57] The raw simplicities of talk are so often overwhelmed with a showy excess that obscures the delicate and exposed points of connection between the lovers. It is in their conversation, however, that we come to understand the texture of their relationship: its insecurities and bombast, its intimacies and evasion of them, its dreams and its poetry, its adventure and neediness, its mutual reliance and dependency. This is where they may be "found out," not in Philo's static tableau but in the time-bound shifts of conversing.

What ruins a conversation? We can establish the conditions for a conversation when we see how and where it goes wrong—when it stops being a conversation. Sometimes the person you are talking to does not listen and vitiates the conditions of conversation. If you condescend, you will quickly abort conversation for it relies on an assumed equality of parties. A certain quality of attention is needed for a conversation to flow and be sustained. Sometimes someone is just waiting their turn to speak, and their impatience is palpable. We all know people like this, and they are not fun to converse with. Conversation depends on a *natural* reciprocity; therein lies its delight. One person is not waiting for the gap in which they can speak but is spurred on to say something in direct response to what it is that someone has just said. In a good conversation, one person's words sponsors (inspires, prompts) another and another responds in kind, leaving full play for the particularity of the other. Where it leads cannot be anticipated: It can be surprising and unexpected, and so frequently good conversation offers something new. It is a medium of self-discovery. It cannot be scripted in advance, as Caesar likes to script his talk, because it is fundamentally free. It depends on a certain kind of trust and intimacy, a delicate balance. You can strike up a conversation or fall into one. Samuel Johnson shows that good conversation is substantial: "We had talk enough but no *conversation*; there was nothing discussed."[58] The delicate balance of a conversation is easily interrupted and destroyed and all the more precious for that: It can transform into a quarrel, for example, as happens quite a lot in *Antony and Cleopatra*. It is a form of dialogue unaccounted for in rhetoric.

Even the simplest neighborly conversation over the fence of our backyards establishes that a conversation is not the actions of two individual people talking but rather a common action. Charles Taylor uses the example of two neighbors discussing the weather. My neighbor and I were perfectly aware of the weather before I said, "Fine weather we're having," but now this is something we attend to together. The conversation has become *our* action and, as Taylor says, opening a conversation inaugurates a common action, one irreducible to my action in talking or yours.[59] Such mutuality is intrinsic to Antony and Cleopatra's relationship. They are, as Antony says, a "mutual pair" (1.1.38). The title of the play belongs to both of them. This makes it distinct from the English neoclassical closet drama Shakespeare knew, focused on either Antony or Cleopatra. (Such drama is also notably declamatory; it is impossible to imagine a conversation in it.) Shakespeare seemed to conceive of the pair as incomprehensible except in relation to each other.[60] "Antony / Will be himself," says Cleopatra, while Antony adds: "but stirred by Cleopatra." (1.1.44–46).

I look more closely at two out of the ten scenes of Antony and Cleopatra conversing: in one scene (act 1, scene 3), they have to accommodate a separation, and in another, they share an almost unbearably intimate scene of shame and belated self-knowledge after the fatal sea battle (act 3, scene 11). In these scenes, we might begin to chart the great open-ended leap into another human being, the space that is made for the soul's growth in this play.[61]

In the first sequence of scenes (act 1, scenes 1 and 3), we see Antony and Cleopatra responding to Rome's pressure. When Antony eventually gives Rome's messengers a hearing, he accepts Rome's reprimand even to its judgment of Cleopatra: "Speak to me home.... Name Cleopatra as she is called in Rome" (1.2.112–12), and like Aeneas, he leaves his queen to report for duty. Cleopatra is never unaware of Rome's power and pull; she is alert to all those moments when a Roman thought strikes Antony (1.2.88) and wants to test out the veracity of his love, the truth of his hyperbolic and extravagant protestations against its judgment: "Let Rome in Tiber melt, and the wide arch / Of the ranged empire fall!" (1.1.34–35). She never ceases to think about Antony during their long stage absences. She never ceases to have love on her mind—love for Antony, all other lovers paling in comparison. But Antony never consciously brings her to mind; he simply and inevitably returns to her. "I will to Egypt" (2.3.37) is spoken after his interview with the soothsayer who advises Antony not to stay by Caesar's side because his "daemon" is afraid of Caesar's (2.3.19) and his luster grows dim at Caesar's side. Enobarbus knows more about him than he knows about himself, but in act 3, scene 11, Antony retrospectively understands the measure of his love for Cleopatra and voices it full-throatedly even in the utter shame of defeat.

When we first see Antony and Cleopatra they are indulging in love talk: "If it be love indeed, tell me how much," opens Cleopatra (1.1.14). Is

Antony's love *love*? If it is, Cleopatra will have it told and retold. Perhaps this is one of love's pleasures—to dwell on its growth and possibilities. Perhaps, however, the "if" entertains doubts as to the nature and quality of Antony's love. From the first, these lovers claim to extend the resources of language to reckon their love. Antony declares that Cleopatra cannot set a bourn on his love: "Thou must needs find out new heaven, new earth" (1.1.17). The extravagantly apocalyptic registers are there, but it is the "finding out" that strikes me. Can these lovers live in this world, or will they, do they, need to find a new one for their love to have a habitation? At this very point, Rome calls upon the pair: "Enter a messenger," a decisive and unwelcome reminder of Rome's impinging reach. It is Antony's curt irritation and dismissal of Rome's messages that appalls Philo and Demetrius.

Cleopatra understands Roman claims chiefly through Fulvia's effect. Fulvia's moods—"perchance she is angry" (1.1.21)—or her scolding can shame or command him. She economically captures Caesar's imperatival speech: "Do this, or this; / Take in that kingdom and enfranchise that," (1.1.22–23) commands either obeyed or disobeyed. Of course, she is taunting and testing as well as ventriloquizing Rome's habitual mode of order and command. Her suspicions are warranted. Her own understanding of marriage incorporates love from the beginning—"Why did he marry Fulvia and not love her?" (1.1.43). This question shows a willful oblivion of the political marital arrangements of Roman polity, or a disdain for them, or simply the assumption that love and marriage do go together.

In fact, Cleopatra perceives entirely accurately that the claims of the political world on Antony are mediated through his (legitimate) marriage to Fulvia. Fulvia is "the married woman": "What says the married woman you may go?" (1.3.21). Not only must she acknowledge that Antony is Fulvia's and that she has no power over him, she must rely alone on his love: "I have no power upon you; hers you are" (1.3.24).

In scene 3, she asks why should she believe Antony's oaths or cries to the gods to witness his truth ("the gods best know") when he has already been false to Fulvia: "Why should I think you can be mine and true— / Though you in swearing shake the throned gods—? Who have been false to Fulvia?" (1.3.27). She rightly understands that his loyalty to her does not have a good precedent in his lack of fidelity to Fulvia and she can also see that the loss of Fulvia barely registers with him.[62] She is therefore right to wonder whether Antony's proclamations may be empty, that the word he has given is at stake. Indeed, in the intervening scene, Antony invites the messenger to give a Roman description of Cleopatra:

"Name Cleopatra as she is called in Rome" (1.2.112). He decides to go to Rome before he knows Fulvia is dead, declaring he must cut his "strong Egyptian fetters" (1.2.123) and break off from the "enchanting Queen" (1.2.135), wishing he had never seen her. No wonder Cleopatra wonders whether Antony's Roman honor and word might be an "excellent falsehood" (1.1.42), his words "mouth-made vows" (1.3.30), his behavior a "scene / Of excellent dissembling" (1.3.80–81).

The first scene ends with a dismissal of the messengers, and Antony invites Cleopatra to a favorite pastime, and to be playmates again. Antony and Cleopatra's pleasures are improvisatory and playful. What they would like to do is "wander through the streets and note the qualities of people" (1.1.54–55). Such an activity is intrinsically uninteresting if you are not to be delighted by the observations of your traveling partner. With the right companion, such simple pleasures are magical. Shakespeare takes this suggestion from North's Plutarch, but in that version, they are cross-dressing for class as slave and chambermaid to "peere into poore men's windows and their shops."[63] Shakespeare is more discreet and sympathetic in providing Antony and Cleopatra with an activity less obviously to be dismissed as hauteur and condescension. It is not merely that Antony is giving Cleopatra what she wants—"last night you did desire it" (1.2.56). What this scene evinces is a mutual delight in an open-eyed curiosity toward others, the possibility of discovery, and a confidant sense that they will find each other's comments remarkable. Antony will later call Cleopatra his "play-fellow." Their pleasure in each other extends and expands their time together: "There's not a minute of our lives should stretch / Without some pleasure now" (1.1.47–48).

In the next scene, in which we find them talking together, Antony has given full hearing to the messengers from Rome. It is clear that such conversations, such mutual delights, are no longer to be possible. Cleopatra knows he has bad news and exasperates him by preventing its delivery. She tells him what he thinks, interrupts him, and casts aspersions on his protestations of love. Nothing, she wants to insist, has changed between them. Recalling him to the memory of love she invokes the "Bliss in our brows bent; none our parts so poor / But was a race of heaven; they are so still" (1.3.37–38). Antony's response is priggish; he makes the kinds of comments one might give at a public assembly but not to a lover: "The strong necessity of time commands / Our services a while, but my full heart / Remains in use with you" (1.3.44–45).

Antony prefers to declare the "necessity" of his departure. He talks of himself in the second-person plural, for he dare not say he wants to leave and evades his responsibility in leaving. Rome commands him as it did Aeneas to leave his Carthaginian queen.

A conversation can degrade into a quarrel, and this is what happens here. Antony no longer finds the "wrangling queen / Whom everything becomes" of the first scene so delightful (1.1.49). "Quarrel no more," says Antony (1.3.67). Because she will hardly give him leave to go, he starkly says: "I'll leave you, lady" (1.3.87). Then, however, the lovers somehow find a way of gracefully taking leave of each other, a real conversational achievement under the circumstances. She cannot yet bear the scourge of his disapproval; she needs to appear well in his eyes: "My becomings kill me when they do not / Eye well to you (1.3.97-99). She reconciles his departure to herself by saying not that Rome or Fulvia summons him but that his honor calls him hence (1.3.99). Antony leaves her with his valediction, forbidding mourning: "Our separation so abides and flies / That thou residing here, goes yet with me / And I, hence fleeting, here remain with thee" (1.3.105-6). What lovers have not had these thoughts? It is their gentle and elderly aubade.

Act 3, scene 11, is one of the play's most daring and delicate scenes. It comes in the wake of the Battle of Actium—that decisive battle in Rome's history depicted on the famous shield of Aeneas in book 8 of the *Aeneid*, inaugurating the empire and one-man rule. Antony has left the battle, a "doting mallard" (3.10.20) flying after Cleopatra's fleet; it is a violation of "experience, manhood, honour," as Scarus describes it (3.10.23). It is a battle of great historic import, but its effects on the lovers are seen to be of overriding importance. Antony and Cleopatra are most divided from each other and most present to each other. It is an unprecedented dialectic of intimacy. The separation and connection tracked so subtly and economically through act 1, scenes 1 and 3, is now revisited but in the face of a devastatingly unglamorous defeat. How does this scene convey such painful raw closeness with so many people on stage?

Antony is alone on stage when Cleopatra enters. They sit at a remove from each other: They cannot, will not, face each other. Each is in torment, but not one they can right now share. Antony is undone by shame, and she by fear of his shame, both by the belated realization of defeat and the reasons for defeat, thus the cost of their bond. Charmian, Iras, and Eros have entered with Cleopatra: The dialogue that ensues between Antony and Cleopatra is impossible without their intervention. Without the insistent help of the attendants who guide them toward each other, they cannot talk to each other at all. Where are the words to be found for such a conversation?

"Nay, gentle madam, to him, comfort him" (3.11.25). Charmian, Iras, and Eros's urgings proceed over the next twenty lines while Antony remains apart and desolate, fixed in his own desperate musings. When Cleopatra moves toward him, the attendants have to rouse him out of his desperate reverie as he ponders his erstwhile strength against the man who had no practice in "the brave squares of war" (3.11.40). Iras urges again: "Go to him, madam; speak to him. / He is unqualitied with very shame" (3.11.43-44). Eros exhorts Antony to comfort her while the queen approaches. Both then are struck dumb; both need rousing. Antony speaks first through his humiliation: "I have offended reputation, / A most unnoble swerving" (3.11.48-49). I imagine Eros's "O, the Queen" draws his attention to Cleopatra. First a question: "O whither hast thou led me, Egypt?" Cleopatra's first words in response are to ask him to "forgive her fearful sails." She adds: "I little thought / You would have followed" (3.11.55-56). This prompts Antony into the astonishing protestation: "Thou knew'st too well / My heart was to thy rudder tied by th'strings / And shouldst tow me after" (3.11.57-59).

Antony has come to know himself in a different way and the knowledge is devastating. Perhaps it is no surprise that there comes a flood of gentle reproaches when he finally does speak with Cleopatra: "Thou knew'st too well . . . you did know / How much you were my conqueror" (3.11.65-66). Cleopatra, unguarded, because there is no precedent in her repertoire for this, can only say, "O, my pardon" and "Pardon, Pardon" (3.11.62, 3.11.69). Is Cleopatra wrong to have thought he would not follow her? Where do right and wrong come in? There are only our fatal ignorances and flighty responses in the moment. Perhaps they are both now discovering the measure of their love.

"Thou knew'st"—"I knew it" is something we often say when we do not know, when events have done their worst and brought us to a realization of what we wished we had known by any other route. It is not clear what Cleopatra knew, what Antony knew, for their love, as most loves, was not sustained by knowledge but only by trust. What is clear now is that they do acknowledge each other and perhaps for the first time in this play. When people say, retrospectively, when all at last is clear, you knew or I knew it, it is because their knowledge is not acknowledged and so that knowledge is useless.

Antony's attempt to comfort her is now heartrending. His prompt is her tears: "Fall not a tear," and one of those tears "rate / All that is won and lost" (3.11.69-70). In the balance, one of her tears falls, and this counterweights everything lost, everything won. He has learned what he values, what is most precious to him. The kiss that comes now must contain the knowledge of the loss and the awareness of all that has just now been acknowledged. The kiss is made in the very face of all the world can throw at them: It is a sad kiss, a kiss of unbearable honesty. It cannot console but does affirm their love's measure. Productions must have the tact and intelligence to respect this intimacy, raw and exposed as it is.[64] The scene ends with a defiant call for that old solution, wine, but the wine is not convivial. It is a welcome to stupor, not festivity.

Living and Dying

Five of the thirteen suicides in the Shakespeare canon take place in *Antony and Cleopatra*.[65] In *The Myth of Sisyphus*, Albert Camus said that the one truly philosophical problem was suicide, because "judging whether life is or is not worth living amounts to answering the fundamental question of philosophy."[66] As Anne Barton shows definitively, Shakespeare offers us in this play the unusual structure of the double catastrophe.[67] The ending may be doubly catastrophic, but the two suicides could not be more differentiated: one a botched Roman attempt, the other a glorious apotheosis.[68] The juxtaposition seems poised to reveal Cleopatra's "toil of grace" (5.3.347) by contrast. The recuperative claims—to the sheer worth of their relationship and to the beauty of her ending—are also a magnificent defense of a theater for mortal bodies and for the embrace of change and transformation. Before we arrive at her defense of theater, we need to see the logic of poor Antony's death.

The action that precipitates their suicides is deliberately murky: Several unanswered questions hang over their deaths. Did Cleopatra betray him? Is she negotiating with Caesar or playing a long game of self-preservation? Antony's terrible military losses are the instigator of his death, but the immediate precipitating factor is Antony's idea that Cleopatra has betrayed him: "To the young Roman boy she hath sold me" (4.12.48). "There is left us / Ourselves to end ourselves" (4.14.21-22), he says. The rationale for Cleopatra's suicide is hotly contested as if her veniality or her attempt at negotiation with Caesar slights her high resolve. Yet Antony's response to the (false) news of her death, Cleopatra's most fatal lie, is immediately touching and generous, setting the tone for the rest of the play. There is simply the urge to talk again one more time no matter the difficulties and obstacles in the way. The two lovers leave the world behind as not worth the living, so both suicides are an indictment of the new world of the universal landlord. Although Shakespeare stages these suicides in utterly different and deliberately polarized ways, they both constitute an interrogation of a fantasy of self-sovereignty that has been in his sights all along in this play.

In Roman stoicism, especially as it became articulated under conditions of tyranny and imperial rule, the greatest empire consists of rule over your own mind: "The greatest empire is to be emperor of oneself."[69] As Rebecca Bushnell has explained: "Stoicism offers an ethics of the imperial self as well as a response to imperialism."[70] Self-sovereignty and autonomy, the autarkic self, are fantasies of avoidance stylizing themselves as freedom.[71] The path to freedom is always open: "Do you ask what path leads to freedom? Any vein in your own body."[72] Seneca's words are gently mocked in Tacitus' description of his suicide in the *Annals*.[73] His suicide is as botched as Antony's death. Seneca did not find freedom in any of his veins for, according to Tacitus, his long habits of fasting had withered his veins, even those in his legs and the back of his knees. His death was long drawn out and slow like Antony's death: He takes poison, but his bloodless legs left him immune to the poison's effect. Eventually, he is placed in a bath of warm water. Between these attempts, he dictates a lengthy missive to his scribes, in Tacitus' mischievous portrayal, and finally, he suffocates in a steam bath after having spattered all the slaves closest to him mightily with water from the bath. Seneca's name was synonymous with suicide: *se necare* (se-necans).[74]

Antony's description of his suicide rehearses a Senecan fantasy. It is Antony's valor not Caesar's, he claims, that has "triumphed on itself" (4.15.16). He describes himself as a "Roman by a Roman valiantly vanquished" (4.15.59-60). He has not been overthrown by Caesar but has only overthrown himself. Cleopatra gently agrees, but the change to the modal auxiliary from Antony's past tense is subtly significant: "So it should be, that none but Antony / Should conquer Antony" (4.16.18-19). This is face-saving, a dying wish to save the appearances of his nobility. The scene of his suicide that we have just witnessed is hard to square with this.

For his first attempt was not in fact to die by his own hand but by the hand of Eros, and Eros kills himself rather than Antony. Because he imagines that both Cleopatra and Eros have now preceded him in death, his suicide is already threatening to be as long drawn out as poor Seneca's. Falling on his sword but with no decisive blow, he too does not yet find freedom in every vein. Even here, he depends on others, first Eros, and then almost any passing soldier who will dispatch him. It is his desperate dependence that leads him to beg any one of the three guards to finish him off, but he comes up short: "*First guard:* Not I! / *Second Guard:* Nor I! / *Third Guard:* Nor any one!" After the three guards run away from the dying Antony, even Decretus will merely steal his sword, the instrument of his "triumph over himself," because it will advance him with Caesar (4.14.113–14). His end is sadly ignominious, and often provokes laughter in the audience, but it is an awkward laughter of discomfort. It cannot altogether shake itself free of the pathos and pain of Antony's abjection. Yet the audience's laughter might derive from the gap between the botched action on stage and Antony's stoical fantasies about his action, which is in line with the play's flirtations with comic idiom.[75]

Even Caesar's response to the news of Antony's death registers what should happen but does not: "The breaking of so great a thing should make / A greater crack" (5.1.14–15).

Antony cannot define his action unilaterally: The stoic fantasy of autonomy is revealed as corrigible, even defeated. Stoic teaching about suicide is "an extreme testimony to the Stoic belief that we are only what we have done for ourselves, that we are not what we have received from others and from the earth in which we live."[76] Before he attempts his stoic suicide, Antony has already been melting, deliquescing in the play's extraordinary images of dissolving and discandying, of losing solidity and shape.[77]

Antony's body in the immediate aftermath of his attempt at suicide is that heavy, not-yet-dead flesh, which does not acquiesce in the nobly stoic end he wills. Moreover, the laboriously unheroic and messy stage business of drawing him up to the monument where Cleopatra is immured for his dying scene utterly denies him his *liebestod* with Cleopatra, as he tries to claim a last dying kiss: "I here importune death awhile, until / Of many thousand kisses, the poor last / I lay upon thy lips" (4.15.21–22). She "dares not" for fear of being taken by Caesar (4.15.24–25). So Antony must be hauled and heaved up to the monument. Cleopatra's "Here's sport indeed!" (4.15.34) is sublimely playful. Antony's weightiness, although recalcitrant, is not lumpen. It erotically recalls her envy of the horse who bears his weight during their long absence: "O happy horse, to bear the weight of Antony!" (1.5.22). But the sport of lovemaking is "all gone into heaviness" (4.15.34), which is sorrow. The gravity of their love is shown side by side with its playfulness: Cleopatra's wit astonishingly even here, even now, especially here and now, accommodates both levity and gravity.

Cleopatra's Revelatory Claims

At the beginning of the play, Antony claims that Cleopatra will have to "find out" a new heaven and a new earth to reveal the extent of their love. The echo is from Revelation 21:1, a text that is resonantly drawn on in Cleopatra's stunning dream of Antony.[78] We have already been told by the disapproving Philo that Antony "oe'r flows the measure"; Antony says he has not "kept my square" to Octavia and vows that what is "to come / Shall all be done by th' rule" (2.3.5–7). Measures are surpassed, and rules are broken: Roman regulation cannot keep up with or get the measure of this love. This includes Antony for much of the play: Enobarbus knows more about him than he knows about himself; he knows, for example, that Antony will return to Cleopatra, that he cannot not return to her, a knowledge Antony belatedly and brokenly acknowledges after Actium. Antony has to find it out.

It is Cleopatra's last act that points us toward that new heaven and earth, one that even Caesar, not being able to contain it, has to acknowledge at the last. Cleopatra's last act is a triumphant claim upon us—a claim that Antony is her husband, the word deferred and uttered for the first time now. We are asked to answer to her claim that her "courage" alone can "prove" her title. Her claims on us in this last act can be understood as aesthetic in just the ways Kant revealed.

Cleopatra's famous conversation with Dolabella prepares us for her audacious, revelatory claim that Antony is her husband. When Cleopatra meets Dolabella, she responds to his confidant address—"Most noble empress, you have heard of me?" (5.2.70)—with a fascinating rebuttal. "No matter, sir," she says, "what I have heard or known" (5.2.71). Who he is and what she knows about him are by the by—except for this one thing she has heard. It is the only thing that matters. She has heard that he laughs at the words of boys and women when they tell their dreams. That is a "trick" of his (5.2.44). To be able to tell anyone anything, they have to credit you, to believe what you say. She wants to be sure he will believe what she says and not dismiss her as he is wont to do with the dreams of women and boys. Dolabella is confused. This is not his world. But Cleopatra wants to tell her dream, her vision of Antony. Despite his threefold attempt at interruption, she does tell her dream. It is the dream of a woman who sees her lover as lighting up her world, even the heavens themselves, and showing the brightness—and the littleness—of "the little O," the earth (5.2.79). The O is the perfect circle of the earth, an O of wonder and perfection resonating in the round sound of her voice (for O is a figure of speech associated with her, too). O, a great, open, and mysterious sound that is also the shape of the very stage on which they stand. It is the wooden O, the O of imaginary puissance, limited only by our imaginations. Cleopatra's dream is a vision of Antony's grandeur and his resonance with the celestial patterns of the world. It is also a paean to a fecundity that depends on death, on reaping to harvest, so it is also implicit with death but with a death that is seasonal and life-giving, like the old Nile itself. It is a dream of Antony's pleasure, his delights that transcended the world yet were of it. All this is evident in the telling of her dream of a man whose legs bestrid the ocean and whose reared arm crested the world. After the recital of her wondrous dream, she invites Dolabella to this *possibility*: "Think you there was or might be such a man / As this I dreamt of?" (5.2.92-93). His "gentle madam" can hardly soften the blow of an abrupt negation: "No" (5.2.93).

Her emphatic response—that he lies up to the hearing of the gods—answers to the paltriness of his world, a world that cannot accommodate the dreams of women, and thus shrinks to the size of a diminished imagination. We might say, to reintroduce the Kantian terminology, that Dolabella's "No" is based on his determinant judgment. He cannot see Antony as a man who bestrid the ocean or whose bounty would only grow and not be diminished by reaping, that is, by those who drew on it. There is no such man, nor could there be in his world—and that is this world. The historical Antony was not that man (and we are in a history play!). He cannot even admit this as a possibility offered in a dream: "Think you there was or *might* be such a man / As this I dreamt of?" (5.2.91-92). That is, like Antigonus in *The Winter's Tale*, he thinks dreams are toys or superstitions and are not to be credited. Cleopatra, as in reflective judgment, is responding to something that is not antecedently defined by a concept. She is grasping after a vocabulary answerable to her response to Antony, to her sense of what is beauteous in him. This is why beauty must be felt for Kant, and why it feels like grace. Cleopatra's dream, and her expression of it, is keeping faith with her response and a means of seeking its realization. (For Kant, a formal condition of beauty is our response to it.)

Dolabella does eventually respond to her claim on him—with something akin to devotion. He talks of Cleopatra's command, "which my love makes religion to obey" (5.2.198), when he tells Cleopatra what she needs to understand: the nature of Caesar's plans for her. Dolabella, despite his "Gentle madam, no!," has experienced her claim as imperatival. Cleopatra's understanding of her place in Rome's eternal theater now inform her anti-Stoic, epiphanic countertheater. Caesar and Cleopatra, as one critic has suggested, are rival triumphal claimants: Cleopatra is to be the "scutcheon" and sign of Caesar's conquest (5.2.135). Her final ceremony of leave-taking, of marriage, of apotheosis is her triumph, outwitting Caesar. It is Shakespeare's audacious counterweight to the victory at Actium celebrated by Vergil and Horace, revealing the blindness of Augustan poetics, all that these men failed to find out about Cleopatra.

Cleopatra is thus a catalyst for an expansion of the realm of morality away from an act of moralized judgment, inviting a vastly enlarged moral imagination. Her last act, with its immortal longings and sensuous haste, its fidelity to the best Antony of her capacious projection, realizes Antony's hyperbolic gestures borrowed from Revelation and makes them good. Cleopatra lays claim to a love of life in its entirety and contrariety, its infinite variety, the sensual and the soulful, the earthbound and the celestial, the dung and the air, as if fecundity, generativity, and creativity emerge from a love of the world, a "yes" to the Roman "no."

I discovered my notes on *Antony and Cleopatra* from the older Arden Shakespeare, 2nd ser., which I studied when I was seventeen years old for my "Advanced Level" English exams. My annotations are meticulous, extensive, touchingly neat, and careful. Despite the studious care of my notes, and my desire to be able to parse every word in the play, I remember having a strong feeling of antipathy for Cleopatra. I needed a well-defended Roman heart in those days. It was not that I admired imperial ambition, but I did seek order. I did need peace, and Cleopatra was not supplying it. I do not think any seventeen-year-old finds old love appealing, especially when it is so flamboyant, so shamelessly erotic. The desires on display embarrassed and dismayed me, and I suppose I might have thought the sublimity of Shakespeare's most poetic play was an excellent cover, undeniably sublime, but a hyperarticulate way of pulling the wool over my not-to-be-fooled eyes.

My response to the play now is more charitable, more open-hearted. I have felt the greater weight and power of empires, and the particular ways they seek to rule our imaginations and bodies. I know, too, that human love is both sublime and ridiculous. I also see that the play incorporates and utterly resituates, in fact exposes, moral purism. It so minutely and innovatively charts the intricate intimacies and transformation of a *mutual* relation, and I take this to be an unprecedented achievement. It revises and explodes the history of the victors even while knowing the measure of their victories. In the freedom and splendor of the imagination, it transcends their worldly empires and shows them to be paltry indeed.

Notes

Preface

1. Rose-Lynn Fisher, *The Topography of Tears* (New York: Bellevue Literary Press, 2017).

Introduction

1. Interview with Cameron Crowe, "Joni Mitchell: 'I'm a fool for love: I make the same mistake over and over,'" *The Guardian*, October 27, 2020, https://www.theguardian.com/music/2020/oct/27/joni-mitchell-interview-archives-early-years-cameron-crowe.
2. The idea of what counts as love is to be distinguished from a Kantian determinative judgment in which what counts as an instance of a concept falls under a self-standing idea or rule. (I pursue this idea further in chapter 6 on *Antony and Cleopatra*.) In that case, I would *already know* what love is and simply need to determine whether this is an instance of it. Instead, our concepts derive from the very fabric of our lives and are fundamentally exposed to experience.
3. Ludwig Wittgenstein, *Culture and Value*, ed. G. H. Von Wright, trans. Peter Winch (Chicago: University of Chicago Press, 1980), 16E.
4. Stanley Cavell, *The Claim of Reason: Wittgenstein, Skepticism, Morality and Tragedy*, 2nd ed. (Oxford: Oxford University Press, 1999), 125, henceforth *CR*. In philosophizing, says Cavell, "I have to bring my own language and life into imagination. What I require is a convening of my culture's criteria, in order to confront them with my words and life as I pursue them and as I may imagine them; and at the same time to confront my words and life as I pursue them with the life my culture's words imagine for me: to confront the culture with itself, along the lines in which it meets in me."
5. Cora Diamond, "Losing Your Concepts," *Ethics* 98, no. 2 (1988): 255–77. Diamond gives examples of conceptual loss as it is differently articulated in the work of Alasdair MacIntyre, John Berger, and Karl Marx, for example, exploring the different conceptual loss resulting from the loss of traditions, or from the inarticulacy of cultural deprivation, or from a present use of words that are inadequate to a human nature from which we are alienated. Her main focus is a general loss of concepts, the loss of a moral and political vocabulary as it is explored in Iris Murdoch's important essays, and the consequent inarticulacy and impoverishment of the language of our conceptual life. Thus, her essay attends to the connection with the way certain philosophical views of language

blind us to our conceptual life. She explores the reasons why "the human good of articulateness, of having the words one needs, is overlooked by philosophers in the analytic tradition" (270). An exploration of living with concepts can be found in Andrew Brandel and Marco Motta, eds., *Living with Concepts: Anthropology in the Grip of Reality* (New York: Fordham University Press, 2021).

6. See Cora Diamond, "Murdoch the Explorer," *Philosophical Topics* 38, no. 1 (Spring 2010): 74n13. Diamond sees one of Iris Murdoch's most important contributions in the reevaluation of midcentury moral philosophy to be the claim that "differences of moral vision and differences of concept are closely tied." In chapter 6 on *Antony and Cleopatra*, I explore different ways of thinking about concepts in relation to Kant's understanding of determinant and reflective judgment.

7. Shakespeare's chronology of plays is notoriously difficult, and my book does not depend on any particular chronological order. Given that both *All's Well That Ends Well* and *Pericles* were composed during the period from 1605 to 1608, no argument can be made for an unbroken focus on tragedy during this time. The priority of *Timon* or *Lear* is still in dispute, and so is the question of whether Shakespeare's last tragedy is *Coriolanus* or *Antony and Cleopatra*. (I bracket the folio attribution of *Cymbeline* for now.) My argument examines the plays under focus as a group not because of a set of shared set of formal features or marks, but rather because they constitute a study of their shared conditions of inheritance, here, an idea of the catastrophic loss of a fundamental set of binding concepts. For this idea of genre, see Stanley Cavell, *Pursuits of Happiness: The Hollywood Comedy of Remarriage* (Cambridge, MA: Harvard University Press, 1981), 28. For a study of tragedy as a set of responses to the idea of social bonds as "fully dissolvable," see Paul Kottman's *Tragic Conditions in Shakespeare: Disinheriting the Globe* (Baltimore, MD: Johns Hopkins University Press, 2009), 4; and his later essay, Paul Kottman, "What Is Shakespearean Tragedy?," in *The Oxford Handbook of Shakespearean Tragedy*, ed. Michael Neill and David. Schalkwyck (Oxford: Oxford University Press, 2016), 3–18. The idea from J. L. Austin that "our word is our bond" leads us to a sense of the depth as well as the fragility of bonds and I return to this question explicitly in the chapter on *Timon of Athens*. For a discussion of "our word is our bond," see J. L. Austin, "Performative Utterances," in *Philosophical Papers* (Oxford, England: Clarendon Press, 1961), 236. Wittgenstein's work deepens our concepts of convention: he reveals that dominant pictures of language tend to miss (while also depending on) the bonds and necessities involved in acts of speech, in the normative reach of words.

8. Ludwig Wittgenstein, *Philosophical Investigations: German Text with an English Translation*, 4th ed., ed. G. E. M. Anscombe, P. M. S. Hacker, and Joachim Schulte (Chichester: Wiley-Blackwell, 2009), henceforth *PI* with the relevant number.

Wittgenstein very often uses ideas of weaving and tapestry to get at the dense interconnections of forms of life and the concepts associated with them. "This complicated form of life" is from fragment i.1; "tapestry" can be found, for example, at fragment i.2. "Criss-cross" and "weave" is a characteristic idiom (e.g., preface, 3, and elsewhere). Also "A main cause of philosophical diseases—a one-sided diet; one nourishes one's thinking with only one kind of example" (*PI*, ¶593).

9. *Macbeth*, ed. Sandra Clark and Pamela Mason, Arden Shakespeare, 3rd ser. (London: Bloomsbury, 2015), 4.3.225–226. All citations from Shakespeare

are from the Arden Shakespeare, Third Series, cited in the first note reference where the edition is first used, by act, scene and line number.

10. *King Lear*, ed. R. A. Foakes, Arden Shakespeare, 3rd ser. (Walton-on-Thames: Thomas Nelson, 1997), 2.2.438.

11. Iris Murdoch, *The Sovereignty of Good* (London: Routledge, 1970), especially the final essay, "The Sovereignty of Good Over Other Concepts." I return to Murdoch's work in chapter 2 on *King Lear*.

12. Raimond Gaita's analysis of remorse can be found in his brilliant chapter, Raimond Gaita, "Remorse and Its Lessons," in *Good and Evil: An Absolute Conception* (London and New York: Routledge, 2004), 43–63.

13. I derive the phrase "excluded and excluding self" from Richard Fleming, *First Word Philosophy: Wittgenstein-Austin-Cavell, Writings on Ordinary Language Philosophy* (Lewisburg, PA: Bucknell University Press, 2004). Fleming is highly alert to the ethical implications of ordinary language philosophy. See Richard Fleming, "Afterword: Demonstrations in Ordinary Ethics," in *First Word Philosophy*, 130–38: "Ordinary ethics . . . is a demonstration of where we answerably stand in the constitutive order of word and world" (130).

14. *Antony and Cleopatra*, ed. John Wilders, Arden Shakespeare, Third Series, (London: Bloomsbury, 1995), 5.2.287.

15. *Begriffsgeschichte* is alive and well in the works of Falko Schmeider; Quentin Skinner's work in intellectual history has been influential in exploring the history of concepts; Thomas Pfau's magisterial book *Minding the Modern Human Agency: Intellectual Traditions, and Responsible Knowledge* (Notre Dame, IN: University of Notre Dame Press, 2015) explores "conceptual amnesia" and excavates the language of responsible agency and its attrition; Jonathan Lear movingly explores the cultural collapse of the Crow Nation in his work *Radical Hope: Ethics in the Face of Cultural Devastation* (Cambridge, MA: Harvard University Press, 2008) and Cora Diamond's insights are visible in the latter two works.

16. G. K. Hunter, "Shakespeare's Last Tragic Heroes," in *Dramatic Identities and Cultural Traditions: Studies in Shakespeare and His Contemporaries—Critical Essays* (New York: Barnes and Noble, 1978), 251.

17. The *Oxford English Dictionary* definition of exile is "banishment to a foreign country" or the person who is so exiled: https://www.oed.com/search/dictionary/?scope=Entries&q=exile. This might define exiles such as Bolingbroke, exiled from England under Richard's orders in *Richard II*, or Kent and Cordelia banished in *King Lear*.

18. Cavell, *CR*, 45.

19. Stanley Cavell, *In Quest of the Ordinary: Lines of Skepticism and Romanticism* (Chicago: University of Chicago Press, 1988), 40.

20. Stanley Cavell, *A Pitch of Philosophy: Autobiographical Exercises* (Cambridge, MA: Harvard University Press, 1994), 118.

21. Raimond Gaita and other philosophers working in the reconceptualization of ethics after Wittgenstein see the seriousness of moral thinking and the attempt at lucidity to be a matter of not losing touch with reality. See Raimond Gaita, introduction to *Ethical Inquiries After Wittgenstein*, Nordic Wittgenstein Studies, ed. Salla Aldrin Salskov, Ondrej Beran, and Nora Hamalainen (Cham: Springer, 2022), 16–17. The ethical possibilities opened up by

Wittgenstein are pursued in many collections; see in addition, *Cora Diamond on Ethics*, ed. Maria Balaska (Cham: Palgrave Macmillan, 2021); *Wittgenstein's Moral Thought*, ed. Reshef Agam-Segal and Edmund Dain (London: Routledge, 2019); *Morality in a Realistic Spirit: Essays for Cora Diamond*, ed. Andrew Gleeson and Craig Taylor (London: Routledge, 2021); and *Ethics After Wittgenstein: Contemplation and Critique*, ed. Richard Amesbury and Hartmut Von Sass (London: Bloomsbury, 2021).

22. Anthony Cascardi says that Shakespeare "explores the full range of the commitments that language entails" and that Shakespeare's power "rests on his ability to envision characters who live out the fate of their words relentlessly, without compromise or escape, or who suffer disastrously from their failure to do so." Anthony Cascardi, "Disowning Knowledge: Cavell and Shakespeare," in *Stanley Cavell*, ed. Richard Eldridge (Cambridge: Cambridge University Press, 2003), 190.

23. Stanley Cavell, *Little Did I Know: Excerpts from Memory* (Stanford, CA: Stanford University Press, 2010), 322: "I can no more take back the word I have given you and you have acted on that I can take back my touch. Each has entered our history." On the boundlessness, unpredictability, and irreversible nature of human action, see Hannah Arendt, *The Human Condition*, 2nd ed. (Chicago: University of Chicago Press, 1998), 190–92, 233–36.

24. *King Lear*, 2.2.73; "intrince" is a Shakespeare coinage.

25. Cavell extends his work in *CR* in *This New Yet Unapproachable America: Lectures After Emerson After Wittgenstein* (Albuquerque, NM: Living Batch, 1989), 36, to suggest that bringing words home is not at all a question of locating their context or conventions, or of finding out what words mean independent of our usage of them. Cavell would thus find the context-hunting of contemporary scholarship necessary but not sufficient to get at what individual speakers are actually saying. It is a question of recalling our criteria—what we count as something on any particular occasion. Recalling what we call and what I call something is a quest of the "ordinary," an attempt to find my voice in relation to my culture's criteria. "Exile," says Cavell, "is under investigation in 'A philosophical problem has the form: 'I don't know my way about'", citing Wittgenstein, *PI* ¶ 123, 36. A grammatical investigation and its eliciting of our criteria is "precisely the philosophical path to this end or disappearance of a philosophical problem" (36).

26. *King Lear*, 1.4.221.

27. For an admirably clear exposition of the ordinary see Fleming, *First Word Philosophy*.

28. Ludwig Wittgenstein, *Culture and Value*, 86E Wittgenstein's remarks on Shakespeare are scrupulously contextualized by Joachim Schulte, "Did Wittgenstein Write on Shakespeare?," *Nordic Wittgenstein Review* 2 (2013): 7–32. *Culture and Value* collects together remarks from Wittgenstein's notebooks posthumously selected by Georg Henrik von Wright. The seven remarks about Shakespeare, dating from 1939 to 1950 were not intended for publication. William Day points out that one can read everything Wittgenstein said about Shakespeare in about five minutes. Day's article speculates interestingly about Wittgenstein's difficulty in hearing "the sound of the raw motives to

skepticism" in Shakespeare's work. See William Day, "To Not Understand, But Not Misunderstand Wittgenstein on Shakespeare," in *Wittgenstein Reading*, ed. Sascha Brue, Wolfgang Huemer, and Daniel Steuer (Berlin: De Gruyter, 2013), 39-49.

29. Ludwig Wittgenstein, *Remarks on the Philosophy of Psychology*, vol 1., ed. G. E. M. Anscombe and G. H. von Wright, trans. G. E. M. Anscombe (Oxford: Basil Blackwell, 1980).

30. Wittgenstein, *Culture and Value*, 84E.

31. Ludwig Wittgenstein, *Lecture on Ethics*, ed. Ermelinda Di Lascio, D. K. Levy, and Edoardo Zamuner (Oxford: Wiley Blackwell, 2014).

32. This vision of language is sometimes called the vision of "ordinary language philosophy." I sometimes use this terminology. The terminology, however, is unsatisfactory and some of my intellectual interlocutors would not recognize themselves under that name. For useful discussion see Sandra Laugier, *Why We Need Ordinary Language Philosophy*, trans. Daniela Ginsburg (Chicago: University of Chicago Press, 2013); Avner Baz, *When Words Are Called For: A Defense of Ordinary Language Philosophy* (Cambridge, MA: Harvard University Press, 2012); and Toril Moi, *Revolution of the Ordinary: Literary Studies after Wittgenstein, Austin, and Cavell* (Chicago: University of Chicago Press, 2017). Moi says she understands ordinary language philosophy as "the philosophical tradition after Ludwig Wittgenstein, J. L. Austin, as continued and extended by Stanley Cavell, specifically through his reading of *Philosophical Investigations*" (1). I will follow her understanding here.

33. Raimond Gaita, *A Common Humanity: Thinking About Love, and Truth and Justice* (New York: Routledge, 1998), xv. See Hilary Putnam, *The Collapse of the Fact/Value Dichotomy and Other Essays* (Cambridge: Harvard University Press, 2002) for an examination of the influential Humean idea that an "ought" cannot be derived from an "is."

34. See Cora Diamond, "We Are Perpetually Moralists: Iris Murdoch, Fact, and Value," in *Iris Murdoch and the Search for Human Goodness*, ed. Maria Antonaccio and William Schweiker (Chicago: University of Chicago Press, 1996), 79-109.

35. Stanley Cavell, *Conditions Handsome and Unhandsome: The Constitution of Emersonian Perfectionism*, (Chicago: University of Chicago Press, 1990), xxix, In his preface to the Italian edition of *The Claim of Reason*, Cavell calls *Conditions Handsome and Unhandsome* a continuation of the neglected part 3 of the CR (omitted from the Italian edition); see *Here and There: Sites of Philosophy* ed. Nancy Bauer, Alice Crary, and Sandra Laugier (Cambridge, MA: Harvard University Press, 2022), 215.

36. Cavell, *Conditions Handsome and Unhandsome*, xxx.

37. The term is Ingeborg Lofgren's coinage in her dissertation "Interpretative Skepticism: Stanley Cavell, New Criticism, and Literary Interpretation" (PhD diss., Uppsala University, 2015). Rita Felski has also and influentially described the limits of a certain attitude taken up in "critique," still the dominant interpretative mode in literary studies in Rita Felski, *The Limits of Critique* (Chicago: University of Chicago Press, 2015).

38. This is the burden of chapter 1 of *CR*, "Criteria and Judgment": "In no case in which (Wittgenstein) appeals to the application of criteria is there a

separate stage at which one might, explicitly or implicitly, appeal to the application of standards" (13).

39. Lofgren, "Interpretative Skepticism," 318, and taking her cue from Wittgenstein's "rough ground" (*PI*, ¶107): In a theoretical idiom we can overlook what our language use actually yields and so we get onto slippery ice "where there is no friction, and so, in a certain sense, the conditions are ideal; but also, just because of that, we are unable to walk. Back to the rough ground!"

40. Stanley Cavell, "The Availability of Wittgenstein's Later Philosophy," in *Must We Mean What We Say?* (Cambridge: Cambridge University Press, second edition, 2002): "Criticism is always an affront, and its only justification lies in usefulness, in making its object available to just response," 46.

41. See especially Toril Moi, "'They Practice Their Trade in Different Worlds': Concepts in Poststructuralism and Ordinary Language Philosophy," *New Literary History* 40, no. 4 (2009): 801–24.

42. Joint Stock began in 1974 and disbanded in 1989. The group is associated with the playwrights David Hare and Caryll Churchill. The groups archives are held in the Special Collections at the University of California at Davis. The influence of this idea is found in publications such as Marina Caldarone and Maggie Lloyd-Williams, *Actions: The Actor's Thesaurus* (London: Drama, 2004).

43. Part 3 of *CR* is almost a book within a book; it is a brilliant analysis of the rationality of morality and a piercing criticism of the available schools of moral philosophy at the time of writing. The fruits of this work are developed in Cavell's later conception of "moral perfectionism."

44. *Hamlet*, ed. Anne Thompson and Neil Taylor, Arden Shakespeare, 3rd ser. (London: Thomson, 2006).

45. Patchen Markell says that the politics of recognition as it has been elucidated by Charles Taylor's influential work is too dependent on a sovereign understanding of agency. See Patchen Markell, *Bound by Recognition* (Princeton, NJ: Princeton University Press, 2003).

1. Coming to Grief in *Hamlet*

1. The *Oxford English Dictionary* gives the first two uses (obsolete) as transitive: (1a) to press heavily upon, as a weight; to burden, and (2) Of persons to harass, gall with hostile action, to hurt, to harm, and so on. https://www.oed.com/dictionary/grieve_v?tab=meaning_and_use#2469167

2. *The Winter's Tale*, ed. John Pitcher, Arden Shakespeare, 3rd. ser. (London: Bloomsbury, 2010), 2.1.98–100.

3. *I Henry IV*, ed. David Scott Kastan Arden Shakespeare, 3rd ser. (London: Bloomsbury, 2002), 4.3.41–42.

4. For a humanistic philosophy of grief, see James Carter, "The Passionate Life: On Grief and Human Experience," in *Moral Powers, Fragile Beliefs: Essays in Moral and Religious Philosophy*, ed. Joseph Carlisle, James C. Carter, and Daniel Whistler (New York: Continuum, 2011). Grief is revelatory: "It reveals to the fullest extent the value of those whom we have lost," 114.

5. *Macbeth*, ed. Sandra Clark and Pamela Mason, Arden Shakespeare, 3rd ser. (London: Bloomsbury, 2015), 4.3.231-32. "Let grief / Convert to anger; blunt not the heart, enrage it." See chapter 4 for further details on this scene.

6. "I cannot but remember such things were / That were most precious to me" (4.3.224-25).

7. *Love's Labour's Lost*, ed. H.R. Woudhuysen, Arden Shakespeare, 3rd ser. (London: Bloomsbury, 2015), 5.2.739.

8. Hermione's "honourable" grief is from *The Winter's Tale* (1.2.111). Constance in *King John* eds. Jesse M. Lander and J. M. Tobin, Arden Shakespeare, 3rd ser. (London: Bloomsbury, 2018) laments that "grief fills the room up of my absent child" (3.4.93). "Patch grief with proverbs" is from Leonato in *Much Ado About Nothing* ed. Claire McEachern, Arden Shakespeare, 3rd ser. (London: Bloomsbury, 2007), (5.1.17). "Grief would have tears and sorrow bids me speak" is the Countess's line in *All's Well That Ends Well* ed. Suzanne Gossett and Helen Wilcox, Arden Shakespeare, 3rd ser. (London: Bloomsbury, 2019), (3.4.42). Cesario's imaginary sister who is herself "sat like Patience on a monument / Smiling at grief" in *Twelfth Night* ed. Keir Elam, Arden Shakespeare, 3rd ser. (London: 2008), (2.4.114-115). Rosalind says to Celia, "And do not seek to take your change upon you, / To bear your griefs yourself and leave me out" in *As You Like It* ed. Juliet Dusinberre, Arden Shakespeare, 3rd ser, (London: Bloomsbury, 2009), (1.3.98-99). Toward the conclusion to confusion in *The Comedy of Errors* ed. Kent Cartwright, Arden Shakespeare, 3rd ser. (London: Bloomsbury, 2017), the abbess sublimely proclaims a festive end: "Go to a gossips' feast, and go with me; / After so long grief, such nativity!" (5.1.408).

9. My citations from *Hamlet* derive from the Arden Shakespeare, 3rd ser., of the second quarto of the play, with references, where appropriate and relevant to the folio text also in Arden Shakespeare, 3rd ser. See *Hamlet*, ed. Ann Thompson and Neil Taylor (London: Thomson, 2006) and *Hamlet: The Texts of 1603 and 1623*, ed. Ann Thompson and Neil Taylor (London: Thomson, 2006). The first folio text (F) lacks about 230 of the second quarto's lines; the second quarto (Q2) lacks about 70 of F's lines. The differences are discussed in the Arden Shakespeare, 3rd ser., second quarto, 82, and by Philip Edwards in his thoughtful edition of *Hamlet* for the New Cambridge Shakespeare (Cambridge: Cambridge University Press, 1985), 8-32; and Stanley Wells and Gary Taylor, *William Shakespeare: A Textual Companion* (New York: W. W. Norton, 1997), 396-402. Wells and Taylor argue that both Q2 and F derive from Shakespeare's foul papers and that *Hamlet* comes closest to *King Lear* in "the scale and complexity of the textual variation apparently resulting from authorial revision" (401).

10. Richard Hooker, *Of the Laws of Ecclesiastical Polity*, ed. W. Speed Hill, Folger Library Edition of *The Works of Richard Hooker*, vol. 5 (Cambridge, MA: Harvard University Press, 1977), 409. Hooker goes on to add "last of all to testifie the care which the church hath to comfort the living, and the hope which wee all have concerning the resurrection of the dead."

11. See Raimond Gaita, "Gypsy Is Old Now," in *The Philosopher's Dog* (New York: Routledge, 2002), 82-83: "The necessity to acknowledge both our commonness and also our radical individuality, and the fact that we cannot

acknowledge one without the other, creates an irresolvable tension between inconsolable aloneness and the consolation to be found in community."

12. I analyze this passage in *Shakespeare and the Grammar of Forgiveness* (Ithaca, NY: Cornell University Press, 2011), 16–20. See also David Schalkwyk, "'Unpacking the Heart': Why It Is Impossible to Say 'I Love You' in Hamlet's Elsinore," in *Shakespeare's "Hamlet": Philosophical Perspectives* (Oxford: Oxford University Press, 2018).

13. The literature charting the transformed language of the post-Reformation death ritual is by now extensive. See, for example, Clive Burgess, "'A Fond Thing Vainly Invented': An Essay on Purgatory and Pious Motive in Later Medieval England," in *Parish, Church and People: Studies in Lay Religion*, ed. S. J. Wright (London: Hutchinson, 1988); David Cressy, *Birth, Marriage, and Death: Ritual, Religion and the Life-Cycle in Tudor and Stuart England* (Oxford University Press, 1997); Peter Marshall, *Beliefs and the Dead in Reformation England* (Oxford: Oxford University Press, 2002); Thomas Laqueur, *The Work of the Dead: A Cultural History of Mortal Remains* (Princeton, NJ: Princeton University Press, 2015).

For penetrating comments about the corpse being the object rather than the subject of address in the second prayerbook of Edward VI, see Eamon Duffy's monumental *The Stripping of the Altars*, 2nd ed. (New Haven, CT: Yale University Press, 2005).

14. "The Ordre for the Buriall of the Dead," in *The Book of Common Prayer: The Texts of 1549, 1559, and 1662*, ed. Brian Cummings (Oxford: Oxford University Press, 2011), 83.

15. In the prayerbooks of 1552 and 1559 of Edward VI and Elizabeth I, the body/soul of the departed has become a third person, talked about, rather than directly addressed, Cummings, *Book of Common Prayer*, 172.

16. Stephen Greenblatt, *Hamlet in Purgatory* (Princeton, NJ: Princeton University Press, 2002); Michael Neill, *Issues of Death: Mortality and Identity in English Tragedy* (Oxford: Clarendon Press, 1999); Susan Zimmerman, *The Early Modern Corpse and Shakespeare's Theater* (Edinburgh: Edinburgh University Press, 2005); Anthony B. Dawson, "The Arithmetic of Memory: Shakespeare's Theater and the National Past," *Shakespeare Survey* 52 (1999): 54–67; Steven Mullaney, *The Reformation of Emotion in the Age of Shakespeare* (Chicago: University of Chicago Press, 2015).

17. This argument is developed in *Phenomenology of Spirit*, trans. A. V. Miller (Oxford: Clarendon Press, 1977), sect. 452.

18. The phrase "exemplary form of social action" is found and developed in J. M. Bernstein, *Torture and Dignity: An Essay on Moral Injury* (Chicago: University of Chicago Press, 2015), 297. "To not give to the body in question the increment of cultural form would make it anomalous: appearing human, but nonetheless not human-just stuff and hence disgusting" (298).

19. The distinction between rites and rights is central in Cora Diamond's important elucidation of Simone Weil's work. See for example, Cora Diamond, "Injustice and Animals," in *Slow Cures and Bad Philosophers: Essays on Wittgenstein, Medicine, and Bioethics*, ed. Carl Elliott (Durham, NC: Duke University Press,

2011), 118–48; Cora Diamond, "The Importance of Being Human," *Royal Institute of Philosophy Supplement* 29 (1991): 35–62.

20. Diamond, "Importance of Being Human," 51. Here, says Diamond, "we can see the depth of the hatred expressing itself in the *denial* of what the soldiers knew human beings extend to other human beings in the face of what death is in our lives."

21. From Stanley Cavell, *In Quest of the Ordinary: Lines of Skepticism and Romanticism* (Chicago: University of Chicago Press, 1994), 75.

22. Cavell, *In Quest of the Ordinary*, 75.

23. Roberto Calasso, *The Unnameable Present* (New York: Farrar, Straus, and Giroux, 2019).

24. Aristotle, *Nicomachean Ethics*, trans. and ed. C. D. C. Reeve (Indianapolis: Hackett, 2024), 4.5.69 (1126b).

25. Saint Thomas Aquinas, *Commentary on Aristotle's "Nicomachean Ethics,"* trans. C. I. Litzinger O.P. (Notre Dame, IN: Dumb Ox, 1964), 257, sect. 804.

26. Aquinas, *Commentary*, 257, sect. 804.

27. Martha Nussbaum, *Anger and Forgiveness: Resentment, Generosity, Justice* (Oxford: Oxford University Press, 2016), 17, 47.

28. "Anger is conceptually linked to helplessness." Nussbaum, *Anger and Forgiveness*, 45.

29. Reuben A. Brower, *Hero and Saint: Shakespeare and the Graeco-Roman Heroic Tradition* (Oxford: Oxford University Press, 1971), 93.

30. Vergil, *Eclogues, Georgics, Aeneid I-VI*, Loeb Classical Library, trans. H. Rushton Fairclough, rev. G. P. Goold (Cambridge, MA: Harvard University Press, 1999), lines 459, 462.

31. *Aeneid*, trans. Robert Fagles (Harmondsworth: Penguin, 2008).

32. In *The Mortal Hero: An Introduction to Homer's "Iliad"* (Berkeley: University of California Press, 1984), Seth L. Schein points out that the violation of Hector's corpse, which offends even the gods, is an offense against the family and community who wish to mourn him: "He is violating the social need on the part of the living to bury the dead with formal, ritual propriety in order to humanize the fact of death." These themes are sounded too in Charles Segal, *The Theme of the Mutilation of the Corpse in the "Iliad,"* Mnemosyne Supplements, no. 17 (Leiden: Brill, 1971); and James M. Redfield, *Nature and Culture in the* Iliad: *The Tragedy of Hector* (Chicago: University of Chicago Press, 1975).

33. "Ter circum Iliacos raptaverat Hectora muros / enanimumque auro corpus vendebat Achilles" (*Aeneid*, 1.483-84). Fairclough translates: "Thrice had Achilles dragged Hector round the walls of Troy and was selling the lifeless body for gold." Vergil now depicts Aeneas responding with a deep groan and the corpse of Hector in the frieze appears to meet his gaze as Priam stretches out his weaponless hands. Leah Whittington comments on Vergil's recollection of Homer: "The ransoming of Hector's body, as Homer presents it, is exceptional and fragile." See Leah Whittington, *Renaissance Suppliants: Poetry, Antiquity, Reconciliation* (Oxford: Oxford University Press, 2016), 71.

34. *Aeneid*, 6.487.

35. *Aeneid*, 1.11. Fairclough frequently translates *ira* as resentment and renders this (rather disappointingly) as "Can heavenly spirits cherish resentment so dire?" Fagles translates the *Iliad*'s *mênis* as "rage."

36. Whittington remarks on the excising of Achilles's response to Priam's supplication from Aeneas emotional response to Priam's outstretched and weaponless hands in the frieze.

37. "The *Iliad*, or the Poem of Force" has been reprinted in Simone Weil and Rachel Bespaloff, *War and the "Iliad,"* trans. Mary McCarthy (New York: NYRB Classics, 2005). Weil's essay was originally published as "L'Iliade, ou, le poème de la force," trans. Mary McCarthy, in *Politics* (1945). I return to this fine essay in chapter 5.

38. *Iliad*, trans. Robert Fagles (Penguin Books, 1990), 24.570-71, 24.591, 24.594-95.

39. Weil and Bespaloff, *War and the "Iliad,"* 79.

40. "Iacet ingens litore truncus, / avulsumque umeris caput et sine nomine corpus" (*Aeneid*, 2.558).

41. *Aeneid*, 2.540-558.

42. *Aeneid*, 12.932-36.

43. Tony Tanner, *Prefaces to Shakespeare* (Cambridge, MA: Harvard University Press, 2010), 491.

44. *Iliad*, 22.309-10.

45. Redfield, *Nature and Culture in* The Iliad, 211.

46. Of course, Marlovian echoes from *Dido, Queen of Carthage* are present in the player's speech. This play works very closely with Vergil's *Aeneid*.

47. Thomas Kyd, *The Spanish Tragedy*, ed. Clara Calvo and Jesus Tronch (London: Bloomsbury, 2013), 4.4.113-14.

48. W. H. Auden, "The Shield of Achilles," in *W. H. Auden: Selected Poems* (New York: Vintage International, 1989), 198-201. The relevant stanza ends: "That girls are raped, that two boys knife a third / Were axioms to him who'd never heard / Of any world where promises were kept / Or one could weep because another wept." Auden writes this poem in 1952, brilliantly reprising Homer's *Iliad* in which Hephaestus forges a mighty shield for Achilles at the behest of his mother, Thetis.

49. Tanya Pollard, *Greek Tragic Women on Shakespearean Stages* (Oxford: Oxford University Press, 2017). 117. Hecuba appeared, of course, in George Chapman's English translation of Homer's *Iliad*, the first seven books of which were published in 1598. Pollard points out that, in 1599, the Admiral's Men staged a series of Trojan-themed plays (*Orestes Furies, Agamemnon*, and Henry Chettle and Thomas Dekker's *Troilus and Cressida*). Pollard's chapter "What's Hecuba to Him?" is an indispensable engagement with *Hamlet* in relation to the tradition of Greek tragedy. See also Louise Schleiner, "Latinized Greek Drama in Shakespeare's Writing of *Hamlet*," *Shakespeare Quarterly* 41, no. 1 (1991): 29-48.

50. Judith Mossman, *Wild Justice: A Study of Euripides Hecuba* (Oxford: Clarendon Press, 1995), 225, 221-23.

51. Philip Sidney, *A Defence of Poetry*, ed. J. A. Van Dorsten (Oxford: Oxford University Press, 1966), 66-67. *Hecuba* is well constructed and comes "to the principal point of that one action which they will represent."

52. Helene Foley, *Euripides: Hecuba* (London: Bloomsbury, 2015).

53. *The Rape of Lucrece*, 1.1448, 1.1458, *The Oxford Shakespeare: Complete Sonnets and Poems* ed. Colin Burrow (Oxford: Oxford University Press, 2002).

54. "Ferrite palmis pectora et planctus date / et justa Troiae facite." *Seneca: Hercules, Trojan Women, Phoenician Women, Medea, Phaedra*, ed. and trans. John Fitch (Cambridge, MA: Harvard University Press, 2002), l, 64–65. Ode 1 is a formal antiphonal lament for Troy, Priam, and Hector.

55. Thompson and Taylor, Arden Shakespeare, 3rd ser., 306.

56. Hecuba bites at the stones thrown by the Thracians and tries to speak but howls through her metamorphosed canine jaws (XIII.565-571). *Ovid: Metamorphosis Books IX-XV*, trans. Frank Justus Miller (Cambridge, MA: Harvard University Press, 1984).

57. Martha Nussbaum, *The Fragility of Goodness: Luck and Ethics in Greek Tragedy and Philosophy* (Cambridge, MA: Cambridge University Press, 1986), 410.

58. Nussbaum, *Fragility of Goodness*, 410. Hecuba wants to make the child killer suffer the same harm of child-killing that she herself has undergone. Her project is both mimetic and revelatory: *Xenia* is a façade: the old *nomos* cannot protect you.

59. Nussbaum, *Fragility and Goodness*, 413.

60. "Revenge attracts because it offers structure and plan without vulnerability." Nussbaum, *Fragility and Goodness*, 410. For an exploration of the dramaturgy of neoclassicism, see Bruce R. Smith, *Ancient Scripts and Modern Experience on the English Stage 1500–1700* (Princeton, NJ: Princeton University Press, 1988).

61. Hamlet's fantasy is a perfectly conventional reading. On tragedy's virtues, for example, see Sidney, *A Defence of Poetry*, 45: "Excellent Tragedy, that openeth the greatest wounds, and showeth forth the ulcers that are covered with tissue, that maketh kings to fear to be tyrants, and tyrants manifest their tyrannical humours."

62. *Hamlet*, 2.1.13. For an in-depth study of the Elizabethan surveillance state, see Curtis C. Breight, *Surveillance, Militarism and Drama in the Elizabethan Era* (New York: St. Martin's, 1996).

63. Rhodri Lewis indefatigably pursues metaphors of predation in *Hamlet* in *Hamlet and the Vision of Darkness* (Princeton, NJ: Princeton University Press, 2017).

64. Try out a thought experiment imagining a form of life in which no one believed anything anyone else said, in which as a matter of course, people routinely or invariably fooled or deceived others.

65. External world skepticism, knowing a table or a tomato is seen as the model for other mind skepticism, knowing people (who talk, converse, and in general have a say in the matter of being known).

66. The philosophical name for this is *skepticism*. For an indispensable redefinition of skepticism, see Stanley Cavell, *The Claim of Reason: Wittgenstein, Skepticism, Morality and Tragedy*, 2nd ed. (Oxford: Oxford University Press, 1999).

67. Richard Moran, *The Exchange of Words: Speech, Testimony, and Intersubjectivity* (Oxford: Oxford University Press, 2018), 70. He suggests that refusing to acknowledge any epistemic stance toward the speaker's words other than as evidence means that the speaker and audience must always be in disharmony

with each other, for in the contexts of telling, promising, and apologizing the speaker is not *presenting* her utterance as evidence," 69.

68. Moran, *Exchange of Words*, 74.

69. J. M. Bernstein, *Torture and Dignity: An Essay on Moral Injury* (Chicago: University of Chicago Press, 2015), 229. I return to the question of trust in chapter 3.

70. Thomas Hobbes, *Leviathan*, ed. Richard E. Flathman and David Johnston (London: W. W. Norton, 1997), chap. 14, 76.

71. Peter Winch, "How Is Political Authority Possible?," *Philosophical Investigations* 25, no. 1 (2002): 29.

72. Olli Lagerspetz, *Trust, Ethics, and Human Reason* (London: Bloomsbury, 2015), 119.

73. That is to say they cannot trust that others are *in* their expressions, that their bodies and words express them, but they must search for a more certain method that sees through, under, or around human expression.

74. Steven G. Affeldt, "Captivating Pictures and Liberating Language: Freedom as the Achievement of Speech in Wittgenstein's *Philosophical Investigations*," *Philosophical Topics* 27, no. 2 (1999): 273.

75. In its profound exploration of the loss of the ability to voice loss in mourning, *Hamlet* might be read as an investigation of the loss of loss. The play inaugurates a dramaturgy enacted in the late tragedies that are the subject of this book.

76. Wittgenstein, *Philosophical Investigations*, ¶363.

77. Telling, suggests Affeldt, involves telling as tallying, counting something as one thing rather than another—bringing objects and experience under concepts and also as recounting or accounting. Thus, telling is telling of "the necessities involved in a wider range of language games." Affeldt, "Captivating Pictures," 273.

78. Affeldt, "Captivating Pictures," 274.

79. I have addressed this issue at greater length in my essay "*Hamlet's* Ethics," in *Shakespeare's Hamlet: Philosophical Perspectives*, ed. Tzachi Zamir (Oxford: Oxford University Press, 2018), 222–46.

80. See Peter Mercer's interesting comments about the kinship of revenge tragedy and satire, in *Hamlet and the Acting of Revenge* (Iowa City: University of Iowa Press, 1987), 91. The satirist and the revenger are isolated and alone, and they inhabit a world dispossessed by vice; they are both truth seekers wishing to tear the mask of the hypocrisy that hides the moral corruption with which they are obsessed. Mercer points out that the satirist looks for the reform and repentance of his audience; the revenger seeks the victim's suffering and death. Is Hamlet shocked out of his mood as satirist by the intimate connection of Yorick with his own history?

81. Tzachi Zamir has noted that "tragedy is the process whereby values and their meanings are crystallized through loss." Tzachi Zamir, "Ethics and Shakespearean Tragedy," in *The Oxford Handbook of Shakespearean Tragedy*, ed. Michael Neill and David Schalkwyk (Oxford: Oxford University Press, 2016), 78. I would add that such losses—to work in a tragic idiom—can never be general; it is only through the most particular realizations of loss that mourning

can bring into play forms of tragic recognition. That *Hamlet* is a play about mourning has been noted by many, whether registered through the loss of a concept of purgatory or through individual practices of mourning.

82. David Farr's RSC production at Stratford on Avon in 2013 with Jonathan Slinger as Hamlet and Pippa Nixon as Ophelia.

83. Charles Taylor, "Iris Murdoch and Moral Philosophy," in *Iris Murdoch and the Search for Human Goodness*, ed. Maria Antonaccio and William Schweiker (Chicago: University of Chicago Press, 1996), 5.

84. F omits the entire soliloquy: "How all occasions..."

85. See Lionel Abel, "Metatheatre," in *Tragedy and Metatheatre: Essays on Dramatic Form*, ed. Martin Puchner (1963; repr., New York: Holmes and Meier, 2003).

86. Taylor, "Iris Murdoch and Moral Philosophy," 20.

87. Nigel Alexander, *Poison, Play, and Duel* (Lincoln: University of Nebraska Press, 1971), 73.

88. Alexander, *Poison, Play, and Duel*, 171.

2. *King Lear* and the Avoidance of Charity

1. Cited in Raimond Gaita, *A Common Humanity: Thinking About Love and Truth and Justice* (London: Routledge, 1998), 26.

2. I have explored the learning of love in an exegetical analysis on a relevant passage of Stanley Cavell's book. Stanley Cavell, *The Claim of Reason: Wittgenstein, Skepticism, Morality and Tragedy*, 2nd ed. (Oxford: Oxford University Press, 1999), 177, henceforth *CR*. See Sarah Beckwith, "Enter the Child: A Scene from *The Claim of Reason*," *Philosophy and Literature* 41, no. 2 (October 2022): 251-62.

3. Cavell, *CR*, 125.

4. This is Wittgenstein's method of investigation of a concept. Ludwig Wittgenstein, *Philosophical Investigations: German Text with an English Translation*, 4th ed., ed. G. E. M. Anscombe, P. M. S. Hacker, and Joachim Schulte (Chichester: Wiley-Blackwell, 2009), henceforth *PI*. We look at what we say about it, because "for a large class of cases of the employment of the word 'meaning'—though not for all—this word can be explained in this way: the meaning of a word is its use in the language" (*PI*, ¶45). For an ordinary language philosopher words bring us a world only in application. See Peter Winch: "We make contact with the world only through the application of language." Peter Winch, "Particularity and Morals," in *Trying to Make Sense* (Oxford: Basil Blackwell, 1987), 170.

5. Eli Friedlander, "Faces of the Ordinary," in *Cavell's "Must We Mean What We Say?" at 50*, ed. Greg Chase, Juliet Floyd, and Sandra Laugier (Cambridge: Cambridge University Press, 2022), 81.

6. See Cavell's extraordinary essay and its companion piece, "Knowing and Acknowledging," show the centrality of Shakespearean tragedy to his path breaking reformulation of skepticism. Stanley Cavell, "Knowing and Acknowledging," in *Must We Mean What We Say? A Book of Essays* (Cambridge: Cambridge University Press, 2002), henceforth *MWM*. The essay is also an exemplary piece of philosophical literary criticism; indeed, as Toril Moi has argued, it is a kind of "phenomenology of criticism." See Toril Moi, "A Phenomenology of Literary

Criticism," in *Wittgenstein and Literary Studies*, ed. Robert Chodat and John Gibson (Cambridge: Cambridge University Press, 2021).

7. My references are from *King Lear*, ed. R. A. Foakes, Arden Shakespeare, 3rd ser. (Walton-on-Thames: Thomas Nelson, 1997). Alexander Pope conflated the quarto and folio texts in 1723, and this practice was followed in most editions until the major editorial revisions of the 1980s. Scholarly consensus now treats the quarto and folio texts as separate versions of the play. The plays have different titles, hundreds of variants. The Quarto has three hundred lines not found in Folio; Folio has more than a hundred not found in Quarto. The Norton Shakespeare, for example, presents both texts. The complex editorial history of the play and the new orthodoxy is established in *The Division of the Kingdoms: Shakespeare's Two Versions of King Lear*, ed. Gary Taylor and Michael Warren (Oxford: Oxford University Press, 1983). In this chapter, I note important differences when relevant.

8. Cavell notes that asides are conventionally both overheard and underheard: overheard by the audience and underheard by all on stage. See Stanley Cavell, "The Interminable Shakespeare Text," in *Philosophy the Day After Tomorrow* (Cambridge, MA: Harvard University Press, 2005), 57.

9. The grammatical point is prior to any psychological application. I do not confine love to an emotion or a feeling. See also David Schalkwyck, who examines love in a Wittgensteinian idiom. David Schalkwyck, *Shakespeare, Love, and Service* (Cambridge: Cambridge University Press, 2008); and David Schalkwyck *Shakespeare, Love and Language* (Cambridge: Cambridge University Press, 2018).

10. First published in *MWM*, 267–353.

11. De Trinitate, Book 9, Chapter 2, Augustine: *On the Trinity* ed. Gareth B. Matthews (Cambridge: Cambridge University Press, 2002), 26.

12. For analyses of charitable relations, see Evan A. Gurney, *Love's Quarrels: Reading Charity in Early Modern England* (Amherst: University of Massachusetts Press, 2018); for charity under the pressure of religious difference, see Alexandra Walsham, *Charitable Hatred: Tolerance and Intolerance in England 1500–1700* (Manchester: Manchester University Press, 2008).

13. John Bossy tracks what he argues is the transformation of a social order based on solidarity to one based on civility. See John Bossy, *Christianity in the West: 1400–1700* (Oxford: Oxford University Press, 1985). See especially his section on "Charity," 140–52. See also John Bossy, "The Mass as a Social Institution 1200–1700," *Past and Present* 100 (August 1983): 29–61. Bossy brilliantly notes (57) that the Lutheran liturgy interprets the PAX (spoken by the priest after fraction) as a peace between God and sinner.

14. For the relation of love to service, see the pioneering article by Jonas A. Barish and Marshall Waingrow, "'Service' in King Lear," *Shakespeare Quarterly* 9, no. 3 (Summer, 1958): 347–55; Schalkwyck, *Shakespeare, Love and Service*, Michael Neill, "Servant Obedience and Master Sins: Shakespeare and the Bonds of Service," in *Putting History to the Question: Power, Politics, and Society in English Renaissance Drama* (New York: Columbia University Press, 2000), 13–48.

15. Augustine, *Concerning the City of God Against the Pagans*, trans. Henry Bettenson (London: Penguin, 1984), book 15, chap. 23, 637.

16. At the same time, as I will show, the question of the corruption of virtue is bound up with what characters can see, with recognition, and the virtue tradition is thus tested and probed for adequacy in new climates.

17. For an excellent phenomenology of love, see Joel Backström, *The Fear of Openness: An Essay on Friendship and the Roots of Morality* (Vasa, Finland: Åbo Akademi University Press, 2007). His way of putting the point about psychology and the grammar of love is this: "Instead of reducing love to psychology, I try to see psychology in the light of love" (118).

18. A point made in Paul Kottman, *Tragic Conditions in Shakespeare: Disinheriting the Globe* (Baltimore, MD: Johns Hopkins University Press, 2009), 81.

19. For the formulation of the "impropriety" of human action, see Patchen Markell, *Bound by Recognition* (Princeton, NJ: Princeton University Press, 2003), 63-64. Impropriety, says Markell, refers not to a contingent moral failing but to a constitutive feature of human action: "The very conditions that make us potent agents—our materiality, which ties us to the causal order of the world, and our plurality, which makes it possible for our acts to be meaningful—also make us potent beyond our own control, exposing us to consequences and implications that we cannot predict and which are not up to us" (63). Markell is working closely with the chapter by Hannah Arendt, "Action," in *The Human Condition* (Chicago: University of Chicago Press, 1998), 175-247. The question of what we do in virtue of speaking runs throughout this book but see especially chapters 4 and 5 on *Macbeth* and *Coriolanus*.

20. The idea of sovereign agency as a fatal misrecognition (but one to which the Western tradition of Hobbes and Locke is blind) derives from Hannah Arendt and is developed with great clarity by Linda Zerilli, *A Democratic Theory of Judgment* (Chicago: University of Chicago Press, 2016).

21. See the excellent essay by Kenneth Graham, "'Without the Form of Justice': Plainness and the Performance of Love in King Lear," *Shakespeare Quarterly* 42, no. 4 (Winter 1991): 442.

22. In the title essay of *MWM*, Cavell explores the "must" in his title "Must We Mean What We Say?" In part, we must because our words necessarily carry implications. Cavell's example is that I must imply something is wrong with the way you dress if I say: "Do you dress like that voluntarily?" But there is also the sense in which we must not always mean what we say because we say things we do not and cannot mean. In this sense, the problem is us: In our self-deception, we refuse to mean what we are actually saying.

23. See Robin Fitzpatrick's comments on the effects of Cordelia's "awesome and wondrous" word *nothing*, "initiating a tempest of uncontainable action." See Robin Fitzpatrick, "Tragedy and Theology in Shakespeare's *Timon of Athens*," in *Christian Theology and Tragedy: Theologians, Tragic Literature and Tragic Theory*, ed. Kevin Taylor and Giles Waller (Farnham: Ashgate, 2011), 97.

24. "And in our faults by lies we flattered be," sonnet 138, *Shakespeare's Sonnets*, ed. Katherine Duncan Jones, Arden 3 ser. (London: Thomas Nelson and Sons Ltd, 1997), 391.

25. Simone Weil, "Love," in *Gravity and Grace*, trans. Emma Crawford and Mario von der Ruhr (London: Routledge, 1952), 65. See also Joel Backström's succinct and probing formulation: "Love and truth go together, but they only

go together in love." Backström, *Fear of Openness*, 108. Backström, glossing Weil's comments in, *The Need for Roots*, trans. A. F. Wills (London: Routledge, 1978), 242: "Truth is the radiant manifestation of reality. Truth is not the object of love but reality. To desire truth is to desire contact with a piece of reality. We desire truth only in order to love in truth. We desire to know the truth about what we love. Instead of talking about love of truth, it would be better to talk about the spirit of truth in love."

26. Anthony Cascardi, "'Disowning Knowledge': Cavell on Shakespeare," in *Stanley Cavell*, ed. Richard Eldridge (Cambridge: Cambridge University Press, 2003), 190.

27. For the necessity of sense and the accompanying pathos of that necessity, see Stanley Cavell, "Counter-Philosophy and the Pawn of Voice," in *A Pitch of Philosophy: Autobiographical Exercises* (Cambridge, MA: Harvard University Press, 1996), 73.

28. Iris Murdoch's essay, "The Idea of Perfection," suggests that "the central concept of morality is the individual knowable by love," and she suggests that this is an "endless task." See Iris Murdoch, *Existentialists and Mystics: Writings on Philosophy and Literature*, ed. Peter Conradi (1964; repr., Harmondsworth: Penguin, 1997), 323, 321.

29. For further exploration, see Jean-Philippe Narboux, "Actions and Their Elaborations," in *Cavell's "Must We Mean What We Say?" at Fifty*.

30. Stanley Cavell, *Little Did I Know: Excerpts from Memory* (Stanford, CA: Stanford University Press, 2010), 322: "I can no more take back the word I have given you and you have acted on that I can take back my touch. Each has entered our history."

31. The previous paragraph is taken from my essay: Sarah Beckwith, "Tragic Implication," in *Cavell's "Must We Mean What We Say?" at Fifty*. The "intrince" holy cords are Kent's explanation for the extravagance of his abuse of Oswald to the Duke of Cornwall. "Such smiling rogues as these / Like rats oft bite the holy cords atwain / Which are too intrince t'unloose" (2.2.71-73). The folio text adds "holy." "Intrince," suggests Foakes, abbreviates "inrinsicate"—an obsolete use which means entangled or involved, *King Lear* ed. R.A. Foakes, Arden 3, footnote 73, p. 229. But the word also includes "intrinsic," "belonging to the thing itself, or by its nature inherent, essential, proper, of its own" (*Oxford English Dictionary*) and this indicates the depth of Oswald's offence against the bonds that bind us, **https://www.oed.com/search/dictionary/?scope=Entries&q=intrinsic**.

32. "Criticism is always an affront, and its only justification lies in its usefulness, in making its object available to just response" (*MWM*, 46).

33. J. L. Austin, "Three Ways of Spilling Ink," in *Philosophical Papers* (Oxford: Clarendon Press, 1961), 273.

34. Austin discusses "linguistic phenomenology" and "what we should say when" as an examination not only of our use of words but the realities we use words to talk about, J. L. Austin, "A Plea for Excuses," in *Philosophical Papers*, 182. Cavell explains why this method will tell us about ourselves as well as the world in "Austin at Criticism" and the title essay of *MWM*.

35. Cavell, "Must We Mean What We Say?," 14.

36. Cavell, *CR*, 179.

37. Cavell explores both the necessity of action and the necessity of sense entailed in our speech acts. Stanley Cavell, "Counter-Philosophy and the Pawn of Voice," in *A Pitch of Philosophy: Autobiographical Exercises* (Cambridge, MA: Harvard University Press, 1994). Our speech acts, being acts, will do things in the world. And they carry necessary implications of use.

38. Niklas Forsberg, *Lectures on a Philosophy Less Ordinary: Language and Morality in J. L. Austin's Philosophy* (London: Routledge, 2022), 179.

39. Romans 13.8: "Owe nothing to any man, but to love one another: for he that loveth another hathe fulfilled the Law." Romans 13:10: "Love doth not evil to his neighbor: therefore is love the fulfilment of the law." *The Geneva Bible: A Facsimile of the 1560 Edition* (Madison: University of Wisconsin Press, 1969).

40. The Lutheran "messenger" in the dialogue is a stand in for English Lutheran infiltration.

41. "Pity would be no more / If we did not make somebody poor." See William Blake, "The Human Abstract," in *The Complete Poetry and Prose of William Blake*, ed. David V. Erdman (New York: Penguin Vintage, 1988).

42. For a fascinating examination of the conviviality and mutuality in charitable relations, see Judith M. Bennett, "Conviviality and Charity in Medieval and Early Modern Europe," *Past and Present* 134 (February 1992): 19–41.

43. Rowan Williams, *Lost Icons: Reflections on Cultural Bereavement* (Edinburgh: T&T Clark, 2000), 77.

44. The priest's prayer to the congregants to come to receive Holy Communion says, for example, "You that truly and earnestly repent you of your sinnes, and be in love and in charite with your neighbours, and entende to lede a newe lyfe. . . . Draw nere and take this holy Sacrament to your comfort." See the 1559 version in *The Book of Common Prayer: The Texts of 1548, 1559, 1662*, ed. Brian Cummings (Oxford: Oxford University Press, 2010), 133.

45. "And yf ye shal perceive your offences to be such, as be not only against God, but also against your neighbours: then ye shal reconcyle youre selves unto them, ready to make restitution and satisfaction according to the uttermost of your powers for all injuries and wronges done by you to any other." *Book of Common Prayer* (1559), 132.

46. On peace and charity, see *The Lay Folks Mass Book (Early English Text Society)*, ed. T. F. Simmons (Oxford: Oxford University Press, 1879), 48–54. See John Bossy, "The Mass as a Social Institution," *Past and Present* 100 (1983): 29–61. For an analysis of charity as a bond of community, see Andy Wood, *Faith, Hope, and Charity: English Neighbourhoods, 1500–1640* (Cambridge: Cambridge University Press, 2020), and especially his depiction of sixteenth-century melancholy about the decline of neighborhood and charitable relations and the pressures of neighborhood in response to the cash nexus. See also Katie Barclay, *Caritas: Neighbourly Love and the Early Modern Self* (Oxford: Oxford University Press, 2021), 9: "Caritas provided an overarching framework for ethical and emotional neighbourly relations."

47. A Dialogue Concerning Heresies III.8," 3–6, in *The Yale Edition of The Complete Works of St. Thomas More*, vol. 6. part 1, ed. Thomas C. Lawler, Germain Marc'hadour, and Richard C. Marius (New Haven, CT: Yale University Press, 1981), 288. See Germain Marc'hadour and Thomas M. C. Lawler, "Scripture in

the Dialogue," in *The Complete Works of St. Thomas More*, vol. 6, part 2, 494–526. More's focus is less on the semantic history of agape and caritas as "what the English words convey" (513).

48. See my essay: Sarah Beckwith, "The Theological Virtues," in *Shakespeare and the Virtues: A Handbook*, ed. Julia Lupton and Donovan Sherman (Cambridge: Cambridge University Press, 2023), 125-36.

49. "Confutation of Tyndale's Answer, II," in *The Complete Works of St. Thomas More*, vol. 8, part 2, ed. Jame P. Lusardi, Louis A. Schuster, Richard C. Marius, and Richard Schoek, 199. For a helpful discussion on Thomas More's quarrel about love with Tyndale, see Evan Gurney, "Thomas More and the Problem of Charity," *Renaissance Studies* 26, no. 2 (2011): 197-217; and Evan Gurney, "Charitable Translation: Thomas More, William Tyndale and the Vagrant Text," in *Love's Quarrels: Reading Charity in Early Modern England* (Amherst: University of Massachusetts Press, 2018), chap. 1.

50. Thomas Lupset, *A Treatise of Charity* (London: Berthelet, 1533), 31. Lupset is making a distinction between agape and eros ("A Dialogue Concerning Heresies," III.8, 287).

51. *A Confutation of Tyndale's Answer, in the Complete Works of Thomas More*, vol 8, part 1, ed. Jame P. Lusardi, Louis, A. Schuster, Richard C. Marius, and Richard Schoek (New Haven, CT: Yale University Press, 1973), 199.

52. Gurney, "Thomas More," 204; More, *Complete Works*, vol. 8, part 1, 199-200.

53. The point is made in Murdoch's famous M and D example. M comes to see D as she is, not simply differently than before, and her task of seeing reality is an "endless one." See Iris Murdoch, "The Idea of Perfection," in *Existentialists and Mystics*, 321. "The realism," she declares, "of a great artist is not a photographic realism, it is essentially both pity and justice." See Iris Murdoch, "The Sovereignty of Good over Other Concepts" in *Existentialists and Mystics*, 371.

54. William Carroll points out that the word *charity* is only used in the subplot "where it refracts the failure of love so evident in the main plot" (202): William Carroll, *Fat King, Lean Beggar: Representations of Poverty in the Age of Shakespeare* (Ithaca, NY: Cornell University Press, 1996).

55. Cavell, *CR*, 437.

56. Kelly S. Johnson, *The Fear of Beggars: Stewardship and Poverty in Christian Ethics* (Grand Rapids, MI: Eerdmans, 2007), 3.

57. Thomas Harman, *A Caveat for Common Cursitors* (1566), in *The Elizabethan Underworld*, ed. A. V. Judges (repr., London: Routledge, 1930), 91.

58. Harman, *Caveat for Common Cursitors*, 62.

59. Thomas Dekker, "O per se O" (1612), in *The Elizabethan Underworld*, 372, 373.

60. Linda Woodbridge, *Vagrancy, Homelessness and English Renaissance Literature* (Chicago: University of Illinois Press, 2001), 205.

61. On charity as a "form of love demanding recognition among different sectors of people," see Kate Crassons, *The Claims of Poverty: Literature, Culture, and Ideology in Late Medieval England* (Notre Dame, IN: University of Notre Dame Press, 2010), 22. For difficulties of recognition, see Crassons, *Claims of Poverty*,

28; and for the classificatory legal apparatus of the Cambridge Statute, see Crassons, *Claims of Poverty*, 82.

62. Paul Slack, *Poverty and Policy in Tudor and Stuart England* (London: Longman, 1988), 25.

63. Jean Améry, *At the Mind's Limits: Contemplations by a Survivor After Auschwitz and Its Realities*, trans. Sidney Rosenfeld and Stella P. Rosenfeld (Bloomington: Indiana University Press, 1980), 40.

64. Simone Weil, "Human Personality," in *Simone Weil: An Anthology*, ed. Sian Miles (New York: Grove Press,1986), 51.

65. Cora Diamond, "Injustice and Animals," in *Slow Cures and Bad Philosophers: Essays on Wittgenstein, Medicine, and Bioethics*, ed. Carl Elliott (Durham, NC: Duke University Press, 2001), 131.

66. Jacobean tragedy is certainly gory, but its violence seems campily grotesque, even complacent when put beside the scene in Lear. Only what is precious can be violated and the scene elicits this sense in us. For a brilliant evocation of what is at stake in the concept of violation, see Christopher Cordner, *Ethical Encounter: The Depth of Moral Meaning*, Swansea Studies in Philosophy (Basingstoke: Palgrave Macmillan, 2002), esp. chap. 1.

67. Diamond, "Injustice and Animals," 131.

68. I borrow from J. M. Bernstein's examination of the phenomenology of torture as a paradigm of moral injury., J. M. Bernstein, *Torture and Dignity: An Essay on Moral Injury* (Chicago: University of Chicago Press, 2015), 104, based on Améry, *At the Mind's Limits*.

69. Bernstein, *Torture and Dignity*, 178.

70. Note change from the quarto: "Mine injurer's meanest dog."

71. The quarto reads: "No, sir, you must not kneel."

72. Echoing, of course, Lear's question: "Is there any cause in nature that make these hard hearts?" (3.5.74-5). See the beautiful analysis of this scene, in Tony Tanner, *Prefaces to Shakespeare* (Cambridge, MA: Harvard University Press, 2010), 549; he supplies Emilia's answer.

73. *Othello*, ed. E.A.J. Honigman (with a new introduction by Ayanna Thompson, Arden Shakespeare, 3rd ser, (London: Bloomsbury, 2016), 3.4.160-1. : "They are not ever jealous for the cause, / But jealous for they're jealous."

74. The folio reads: "Pray you now."

75. For an excellent essay on the language of bearing, taking up, and so on in *King Lear*, see Jason Crawford, "Shakespeare's Liturgy of Assumption," *Journal of Medieval and Early Modern Studies* 49, no. 1 (2019): 57–84.

76. The latter is James Wetzel's beautiful phrase. See James Wetzel, "A Meditation on Hell" in *Parting Knowledge: Essays After Augustine* (Eugene: Cascade, 2013), 173.

77. Shakespeare never tried to justify the ways of God to men or, therefore, to disabuse us of such justifications.

78. For an excellent examination of the pervasive theme of weight in Augustine's conception of love, see Eric Gregory, *Politics and the Order of Love: An Augustinian Ethic of Democratic Citizenship* (Chicago: University of Chicago Press, 2010), 246, 248.

79. Foakes makes this point in his footnotes to the stage direction in 5.3.

80. Wittgenstein, *PI*, ¶ 66.

81. Paul Fiddes, *More Things in Heaven and Earth: Shakespeare, Theology, and the Interplay of Texts* (Charlottesville: University of Virginia Press, 2022), 142. Lear's entry with Cordelia dead in his arms is the pose of faithful love, the "something" that comes out of nothing, reversing, "nothing will come of nothing." For a response to this scene, see Charles Altieri, "How Can Act 5 Forget Lear and Cordelia?" in *Shakespeare Up Close: Reading Early Modern Texts*, ed. Russ McDonald, Nicholas D. Nace, and Travis D. Williams (New York: Bloomsbury, 2013), 309-16. He explores the world of value not accessible to either sentimentalizing or ironizing readings. "Lear's repeated imperatives," he argues, "suggest that there is something significant just in the spectacle Cordelia becomes in the end, framed by her love and fidelity and honored by his capacity to enter into the space that his love and fidelity have the strength to compose" (315).

82. Cited in Gregory, *Politics and the Order of Love*, 252.

83. Williams, *Lost Icons*, 56; John Burnaby, *Amor Dei: A Study of the Religion of St. Augustine* (1938; repr., Eugene: Wipf & Stock, 2007).

84. For an exceptional essay, see Cora Diamond, "The Difficulty of Reality and the Difficulty of Philosophy," in *Philosophy and Animal Life*, ed. Stanley Cavell, Cora Diamond, Ian Hacking, John McDowell, and Cary Wolfe (New York: Columbia University Press, 2008), 43-90.

85. I have found Camilla Kronqvist's work on these issues very illuminating. See, especially, Camilla Kronqvist, "Our Struggles with Reality," in *Emotions and Understanding: Wittgensteinian Perspectives*, ed. Ylva Gustafsson, Camilla Kronqvist, and Michael McEachrane (Basingstoke: Palgrave Macmillan, 2009), 202-20. I am grateful to Salla Peltonen for drawing Kronqvist's work to my attention. For concepts and literature especially in the work of Iris Murdoch and Cora Diamond, also see Niklas Forsberg *Language Lost and Found: On Iris Murdoch and the Limits of Philosophical Discourse* (New York: Bloomsbury, 2013).

86. This is usefully explored in Patrick Rogers Horn, *Gadamer and Wittgenstein on the Unity of Language: Reality and Discourse Without Metaphysics* (Aldershot: Ashgate, 2005), 124-5, 127. Also see the very important chapter by Rush Rhees, "Understanding What Is Said," in *Wittgenstein and the Possibility of Discourse*, ed. D. Z. Phillips (Cambridge: Cambridge University Press, 1998), esp. 160, 163.

87. Peter Winch, "Understanding a Primitive Society," in *Rationality: Key Concepts in the Social Sciences*, ed. B. R. Wilson. Oxford: Blackwell, 1974. For comments on this citation from Winch, see Kronqvist, "Our Struggles with Reality," 205.

88. Niklas Forsberg, *Language Lost and Found*, 85.

3. Benefits and Bonds

1. *The Geneva Bible: A Facsimile of the 1560 Edition* (Madison: University of Wisconsin Press, 1969). The Vulgate has: "quid enim boni habes quod non accepisti?" (What aspect of the good do you have that you have not received?) See *Biblia Sacra Vulgata*, 5th ed., ed. B. Fischer, I. Gribomont, H. F. D. Sparks, and W. Thiele (Stuttgart: Deutsche Bibelgesellschaft, 2007). I like this translation for bringing out the recognition of the good, importantly highlighted when

it comes to the translation of benefit/beneficium. In his book, John Barclay comments that "Augustine finds nothing that falls outside of the reach of this Pauline question" (91). See John Barclay, *Paul and the Gift* (Grand Rapids, MI: Eerdmans, 2015).

2. I use the Arden 3rd ser. edition for all citations in this chapter and throughout. *Timon of Athens*, ed. Anthony B. Dawson and Gretchen E. Minton, Arden Shakespeare, 3rd ser. (London: Bloomsbury, 2008). The play is variously dated, so it is hard to determine precisely where it works with my grouping chronologically. Does it come before or after *Lear*? A plausible date of early 1606 puts it very near *Macbeth* and *Coriolanus* and possibly *Antony and Cleopatra*. However we determine this, *Timon* makes a cluster with this extraordinary group of late tragedies, and its investigation of the depth of bonds is revelatory of all the plays in my group and book.

3. J. L. Austin says, "Accuracy and morality alike are on the side of the plain saying: our word is our bond" (10). See J. L. Austin, *How to Do Things with Words*, ed. J. O. Urmson and Marina Sbisa (Cambridge, MA: Harvard University Press, 1962). If we have given our word, our "inner state" of reservation cannot cancel out the pledge. Austin is precisely not hiving off a special class of commissives here—although he will investigate that class later on in his lectures. He locates ties of claim and obligation in *us* and in the giving and taking of words.

4. On Timon's extremes, Apemantus comment is apt: "The middle of humanity thou never knewst, but the extremity of both ends" (4.3.300-301).

5. These expectations are tacit—importantly so—but they are revealed retrospectively. Timon says to Flavius that his impoverishment is a test for his friends, and he is confident that he is "wealthy in his friends" (2.2.184).

6. Karl Marx quotes *Timon* in *Economic and Philosophic Manuscripts of 1844*, Collected Works 3 (New York: International Press, 1976), 323-25. Money is "the bond of all bonds. Can it not dissolve and bind all ties?" See also Karl Marx, *Capital*, trans. Eden Paul and Cedar Paul (London: J. M. Dent, 1974): "Modern society which, when still in its infancy, pulled Pluto by the hair of his head out of the bowels of the earth, acclaims gold, its Holy Grail, as the glittering incarnation of its inmost vital principle" (3). Jowett, who cites these passages in his edition of the play, also points out that "gold" is used thirty-six times in this play, and of these, only three can be ascribed to Middleton. See *Timon of Athens*, ed. John Jowett (Oxford: Oxford University Press, 2004), 55. The gold Timon finds in the earth after his exile is ambiguously a product of culture and nature; mined gold or coins are variously used in production.

7. The expression is Kent's, *King Lear*, ed. R. A. Foakes, Arden Shakespeare, 3rd ser. (Walton-on-Thames: Thomas Nelson, 1997), 2.2.68.

8. Una Ellis Fermor makes the case for incompletion. See Una Ellis Fermor, "*Timon of Athens:* An Unfinished Play," *The Review of English Studies* 18, no. 71 (July 1942): 270-83. The Alcibiades subplot is murky and full of gaps; we do not hear about the death of the friend for whom Alcibiades pleads in act 3, and Alcibiades military role is not well motivated or anticipated; the characters of the friends are sometimes named, sometimes not; the play offers us multiple epitaphs, and so on. Dawson and Minton discuss these questions (8-9) and argue that the play was "at some point abandoned by its authors, perhaps set

aside for revision, and later neglected" (10). Jowett finds this only a "mythical truth" in his edition (1).

9. For questions of joint authorship see the discussion of the play in John Jowett, "Canon and Chronology," in *Thomas Middleton and Early Modern Textual Culture: A Companion to the Collected Works*, ed. Gary Taylor and John Lavagnino (Oxford: Clarendon, 2007), 356–358. Middleton, the younger playwright, was responsible for about a third of the play, and there is some scholarly discussion about determining the exact parameters of this exercise in joint authorship. Jowett includes a chart assessing attribution to Middleton in his edition of *Timon*, giving to Middleton some role in scenes 1, 4, 11, and 12, and 17, and the entirety of scenes 2.6-10. Jowett leaves the division into scenes intact, but in the act divisions used by most editors after the eighteenth century, this corresponds to the first three scenes in act 3 and much of act 4. For further discussion, see Dawson and Minton, Arden 3rd ser. edition, which includes a vital treatment about the process of sharing in joint authorship, which was a key feature of the Elizabethan and Jacobean stage (6).

10. See Stanley Cavell, *Conditions Handsome and Unhandsome: The Constitution of Emersonian Perfectionism* (Chicago: University of Chicago Press, 1990), 25.

11. Genre is not a list of characteristics by which a work is entered under a description such that it counts if it has these particular features. It is best seen as a response to a set of conditions which it works through. As Cavell says in *Pursuits of Happiness*, it has no history, only a birth and a logic. Members of the genre share the inheritance of these conditions and "each member of the genre shares the responsibility of its inheritance" (28). Stanley Cavell, *Pursuits of Happiness: The Hollywood Comedy of Remarriage* (Cambridge, MA: Harvard University Press, 1981). Paul Kottman has brilliantly pursued a similar idea of genre. See Paul Kottman, *Tragic Conditions in Shakespeare: Disinheriting the Globe* (Baltimore, MD: Johns Hopkins University Press, 2009), 1–22; and, in a more Hegelian direction, see Paul Kottman "What Is Tragedy?," in *The Oxford Handbook of Shakespearean Tragedy*, ed. David Schalkwyk and Michael Neill (Oxford: Oxford University Press, 2016), 3–18.

12. I am in dialogue with two very different books on social and verbal bonds. Kottman's *Tragic Conditions* reads Shakespearean tragedy as a response to the realization that the social and authoritative bonds by which we had understood ourselves—bonds of kinship, civic, economic or political relations, are "fully dissolvable" (4). How we inherit the world, and pass it on become bewilderingly opaque and unsettled and Shakespeare's tragedies work through this realization. John Kerrigan takes a comprehensive look at a range of speech acts, such as oaths and vows, to analyze what he calls Shakespeare's *binding* language. See John Kerrigan, *Shakespeare's Binding Language* (Oxford: Oxford University Press, 2016).

I have learned much from these stimulating books. Succinctly, I find Kottman's "fully dissolvable" to be too absolute and that Shakespeare's sense of bonds goes deeper. And I find that Kerrigan's understanding of binding language is too restricted to oaths, vows, and promises as the main route to commitment. I will examine the bonds we are (already) in, and the ways we commit ourselves in language.

13. The citation from *Twelfth Night* is from *Twelfth Night* Arden 3, ed. Keir Elam (London: Bloomsbury, 2008). A written bond was the default mode of contractual agreements by this time. Such documents could be known as a "recognizance," "a promissory note," a "seal" and sometimes a "bill" as used with great dramatic effectiveness in act 3, scene 4, where the pun weaponizes the bonds. (Bills are also a kind of long-handled weapon.) See Amanda Bailey, *Of Bondage: Debt, Property, and Personhood in Early Modern England* (Philadelphia: University of Pennsylvania Press, 2013), 5. The bond, she says is both the legal instrument of binding and proof that the debtor was so bound.

14. A. D. Nuttall, *Timon of Athens*, Twayne's New Critical Introductions to Shakespeare (Boston: Twayne, 1989), 126.

15. Nuttall, *Timon of Athens*, 125, seeing Timon as taking up crucial, unfinished investigations of *The Merchant of Venice* (see the famous trial scene of act 4.scene 1, *The Merchant of Venice* ed. John Drakakis, Arden Shakespeare, 3rd ser. (London: A & C. Black Publishers, 2010).). See also Elizabeth Fowler, "Toward a History of Performativity: Sacrament, Social Contract, and *The Merchant of Venice*," in *Medieval Shakespeare*, ed. Curtis Perry and John Watkins (Oxford: Oxford University Press, 2009), 68–77.

16. *Cymbeline*, Arden 3rd ser., ed. Valerie Wayne (London: Bloomsbury, 2017).

17. An important starting point for thinking through disagreement about the language of promise and contract is Victoria Kahn, *Wayward Contracts: The Crisis of Political Obligation in England 1640–1674* (Princeton, NJ: Princeton University Press, 2004), esp. introduction, 1–28. There is a large literature on the importance of covenantal theology in Calvinist thought and the movement from the unilateral understanding of the covenant of grace (God's one-sided gift in which only one-sidedness preserved the very notion of gratuity) and to a more contractarian understanding of the obligations of the chosen. The market-driven operations of credit and the theology of grace provide a richly ambiguous context for questions of what we owe and what we own. For an increasingly contractarian world, see David Zaret, *The Heavenly Contract: Ideology and Organization in Pre-Revolutionary Puritanism* (Chicago: University of Chicago Press, 1985).

18. On usury, see R. H. Tawney's introduction to Thomas Wilson's *A Discourse on Usury* (New York: Harcourt, Brace, 1925). For John Shakespeare's debt and involvement in usurious practices, see Park Honan, "John Shakespeare's Fortunes," in *Shakespeare: A Life* (Oxford: Oxford University Press, 1998), 36–42.

19. Jowett, *Timon of Athens*, 8.

20. Annette Baier, *Postures of the Mind: Essays on Mind and Morals* (Minneapolis: University of Minnesota Press, 1985): "The second person, the pronoun of mutual address, introduces us to the first and third . . . We are second persons before we are first or third persons" (90).

21. Patchen Markell, "Conclusion: Towards a Politics of Acknowledgment," in *Bound by Recognition* (Princeton, NJ: Princeton University Press, 2003), 177–89.

22. Ventidius's messenger says, "Your lordship ever binds him" (1.1.107). Lucilius says that everything that falls into his keeping will be owed to Timon, hyperbolically expressing it as an optative, introduced with two negatives

(1.1.154–55): "Never may / That state or fortune fall into my keeping / Which is not owed to you."

23. *The Geneva Bible* gives a fascinating gloss that shows a financial metaphor underlying the notion of Christ's redemption (etymologically, buying back): "Not hoping for profite, but to lose the stocke and principal forasmuch as Christ bindeth himself to repay the whole with a more liberal interest."

24. Marcel Mauss, *The Gift*, ed. and trans. Jane I. Guyer (Chicago: HAU Books, 2016), 73.

25. *Of Benefits*, 1.3.2–5. I use *Seneca: On Benefits*, trans. Miriam Griffin and Brad Inwood (Chicago: University of Chicago Press, 2011), checked against the Loeb edition of the Latin text, *Seneca: Moral Essays*, vol. 3, trans. John W. Basore (Cambridge, MA: Harvard University, 1953). John Wallace first made the most extensive claims for Seneca's importance in *Timon*. See John Wallace, "*Timon of Athens* and the Three Graces: Shakespeare's Senecan Study," *Modern Philology* 83, no. 4 (May 1986): 349–63. It will become apparent that I do not agree with Wallace's Hobbesian conclusions.

26. Hannah Arendt, *The Human Condition* (Chicago: University of Chicago Press, 1958), 175. Sovereign agency belongs to the self-determining, self-sufficient, and masterful subject, a concept under such profound, excoriating scrutiny in the late tragedies. This idea of human agency is so deeply rooted in our culture and in liberal political theory that it is often simply assumed; yet it is a version of self that radically underestimates and misconstrues the depth of our agreements with each other, therefore the human condition of plurality.

27. Romand Coles, *Rethinking Generosity: Critical Theory and the Politics of Caritas* (Ithaca, NY: Cornell University Press, 1997), vii.

28. It is arguable, of course, that such a claim rests precisely on an understanding of possession that the gift contests, but it is part of the play's gloss on bonds to show that Timon has been oblivious to the written bonds that will soon fall fast and thick upon him.

29. Flavius lets us the audience know in his aside (1.2.160) that Timon cannot fund his generosity—it is empty. He speaks in further asides at 1.2.194-208 and 2.2.1-9. He tries to speak to Timon (1.2.178) and finally in act 2. scene 2. It becomes clear that he has managed to communicate the parlous state of Timon's finances. Timon reproaches him but he crucially says: "You would not hear me" (2.2.127). He has denied all requests from Flavius to address his situation, so his denial of Flavius and his denial of his true status are interwoven because he has stopped the only honest path of words.

30. The language of "breeding" smacks of usury.

31. Usury presented a problem for as long as it was regarded as a religio-ethical issue and before it could be justified on economic grounds. The arguments in parliament over usury (1571, 1604, 1606, 1614, 1621, 1624) while initially dominated by scholastic language ignored God almost entirely by 1624. See Norman Jones, *God and the Moneylenders: Usury and Law in Early Modern England* (Oxford: Blackwell, 1989).

32. Regina Schwartz, *Loving Charity, Living Shakespeare* (Oxford: Oxford University Press, 2016), 69.

33. For the textual transmission see L. D. Reynolds, *Texts and Transmission: A Survey of the Latin Classics* (Oxford: Oxford University Press, 1983), 363–65.

34. Erasmus's edition dates from 1529; Marc-Antoine Muret's partial edition is 1585; and Lipsius's version is 1605. Arthur Golding's *The Woorke of the Excellent Philosopher Lucius Annaeus Seneca concerning Benefyts* was published in 1577–1578. Thomas Lodge's translation (1614, therefore postdating Shakespeare and Middleton's play) is based on Justus Lipsius's edition. For the wider context, see Jill Kraye, "Moral Philosophy," in *The Cambridge History of Renaissance Philosophy*, ed. C. B. Schmitt, Quentin Skinner, Eckerd Kessler, and Jill Kraye (Cambridge: Cambridge University Press, 2008), 303–86; and Roland Mayer, "Seneca Redivivus: Seneca in the Medieval and Renaissance World," in *The Cambridge Companion to Seneca*, ed. Shadi Bartsch and Alessandro Schiesaro (Cambridge: Cambridge University Press, 2015), 277–88. Seneca was essentially a "moral authority for the medieval reader" (Mayer, "Seneca Redivivus," 279).

35. Geoffrey Bullough does not cite Seneca's treatise. See Geoffrey Bullough, *Narrative and Dramatic Sources of Shakespeare*, vol. 6 (London: Routledge, 1966), 225–345. John M. Wallace's "*Timon of Athens* and the Three Graces" is the first study that argues that Shakespeare's ideas about benefits are indebted to Seneca's study. See also Richard Finkelstein, "*Amicitia* and *Beneficia* in *Timon of Athens*," *Studies in Philology* 117, no. 4 (Fall 2020): 801–25.

36. Also sometimes translated as charity or an act of kindness.

37. For the significance of these kinds of differences, see J. L. Austin, "A Plea for Excuses," in *Philosophical Papers*, 3rd ed., ed. J. O. Urmson and G. J. Warnock (Oxford: Oxford University Press, 1979), 175–204. See "Our common stock of words embodies all the distinctions men have found worth drawing, and the connexions they have found worth marking, in the lifetimes of many generations" (182). For an elaboration of these possibilities, see also Sarah Beckwith, "A Vision of Language for Literary Historians: Forms of Life, Context, Use," in *Wittgenstein and Literary Studies*, ed. Robert Chodat and John Gibson (Cambridge, MA: Cambridge University Press, 2022), 82–103.

38. Felicity Heal beautifully charted the language of bribe and gift in Jacobean vocabulary and institutions. Felicity Heal, *The Power of Gifts: Gift Exchange in Early Modern England* (Oxford: Oxford University Press, 2014). See especially "Bribes and Benefits," 188–206.

39. "A benefit cannot be touched with one's hand; the business is carried out with the mind" (1.5.1) translating "Non potest beneficium manu tangi: res animo geritur."

40. Seneca is concerned with ingratitude and investigates it at length, see 1.10.3, 2.25.1, and in much of book 4. Seneca understands ingratitude to be one of the most common vices (1.1.1), and also a monstrous and devastating vice, breaking the very ligatures of society.

41. On gifts to self (5.7–11), on slaves as donors (3.18.1), on son and father (3.35.4).

42. There is no induction into an office of giving or donation. Giving, receiving, and reciprocating are in the fabric of our interwoven lives and language. On the office of promising, see Stanley Cavell, *The Claim of Reason: Wittgenstein, Skepticism, Morality and Tragedy*, 2nd ed. (Oxford: Oxford University Press, 1999),

part 3, chap. 11, "Rules and Reasons," 297, henceforth *CR*, for Cavell's criticism of Rawls who calls promising an "office." "Virtue is satisfied with the bare person" (3.18.2) translating "nudo homine contenta est." In *Timon*, Lucullus to whom Timon has given in abundance, says to one of Timon's servants in response to a request for a loan: "thou know'st well enough, although thou com'st to me, that this is no time to lend money, especially upon bare friendship without security" (3.1.40–43).

43. I am indebted to Jean-Joseph Goux's essay, "Seneca Against Derrida: Gift and Alterity," which first made me understand Seneca's importance. Goux's concern is to explore gift and alterity against Derrida's influential understandings of the gift as aporetic, impossible. Goux uses Seneca's idea that there cannot be a gift without others to suggest that the gift gives the other because "to give and open yourself to the existence of others is the same thing." Seneca thus demonstrates that "the possibility of the gift refutes solipsism" (160). See Jean-Joseph Goux, "Seneca Against Derrida: Gift and Alterity," in *The Enigma of the Gift and Sacrifice*, ed. Jean-Joseph Goux, Edith Wyschogrod, and Eric Boynton (New York: Fordham University Press, 2002), 148–60.

44. A benefit is intrinsically social (5.10.1), requiring the involvement of others.

45. *On Benefits*, 1.4.3: "People must be taught to give benefits freely, receive them freely, and return them freely" (22).

46. See Jonathan Lear's wonderful meditation, "Gratitude and Meaning" that ends his book. Jonathan Lear, *Imagining the End: Mourning and Ethical Life* (Cambridge, MA: Harvard University Press, 2022), 126: "Gratitude protects the realm of generosity by recognizing it as such and not treating the benefaction as part of the normal economy of gift and (expected) reciprocation."

47. For an excellent treatment of the gift, and the problems with the "pure" gift, see Barclay, *Paul and the Gift*, 23, 51, and the helpful "The Lexicon of Gift" at the end of his book. The "pure" gift is "free" from obligation, unreciprocated, given without a return (52). For Derrida's exploration of the "pure" gift, see Derrida, *Given Time: 1. Counterfeit Money*, trans. Peggy Kamuf (Chicago: University of Chicago Press, 1992): and Derrida, *The Gift of Death*, trans. David Wills (Chicago: University of Chicago Press, 1995), which has been hugely influential in literary studies, anthropology, and theology. Derrida's idea of the gift as one that must involve "no reciprocity, return, exchange, countergift, or debt" (*Given Time*, 12) is taken up with trenchant clarity by Ken Jackson. See Ken Jackson, "'One Wish' or the Possibility of the Impossible: Derrida, the Gift, and God in *Timon of Athens*," *Shakespeare Quarterly* 52, no.1 (Spring 2001): 34–66.

48. How it got to be a scandal is the story told in Coles, *Rethinking Generosity*, and Barclay, *Paul and the Gift*.

49. Derrida, *Given Time*, 12. On Derrida's account, the gift is vitiated by the mere recognition that it is gifted by either the giver or the receiver. Derrida's insists "for there to be a gift, it is necessary that the donee does not give back, amortize, reimburse, acquite himself, enter into a contract, and that he never have contracted a debt" (13).

50. See Adriaan Peperzak, "Giving," in *The Enigma of Gift and Sacrifice*, ed. Edith Wyschogrod, Jean-Joseph Goux, and Eric Boynton (New York: Fordham

University Press, 2002), 161-75. Peperzak helpfully points out that for a phenomenology of giving, it is not necessary to establish the purest form of it as an empirical fact, and that the rareness of generosity is not a revelation, but that its corruptions are also identifiable and must be (163). For example, the fact that we can compare more and less generous givers shows that we already have an idea of a genuine act of generosity. There is no room for gratitude in Derrida's understanding of the gift, because giving is actually destroyed by gratitude.

51. Of course, this language was made familiar in the central practices (and controversies) around the Eucharist, drawing on the Greek word for thanksgiving, see Barclay, "Lexicon of the Gift," in *Paul and the Gift*, 575. In Latin, gratia can also serve as grace given and thanks in response to it. Barclay points out that in English "gift" captures only one side of the favor or benefit, whereas "grace" covers all three moments in the circle of the gift: "the graciousness of the giver, the grace conveyed, and the gratitude returned," 582. For an exploration of the play's "anti-graces," see A. D. Nuttall, "Timon Says Grace: The Parodic Eucharist," in *Timon of Athens*, 113-35. The play's antigraces can be found in 1.2.63-72 and 3.7.69-83.

52. Peter Leithart, *Gratitude: An Intellectual History* (Waco, TX: Baylor University Press, 2014), 11.

53. Aristotle's magnanimous, great-souled, or proud man (megalopsuchia) "is the sort of man to confer benefits but is ashamed of receiving them; for one is the mark of the superior, the other of an inferior." *Nicomachean Ethics*, trans. David Ross (Oxford: Oxford University Press, 1998), book 4:1124b.

54. Annette Baier, "Trust and Antitrust," *Ethics* 96, no. 2. (January 1986), 149. Also cited in J. M. Bernstein, *Torture and Dignity: An Essay on Moral Injury* (Chicago: University of Chicago Press, 2015). Bernstein makes these distinctions relevant to Timon's sense of betrayal: "One of the reasons why destructions of trust tend to be so disturbing is that, unlike contracts that are explicit, linear, and specific, trust relations tend to be implicit, that is, there is no specific thing we had trusted the other to do or forgo from doing" (227).

55. "The child learns by believing the adult. Doubt comes after belief." See Ludwig Wittgenstein, *On Certainty*, ed. G. E. M. Anscombe and G. H. Wright (New York: Harper and Row, 1969), ¶160, 23e.

56. Knud Ejler Løgstrup, *The Ethical Demand*, trans. Theodro I. Jensen, Gary Puckering, and Eric Watkins (Notre Dame: University of Notre Dame Press, 1997), 18. As Alasdair MacIntyre and Hans Fink say in their introduction, Løgstrup understands life as a gift, and it is "a precondition of any cultural ordering that the basic expression of life is to give and receive" (xxi). For a further investigation of giving and receiving (uncalculated, unpredicted), see Alasdair MacIntyre, *Dependent Rational Animals: Why Human Beings Need the Virtues* (Chicago: Open Court, 1999), 100, 116, 144.

57. In addition to Løgstrup, a variety of philosophers have explored trust and shown why it has been invisible—and sometimes frankly unthinkable—in the dominant traditions of philosophy. See C. A. J. Coady, *Testimony: A Philosophical Study* (Oxford: Clarendon Paperbacks, 1992); Benjamin McMyler, *Testimony, Trust, and Authority* (Oxford : Oxford University Press, 2011); Olli Lagerspetz,

Trust, Ethics, and Human Reason (London: Bloomsbury, 2015); Annette Baier, *Moral Prejudices: Essays on Ethics* (Cambridge, MA: Harvard University Press, 1994); Richard Moran, *The Exchange of Words: Speech, Testimony, and Intersubjectivity* (Oxford: Oxford University Press, 2018); and Lars Hertzberg, "On the Attitude of Trust," *Inquiry* 31 (1994), 307-22. The difficulties of recognizing trust come about because it is what we tacitly take for granted but also because the modern philosophical tradition privileges "epistemic autonomy." See McMyler, *Testimony, Trust, and Authority*, 196.

58. Hortensius certainly compares his lord's ingratitude to "stealth" at 3.4.27. And the exchange between the three strangers in 3.2 is a vital part of the play's ethical landscape.

59. For some fine distinctions, see Regina Schwartz, *Living Shakespeare* (Oxford: Oxford University Press), 69-70. She offers a textbook definition of a contract as a "promise that the law will enforce." J. M. Bernstein in his chapter on "Trust as Mutual Recognition" in *Torture and Dignity* has suggested that social contract theory is "a way of both affirming and denying the necessity of recognition for everyday life." It considers the parties to the contract to be fully formed, and understands them as self-sufficient apart from the contract (224).

60. Avishai Margalit, *On Betrayal* (Cambridge, MA: Harvard University Press, 2017), 90-11, 154.

61. The word "truster" in the sense of believer, as the Arden note reminds us, does occur in *Hamlet* (1.2.172) but this is the only use in the sense of creditor in the canon of plays. "Truster" surely carries the sense of credit not alone in the financial sense but as in Pericles's use of it to Marina that he will "credit her relation" (*Pericles*, 5.1.114). Suzanne Gossett (Walton-on-Thames: Thomas Nelson, 2004).

62. Lucilius, Flaminius, and Servilius serve Timon. Philotous, Lucius, Hortensius, Titus, and Caphis are named and there are two servants of Varro, one of Isodore. These serve the play's creditors, but their loyalties do not always lie with them. For example, when the servants of Isodore and Varro meet to collect dues from Timon, Caphis's pun, "Would we were all discharged," can be taken to express a hope that their dues be paid, but it can just as easily indicate a reluctance to perform the duty (2.2.14).

63. For the ethical fellowship of the servants, see Ellorashree Maitra, "Toward an Ethical Polity: Service and the Tragic Community in *Timon of Athens*," *Renaissance Drama* 41, no. 12 (Fall 2013): 173-98; Michael Noschka, "Thinking Hospitably with *Timon of Athens*: Towards an Ethics of Stewardship," in *Shakespeare and Hospitality: Ethics, Politics, and Exchange*, ed. David Goldstein and Julia Reinhard Lupton (London: Routledge, 2019), 242-64; and David Schalkwyck, *Shakespeare, Love and Service* (Cambridge: Cambridge University Press, 2009).

64. *Summa Theologica* 2-2, 106, resp. obj. 3. All quotations are from St. Thomas Aquinas, *Summa Theologica*, the Complete English Edition, 5 vols. trans. Fathers of the English Dominican Province (Notre Dame, IN: Christian Classics, 1981), henceforth *ST*. Citations from the *Summa* use the following abbreviations following the architecture of the work. 2.2 specifies the second part of the second part, 106 specifies the question addressed, followed by a number for the

article, s.c. for sed contra (on the contrary)and resp.obj. specifies response to the objection.

65. Aquinas, *ST* 2-2, 106, 3, resp. obj. 5.
66. Aquinas, *ST* 2-2, 106, 5, s.c.
67. Aquinas, *ST* 2-2, 106, s.c.
68. Andrew Galloway, "The Making of a Social Ethic in Late-Medieval England: From Gratitudo to 'Kyndenesse,'" *Journal of the History of Ideas* 55, no. 4. (July 1994): 365–83. The most probing exploration of "kyndeness" before Shakespeare is Langland's *Piers Plowman* B and C-Texts. See *William Langland, Piers Plowman: The B Version*, eds. George Kane and E.Talbot Donaldson, rev. ed. (London: Athlone, 1988, and *Piers Plowman, by William Langland: An Edition of the C-Text*, ed. Derek Pearsall, 2nd (York Medieval Texts, 2nd ser. (Exeter: University of Exeter Press, 1994).
69. Galloway points out that "exploring the double-entendre of both the 'natural' and the 'moral' meanings of 'kyndenesse' must rank among the favorite verbal games of Middle English religious writers." See Galloway, "The Making of a Social Ethic," 373.
70. A decidedly Christian language is here invoked as it is in the play's eucharistic references.
71. *2 Henry IV*, ed. James C. Bulman, Arden Shakespeare, 3rd ser, (London: Bloomsbury, 2016), 5.5.46.
72. For the tears, see James Kuzner, *Shakespeare as a Way of Life: Skeptical Practice and the Politics of Weakness* (New York: Fordham University Press, 2016). Kuzner gives us a marvelous account of his experience of reading *Timon*. And see Maurice Hunt, "Qualifying the Good Steward of Shakespeare's *Timon of Athens*," *English Studies* 82, no. 6 (2001): 507–20, 511. The tears are Virgil's *lacrimae rerum*, "sad, wise tears for the human condition of ingratitude." I would add that they are tears for his failure to see his honest servant, for the kind of failure that is.
73. *Twelfth Night*, ed. Keir Elam, Arden Shakespeare, 3rd ser, (London: Bloomsbury, 2008), 2.3.111. *King Lear* Q, 3.7.79.
74. "Here, take," says Timon (4.3.519). The Arden editors assume Flavius does take the gold because the Painter thinks (5.1) that the rumours that the steward has gold are true. Karl Klein notes John Woodvine's moving and quiet return of the poisoned gift to Michael Pennington's Timon in Greg Doran's 1999 Royal Shakespeare Theatre production. See *Timon of Athens*, ed. Karl Klein (Cambridge, MA: Cambridge University Press, 2001), 50.
75. On the work of differences see Austin, "A Plea for Excuses." The epigraph Wittgenstein once thought of using for the *Philosophical Investigations* was from *King Lear*. "I'll teach you differences." See Ludwig Wittgenstein, *Philosophical Investigations: The German Text with an English Translation*, 4th ed., ed. G. E. M. Anscombe, P. M. S. Hacker, and Joachim Schulte (Chichester: Wiley-Blackwell, 2009), henceforth *PI*. The hope was that distinctions in ordinary usage and reminders about how we came to learn such distinctions might help us find our way home when we are exiled from our own words, when we are lost and wandering. His aim was to restore us to our responsibilities in talking, our (internally related) responsiveness to each other, and our responsibility to the

ways our words bind us, thus all at once to the significance of our words to each other and to the worth of speech. Without these differences and distinctions there would be nothing to say.

76. Stanley Cavell, "Performative and Passionate Utterance," in *Philosophy the Day After Tomorrow* (Cambridge, MA: Harvard University Press, 2005), 187.

77. Cavell, CR, 268. Part 3 constitutes a brilliant, sustained critical analysis of the major schools of moral philosophy in its contemporary forms. Cavell comments on part 3 in the introduction to the Italian edition of CR, which omitted this section. He felt that he had not yet brought out the full moral implication of Wittgenstein's *PI*, a project continued years later in part 4, and continued in Cavell's conception of perfectionism in *Conditions Handsome and Unhandsome* and subsequent works.

78. Austin outlines the conditions of illocutionary speech initially in Austin, *How to Do Things with Words*. Cavell ponders Austin's neglect of the perlocutionary (what we do by rather than in virtue of speaking), and accounts for the disanalogies with Austin's procedure. He begins this analysis in Stanley Cavell, "Counter Philosophy and the Pawn of Voice," in *A Pitch of Philosophy: Autobiographical Exercises* (Cambridge, MA: Harvard University Press, 1994), 53–128, and develops it in "Performative and Passionate Utterance."

79. Cavell, "Performative and Passionate Utterance," 185.

80. Cavell says something he wants from moral theory is "a systematic recognition of speech as confrontation, as demanding, as owed"—and not alone in the form of moral reasons. Cavell, "Performative and Passionate Utterance," 187.

4. Losing the Name of Action

1. For vital reflections on the question of the human as a question of *recognition* to which I return later in the chapter, see Stanley Cavell, *The Claim of Reason: Wittgenstein, Skepticism, Morality and Tragedy*, 2nd ed. (Oxford: Oxford University Press, 1999), henceforth CR; Cora Diamond, "The Importance of Being Human," in *Human Beings*, ed. David Cockburn (Cambridge: Cambridge University Press, 1991); and Niklas Forsberg, *Language Lost and Found: On Iris Murdoch and the Limits of Philosophical Discourse* (New York and London: Bloomsbury, 2013).

2. John Berger and Jean Mohr, *A Fortunate Man: The Story of a Country Doctor* (1967; repr., Vintage, 1997), 166.

3. "Being human is aspiring to be human . . . since it is not aspiring to being the only human, it is an aspiration on behalf of others as well." Stanley Cavell, CR, 399.

4. *Merriam-Webster* defines scare quotes as "quotation marks used to express esp. skepticism or decision concerning the use of the enclosed word or phrase." https://www.merriam-webster.com/dictionary/scare%20quotes?src=search-dict-box, accessed Febrary 21st, 2025.

5. https://www.oed.com/dictionary/scare-quotes_n?tab=meaning_and_use#24148539, accessed February 21st, 2025.

6. Missouri's republican senate candidate in 2012 said that women who suffer "legitimate rape" rarely get pregnant. A public outcry led to his withdrawal from the Senate race. See *New York Times*, "Rep. Todd Akin: The Statement

and the Reaction," August 10, 2012, https://www.nytimes.com/2012/08/21/us/politics/rep-todd-akin-legitimate-rape-statement-and-reaction.html.

7. For some reflections on the question of the human, see "Introduction: Cavell, Literary Studies, and the Human Subject: Consequences of Skepticism," in *Stanley Cavell and Literary Studies: Consequences of Skepticism*, ed. Richard Eldridge and Bernard Rhie (New York: Bloomsbury, 2011), 5. See also Richard Eldridge, *Leading a Human Life: Wittgenstein, Intentionality, and Romanticism* (Chicago: University of Chicago Press, 1997).

8. In her introduction to Hannah Arendt's *The Human Condition*, Margaret Canovan has said: "Human animals unconscious of their capacities and responsibilities are not well-fitted to take charge of earth-threatening powers" (xi). Margaret Canovan, introduction to *The Human Condition*, 2nd ed., by Hannah Arendt, (Chicago: University of Chicago Press, 1998).

9. For the idea of Shakespeare and the "invention" of the human, See Harold Bloom, *Shakespeare: The Invention of the Human* (New York: Riverhead Trade, 1999).

10. Cora Diamond, "The Importance of Being Human," in *Human Beings*, ed. David Cockburn (Cambridge: Cambridge University Press, 1991), 35–62.

11. Ludwig Wittgenstein, *Philosophical Investigations: The German Text with an English Translation*, 4th ed., ed. G. E. M. Anscombe, P. M. S. Hacker, and Joachim Schulte (Chichester: Wiley-Blackwell, 2009), henceforth PI, ¶287: "How am I filled with pity *for this human being?* How does it come about what the object of my pity is? (Pity, one might say, is one form of being convinced that someone else is in pain."

12. I am indebted throughout to Raimond Gaita for his compelling understanding of lucid remorse as "an encounter with the reality of the ethical." See Raimond Gaita, *Good and Evil: An Absolute Conception* (London: Routledge, 2004), xiv.

13. For the desiccation of the concept of human action at the hands of moral theory, see Iris Murdoch, "Against Dryness," in *Existentialists and Mystics: Writings on Philosophy and Literature*, ed. Peter Conradi (Harmondsworth: Penguin, 1997). For a brilliant exploration of human agency taking up some of Murdoch's perceptions, see Thomas Pfau, *Minding the Modern: Human Agency, Intellectual Traditions, and Responsible Knowledge* (Notre Dame, IN: University of Notre Dame Press, 2013). R. F. Holland also explored the poverty of moral theory (particularly utilitarianism) when it comes to envisaging evil. See R. F. Holland, "Good and Evil in Action," in *Against Empiricism: On Education, Epistemology, and Value* (Totowa, NJ: Barnes and Noble, 1980), 110–25. "Utilitarianism," Holland claims, "gives us a myopic, misleading picture of the way that good and evil enter into action" (110–11). Raimond Gaita acknowledges Holland's profound influence on his own work; see Gaita, *Good and Evil*, xi. The book began life as a dissertation supervised by Holland.

14. This reference to his murder of Duncan or to his other murders as an unspecified "it" is a characteristic locution for Macbeth (e.g., see 1.4.50, 2.1.62). All citations are from *Macbeth*, ed. Sandra Clark and Pamela Mason, Arden Shakespeare, 3rd ser. (London: Bloomsbury, 2015).

15. The *Oxford English Dictionary* records this as the first citation for the meaning of "the taking of a life by treacherous violence," as recorded in the notes of the

Arden, 3rd ser. https://www.oed.com/dictionary/assassination_n?tab=meaning_and_use#37063784, accessed February 21, 2025.

16. Arendt, *Human Condition*, part 5, 192.

17. My phrase recalls the Captain's fearsome description of Macbeth the warrior, "Valour's minion" who "carved out his passage" with "his brandished steel" (1.2.16, 1.2.19). This passage through enemy bodies is glorified by the King and his witnesses, the not-so-latent violence disciplined to the king's cause. The adjacent play, *Coriolanus*, explores this world of uncontainable and deathly force, as I show in chapter 5.

18. "Be-all and end-all" is another remarkable coinage, luminously revealing his own wishful logic.

19. Cavell, *CR*, 110. Cavell is importantly getting at the depth of convention in human life. To Cavell's succinct formulation, we might add the vital idea that acts come under descriptions, and "do not come named for assessment, nor, like apples, ripe for grading." See Cavell, *CR*, 265. For a helpful elaboration of this dimension of Cavell's work, see Jean-Philippe Narboux, "Actions and Their Elaboration," in *Cavell's "Must We Mean What We Say?" at 50*, ed. Greg Chase, Juliet Floyd, and Sandra Laugier (Cambridge: Cambridge University Press, 2022), 56–76.

20. Tony Tanner, *Prefaces to Shakespeare* (Cambridge, MA: Harvard University Press, 2010): "Most tragic heroes, from Oedipus on, have, for a variety of reasons, ever but slenderly known themselves, and when self-knowledge does finally break in, or through, it is invariably at ruinous cost" (563).

21. James Calderwood, *If It Were Done: Macbeth and Tragic Action* (Cambridge, MA: University of Massachusetts Press, 1986). I have found this excellent study very helpful.

22. For a beautifully understated but trenchant analysis, see what is perhaps one of the best essays ever written on the philosophy of action: J. L. Austin, "A Plea for Excuses," in *Philosophical Papers*, ed. J. O. Urmson and G. J. Warnock (Oxford: Clarendon, 1961); see 202, for our language helping us to mistake causes for reasons. For the transition from action to behaviour and its disastrous *ethical* consequences, see Charles Taylor, *The Explanation of Behaviour* (London: Routledge and Kegan Paul, 1980); and Charles Taylor, introduction to *Philosophical Papers: Human Agency and Language*, vol. 1 (Cambridge: Cambridge University Press, 1985), 2. See also Pfau, *Minding the Modern*; and the still highly relevant, Peter Winch, *The Idea of a Social Science and Its Relevance to Philosophy* (London: Routledge and Kegan Paul, 1958).

23. Alasdair MacIntyre, *After Virtue: A Study in Moral Theory*, 2nd ed. (Notre Dame, IN: University of Notre Dame Press, 1984). When an occurrence is described as an action, it brings in the question of accountability and responsibility. "When an occurrence is apparently the intended action of a human agent, but nonetheless we cannot so identify it, we are both intellectually and practically baffled" (209). For a good essay on this aspect of MacIntyre's thought, see Stanley Hauerwas, "The Virtues of Alasdair MacIntyre," *First Things*, October 2007, https://www.firstthings.com/article/2007/10/the-virtues-of-alasdair-macintyre.

24. My citations are from *St. Thomas Aquinas: Summa Theologica*, Complete English Edition, trans. the Fathers of the English Dominican Province, 5 vols. (Notre Dame, IN: Christian Classics, 1948). *The Treatise on Human Acts* within the *Summa* takes up the first twenty-one quaestiones of the *Prima Secundae* of the *Summa*. Aquinas precisely differentiates human acts as those emerging from the deliberation of reason. Human acting is purposive in this tradition and should not be confused with mere motion or happening. Acting is precisely then not reacting to external stimuli in the manner of behaviorism. Although behaviorism is technically a branch of psychology, outmoded in its most notorious forms (e.g., B. F. Skinner), it stands here for a much broader intellectual phenomenon. I invoke it for a kind of scientism that takes out the role of intention and purpose from human agency and thus evacuates questions of meaning and value central to the self-interpreting creatures we are. See Charles Taylor, "What Is Human Agency?," in *Philosophical Papers*, 15–44. See Taylor's introduction for a devastating critique of behaviorism. G. E. M. Anscombe was Taylor's adviser in Oxford during the 1950s. For a perceptive examination of the attempt to understand reading and criticism from the perspectives of the natural and social sciences, see Robert Chodat, "Appreciating Material: Criticism, Science, and the Very Idea of Method," in *Wittgenstein and Literary Studies*, ed. Robert Chodat and John Gibson (Cambridge: Cambridge University Press, 2022), 62–81.

25. Charles R. Pinches brings this out very clearly in his book. See Charles R. Pinches, *Theology and Moral Action: After Theory in Christian Ethics* (Grand Rapids, MI: Eerdmans, 2002), see esp. 90, 101, 106: "The realms of morality and human acts are exactly co-extensive." Pinches contrasts this with a strand of moral philosophy that extrinsically brings to bear something called "morality" onto human action. Once again, we can see why the naming of actions and their elaboration is so vital (91).

26. "Intentional actions" are ones to which a certain sense of the question "why?" has application. See G. E. M. Anscombe, *Intentions* (Oxford: Blackwell, 1963), 11. Anscombe shows herself to be a deeply Thomistic thinker. Human acting is directed toward an end (an end we think is good) and so it is dependent on understanding as well as will.

27. Of course, we can be deceived about our own intentions: Our self-knowledge is far from perfect. For us, things come under certain descriptions, and naming actions is a "most sensitive occupation." Stanley Cavell, *Must We Mean What We Say? A Book of Essays* (Cambridge: Cambridge University Press, 2002), 35.

28. Ilham Dilman, *Raskolnikov's Rebirth: Psychology and the Understanding of Evil* (Chicago: Open Court, 2000), 112.

29. The "sweet oblivious antidote" is what he hopes the Doctor can minister to his wife, tormented by an endlessly recurring nightmare, an exacting and horrifying nightly reprise of the murders.

30. We might see this as part of the willful thoughtlessness the play explores. Thinking, as Hannah Arendt established, is intrinsically dialogical: It is always thinking with. Macbeth's desire is for solitude. He seeks out only the three

weird sisters and the secret knowledge he imagines can make him invulnerable. Arendt explores thinking and thoughtlessness; see, most famously, Hannah Arendt, *Eichmann in Jerusalem: A Report on the Banality of Evil* (New York: Penguin, 1964); and Hannah Arendt, *The Life of the Mind* (New York: Harcourt, 1978). For reflections on this topic, see Maria Balaska, "When a Mind Goes Up in Smoke: Thinking of Evil and Thinking," in *Cora Diamond on Ethics*, ed. Maria Balaska (Chan: Palgrave Macmillan, 2021), 247–67.

31. The denaturing of human action is once again apparent. In suggesting that "returning" were as "tedious" as proceeding, the point of acting is lost. It is a horrifying image of numbness, as if Macbeth is anesthetized to his own actions: The way forward and the way back are alike steeped in blood.

32. The Portrait of Macbeth is not moralistic, for we might recognize our chronic proneness to self-deception, the ease with which, as the creatures we are, we slide into it with such alarming ease—and sincerity!

33. Herbert Fingarette has given us a wonderfully clear picture of self-deception. He also shows why certain philosophical pictures of the self will remain puzzled in the face of the paradox of self-deception. See Herbert Fingarette, *Self-Deception* (1969; repr., Berkeley: University of California Press, 2000), 38–39. For a far-reaching use of Fingarette's ideas on self-deception, see David Burrell and Stanley Hauerwas, "Self-Deception and Autobiography: Theological and Ethical Reflections on Speer's *Inside the Third Reich*," *Journal of Religious Ethics* 2, no. 1 (Spring 1974): 99–117.

34. On losing concepts, see Forsberg, *Language Lost and Found*; and for her seminal essay, see Cora Diamond, "Losing Your Concepts," *Ethics* 98, no. 2 (1988). One of Forsberg's key points is that it may be hard to see when we might be losing our grip of a concept and speaking only under the illusion of sense because "words are worn and torn and so turned (differently)." They are "changed but not necessarily exchanged since words may look the same when their concepts change"—and because this is so "it is oftentimes hard to come to see that one may fail in the command of one's own language" (1).

35. I borrow this term from Holland, "Good and Evil in Action," 118. The sense of the priority of good over evil is Augustinian: Goodness is creative, and evil can only be a privation of the good, being in itself nothing.

36. Macbeth's claim that his "violent love . . . Outran the pauser reason" (2.3.111–12) is his cover-up for his murder of the grooms when the murder of Duncan is discovered.

37. Of course, at this point Lady Macbeth seems to have a limited imagination of "illness." She seems to see it here as that "necessary" evil that courage and will can supply to get what you want. It hardly needs saying that this is a radical miscontrual of courage, of evil, and the nature of the murder she contemplates. Macbeth's paltry "bring forth man-children only" (1.7.74) shows him as feebly complicit in this fatal misunderstanding of masculine courage. (Compare this: "What the self-deceiver lacks is not integrity or sincerity but the courage and skill to confront the reality of his or her situation"; Burrell and Hauerwas, "Self-Deception and Autobiography," 105.) Duncan is, like the Prince of Cumberland a "step" they must o'erleap because it stands in their way. Whatever boldness they have is hectic, feverish, intoxicated with drink,

driven and riven not with cruelty or calculation but with a terrible mutual incitement. I think it is obvious that neither would have committed murder without the other: Their act, as the play abundantly dramatizes, leaves them both with blood on their hands that they can never clear. Macbeth cannot outsource his responsibility to his wife, or to the Weird Sisters: The play presents this as a temptation and a confusion but an evasion of a responsibility that can only coherently be assumed singly.

38. James Wetzel points out that Dante cannot locate himself in the "selva oscura" by "recalling the moment and motive of his entry." James Wetzel, "A Meditation on Hell," *Parting Knowledge: Essays After Augustine* (Eugene: Cascade Books, 2013), 162. *Macbeth,* as I have been arguing, shows that self-forgetfulness and its consequences in action. Augustine's famous meditation on the stolen pears he did not even really want or need is also a meditation on evil's perversity.

39. Primo Levi, *Survival in Auschwitz* (New York: Collier, 1993), 29.

40. *The Comedy of Dante Alighieri the Florentine* (Harmondsworth: Penguin, 1949), 68. I thank David Burrell for this reference. See David Burrell, *Aquinas, God, and Action* (Scranton: University of Scranton Press, 2008), 136.

41. Augustine, *Concerning the City of God Against the Pagans*, trans. Henry Bettenson (London: Penguin Classics, 1984), book 12.7, 480.

42. *City of God*, 12.7, 480. It is certainly an intelligible statement for *Macbeth*. It is notorious that Macbeth's language uncannily echoes the language of the weird sisters from the beginning of the play. The incantatory "fair is foul, and foul is fair" (1.1.9) with its alliterative chiasmus attempts to reverse good's priority by negating distinction. If fair is foul, and foul is fair, moral discernment is impossible. This is not quite like Milton's later Satanic, "Evil be thou my good," which immediately succeeds "all good to me is lost," for there the distinction is still clear. John Milton *Paradise Lost*, book 4, 109-110, *The Complete Poetry and Essential Prose of John Milton* eds. William Kerrigan, John Rumrich, and Stephen M. Fallon (New York: Modern Library, 2007), 388. Macbeth's "This supernatural soliciting/Cannot be ill; cannot be good" (1.3.132-33) shows the preliminary moves toward the negation of distinction.

43. Charles T. Matthewes, *Evil and the Augustinian Tradition* (Cambridge: Cambridge University Press, 2001), 79. The Augustinian tradition continues in Hannah Arendt's work. One of Arendt's early works was her Heidelberg dissertation, an account of love in Augustine, which she took with her from her exile in France to New York. It is now translated as *Love and Saint. Augustine*, ed. and trans. Joanna Vecchiarelli Scott and Judith Chelius Stark (Chicago: University of Chicago Press, 1996). In *Eichmann in Jerusalem*, Arendt's picture of Eichmann's evil arguably remains Augustinian. A better understanding of this dimension of her thought might qualify the outrage engendered by her talk of evil's "banality." Of course, Augustine could not have anticipated the particular horrors of totalitarian thoughtlessness, but her thinking is importantly different from many other post-Auschwitz analysts.

44. Gaita, *Good and Evil*, xxi. Judi Dench's outstanding performance as Lady Macbeth was in Trevor Nunn's Royal Shakespeare production (with Ian McKellen as Macbeth) in 1976. My attendance at this production in London that year transformed my sense of the possibilities of theater utterly and forever.

45. The prior nature of a good to be violated is apparent, though conceived terribly as an obstacle to her "fell purpose." "Compunctious visitings of nature" are glossed as menstruation in the Arden, 3rd ser., but surely stand as much for the naturalness of compassion for the living, as well as the for the pricking conscience.

46. Thanks to Thomas Pfau for the reference to Emily Dickinson's poem. It can be found in *The Complete Poems of Emily Dickinson*, ed. Thomas H. Johnson (San Francisco: Back Bay, 1976), 365. Raimond Gaita, "Ethical Individuality," in *Value and Understanding: Essays for Peter Winch* (London: Routledge, 1990), 137.

47. Gaita, *Good and Evil*, 52. Gaita finds remorse as "an astonishing encounter with the reality of the ethical" (xiv).

48. Wittgenstein, *PI*, ¶287: "How am I filled with pity *for this human being*? How does it come about what the object of my pity is? (Pity, one may say, is one form of being convinced that someone else is in pain.)"

49. Gaita, *Good and Evil*, 177–78.

50. Wittgenstein, *PI*, ¶286. Wittgenstein is combatting the pervasive idea of the body as a veil or mask that we must get beyond to be certain of say, pain. Cavell's gloss on this remark in is: "to withhold, or hedge our concepts of psychological states to given creatures, on the ground that my criteria cannot reach to the inner life of the creature is specifically to withhold the source of my idea that living creatures are things that feel: it is to withhold myself, to reject my response to anything as a living being" (*CR*, 83–84).

51. Gaita, "Ethical Individuality," 127. Rowan Williams calls remorse a lost icon, along with childhood, and charity, by which he means an understanding and way of perceiving a pattern of human behavior that condition the possibility of recognizably human conversations. In cases in which certain things, such as marking deaths in ritual, or respecting the latency of childhood, or the making of promises do not obtain, we might find it hard to stay within a recognizably human conversation. Lost icons are concepts in danger and Williams's task is to show the costs of that loss. See Rowan Williams, *Lost Icons: Reflections on Cultural Bereavement* (Edinburgh: T &T Clark, 2000).

52. It reprises in an altogether different register her words to her husband in the third act, her wan attempt at reassurance: "What's done is done" (3.2.13), uttered just at the point at which she may be on the brink of perceiving how useless and ineffective those words are, and how also untrue. What's done can't be undone, but the action is far from finished in consequence, and in this sense, it is not "done" at all.

53. Lady Macbeth was going to die sooner or later. Lady Macbeth should have died at a more convenient time (to mourn her?). Both readings cauterize natural response.

54. The *OED* gives these compounds for remorse—remorse-filled, remorse-smitten, remorse-stirred, remorse-stricken, remorse-stung. The biting nature of remorse is closely associated with the medieval discourse of conscience. Remorse is "agenbite" as one medieval treatise has it: It is "again-biting." It is sharp and stinging: a "pricke" of conscience (https://www.oed.com/dictionary/remorse_n?tab=meaning_and_use#26042706, accessed February 21, 2025.

55. Gaita, *Good and Evil*, 59.

56. The weird sisters too sometimes think about deeds intransitively: "I'll do, I'll do, and I'll do" (1.3. 10) or without name as when in 4.1. they respond to Macbeth's question, "What is't you do" with the reply: "A deed without a name" (4.1.63-64).

57. Gaita, *Good and Evil*, 63.

58. This is, of course, how Lady Macbeth greets Macbeth when they meet for the first time in the play. This is the place to which his letters with the "intelligence" of the weird sisters have "transported" her.

59. Williams, *Lost Icons*, 109. This picture of the will is intrinsically bound up with the negation of time. An atemporal self does not have to be connected with the lives of others. Macbeth's reading of the weird sister's equivocations as prophecies and predictions is an evasion of his temporal self.

60. See the epigraph by Murdoch, *Existentialists and Mystics*: "Man is a creature who makes pictures of himself, and then comes to resemble the picture," from "Metaphysics and Ethics" in the same volume. She has in her sights the concept of a deracinated will. Shakespeare's philosophical understanding of such a picture is that it is potentially murderous, extinguishing others metaphorically, and in the case of Macbeth, literally: "How does one become Thane of Cawdor? By his death. How does one become king? By killing him. How does one become an earl, as at the end of the play? By killing." *Macbeth: Texts and Contexts*, ed. William C. Carroll (New York: St. Martin's, 1999), 20.

61. *Hamlet*, ed. Ann Thompson and Neil Taylor, Arden Shakespeare, 3rd ser. (London: Bloomsbury, 2006), 3.1.55.

62. Pfau, *Minding the Modern*, see esp. 3: "to work with concepts ... means to enter into an ethical—as opposed to a straightforwardly pragmatic—relation to the reality that these concepts *prima facie* allow us to apprehend"; Cora Diamond, "Losing Your Concepts."

63. Murdoch, "Against Dryness," 290. The differences in conceptual amnesia in the work of MacIntyre (whose chief concern is the radical attenuation of an understanding of virtue) and Murdoch are certainly worth exploring as are implications of their Aristotelian and Platonic lineages, but they cannot be my central concern. Diamond undertakes some distinctions between a MacIntyrean understanding of the loss of concepts and conceptual loss in Murdoch in "Losing Your Concepts." Nevertheless, immediately preceding the words I have cited, Murdoch asks, "What have we lost here? And what have we perhaps never had?" Murdoch also suggests that we have stripped ourselves of concepts in morals and politics, and (relevant here) that the ones we have cannot imagine evil (294). I cannot do more than allude to the riches on offer in Pfau's extraordinary book, a rich investigation of agency, its attenuation in modernity, and its related concepts.

64. Forsberg, *Language Lost and Found*, 62. Forsberg points out that for Murdoch (and I add, for Diamond), loss of concepts cannot be understood in a purely historical way—that is, as if some concepts had application in a former period and now do not. See my introduction.

65. Murdoch's understanding of conceptual amnesia is superbly elucidated by Forsberg, *Language Lost and Found*, see esp. 171.

66. For an excellent elucidation of Murdoch and the idea of choice, see Susan Wolf, "Loving Attention: Lessons in Love from *The Philadelphia Story*," in *Understanding Love: Philosophy, Film, and Fiction*, ed. Susan Wolf and Christopher Grau (Oxford: Oxford University Press, 2014).

67. Forsberg, *Language Lost and Found*, 132; for the idea of comprehension as merely regional, see 133.

68. Gaita, *Good and Evil*, chap. 4.

69. G. Wilson Night, "Macbeth and the Metaphysic of Evil," in *The Wheel of Fire: Interpretations of Shakespearean Tragedy* (1930; repr., London:, 1989).

70. Gaita, *Good and Evil*, 68.

71. Gaita, *Good and Evil*, 71.

72. Cavell, *CR*, part 3, 247, for a brilliant critique of the focus on the constricted question "what ought to be done."

73. Forsberg, *Language Lost and Found*, 171: "A loss of concepts is, at bottom, due to a lack, or a distorted form of self-understanding. This lack or these distortions are in turn related, but not reducible to misunderstandings of our language."

74. See Cavell, *CR*, 324, Cavell's critique of Rawls, and his elucidation of specifically moral claims: "What you are said to do can have various descriptions; under some you will know that you are doing it, under others you will not, under some your act will seem unjust to you, under others not. What alternatives we can and must take are not fixed, but chosen; and thereby fix us."

75. Lars Hertzberg, "Gaita on Recognizing the Human," in *Ethics, Philosophy and a Common Humanity*, ed. Christopher Cordner (London: Routledge, 2010), 7–20.

76. Mark Doty, *The Art of Description: Word into World* (Minneapolis, MN: Graywolf, 2010), 65: "Description is an *art* to the degree it gives us not just the world but the inner life of the witness." In literary criticism, the art of description has been neglected and despised for too long and precisely because of the assumptions Murdoch criticizes. Description is on this account obvious and banal because what is self-evidently there is not related to our vision of it; what we see is irrelevant to the kinds of people we are.

77. Gaita, *Good and Evil*, xiv; see also 61: "Remorse is a central and inexpungeable determinant of what it is for something to be a moral matter."

78. For Murdoch understanding the reality of another person is the work of love, justice, and pity, all essential to the vision of Shakespeare's late tragedies. Gaita's vital commentary on this comment is that love, justice, and pity are *forms of understanding* not consequences of it. See Hertzberg, "On Recognizing the Human" in *Ethics, Philosophy and a Common Humanity*, ed. Christopher Cordner (London: Routledge, 2011), 7.

79. A point that Gaita makes about Oedipus; Gaita, *Good and Evil*, 44. The chorus, he says, holds Oedipus responsible for his unintentional deeds, and does so through their pity for what he had become. Pity is part of their "lucid response to the significance of what he did" (44).

80. Murdoch, "Against Dryness," 293.

81. Murdoch, "Against Dryness," 293.

82. See Yaniv Iczkovits, *Wittgenstein's Ethical Thought* (Basingstoke: Palgrave Macmillan, 2012), 145.

83. Michael Boyd's fabulously inventive production doubled the actors playing Macduff's children for the weird sisters, who appeared hanging down on nooses in the second appearance of the weird sisters (the first scene was cut). The production kept "the eye of childhood" resolutely to the fore.

84. "The responsibility of responsiveness" is a key idea in Cavell's interpretation of Wittgenstein and Austin. For the phrase in Cavell's work, see Stanley Cavell, *A Pitch of Philosophy: Autobiographical Exercises* (Cambridge, MA: Harvard University Press, 1996), 126.

85. Malcolm is obtuse to Shakespeare's astonishing uncoupling of grief and anger, his turning inside out of the revenge tradition and he talks as if revenge can cure grief: "Let's make us medicines of our great revenge / To cure this deadly grief."

86. Cora Diamond's essay beautifully explores how ethics is utterly interwoven with explorations of how concepts work in our lives. See Cora Diamond, "Suspect Notions and the Concept Police," in *Cora Diamond on Ethics*, ed. Maria Balaska (Cham: Palgrave Macmillan, 2021), 17.

87. Tragedy again stands as a corrective to some forms of moral philosophy, an alternative form of it.

88. Cavell, *CR*, 399.

89. Czeslaw Milosz, "One More Day," in *New and Collected Poems, 1931–2001* (New York: Harper Collins, 2001), 418–19. Milosz's poem is, of course, deeply Augustinian: "Or should we say plainly that good is on the side of the living / And evil on the side of a doom that lurks to devour us." It is also deeply Platonic: "And when people cease to believe that there is good and evil / Only beauty will call to them and save them / So that they will still know how to say: this is true and that is false."

90. The play, as many have noted, is haunted by children—the children the Macbeths notoriously do not have; the children of those who are prophesied to be future kings (Banquo's lineage, childish apparitions); the children murdered at Fife; and young Siward toward the play's end. Some productions portray the weird sisters as children to highlight this strong strand of the play. The imaginary baby at Lady Macbeth's breast from whom she plucks the nipple depends entirely on the idea of "the milk of human kindness" (1.5.17), that we take in human kindness with our milk, as Milosz's poem suggests.

91. Cavell, *CR*, 397.

92. Wittgenstein, *PI*, ¶283.

93. See Peter Winch, "Eine Einstellung Zur Seele" in *Trying to Make Sense* (Oxford: Basil Blackwell, 1987).

94. For the interdependence of concept and response, see Gaita, *Good and Evil*, 188.

95. The key discussion is Cavell's discussion of the slaveholder; see Cavell, *CR*, 372; and Gaita, *Good and Evil*, 173.

96. On treating people as people, with startlingly lucid and extended examples, see the discussion of "the vanishing of the human": Cavell, *CR*, 468.

97. "Criticism is always an affront, and its only justification lies in its usefulness, in making its object available to just response": Cavell, "The Availability of Wittgenstein's Philosophy," in *Must We Mean What We Say?*, 46.

5. Coriolanus

1. It is hard to know what to call Coriolanus, as the question of what he is called—and the relation of naming to identity—is central to the play. The speech headings change to read Coriolanus after he receives his new name at Corioles (1.9.62–64). Before that, he is Caius Martius. It is an option to follow this naming precisely by calling him Caius Martius only before his renaming, but I use the names interchangeably.

2. The Oxford editors in their essay "The Canon and Chronology of Shakespeare's Plays" say that stylistic tests uniformly put the play after *Lear*, *Macbeth*, and *Anthony and Cleopatra*. In both plays, one can see the final experimentations in the form of late tragedy, with *Antony and Cleopatra* introducing the eradication of solid and single *Antony*, and *Coriolanus* definitely diagnosing the fantasy of the private linguists that in some ways underwrites them all. See *William Shakespeare: A Textual Companion*, ed. Stanley Wells and Gary Taylor, with John Jowett and William Montgomery (Oxford: Oxford University Press, 1997), 131.

3. Stanley Cavell, *The Claim of Reason: Wittgenstein, Skepticism, Morality and Tragedy*, 2nd ed. (Oxford: Oxford University Press, 1999), 297, henceforth *CR*. In part 3 of *CR*, Cavell takes issue with John Rawls characterization of promising as an office ("Two Concepts of Rules") in the following terms: "And to call being a promisor an 'office' (28n25) can only, I think, mislead. For it is obviously unlike other offices which are established within practices: there is no special procedure for entering it (e.g. no oaths!), no established routes for being selected or training yourself for it, etc. If it is an office, it is one any normal adult is competent to hold and can hold merely by putting himself in it with respect to anyone with whom he is in, or with whom he might create, a certain form of relationship. And it is critical to the concept of moral responsibility that it should be so" (297).

My preliminary investigation of the grammar of asking is influenced here both overall, and here locally by Ludwig Wittgenstein, Stanley Cavell, and Steven Affeldt's helpful thoughts about the language game of telling. See Ludwig Wittgenstein, *Philosophical Investigations: The German Text with an English Translation*, 4th ed., ed. G. E. M. Anscombe, P. M. S. Hacker, and Joachim Schulte (Chichester: Wiley-Blackwell, 2009), henceforth *PI*, ¶363; Cavell, *CR*, 93; and Steven Affeldt, "Captivating Pictures and Liberating Language: Freedom as the Achievement of Speech in Wittgenstein's *Philosophical Investigations*," *Philosophical Topics* 27, no. 2 (Fall 1999): 255–85, esp. 273–75.

4. All citations from *Coriolanus* are from *Coriolanus*, ed. Peter Holland, Arden Shakespeare, 3rd ser. (London: Bloomsbury, 2013). For some fine analyses of *Coriolanus* and the speech act of asking, see Stanley Fish, "How to Do Things with Austin and Searle," in *MLN* 91, no. 5 (October 1976): 983–1025, republished in *Is There a Text in This Class?: The Authority of Interpretive Communities*

(Cambridge, MA: Harvard University Press, 1980), 197–245. There are, however, some consequential differences between Fish's version of what he calls "speech act theory" and my understanding of ordinary language philosophy that will emerge more clearly. To put it succinctly, Fish's understanding of convention is very different from the question of convention as it is developed in Cavell's reading of Wittgenstein.

For Wittgenstein, on Cavell's understanding, convention is natural, built into our most basic and instinctual responses to each other, and therefore it is not something we *decide*, but rather it is something we live in our forms of life. It is something we cannot fail to know but about which we need to be reminded. For a detailed and important elaboration see Cavell, *CR*, "Natural and Conventional," chap. 5, 86–125. Wittgenstein, as Cavell says, writes that "if language is to be a means of communication there must be agreement not only in definitions but also (queer as this may sound) in judgments" (*PI*, ¶242), and Cavell's gloss on this remark underlines that the agreement is *in* not *on* judgments. This is part of the burden of the first chapter of *CR*. It is precisely this difference that Fish does not discern when he assimilates conventions to things we agree and decide *on*. The upshot of Cavell's reading is not, as Affeldt puts it, "that our shared language is the ground of our intelligibility." Rather, "our intelligibility to each other depends continuously, from moment to moment and in each act of speech, upon our agreement in judgment. . . . Our language is the vehicle through which, or the medium within which, we continuously undertake to make ourselves intelligible to one another by projecting the ground that we individually, at a given moment, occupy." Steven Affeldt, "The Ground of Mutuality: Criteria, Judgment, and Intelligibility in Stephen Mulhall and Stanley Cavell," *European Journal of Philosophy* 6, no. 1 (1998): 1–31, here 23.

Furthermore, Fish treats Austin as if he were John Searle and treats his vision of language as a theory about a particular class of speech acts called "performatives." John Searle in attempting to systematize Austin missed the revolution in his thinking. Searle, unlike Austin, assumes that meaning and use can be separated, imagining that sense is one thing and the use we make of words is another. My understanding of Austin sees him as inaugurating a revolution carried on by Wittgenstein and made available in Cavell's extension and understanding of both thinkers. See Niklas Forsberg, *Lectures on a Philosophy Less Ordinary: Language and Morality in J. L. Austin's Philosophy* (Abingdon: Routledge, 2022), 140n98, 171, 190–91. Cavell takes issue with Fish's distinctions between literary language and ordinary language. Stanley Cavell, "The Politics of Interpretation: Politics as Opposed to What?," in *Themes Out of School: Effects and Causes* (Chicago: University of Chicago Press, 1984), 34–39. For the "revolution" see Toril Moi, *Revolution of the Ordinary: Literary Studies After Wittgenstein, Austin, and Cavell* (Chicago: University of Chicago Press, 2017); and Sandra Laugier, introduction to *Must We Mean What We Say?*, trans. Sandra Laugier, *Critical Inquiry* 37, no. 4 (Summer 2011): 627–51; and Sandra Laugier, introduction to *Cavell's "Must We Mean What We Say?" at 50*, ed. Greg Chase, Juliet Floyd, and Sandra Laugier (Cambridge: Cambridge University Press, 2022).

5. For an extremely useful essay, see Sandra Laugier, "Wittgenstein and Cavell: Anthropology, Skepticism, and Politics," in *The Claim to Community: Essays on Stanley Cavell and Political Philosophy*, ed. Andrew Norris (Stanford, CA: Stanford University Press, 2006), 19–37, esp. 31, where the parallel between ordinary language and political language is made apparent.

6. Sicinius suggests he solicits them "in free contempt" (2.2.198). "Have you" he asks, "Ere now, denied the asker, and now again, / Of him that did not ask but mock, bestow / Your sued-for tongues?" (2.3.203-5).

7. "Plutarch's Lives of Noble Grecians and Romans," trans. Thomas North, in *Narrative and Dramatic Sources of Shakespeare*, vol. 5, ed. Geoffrey Bullough (London: Routledge, 1966), 506.

8. For some of the larger issues, see Affeldt, "Ground of Mutuality."

9. Caius Martius is equally disgusted by the idea of praise and cannot "idly sit" to hear his "nothings monstered" (2.2.73-74). Later, as he joins Aufidius's forces, he is described by Cominius as "a kind of nothing, titleless / Till he had forged himself a name o'the fire / Of burning Rome" (4.7.211-13), where he aspires to the impossible status of namelessness, and the fantasy of naming himself without others.

10. For "grounds of intelligibility," which we project in every speech act, see Affeldt, "Ground of Mutuality."

11. Of course, the logic of the first watch, which is initially Coriolanus's, is precisely what will be subverted in the supplication scene. The petitioners are old women and nonwarriors, those who do not fight but who must plead and, by these means, bring about a peace that "convenes" together.

12. Fish, "How to Do Things with Austin and Searle," 1000.

13. Wittgenstein, *PI*, ¶243. These remarks are collectively known as the "private language argument" and are often capitalized in the philosophical literature and given the abbreviated designation PLA (*PI*, ¶243–315). For the designation "argument," see, for example, Anthony Kenny, *Wittgenstein* (London: Allen Lane, 2005), chap. 10; G. P. Baker "The Private Language Argument," *Language and Communication* 18 (1998): 325–56; Hans-Johann Glock, *A Wittgenstein Dictionary* (Oxford: Blackwell, 1996), 309–15; and G. P. Baker and P. M. S. Hacker, *Wittgenstein: Rules, Grammar and Necessity*, vol. 2 of *An Analytical Commentary on the Philosophical Investigations*, 2nd ed. (Oxford: Wiley-Blackwell, 2009), 2:158–68.

Wittgenstein's remarks in *PI* come after a long section on rules (*PI*, ¶185–242) and before further remarks on thinking and on states of consciousness. They are part and parcel of an investigation of language and meaning, including almost a linguistic anthropology for human creatures. In his preface, Wittgenstein says that "the same or almost the same points were always being approached from fresh directions, and new sketches made," sketches of "landscapes "criss-crossing in every direction over a wide field of thought" (*PI*, 3e).

14. "Immediately after introducing the idea, Wittgenstein goes on to argue that there cannot be such a language. . . . The importance of drawing philosophy's attention to a largely un-heard of notion and then arguing that it is unrealizable lies in the fact that an unformulated reliance on the possibility of a private language is arguably essential to mainstream epistemology, philosophy

of mind and metaphysics from Descartes to versions of the representational theory of mind which became common in late twentieth century cognitive science." Stewart Candlish and George Wrisley, "Private Language," *Stanford Encyclopedia of Philosophy*, July 26, 1996, substantive revision, July 30, 2019, https://plato.stanford.edu/entries/private-language.

15. Cavell, *CR*, 343–54.

16. Cavell, *CR*, 343: "The dependence of reference upon expression in naming our states of consciousness, is, I believe, the specific moral of Wittgenstein's inventions containing the so-called language argument."

17. Cavell, *CR*, 344, 348, 351–52.

18. Cavell, *CR*, 343.

19. Sandra Laugier, *Wittgenstein: Le Mythe de L'Inexpressivité* (Paris: Vrin, 2010), 14. The latter phrase belongs to Peter Dula, "Private Languages," in *Cavell, Companionship, and Christian Theology* (Oxford: Oxford University Press, 2010), chap. 3. Richard Eldridge finds that the private language fantasy is a fantasy about the "acquisition of authority"; "one sustains—if it is possible—a conceptual life apart from the accommodations to any public practice." See Richard Eldridge, *Leading a Human Life: Wittgenstein, Intentionality, and Romanticism* (Chicago and London: University of Chicago Press, 1997), 243, 268. Cavell says that it is his goal "to reinsert the voice in philosophical thinking"; see Stanley Cavell, *Contesting Tears: The Hollywood Melodrama of the Unknown Woman* (Chicago and London: University of Chicago Press, 1997), 63. He also finds Wittgenstein as a philosopher more "attuned to the human voice than any other I can think of" (Cavell, *CR*, 5) and in his foreword, he finds the human voice "is being returned to moral assessments of itself" (Cavell, *CR*, xvi).

20. Cavell addresses the question of private language; see Stanley Cavell, *Coriolanus*, "*Coriolanus* and Interpretations of Politics ('Who does the wolf love?')," in *Themes Out of School: Effects and Causes* (Chicago: University of Chicago Press, 1984), 61. Wittgenstein's articulations of the fantasy of a private language are part of his redefinition of skepticism as a kind of narcissism, "a kind of denial of an existence shared with others."

21. Robert Miola, *Shakespeare's Rome* (Cambridge: Cambridge University Press: 1983); Paul Cantor, *Shakespeare's Rome: Republic and Empire* (Ithaca, NY: Cornell University Press, 1976), and Gail Kern Paster, "'To Starve with Feeding': The City in *Coriolanus*," *Shakespeare Studies* 11 (1978): 123–44.

22. Cavell, *CR*, 25.

23. Both meanings are available in the early 1600s.

24. Note Martius's characteristic reduction of their voices as explosive hot air rather than reasoned speech.

25. Force and political recognition are at issue in Plutarch's account, too. For Plutarch, one large question is whether "valliantnes," "honoured in Rome above all other vertues" should be accorded that status. For Coriolanus is seen as unyielding, and "churlish, uncivill, and altogether unfit for any man's conversation." This would make civility, the capacity for talking, for conversation central to political life, for the ability of a group of people to so much as form a polis; see Bullough, *Narrative and Dramatic Sources of Shakespeare*, 506.

26. See Naomi Scheman, "A Storied World: On Meeting and Being Met," in *Stanley Cavell and Literary Studies: Consequences of Skepticism*, ed. Richard Eldridge and Bernie Rhie (New York: Continuum, 2011), 96.

27. Andrew Norris, *Becoming Who We Are: Politics and Practical Philosophy in the Work of Stanley Cavell* (Oxford: Oxford University Press, 2017), 115. He cites Cavell, *CR*, 19: "The only source of confirmation . . . is ourselves. And each of us is fully authoritative in this struggle."

28. Hannah Arendt, *The Human Condition* (Chicago: University of Chicago Press, second edition, 1998), 175, henceforth *HC*.

29. Arendt uses the term *men* where we might now prefer a more inclusive term.

30. Arendt, *HC*, 176.

31. Cavell, *CR*, 27.

32. See, for example, Miola, *Shakespeare's Rome*: "[Shakespeare] seeks in *Coriolanus* to explore the purpose, nature, and problems of political order" (165).

33. The political nature of the play is noted by many critics. Rossiter calls it "Shakespeare's only great political play." A. P. Rossiter *Angel with Horns and Other Shakespearean Lectures* (New York: Theater Arts, 1961), 235-52.

34. "The Romane Historie of T. Livy" was translated by Philemon Holland and published in 1600. The discussion of the management of the plebs begins in book 1.

35. Niccolo Machiavelli, *The Discourses*, trans. Leslie Walker, ed. Bernard Crick (London: Penguin, 1983), book 1, 3-5.

36. Discussions of republicanism in a growing body of literature include Andrew Hadfield (who does not discuss *Coriolanus*), *Shakespeare and Republicanism* (Cambridge: Cambridge University Press, 2005); James Kuzner, *Open Subjects: English Renaissance Republicans, Modern Selfhoods, and the Virtue of Vulnerability* (Edinburgh: Edinburgh University Press, 2011); and Patrick Gray, *Shakespeare and the Fall of the Roman Republic: Selfhood, Stoicism, and Civil War* (Edinburgh: Edinburgh University Press, 2019). For Tacitus's major influence in the early seventeenth century, see Peter Burke, "Tacitus, Skepticism, and Reason of State," in *Cambridge History of Political Thought 1450–1700*, ed. J. H. Burns (Cambridge: Cambridge University Press, 2008), 477-98.

37. Cavell suggests that talking, claiming, calling, and counting are the major modes in which we word the world, (*CR*, 94).

38. *The Tragedy of Coriolanus*, ed. R. B. Parker (Oxford: Oxford University Press, 1994), 83n4.

39. Fish's concept of "interpretative communities" thinks of convention as something more like contract. Cavell's idea of agreements "in" and not about judgments sounds a deeper conception of convention as what we cannot possibly all have agreed in advance, but which concerns a shared form of life. For an elucidation of Wittgenstein's understanding of agreement in judgment and forms of life, see Cavell, *CR*, chap. 5. See also Sandra Laugier, "Voice as Form of Life and Life From," *Nordic Wittgenstein Review* (2015): 63-81. I chart my understanding of this difference in detail; see Sarah Beckwith, "A Vision of Language for Literary Historians: Forms of Life, Context, Use," *Wittgenstein and Literary*

Studies, ed. Robert Chodat and John Gibson (Cambridge: Cambridge University Press, 2022), 82-103.

40. Stanley Cavell, "Declining Decline: Wittgenstein as a Philosopher of Culture," in *This New Yet Unapproachable America: Lectures after Emerson after Wittgenstein* (Albuquerque, NM: Living Batch, 1989), 48. This essay, along with Cavell's chapter "Natural and Conventional" in *CR*, is one of the most original and profound readings of "forms of life." Cavell expounds an idea of culture as a "system of modifications of our lives as talkers." He writes: "Culture as a whole is the work of our life with language, it goes with language, it is languages's manifestation or picture or externalization" (*CR*, 48).

41. Cavell, *CR*, 17. Criticism of the play has been fruitfully preoccupied by the speech act of naming. See especially Gordon, D. G. "Name and Fame: Shakespeare's *Coriolanus*." In *The Renaissance Imagination: Essays and Lectures by D. G. Gordon*, ed. Stephen Orgel. Berkeley: University of California Press, 1975. 40-57. I am arguing that an exclusive focus on naming obscures the way the play is involved in a much more fundamental examination of linguistic agency.

42. Cavell, *CR*, 35, 94.

43. J. L. Austin, "A Plea for Excuses" in *Philosophical Papers* (Oxford: Clarendon, 1961), henceforth *PP*, 182: "Our common stock of words embodies all the distinctions men have found worth drawing, in the lifetimes of many generations." See also Cavell, *CR*, 94.

44. Laugier, "Wittgenstein and Cavell, 34.

45. Paul Standish, "Democratic Participation in the Body Politic," *Educational Theory* 55, no. 4 (July 2005), 374: "Language is the epitome of community because in talking we are already exposed to others."

46. Cavell, *CR*, 14.

47. The first citizen in act 1, scene 1, does not appear to be the same first citizen as in subsequent scenes, so first citizen designates only who speaks first and second.

48. Not all readings of the play see Coriolanus's death as a sacrifice, of course. One powerful version of this reading is Philip Brockbank's in his Arden, 2nd ser. edition of *Coriolanus*. In this reading, Coriolanus dies for the city that has worshipped glory, yet failed to understand its need of the warrior Coriolanus in Rome. His death is at once the inevitable climax of that failure of recognition, and a punishment for a mode of life which cannot make peace with "the more vulnerable claims of human community." That community is therefore "purged, chastened, shamed, and renewed." *Coriolanus*, ed. Philip Brockbank, Arden Shakespeare, 2nd ser. (London: Methuen & Co, 1976), 66.

49. "It is held / That valour is then chiefest virtue and / Most dignifies the haver" (2.2.81-83). Although the speech goes on to name Martius's deeds of valour, it continues, "If it be." The "if" invites us to consider the conditions under which valor might be the chiefest virtue and thus challenges the connections between virtue, valor and worth.

50. Hannah Arendt, *On Violence* (Orlando, FL: Harcourt, 1969), 56: "Power and Violence are opposites.... Violence appears where power is in jeopardy, but left to its own course it ends in power's disappearance." On the confusion of power, violence and authority, see Hannah Arendt, "What Is Authority?," in *Between Past and Future* (London: Penguin, 1977), 92.

51. Michael Mann, *On Wars* (New Haven, CT: Yale University Press, 2023), 10. Mann distinguishes military from other forms of power (ideological, economic, and political) in his previous work. See Michael Mann, *The Sources of Social Power*. 3 vols. Second ed. (Cambridge: Cambridge University Press, 2012).

52. Simone Weil and Rachel Bespaloff, *War and the Iliad*, trans. Mary McCarthy (New York: New York Review of Books, 2005), 3, 7-8, 11, 26, 11.

53. When he returns home from Corioles, Volumnia exclaims: "O, he is wounded, I thank the gods for't." Menenius shares the feeling, though modifies it—"the wounds become him" as long as they are "not too much" and as long as he brings home a victory in his pocket (2.1.118-20).

54. Reuben Brower calls Coriolanus "Achilles in the Forum" in his interesting chapter on the play; see Reuben Brower, *Hero and Saint: Shakespeare and the Graeco-Roman Heroic Tradition* (Oxford: Oxford University Press, 1971), 363.

55. The phrase is from Gordon Braden's excellent book; see Gordon Braden, *Renaissance Tragedy and the Senecan Tradition: Anger's Privilege* (New Haven, CT: Yale University Press, 1985), 2.

56. For Hannah Arendt on natality, see *HC*; for the development of the concept in her thinking, see Patricia Bowen-Moore, *Hannah Arendt's Philosophy of Natality* (New York: St. Martin's Press, 1989).

57. Wilfrid Owen, "I am the enemy you killed, my friend," from "Strange Meeting," in *The Poems of Wilfrid Owen*, ed. Jon Stallworthy (New York: W.W. Norton, 1986).

58. Seneca, *Moral and Political Essays*, ed. John M. Cooper and J. F. Pocope (Cambridge: Cambridge University Press, 1995), 131.

59. In their edition of Shakespeare's complete works published in 1914, Charlotte Porter and Helen Clark see the play as structured around five acts showing Coriolanus as "soldier," "candidate," "foe to the public weal," then "avenger," and finally Coriolanus as Human." Cited in Holland, Arden Shakespeare, 3rd ser., 110.

60. Leah Whittington, *Renaissance Suppliants: Poetry, Antiquity, Reconciliation* (Oxford: Oxford University Press, 2016), 138. This, she says, cannot be said of any other play in the Shakespeare canon. Whittington learnedly shows the genesis of this focus in Plutarch and in the wider literary and visual culture in her chapter, "Constraint and Coercion in Shakespeare." Most tellings render the scene a "moral tale about anger, estrangement, and reintegration" but Shakespeare creates of it a tragedy (141). Shakespeare's profound originality, I want to add, makes it a tragedy motivated by the relinquishment and adoption of human kindness.

61. Rachel Bespaloff, "On the *Iliad*," in Weil and Bespaloff, *War and the Iliad*, 79. Bespaloff's stunning chapter "Priam and Achilles Break Bread" is part of a meditation on the *Iliad*, contemporaneous with Weil's essay, which was her way of facing the catastrophe of war.

62. For a reassessment of selfhood and the role of vulnerability, see Kuzner, *Open Subjects*, and Gray, *Shakespeare and the Fall of the Roman Republic*.

63. Bullough, *Narrative and Dramatic Sources of Shakespeare*, 539.

64. We may want to recall here the homosocial reunion of Aufidius with Coriolanus. Aufidius "more dances his rapt heart" when he first recognizes Coriolanus and becomes allied with him, than when he saw his wedded mistress astride his threshold (4.5.118-120). Aufidius might well feel displaced as he witnesses this particular kiss!

65. Holland, Arden Shakespeare, 3rd ser., 390. He notes Doran's 2007 production in which the actor Will Houston speaks the line "O, a kiss" not as a response to a kiss, but a longing for one that never happens.

66. *Coriolanus*, ed. Lee Bliss (Cambridge: Cambridge University Press, 2000), 253.

67. Weil and Bespaloff, *War and the Iliad*, 4.

68. Raphael Lyne, "The Shakespearean Grasp," *Cambridge Quarterly* 42, no. 1 (March 2013): 38-61, suggests—against the idea that the stage direction is authorial—that it is the prompter who might most benefit from this stage direction to prevent a vital dramatic moment being ruined or talked over, with the implication that the folio version is quite close to the prompt book, but Lyne also says this argument is both beguiling and circular. For another analysis, see Jarrett Walker, "Voiceless Bodies, Bodiless Voices: The Drama of Human Perception in *Coriolanus*," *Shakespeare Quarterly* 43 (1992): 180.

69. In his essay on *Coriolanus*, Cavell understands this speech as "expressing the silence with which this son holds, and then relinquishes, his mother's hand." Stanley Cavell, *Disowning Knowledge in Seven Plays of Shakespeare*, updated ed. (Cambridge: Cambridge University Press, 2003), 160.

70. Narrative and Dramatic Sources of Shakespeare ed., Geoffrey Bullough, vol. 5, *The Roman Plays* (NY: Columbia University Press, 1966), 541.

71. The softness is appropriate to the scene's dynamic. Martius has already described himself as "melting" (5.3.27) when he sees them first approach, as if here like Anthony, he cannot maintain and sustain his former shape, his body-armour.

72. See Jan H. Blits, *Spirit, Soul, and City: Shakespeare's Coriolanus* (Lanham, MD: Lexington, 2006), 216: "In *Coriolanus* hands are often synecdoches for the grip of force or necessity, especially in matters of death." See also Lyne, "Shakespearean Grasp."

73. Heather James nicely says: "What brings him to man's estate and the threshold of tragedy is his consent to identifying with the members of society who are forced to depend on others." Heather James, "A Modern Perspective: *Coriolanus*," Folger Shakespeare Library, accessed February 9, 2025, https://www.folger.edu/explore/shakespeares-works/coriolanus/coriolanus-a-modern-perspective.

74. Christina Luckyj examines four productions in which Volumnia's silence after act 5, scene 3, is interpreted "as devastation." They are as follows: Old Vic, 1954; Royal Shakespeare Company, 1972; Stratford, Ontario, 1981; and the National Theatre, 1984. In "Volumnia's Silence," *Studies in English Literature, 1500–1900* 31, no. 2 (1991): 340.

75. Wittgenstein, *PI*, ¶287.

76. An important distinction maintained and developed in Raimond Gaita, *A Common Humanity: Thinking About Love and Truth and Justice* (London and New York: Routledge, 1998).

77. For some useful reflections on Cavell's humanism, see Bernie Rhie and Richard Eldridge, introduction to *Stanley Cavell and Literary Studies: Consequences of Skepticism* (New York: Continuum, 2011), 4.

78. John Berger, with photographs by Jean Mohr, *A Fortunate Man: The Story of a Country Doctor* (1967; repr., New York: Vintage International, 1997), 116.

79. The apt terminology of "man-child" is introduced by Volumnia. "I sprang not more in joy at first hearing he was a man-child than now in first seeing he had proved himself a man" (1.3.15–7). She means, of course, that she rejoices he was born male, but the history of his childhood is notably emphasized in the play, as is the idea that he is so often seen in relation to his mother, therefore as a child, her child. The first citizen observes in the very first scene that he fights the wars "to please his mother, and to be partly proud" more than for his country (1.1.35–36).

80. Bullough, *Narrative and Dramatic Sources of Shakespeare*, 539.

81. I am going against quite a strong critical consensus. Janet Adelman's strong psychoanalytic reading led the way. Her argument is as rich as it has been influential and I am in sympathy with much of it but not with this: "Just as his child entered the scene holding Volumnia's hand, so Coriolanus again becomes a child, holding his mother's hand": Janet Adelman, *Suffocating Mothers: Fantasies of Maternal Origin in Shakespeare's Plays, Hamlet to The Tempest* (New York and London: Routledge, 1992), 161. Among many other examples, see Michael Long, *The Unnatural Scene: A Study in Shakespearean Tragedy* (London: Methuen, 1976), 78. Long finds Aufidius's slur perfectly valid; the man child has never been adult, as the first citizen hints at the play's beginning. Lucy Munro, in a fascinating essay on the discrepancy between actor and role so prevalent in the Children's Companies, yet unavailable to Shakespeare, says his "political childishness" is evident throughout the play; see Lucy Munro, "*Coriolanus* and the Little Eyases: The Boyhood of Shakespeare's Hero," in *Shakespeare and Childhood*, ed. Kate Chedgzoy, Suzanne Greenhalgh, and Robert Shaughnessy (Cambridge: Cambridge University Press, 2007), 78. Kenneth Gross discusses Coriolanus's buried impulses as more infantile than heroic; see Kenneth Gross *Shakespeare's Noise* (Chicago: University of Chicago Press, 2001), 133.

82. See Jessica Wolfe, *Homer and the Question of Strife from Erasmus to Hobbes* (Toronto: University of Toronto Press, 2015), 294.

6. Antony and Cleopatra

1. Cicero, *Letters to Atticus*, vol. 1, ed. and trans. D. R. Shackleton Bailey, Loeb Classical Library (Cambridge, MA: Harvard University Press, 1999), 15:15: "I can't stand the Queen."

2. Horace's "Cleopatra Ode," Ode 1.37.21; http://www.perseus.tufts.edu/hopper/text.jsp?doc=Perseus:text:1999.02.0024:book=1:poem=37. "Fatale

monstrum" is best translated as a "doom-laden portent." Lawrence Rhu has pointed out to me in a private communication that the stanzas after this include admiration for Cleopatra's regal stoicism.

3. *The Aeneid*, trans, Robert Fagles (New York: Penguin, 2006), 8:808, 264, translating Virgil's *"sequiturque (nefas) Aegyptia coniunx."* (*Coniunx* can be translated as wife or woman. I will show why that distinction might be important.)

4. For the difference between the moralizer and the moralist, see Stanley Cavell, *The Claim of Reason: Wittgenstein, Skepticism, Morality and Tragedy*, 2nd ed. (Oxford: Oxford University Press, 1999), henceforth *CR*, 326: "What is required in confronting another person is not your liking him or her but your being willing, from whatever cause, to take his or her position into account, and bear the consequences. If the moralist is the human being who best grasps the human position, teaches us what our human position is, better than we know, in ways we cannot escape but through distraction and muddle, then our first task, in subjecting ourselves to judgment is to tell the moralist from the moralizer."

Raimond Gaita has remarked that "the estrangement from morality of morally serious people—is a mark of the times." Raimond Gaita, *A Common Humanity: Thinking about Love and Truth and Justice* (London: Routledge, 1998), xv. Gaita significantly stages his reflections as encounters. My reflections in this chapter develop the idea that judgment is not located in particular acts of judgment, moralized or otherwise (although that reduction is indeed closely connected with the moralization of moral theory), but it is pervasive in our using criteria to make the distinctions we habitually make in speaking. It is these encounters and responses rather than any moralized framing to which I pay attention.

5. Philo's "Nay" (1.1.1); Dolabella's "Gentle Madam, No" (5.2.93). All quotations are from the *Antony and Cleopatra*, ed. John Wilders, Arden Shakespeare, 3rd ser. (London: Routledge, 1995).

6. For a detailed and compelling analysis of an Augustan attempt to possess time and space in an imperial theater, see William Junker, "The Image of Both Theaters: Empire and Revelation in Shakespeare's *Antony and Cleopatra*," *Shakespeare Quarterly* 66, no. 2. (Summer 2015): 167–87. Cleopatra's competing model discloses a history of what "might be" over "the history of what merely was" (168; 5.2.91-92). For Augustan innovations in triumphal theater, see Mary Beard, *The Roman Triumph* (Cambridge, MA: Harvard University Press, 2007). After his extravagant triumph of 29 BCE, Augustus restricts triumphal theater to the emperor and his family, and he characteristically refused the triumphs offered to himself and his family. For Cleopatra's "witty appropriations of triumph," see Anthony Miller, *Roman Triumphs and Early Modern English Culture* (Houndmills: Palgrave, 2001), 128, 133.

7. Directors often stage a kiss at "to do thus" (1.1.38). There is no such direction in the folio. "Thus" might be a more general sweep of the terrain to encompass their self-styled grandeur or magnitude, or it might indeed be Antony's way of stopping Cleopatra's mouth.

8. I take this latter phrase from Christopher Cordner, "Moral Philosophy in the Midst of Things," in *A Sense for Humanity: The Ethical Thought of Raimond Gaita*, ed. Craig Taylor and Melinda Graefe (Clayton, Australia: Monash University, 2014), 128. Cordner is describing a moral philosophy that merges out

of moral encounter, one that does not illustrate a given concept (as in Kant's determinate judgment) but is shaped by an example as in reflective judgment. I pursue some of these distinctions, useful as they are for catching the imaginative provocations of this play.

9. For Craig Taylor, it is a feature of moralism to occlude the ways in which responses such as pity and other immediate responses act as forms of moral recognition. This kind of responsiveness is a dimension of moral thought. See Craig Taylor, *Moralism: A Study of a Vice* (Montreal, Canada: McGill-Queen's University Press, 2012), vii, ix.

10. For a careful and comprehensive argument that moral thinking goes "beyond judgment," see Alice Crary, *Beyond Moral Judgment* (Cambridge, MA: Harvard University Press, 2007). I return to these themes later in the chapter. Vivasvan Soni and Thomas Pfau have brought judgment back into critical focus in their collection, *Judgment and Action: Fragments Toward a History* (Evanston, IL: Northwestern University Press, 2018). Signs that scholars and critics are beginning to pay attention to this crucial humanistic concept are evident in the publications by Michael W. Clune, *A Defense of Judgment* (Chicago: University of Chicago Press, 2021); and D. N. Rodowick, *An Education in Judgment: Hannah Arendt and the Humanities* (Chicago: University of Chicago Press, 2021).

11. John Danby, "*Antony and Cleopatra*: A Shakespearian Adjustment," first published in *Scrutiny* (1949). I use the version reprinted in *Antony and Cleopatra: New Casebooks*, ed. John Drakakis (London: Red Globe, 1994), 33–55.

12. Other critics have brilliantly taken up Danby's cue; see, for example, Janet Adelman, *The Common Liar: An Essay on Antony and Cleopatra* (New Haven, CT: Yale University Press, 1973); and Barbara J. Bono, *Literary Transvaluation: From Vergilian Epic to Shakespearean Tragi-comedy* (Berkeley: University of California Press, 1984).

13. Danby, "*Antony and Cleopatra*: A Shakespearean Adjustment," 36, 35, 45.

14. Danby, "*Antony and Cleopatra*: A Shakespearean Adjustment," 35, 36, 40.

15. Adelman, *The Common Liar*, 20, cited in Wilders, *Antony and Cleopatra*, 42.

16. Danby, "*Antony and Cleopatra*: A Shakespearean Adjustment," 24, 27, 30. In Wilders's Arden Shakespeare, 3rd ser., he devotes a sequence of his introduction to "the question of moral judgement." See Wilders, *Antony and Cleopatra*, 38–43.

17. Barbara Bono also finds a "crisis of belief" present in almost all of Shakespeare's plays, but "absolutely central to *Antony and Cleopatra*" (*Literary Transvaluation*, 12). She charts as carefully and convincingly as Danby and Adelman the way in which the play both "demands that we make judgments even as it frustrates our ability to judge rationally" (*Literary Transvaluation*, 14).

18. Bono, *Literary Transvaluation*, 39.

19. The crisis of judgment is identifiable under many descriptions and on the basis of some characteristic oppositions between fact and value, objective and subjective, ought and is, and descriptive and evaluative. It appears in many different guises, dogmatism and skepticism, for example.

20. Vivasvan Soni, "Introduction: The Crisis of Judgement," *Eighteenth Century* 51, no. 3 (Fall 2010): 261–88. The question of judgment is now explored in Thomas Pfau, *Minding the Modern: Human Agency, Intellectual Traditions, and*

Responsible Knowledge (Notre Dame, IN: University of Notre Dame Press, 2013); Linda Zerilli, *A Democratic Theory of Judgment* (Chicago: University of Chicago Press, 2016); and Kevin Curran, ed., *Shakespeare and Judgment* (Edinburgh: Edinburgh University Press, 2016).

21. I differentiate this from a realization that judgment is often tragic, which is precisely what tragedy will sometimes reveal.

22. Conant's idiom is a Wittgensteinian and Austinian one in which the pressures of "philosophy" are taken to remove the context of use which makes concepts intelligible. That is why he wants to put us back in contact with the way we actually use "perspective"—that is, when we invoke it, what it does in our speech. See James Conant, "The Dialectic of Perspectivism, I," *SATS: Nordic Journal of Philosophy* 6, no. 2 (2005): 5–50.

23. Conant, "The Dialectic of Perspectivism, I," 15.

24. Conant, "The Dialectic of Perspectivism, I," 12.

25. Wilders, *Antony and Cleopatra*, 41.

26. Soni, "Introduction: The Crisis of Judgment," 262-63.

27. Immanuel Kant, *Critique of the Power of Judgment*, ed. Paul Guyer (Cambridge: Cambridge University Press, 2000).

28. Andrew Norris, "Skepticism and Critique in Arendt and Cavell," *Philosophy and Social Criticism* 44, no. 1 (2018), 81. Arendt's Kantian work on judgment begins with *Hannah Arendt's Lectures on Kant's Political Philosophy*, ed. Ronald Beiner (Chicago: University of Chicago Press, 1992), and had she not died, was to be continued in the third part of *Life of the Mind*. For the Kantian underpinnings of Hannah Arendt's late work, see Zerilli, *Democratic Theory of Judgment*. Kant's influence is all pervasive in Cavell's work, implicit in the very title of *The Claim of Reason* and explicitly addressed in Stanley Cavell, "Aesthetics Problems of Modern Philosophy," in *Must We Mean What We Say?* (Cambridge: Cambridge University Press, 2002). I am indebted to Keren Gorodeisky and Arata Hamawaki for educating me on the Kantian dimensions of Cavell's work both in person and in print. See especially Arata Hamawaki, "Kant on Beauty and the Normative Force of Feeling," *Philosophical Topics* 34, nos. 1 and 2 (Spring and Fall 2006): 107–44; and Arata Hamawaki, "Philosophic and Aesthetic Appeal: Stanley Cavell on the Irreducibility of the First Person in Aesthetics and in Philosophy," in *Cavell's "Must We Mean What We Say?" at 50*, ed. Greg Chase, Juliet Floyd, and Sandra Laugier (Cambridge: Cambridge University Press, 2022), 103-20.

29. Arendt's project was sponsored by her sense that after the camps and horrors of twentieth-century totalitarianism, there was no guarantee in legal frameworks, or in universal human rights, but only in the capacity for judgment, which was so alarmingly atrophied in the likes of Eichmann. Arendt studied the conditions of such atrophy and sought, in her unfinished third volume of *The Life of the Mind*, to examine and retrieve this essential faculty. Cavell's Kantianism underlines the whole project of *CR*.

30. Kant, "Analytic of the Aesthetic Power of Judgment," *Critique of the Power*, 89. In Kant's lingo he says that the determining ground of an aesthetic judgment "cannot be other than subjective."

31. Kant, *Critique of the Power*, 97, for "Subjective universality"; for the demand on everyone, 98.

32. J. M. Bernstein, "Aesthetics, Modernism, Literature: Cavell's Transformations of Philosophy," in *Stanley Cavell*, ed. Richard Eldridge (Cambridge: Cambridge University Press, 2003), 107.

33. Ludwig Wittgenstein, *Philosophical Investigations: The German Text with an English Translation*, 4th ed., ed. G. E. M. Anscombe, P. M. S. Hacker, and Joachim Schulte (Chichester: Wiley-Blackwell, 2009), henceforth *PI*, ¶68. See Stanley Cavell, "The Availability of Wittgenstein's Later Philosophy," in *Must We Mean What We Say? A Book of Essays* (Cambridge: Cambridge University Press, 2002); and Cavell, *CR*, 188.

34. See Stanley Cavell, *Pursuits of Happiness: The Hollywood Comedy of Remarriage* (Cambridge, MA: Harvard University Press, 1981). The phrase is the title chapter for Cavell's essay on *The Philadelphia Story*.

35. Sandra Laugier, "What Matters: The Ethics and Aesthetics of Importance," in *Stanley Cavell on Aesthetic Understanding*, ed. Gary L. Hagberg (London: Palgrave Macmillan, 2018), 169. Laugier judges it to be one of Cavell's greatest accomplishments to show "that truth and importance are one and the same, or that importance is just as important as truth, and just as demanding and precise a concept" (171).

36. Richard Eldridge, *Leading a Human Life: Wittgenstein, Intentionality, and Romanticism* (Chicago: University of Chicago Press, 1997), 214–15.

37. For important inquiries on this central concept in the humanities, see Soni, "Introduction: The Crisis of Judgment"; Pfau, *Minding the Modern*; Zerilli, *Democratic Theory of Judgement*; and Soni and Pfau, *Judgment and Action*.

38. Ludwig Wittgenstein, *Tractatus-Logico-Philosophicus*, trans. C. K. Ogden (New York: Dover, 1999), 6.43, 106.

39. Madeline Doran, "High Events Such as These: The Language of Hyperbole," in *Shakespeare's Dramatic Language: Essays* (Madison: University of Wisconsin Press, 1976), 154–81.

40. Russ McDonald remarks that the surrender of son to mother in *Coriolanus* ("he holds her by the hand, silent") is a profound shift from the "masculine verbal purist" to the feminine verbal seducer in *Antony and Cleopatra*, as "Cleopatra inserts herself into and transforms what might be-as it is in Plutarch and other neoclassical versions, the single tragedy of Antony." Russ McDonald, *Shakespeare's Late Style* (Cambridge: Cambridge University Press, 2006), 70.

41. Wilders, *Antony and Cleopatra*, 25.

42. John Milton, *The Doctrine and Discipline of Divorce*. In *The Complete Poetry and Essential Prose of John Milton*. Ed. William Kerrigan, John Rumrich, and Stephen M. Fallon. (New York: Modern Library, 2007), 866.

43. Milton, *Doctrine and Discipline*, 866.

44. Cavell, *Pursuits of Happiness*, 19.

45. Stanley Cavell, *Disowning Knowledge: In Seven Plays of Shakespeare*, 2nd ed. (Cambridge: Cambridge University Press, 2012), 18.

46. Cavell, *Pursuits of Happiness*, 53. Cavell also says that in the remarriage comedies a "criterion is being proposed for the success or happiness of a society, namely that it is happy to the extent that it provides conditions that permit conversations of this character, or a moral equivalent of them, between its citizens," 32.

47. Ludger Viefhues-Bailey, *Beyond the Philosopher's Fear: A Cavellian Reading of Gender, Origin and Religion in Modern Skepticism* (London: Routledge, 2007), 98.

48. Stanley Cavell, *Contesting Tears: The Hollywood Melodrama of the Unknown Woman* (Chicago: University of Chicago Press, 1989), 30.

49. Robert Ornstein, "Love and Art in *Antony and Cleopatra*," in *Twentieth Century Interpretations of Antony and Cleopatra*, ed. Mark Rose (Englewood Cliffs, NJ: Prentice-Hall, 1977), 95.

50. North's translation of Plutarch's "The Life of Marcus Antonius," in *Lives of the Noble Grecians and Romans*, is reproduced from Geoffrey Bullough, *Narrative and Dramatic Sources of Shakespeare*, vol. 5 (London: Routledge and Kegan Paul), 289.

51. Bullough, *Narrative and Dramatic Sources of Shakespeare*, 275. My point is the extraordinary, vital, and ambitious claims they make for their love, but Tony Tanner sees in this phrase an invention of language, "using language as a repository of possibilities, trying to transcend the limitations of the available formulations, rehearsing reality by stretching language in new directions and combinations." Tony Tanner, *Prefaces to Shakespeare* (Cambridge, MA: Harvard University Press, 2010), 622.

52. For Cinthio, see Bullough, *Narrative and Dramatic Sources of Shakespeare*, 346; for Garnier, see Bullough, *Narrative and Dramatic Sources of Shakespeare*, 372.

53. Scenes of conversation: 1.1, 1.3, 3.7, 3.11, 3.13, 4.2, 4.4, 4.8, 4.12, 4.15. Emrys Jones has shown how the play's movement is obscured in the editorial addition of acts to the play's seamless movement. The far-flung and rapidly alternating locales in short, sometimes tiny scenes makes way for a more concentrated focus on Actium, Alexandria, and the monument, culminating in the focus on the play's longest scene, which requires our utmost attention: The scene that "ends all other deeds" (5.1.5). See Emrys Jones, *Scenic Form in Shakespeare* (Oxford: Clarendon, 1971), 225–65. Jones suggests that this allows for the alternation of intimacy and detachment in relation to the play's chief pair; see Jones, *Scenic Form*, 239.

54. See Jones, *Scenic Form*, 7–8.

55. Bullough, *Narrative and Dramatic Sources of Shakespeare*, 275. He also mentions that her voice was "an instrument of musicke to divers sports and pastimes, the whiche she easely turned to any language that pleased her." She has learned many languages and converses easily in them, but it is Shakespeare who takes up and explores the mutuality of conversation and how central it is to their love. Plutarch is as disdainful as the Romans in his condemnation of their pastimes as "idle," wasting as he puts it, "the most pretious thing a man can spende" (275). Time is not *spent* by Antony and Cleopatra when they are together; it is stretched and distended by their mutual pleasure.

56. *The Oxford Shakespeare: The Tragedy of Antony and Cleopatra*, ed. Michael Neill (Oxford: Oxford University Press, 1994), 211. I prefer this to Wilders's "satisfy his appetite," 161.

57. *Antony and Cleopatra* is notoriously hard to play, and there have been many unsuccessful stage productions. The raw simplicities of Antony and Cleopatra's talk are saturated with a showy excess that obscures the delicate and exposed points of connection between the lovers. This is not to say that the

lovers are not self-regarding, grandiose, or histrionic, nor that their relationship is not thoroughly erotic, suffused with desire and vitality; it is to point to a significant dramatic and philosophical *achievement* of the play in showing what it means to converse.

58. James Boswell, *The Life of Samuel Johnson*, ed. David Womersley (London: Penguin, 2008), 867.

59. Charles Taylor makes this point and uses this example in "Cross-Purposes: The Liberal-Communitarian Debate," in *Philosophical Arguments* (Cambridge, MA: Harvard University Press, 1995), 189. Taylor's point is that the dominant atomized picture of agency makes some dimensions of conversation obscure. This is a point made too in Rowan Williams, *Lost Icons: Reflections on Cultural Bereavement* (Edinburgh: Clark, 2000), 81.

60. Robert Garnier's play, *M. Antoine* (1578) was translated by Mary Herbert (Sidney), The Countess of Pembroke as *Antonius* (1592), and Samuel Daniel's version was *The Tragedie of Cleopatra* (1594). The declamatory style rules out the very notion of conversation, but Shakespeare finds an idiom for it in his dramatic poetry.

61. I borrow these last phrases from Claire Carlisle, *The Marriage Question: George Eliot's Double Life* (New York: Farrar, Straus, and Giroux, 2023), ix, 266. Her wonderful book is relevant to my reading of Shakespeare's play, because Carlisle claims George Eliot as a philosophical writer and explores her brilliant novelistic investigation of marriage. "There is something dazzling about marriage—that leap into the open-endedness of another human being" is the first sentence of the preface to her book. The last quotation comes from the book's closing pages: "[Eliot] searched for truths not in order to form crisp definitions or moral judgments, but to make peace for souls to grow, to stay curious, to feel alive." Shakespeare, I think, is profoundly interested here in the "growth of souls" through a loving relationship, and this, as a very principle of life, is what makes life worth living, therefore worth dying for.

62. Of course this is a double-bind. It would not go down too well to mourn her in front of Cleopatra.

63. Bullough, *Narrative and Dramatic Sources of Shakespeare*, 276.

64. On the subject of the kisses in this play, see Bernard Beckerman, "Past the Size of Dreaming," in *Twentieth Century Interpretations of Antony and Cleopatra*, ed. Mark Rose (Englewood Cliffs, NJ: Prentice Hall, 1977), 110.

65. *Romeo and Juliet* ends with two; *Julius Caesar* with three; *Othello*, *Macbeth*, and *Hamlet* with one a piece. In *Antony and Cleopatra*, the deaths by suicide include Enobarbus (4.9), Antony (4.14), and Cleopatra, Charmian, and Iras (5.2).

66. Cited in *The Oxford Book of Death*, ed. D. J. Enright (Oxford: Oxford University Press, 1983), 85.

67. Anne Barton, "'Nature's Piece Against Fancy': The Divided Catastrophe of *Antony and Cleopatra*" (inaugural lecture, Bedford College, 1973); reprinted in *Essays, Mainly Shakespearean* (Cambridge: Cambridge University Press, 1994), 113-35.

68. On the unusual structure of the divided catastrophe see Barton, "Nature's Piece Against Fancy."

69. "Imperare sibi maximum imperium est," Seneca, epistle 113.31, in *Seneca: Epistles 93–124* trans. Richard M. Gummere (Cambridge, MA: Harvard University Press, 1925), 298.

70. Rebecca Bushnell, *Tragedies of Tyrants: Political Thought in the English Renaissance* (Ithaca, NY: Cornell University Press, 1990), 31.

71. In Gordon Braden's classic study of Seneca's influence on Renaissance drama, he calls stoicism a philosophy of the will; see Gordon Braden, *Renaissance Tragedy and the Senecan Tradition: Anger's Privilege* (New Haven, CT: Yale University Press, 1985).

72. Seneca, "*De Ira*," in *Anger, Mercy, Revenge*, trans. Robert A. Kaster and Martha Nussbaum (Chicago: University of Chicago Press, 2010), 76.

73. Tacitus's description is in *Annals*, vol. 15, trans. A. J. Woodman (Indianapolis: Hackett, 2004), 64–67.

74. See James Ker, *The Deaths of Seneca* (Oxford: Oxford University Press, 2009). Medieval legendary material had Seneca's name as a kind of prophecy, killing himself (se-necans), Jacobus de Voragine, *Legenda Aurea*, ed. Georg Theodor Graesse (Dresden, 1846), Chap. LXXXIX, 3.

75. The play frequently flirts with comedy.

76. Robert Sokolowski, *Moral Action* (Bloomington: Indiana University Press, 1985), appendix A, 198.

77. "Here I am Antony / Yet cannot hold this visible shape" (4.14.13-4). The image here of the clouds and their vaporous shape-shifting leads to indistinction "like water is in water" (4.14.10–11). The stoic suicide cannot possibly prevail amidst this deliquescence.

78. Explorations of the use of revelation in *Antony and Cleopatra* include Hannibal Hamlin, *The Bible in Shakespeare* (Oxford: Oxford University Press, 2018), 214; and Adrian Streete, "The Politics of Ethical Presentism: Appropriation, Spirituality, and the Case of *Antony and Cleopatra*," *Textual Practice* 22 (2008): 405–31.

Bibliography

Shakespeare Editions

Plays

Shakespeare, William. *All's Well that Ends Well*. Eds. Suzanne Gossett and Helen Wilcox. Arden Shakespeare, 3rd ser. London: Bloomsbury, 2019.
Shakespeare, William. *Antony and Cleopatra*. Ed. John Wilders. Arden Shakespeare, 3rd ser. London: Bloomsbury, 1995.
Shakespeare, William. *As You Like It*. Ed. Juliet Dusinberre. Arden Shakespeare, 3rd ser. London: Bloomsbury, 2006.
Shakespeare, William. *The Comedy of Errors*. Ed. Kent Cartwright. Arden Shakespeare, 3rd ser. London: Bloomsbury, 2017.
Shakespeare, William. *Coriolanus*. Ed. Lee Bliss. Cambridge: Cambridge University Press, 2000.
Shakespeare, William. *Coriolanus*. Ed. Philip Brockbank. Arden Shakespeare, 2nd ser. London: Methuen, 1976.
Shakespeare, William. *Coriolanus*. Ed. Peter Holland. Arden Shakespeare, 3rd ser. London: Bloomsbury, 2013.
Shakespeare, William. *Cymbeline*. Ed. Valerie Wayne. Arden Shakespeare, 3rd ser. London: Bloomsbury, 2013.
Shakespeare, William. *Hamlet*. Ed. Anne Thompson and Neil Taylor. Arden Shakespeare, 3rd ser. London: Thomson, 2006.
Shakespeare, William. *Hamlet, Prince of Denmark*. The New Cambridge Shakespeare, ed. Philip Edwards. Cambridge: Cambridge University Press, 1985.
Shakespeare, William. *King Henry IV, Part 1*. Ed. David Kastan. Arden Shakespeare, 3rd ser. London: Bloomsbury, 2002,
Shakespeare, William. *King Henry IV, Part 2*. Ed. James C. Bulman. Arden Shakespeare, 3rd ser. London: Bloomsbury, 2016.
Shakespeare, William. *Love's Labour's Lost*. Ed. H.R. Woodhuysen. Arden Shakespeare, 3rd ser. London: Bloomsbury, 2015.
Shakespeare, William. *Macbeth*. Ed. Sandra Clark and Pamela Mason. Arden Shakespeare, 3rd ser. London: Bloomsbury, 2015.
Shakespeare, William. *Much Ado About Nothing*. Ed. Claire McEachern. Arden Shakespeare, 3rd ser. London: Bloomsbury, 2006.
Shakespeare, William. *The Norton Shakespeare*. 3rd ed. Ed. Stephen Greenblatt. New York: W. W. Norton, 2016.
Shakespeare, William. *Othello*. Ed. E.A. J. Honigman. Arden Shakespeare, 3rd ser. London: Bloomsbury, 2008.

Shakespeare, William. *Pericles*. Ed. Suzanne Gossett. Arden Shakespeare, 3rd ser. London: Bloomsbury, 2004.
Shakespeare, William. *Timon of Athens*. Ed. Anthony B. Dawson and Gretchen E. Minton. Arden Shakespeare, 3rd ser. London: Bloomsbury, 2008.
Shakespeare, William. *Timon of Athens*. Ed. John Jowett. Oxford: Oxford University Press, 2004.
Shakespeare, William. *Timon of Athens*. Ed. Karl Klein. Cambridge: Cambridge University Press, 2001.
Shakespeare, William. The Tragedy of Antony and Cleopatra. Ed. Michael Neill. Oxford: Oxford University Press, 1994.
Shakespeare, William. *The Tragedy of Coriolanus*. Ed. R. B. Parker. Oxford: Oxford University Press, 1994.
Shakespeare, William. *Twelfth Night*. Ed. Keir Elam. Arden Shakespeare, 3rd ser. London: Bloomsbury, 2008.
Shakespeare, William. *The Winter's Tale*. Ed. Sandra Clark and Pamela Mason. Arden Shakespeare, 3rd ser. London: Bloomsbury, 2015.

Poetry

Shakespeare, William. *Complete Sonnets and Poems*. Ed. Colin Burrow. Oxford: Oxford University Press, 2002.
Shakespeare, William. *Shakespeare's Sonnets*. Ed. Katherine Duncan-Jones. Arden Shakespeare, 3rd Ser. London: Thomas Nelson and Sons Ltd, 1998.

Abel, Lionel. "Metatheatre." In *Tragedy and Metatheatre: Essays on Dramatic Form*, ed. Martin Puchner. New York: Holmes and Meier, 2003.
Adelman, Janet. *The Common Liar: An Essay on* Antony and Cleopatra. New Haven, CT: Yale University Press, 1973.
Adelman, Janet. *Suffocating Mothers: Fantasies of Maternal Origin in Shakespeare's Plays*, Hamlet *to* The Tempest. New York: Routledge, 1992.
Affeldt, Steven G. "Captivating Pictures and Liberating Language: Freedom as the Achievement of Speech in Wittgenstein's *Philosophical Investigations*." *Philosophical Topics* 27, no. 2 (1999): 255–85.
Affeldt, Steven G. "The Ground of Mutuality: Criteria, Judgment, and Intelligibility in Stephen Mulhall and Stanley Cavell." *European Journal of Philosophy* 6, no. 1 (1998): 1–31.
Agam-Segal, Reshef, and Edmund Dain, eds. *Wittgenstein's Moral Thought*. London: Routledge, 2019.
Alexander, Nigel. *Poison, Play, and Duel*. Lincoln: University of Nebraska Press, 1971.
Altieri, Charles. "How Can Act 5 Forget Lear and Cordelia?" In *Shakespeare Up Close: Reading Early Modern Texts*, ed. Russ McDonald, Nicholas D. Nace, and Travis D. Williams. New York: Bloomsbury, 2013.
Améry, Jean. *At The Mind's Limits: Contemplations by a Survivor After Auschwitz and Its Realities*. Trans. Sidney Rosenfeld and Stella P. Rosenfeld. Bloomington: Indiana University Press, 1980.

Amesbury, Richard, and Harmut Von Sass, eds. *Ethics After Wittgenstein: Contemplation and Critique*. London: Bloomsbury, 2021.
Anscombe, G. E. M. *Intentions*. Oxford: Blackwell, 1963.
Aquinas, Saint Thomas. *Commentary on Aristotle's Nicomachean Ethics*. Trans. C. I. Litzinger, O. P. Notre Dame, IN: Dumb Ox, 1964.
Aquinas, Saint Thomas. *Summa Theologica*. 5 vols., trans. Fathers of the Dominican Province. Notre Dame, IN: Christian Classics, 1948.
Arendt, Hannah. *Between Past and Future*. London: Penguin, 1977.
Arendt, Hannah. *Eichmann in Jerusalem: A Report on the Banality of Evil*. New York: Penguin, 1964.
Arendt, Hannah. *Hannah Arendt: Lectures on Kant's* Political Philosophy. Ed. Ronald Beiner. Chicago: University of Chicago Press, 1992.
Arendt, Hannah. *The Human Condition*. Chicago: University of Chicago Press, 1958.
Arendt, Hannah. *The Life of the Mind*. New York: Harcourt, 1978.
Arendt, Hannah. *Love and Saint Augustine*. Trans. and ed. Joanna Vecchiarelli Scott and Judith Chelius Stark. Chicago: University of Chicago Press, 1996.
Arendt, Hannah. *On Violence*. Orlando, FL: Harcourt, 1969.
Aristotle. *The Nicomachean Ethics*. Trans. and ed. C. D. C. Reeve. Indianapolis, IN: Hackett, 2024.
Aristotle. *The Nicomachean Ethics*. Trans. David Ross. Oxford: Oxford University Press, 1998.
Auden, W. H. *W. H. Auden: Selected Poems*. New York: Vintage, 1989.
Augustine. *Concerning the City of God Against the Pagans*. Trans. Henry Bettenson. London: Penguin, 1984.
Austin, J. L. *How to Do Things with Words*. Ed. J. O. Urmson and Marina Sbisa. Cambridge, MA: Harvard University Press, 1962.
Austin, J. L. *Philosophical Papers*. Oxford: Clarendon, 1961.
Austin, J. L. "A Plea for Excuses." In *Philosophical Papers*. 3rd ed., ed. J. O. Urmson and G. J. Warnock. Oxford: Oxford University Press, 1961.
Backström, Joel. *The Fear of Openness: An Essay on Friendship and the Roots of Morality*. Turku: Åbo Akademi University Press, 2007.
Baier, Annette. *Moral Prejudice: Essays on Ethics*. Cambridge, MA: Harvard University Press, 1994.
Baier, Annette. *Postures of the Mind: Essays on Mind and Morals*. Minneapolis: University of Minnesota Press, 1985.
Baier, Annette. "Trust and Antitrust." *Ethics* 96, no. 2 (1986): 231–60.
Bailey, Amanda. *Of Bondage: Debt, Property, and Personhood in Early Modern England*. Philadelphia: University of Pennsylvania Press, 2013.
Baker, G. P. "The Private Language Argument." *Language and Communication* 18 (1998): 325–56.
Baker, G. P., and P. M. S. Hacker. *Wittgenstein: Rules, Grammar and Necessity*. Vol. 2 of *An Analytical Commentary on the Philosophical Investigations*. 2nd ed. Oxford: Wiley-Blackwell, 2009.
Balaska, Maria, ed. *Cora Diamond on Ethics*. Cham: Palgrave Macmillan, 2021.
Balaska, Maria, ed. "When a Mind Goes Up in Smoke: Thinking of Evil and Thinking." In *Cora Diamond on Ethics*, ed. Maria Balaska. Cham: Palgrave Macmillan, 2021.

Barclay, Katie. *Caritas: Neighbourly Love and the Early Modern Self.* Oxford: Oxford University Press, 2021.

Barclay, Paul. *Paul and the Gift.* Grand Rapids, MI: W. B. Eerdmans, 2015.

Barish, Jonas A., and Marshall Waingrow. "'Service' in *King Lear.*" *Shakespeare Quarterly* 9, no. 3 (1958): 347-55.

Barton, Anne. "'Nature's Piece Against Fancy': The Divided Catastrophe in *Antony and Cleopatra.*" In *Essays, Mainly Shakespearean.* Cambridge: Cambridge University Press, 1994.

Bauer, Nancy, Alice Crary, and Sandra Laugier, eds. *Here and There: Sites of Philosophy.* Cambridge, MA: Harvard University Press, 2022.

Baz, Avner. *When Words Are Called For: A Defence of Ordinary Language Philosophy.* Cambridge, MA: Harvard University Press, 2012.

Beard, Mary. *The Roman Triumph.* Cambridge, MA: Harvard University Press, 2007.

Beckerman, Bernard. "Past the Size of Dreaming." In *Twentieth Century Interpretations of* Antony and Cleopatra, ed. Mark Rose. Englewood Cliffs, NJ: Prentice Hall, 1977.

Beckwith, Sarah. "Enter the Child: A Scene from *The Claim of Reason.*" *Philosophy and Literature* 41, no. 2 (2022): 251-62.

Beckwith, Sarah. "*Hamlet's* Ethics." In *Shakespeare's Hamlet: Philosophical Perspectives*, ed. Tzachi Zamir. Oxford: Oxford University Press, 2018.

Beckwith, Sarah. *Shakespeare and the Grammar of Forgiveness.* Ithaca, NY: Cornell University Press, 2011.

Beckwith, Sarah. "The Theological Virtues." In *Shakespeare and the Virtues: A Handbook*, ed. Julia Reinhard Lupton and Donovan Sherman. Cambridge: Cambridge University Press, 2023.

Beckwith, Sarah. "Tragic Implication." In *Cavell's* Must We Mean What We Say? *at 50*, ed. Greg Chase, Juliet Floyd, and Sandra Laugier. Cambridge: Cambridge University Press, 2022.

Beckwith, Sarah. "A Vision of Language for Literary Historians: Forms of Life, Context, Use." In *Wittgenstein and Literary Studies*, ed. Robert Chodat and John Gibson. Cambridge: Cambridge University Press, 2022.

Bennett, Judith M. "Conviviality and Charity in Medieval and Early Modern Europe." *Past and Present* 134 (1992): 19-41.

Berger, John, and Jean Mohr. *A Fortunate Man: The Story of a Country Doctor.* New York: Vintage, 1997.

Bernstein, J. M. "Aesthetics, Modernism, Literature: Cavell's Transformations of Philosophy." In *Stanley Cavell*, ed. Richard Eldridge. Cambridge: Cambridge University Press, 2003.

Bernstein, J. M. *Torture and Dignity: An Essay on Moral Injury.* Chicago: University of Chicago Press, 2015.

Bespaloff, Rachel. "On the *Iliad.*" In *War and the* Iliad, by Simone Weil and Rachel Bespaloff. Trans. Mary McCarthy. New York: New York Review of Books, 2005.

Blake, William. *The Complete Poetry and Prose of William Blake.* Ed. David V. Erdman. New York: Penguin Vintage, 1988.

Blits, Jan H. *Spirit, Soul, and City: Shakespeare's Coriolanus.* Lanham, MD: Lexington, 2006.

Bloom, Harold. *Shakespeare: The Invention of the Human.* New York: Riverhead, 1999.

Bono, Barbara J. *Literary Transvaluation: From Vergilian Epic to Shakespearean Tragicomedy*. Berkeley: University of California Press, 1984.
Bossy, John. *Christianity in the West: 1400–1700*. Oxford: Oxford University Press, 1985.
Bossy, John. "The Mass as a Social Institution 1200–1700." *Past and Present* 100 (1983): 29–61.
Boswell, James. *The Life of Johnson*. Ed. David Womersley. London: Penguin, 2008.
Bowen-Moore, Patricia. *Hannah Arendt's Philosophy of Natality*. New York: St. Martin's Press, 1989.
Braden, Gordon. *Renaissance Tragedy and the Senecan Tradition: Anger's Privilege*. New Haven, CT: Yale University Press, 1985.
Brandel, Andrew, and Marco Motta, eds. *Living with Concepts: Anthropology in the Grip of Reality*. New York: Fordham University Press, 2021.
Breight, Curtis C. *Surveillance, Militarism, and Drama in the Elizabethan Era*. New York: St. Martin's Press, 1996.
Brower, Reuben A. *Hero and Saint: Shakespeare and the Graeco-Roman Heroic Tradition*. Oxford: Oxford University Press, 1971.
Bullough, Geoffrey, ed. *Narrative and Dramatic Sources of Shakespeare*. Vol. 5. London: Routledge, 1966.
Bullough, Geoffrey, ed. *Narrative and Dramatic Sources of Shakespeare*. Vol. 6. London: Routledge, 1966.
Burgess, Clive. "'A Fond Thing Vainly Invented': An Essay on Purgatory and Pious Motive in Later Medieval England." In *Parish, Church, and People: Studies in Lay Religion*, ed. S. J. Wright. London: Hutchinson, 1988.
Burke, Peter. "Tacitus, Skepticism, and Reason of State." In *Cambridge History of Political Thought 1450–1700*, ed. J. H. Burns. Cambridge: Cambridge University Press, 2008.
Burnaby, John. *Amor Dei: A Study of the Religion of St. Augustine*. Eugene, OR: Wipf & Stock, 2007.
Burrell, David. *Aquinas: God, and Action*. Scranton, PA: University of Scranton Press, 2008.
Burrell, David, and Stanley Hauerwas. "Self-Deception and Autobiography: Theological and Ethical Reflections on Speer's *Inside the Third Reich*." *Journal of Religious Ethics* 2, no. 1 (1974): 99–117.
Bushnell, Rebecca. *Tragedies of Tyrants: Political Thought in the English Renaissance*. Ithaca, NY: Cornell University Press, 1990.
Calasso, Roberto. *The Unnameable Present*. New York: Farrar, Straus and Giroux, 2019.
Caldarone, Maria, and Maggie Lloyd-Williams. *Actions: The Actor's Thesaurus*. London: Drama, 2004.
Calderwood, James. *If It Were Done: Macbeth and Tragic Action*. Cambridge, MA: University of Massachusetts Press, 1986.
Calderwood, James. "Wordless Meanings and Meaningless Words." *Studies in English Literature* 6 (1966): 211–24.
Candlish, Stewart, and George Wrisley. "Private Language." *Stanford Encyclopedia of Philosophy*, July 26, 1996; substantive revision July 30, 2019. https://plato.stanford.edu/entries/private-language.
Cantor, Paul. *Shakespeare's Rome: Republic and Empire*. Ithaca, NY: Cornell University Press, 1976.

Carlisle, Claire. *The Marriage Question: George Eliot's Double Life*. New York: Farrar, Straus and Giroux, 2023.
Carroll, William. *Fat King, Lean Beggar: Representations of Poverty in the Age of Shakespeare*. Ithaca, NY: Cornell University Press, 1996.
Carroll, William, ed. *Macbeth: Texts and Contexts*. Boston: Bedford/St. Martin's, 1999.
Carter, James. "The Passionate Life: On Grief and Human Experience." In *Moral Powers, Fragile Beliefs: Essays in Moral and Religious Philosophy*, ed. Joseph Carlisle, James C. Carter, and Daniel Whistler. New York: Continuum, 2011.
Cascardi, Anthony. "'Disowning Knowledge': Cavell on Shakespeare." In *Stanley Cavell*, ed. Richard Eldridge. Cambridge: Cambridge University Press, 2003.
Cavell, Stanley. *The Claim of Reason: Wittgenstein, Skepticism, Morality, and Tragedy*. 2nd ed. Oxford: Oxford University Press, 1999.
Cavell, Stanley. *Conditions Handsome and Unhandsome: The Constitution of Emersonian Perfectionism*. Chicago: University of Chicago Press, 1990.
Cavell, Stanley. *Contesting Tears: The Hollywood Melodrama of the Unknown Woman*. Chicago: University of Chicago Press, 1996.
Cavell, Stanley. *Disowning Knowledge in Seven Plays of Shakespeare*. Cambridge: Cambridge University Press, 2012.
Cavell, Stanley. *In Quest of the Ordinary: Lines of Skepticism and Romanticism*. Chicago: University of Chicago Press, 1988.
Cavell, Stanley. *Little Did I Know: Excerpts from Memory*. Stanford, CA: Stanford University Press, 2010.
Cavell, Stanley. *Must We Mean What We Say?: A Book of Essays*. Updated ed. Cambridge: Cambridge University Press, 2002.
Cavell, Stanley. *Philosophy the Day After Tomorrow*. Cambridge, MA: Harvard University Press, 2005.
Cavell, Stanley. *A Pitch of Philosophy: Autobiographical Exercises*. Cambridge, MA: Harvard University Press, 1994.
Cavell, Stanley. *Pursuits of Happiness: The Hollywood Comedy of Remarriage*. Cambridge, MA: Harvard University Press, 1981.
Cavell, Stanley. "A Reply to Four Chapters." In *Wittgenstein and Skepticism*, ed. Denis McManus. London: Routledge, 2004.
Cavell, Stanley. *Themes Out of School: Effects and Causes*. Chicago: University of Chicago Press, 1984.
Cavell, Stanley. *This New Yet Unapproachable America: Lectures After Emerson After Wittgenstein*. Albuquerque, NM: Living Batch, 1989.
Chase, Greg, Juliet Floyd, and Sandra Laugier. Introduction to *Cavell's* Must We Mean What We Say? *at 50*, ed. Greg Chase, Juliet Floyd, and Sandra Laugier. Cambridge: Cambridge University Press, 2022.
Chodat, Robert. "Appreciating Material: Criticism, Science, and the Very Idea of Method." In *Wittgenstein and Literary Studies*, ed. Robert Chodat and John Gibson. Cambridge: Cambridge University Press, 2022.
Cicero. *Letters to Atticus*. Loeb Classical Library, trans. and ed. D. R. Shackleton Bailey. Cambridge, MA: Harvard University Press, 1999.
Clune, Michael W. *A Defense of Judgment*. Chicago: University of Chicago Press, 2021.

Coady, C. A. J. *Testimony: A Philosophical Study*. Oxford: Clarendon, 1992.
Coles, Romand. *Rethinking Generosity: Critical Theory and the Politics of Caritas*. Ithaca, NY: Cornell University Press, 1997.
Conant, James. "The Dialectic of Perspectivism, I." *SATS: Nordic Journal of Philosophy* 6, no. 2 (2005): 5–50.
Cordner, Christopher. *Ethical Encounter: The Depth of Moral Meaning*. Swansea Studies in Philosophy. Basingstoke: Palgrave Macmillan, 2002.
Cordner, Christopher. "Moral Philosophy in the Midst of Things." In *A Sense of Humanity: The Ethical Thought of Raimond Gaita*, ed. Craig Taylor and Melinda Graefe. Clayton, AU: Monash University Publishing, 2014.
Crary, Alice. *Beyond Moral Judgement*. Cambridge, MA: Harvard University Press, 2007.
Crassons, Kate. *The Claims of Poverty: Literature, Culture and Ideology in Late Medieval England*. Notre Dame, IN: University of Notre Dame Press, 2010.
Crawford, Jason. "Shakespeare's Liturgy of Assumption." *Journal of Medieval and Early Modern Studies* 49, no. 1 (2019): 57–84.
Cressy, David. *Birth, Marriage, and Death: Ritual, Religion, and the Life-Cycle in Tudor and Stuart England*. Oxford: Oxford University Press, 1997.
Cummings, Brian, ed. *The Book of Common Prayer: The Texts of 1549, 1559, and 1662*. Oxford: Oxford University Press, 2011.
Curran, Kevin, ed. *Shakespeare and Judgment*. Edinburgh: Edinburgh University Press, 2016.
Danby, John. "*Antony and Cleopatra*: A Shakespearean Adjustment." In *Antony and Cleopatra: New Casebooks*, ed. John Drakakis. London: Red Globe, 1994.
Dante, Alighieri. *The Comedy of Dante Alighieri the Florentine*. Trans. Dorothy Sayers. Harmondsworth: Penguin, 1949.
Dawson, Anthony. "The Arithmetic of Memory: Shakespeare's Theater and the National Past." *Shakespeare Survey* 52 (1999): 54–67.
Day, William. "To Not Understand, but Not Misunderstand Wittgenstein on Shakespeare." In *Wittgenstein Reading*, ed. Sascha Brue, Wolfgang Huemer, and Daniel Steuer. Berlin: De Gruyter, 2013.
Dekker, Thomas. "O per se O." In *The Elizabethan Underworld*, ed. A. V. Judges. London: Routledge, 1930.
Derrida, Jacques. *The Gift of Death*. Trans. David Wills. Chicago: University of Chicago Press, 1995.
Derrida, Jacques. *Given Time I: Counterfeit Money*. Trans. Peggy Kamuf. Chicago: University of Chicago Press, 1992.
Diamond, Cora. "The Difficulty of Reality and the Difficulty of Philosophy." In *Philosophy and Animal Life*, by Stanley Cavell, Cora Diamond, John McDowell, Ian Hacking, and Cary Wolfe. New York: Columbia University Press, 2008.
Diamond, Cora. "The Importance of Being Human." In *Human Beings*, ed. David Cockburn. Cambridge: Cambridge University Press, 1991.
Diamond, Cora. "Injustice and Animals." In *Slow Cures and Bad Philosophers: Essays on Wittgenstein, Medicine, and Bioethics*, ed. Carl Elliott. Durham, NC: Duke University Press, 2001.
Diamond, Cora. "Losing Your Concepts." *Ethics* 98, no. 2 (1988): 255–77.

Diamond, Cora. "Murdoch the Explorer." *Philosophical Topics* 38, no. 1 (2010): 51–85.
Diamond, Cora. "Suspect Notions and the Concept Police." In *Cora Diamond on Ethics*, ed. Maria Balaska. Cham: Palgrave Macmillan, 2021.
Diamond, Cora. "'We Are All Perpetually Moralists': Iris Murdoch, Fact, and Value." In *Iris Murdoch and the Search for Human Goodness*, ed. Maria Antonaccio and William Schweiker. Chicago: University of Chicago Press, 1996.
Dickinson, Emily. *The Complete Poems of Emily Dickinson*, ed. Thomas H. Johnson. San Francisco: Back Bay, 1976.
Dilman, Ilham. *Raskolnikov's Rebirth: Psychology and the Understanding of Evil*. Chicago: Open Court, 2000.
Doran, Madeline. "High Events Such as These: The Language of Hyperbole." In *Shakespeare's Dramatic Language: Essays*. Madison: University of Wisconsin Press, 1976.
Doty, Mark. *The Art of Description: Word Into World*. Minneapolis, MN: Graywolf, 2010.
Duffy, Eamon. *The Stripping of the Altars: Traditional Religion in England 1400–1580*. 2nd ed. New Haven, CT: Yale University Press, 2005.
Dula, Peter. *Cavell, Companionship, and Christian Theology*. Oxford: Oxford University Press, 2010.
Eldridge, Richard. *Leading a Human Life: Wittgenstein, Intentionality, and Romanticism*. Chicago: University of Chicago Press, 1997.
Eldridge, Richard, and Bernie Rhie, eds. *Stanley Cavell and Literary Studies: Consequences of Skepticism*. New York: Continuum, 2011.
Ellis-Fermor, Una. "*Timon of Athens*: An Unfinished Play." *Review of English Studies* 18, no.71 (1942): 270–83.
Enright, D. J., ed. *The Oxford Book of Death*. Oxford: Oxford University Press, 1983.
Felski, Rita. *The Limits of Critique*. Chicago: University of Chicago Press, 2015.
Fiddes, Paul. *More Things in Heaven and Earth: Shakespeare, Theology, and the Interplay of Texts*. Charlottesville: University of Virginia Press, 2022.
Fingarette, Herbert. *Self-Deception*. Berkeley: University of California Press, 2000.
Finkelstein, Richard. "*Amicitia* and *Beneficia* in *Timon of Athens*." *Studies in Philology* 117, no. 4 (2020): 801–25.
Fischer, B., I. Gribomont, H. F. D. Sparks, and W. Thiele, eds. *Biblia Sacra Vulgata*. 5th ed. Stuttgart: Deutsche Bibelgesellschaft, 2007.
Fish, Stanley. "How to Do Things with Austin and Searle: Speech Act Theory and Literary Criticism." *Modern Language Notes* 91, no. 5 (1976): 983–1025.
Fish, Stanley. *Is There a Text in This Class? The Authority of Interpretive Communities*. Cambridge, MA: Harvard University Press, 1980.
Fitzpatrick, Robin. "Tragedy and Theology in Shakespeare's *Timon of Athens*." In *Christian Theology and Tragedy: Theologians, Tragic Literature and Tragic Theory*, ed. Kevin Taylor and Gary Waller. Farnham: Ashgate, 2011.
Fleming, Richard. *First Word Philosophy: Wittgenstein-Austin-Cavell, Writings on Ordinary Language Philosophy*. Lewisburg, PA: Bucknell University Press, 2004.
Foley, Helene. *Euripides: Hecuba*. London: Bloomsbury, 2015.
Forsberg, Niklas. *Language Lost and Found: On Iris Murdoch and the Limits of Philosophical Discourse*. New York: Bloomsbury, 2013.

Forsberg, Niklas. *Lectures on a Philosophy Less Ordinary: Language and Morality in J. L. Austin's Philosophy*. London: Routledge, 2022.
Fowler, Elizabeth. "Towards a History of Performativity: Sacrament, Social Contract, and *The Merchant of Venice*." In *Shakespeare and the Middle Ages*, ed. Curtis Perry and John Watkins. Oxford: Oxford University Press, 2009.
Friedlander, Eli. "Faces of the Ordinary." In *Cavell's Must We Mean What We Say? at Fifty*, ed. Greg Chase, Juliet Floyd, and Sandra Laugier. Cambridge: Cambridge University Press, 2022.
Gaita, Raimond. *A Common Humanity: Thinking About Love and Truth and Justice*. New York: Routledge, 1998.
Gaita, Raimond. "Ethical Individuality." In *Value and Understanding: Essays for Peter Winch*, ed. Raimond Gaita. London: Routledge, 1990.
Gaita, Raimond. *Good and Evil: An Absolute Conception*. London: Routledge, 2004.
Gaita, Raimond. *The Philosopher's Dog*. New York: Routledge, 2002.
Galloway, Andrew. "The Making of a Social Ethic in Late-Medieval England: From *Gratitudo* to 'Kyndnesse.'" *Journal of the History of Ideas* 55, no. 3 (1994): 365–83.
The Geneva Bible: A Facsimile of the 1560 Edition. Madison: University of Wisconsin Press, 1969.
Gleeson, Andrew, and Craig Taylor, eds. *Morality in a Realistic Spirit: Essays for Cora Diamond*. London: Routledge, 2021.
Glock, Hans-Johann. *A Wittgenstein Dictionary*. Oxford: Blackwell, 1996.
Gordon, D. G. "Name and Fame: Shakespeare's *Coriolanus*." In *The Renaissance Imagination: Essays and Lectures by D. G. Gordon*, ed. Stephen Orgel. Berkeley: University of California Press, 1975.
Goux, Jean-Joseph. "Seneca Against Derrida: Gift and Alterity." In *The Enigma of the Gift and Sacrifice*, ed. Jean-Joseph Goux, Edith Wyschogrod, and Eric Boynton. New York: Fordham University Press, 2002.
Graham, Kenneth. "'Without the Form of Justice': Plainness and the Performance of Love in *King Lear*." In *Shakespeare Quarterly* 42, no. 4 (1991): 438–61.
Gray, Patrick. *Shakespeare and the Fall of the Roman Republic: Selfhood, Stoicism, and Civil War*. Edinburgh: Edinburgh University Press, 2019.
Greenblatt, Stephen. *Hamlet in Purgatory*. Princeton, NJ: Princeton University Press, 2002.
Gregory, Eric. *Politics and the Order of Love: An Augustinian Ethic of Democratic Citizenship*. Chicago: University of Chicago Press, 2010.
Gross, Kenneth. *Shakespeare's Noise*. Chicago: University of Chicago Press, 2001.
Gurney, Evan A. *Love's Quarrels: Reading Charity in Early Modern England*. Amherst: University of Massachusetts Press, 2018.
Gurney, Evan A. "Thomas More and the Problem of Charity." *Renaissance Studies* 26, no. 2. (2011): 197–217.
Hadfield, Andrew. *Shakespeare and Republicanism*. Cambridge: Cambridge University Press, 2005.
Hagberg, Gary L., ed. *Stanley Cavell on Aesthetic Understanding*. London: Palgrave Macmillan, 2018.
Hamawaki, Arata. "Kant and Beauty and the Normative Force of Feeling." *Philosophical Topics* 34, nos. 1–2 (2006): 107–44.

BIBLIOGRAPHY

Hamawaki, Arata. "Philosophical and Aesthetic Appeal: Stanley Cavell on the Irreducibility of the First Person in Aesthetics and in Philosophy." In *Cavell's* Must We Mean What We Say? *at Fifty*, ed. Greg Chase, Juliet Floyd, and Sandra Laugier. Cambridge: Cambridge University Press, 2022.
Hamlin, Hannibal. *The Bible in Shakespeare*. Oxford: Oxford University Press, 2018.
Harman, Thomas. "A Caveat for Common Cursitors." In *The Elizabethan Underworld*, ed. A. V. Judges. London: Routledge, 1930.
Hauerwas, Stanley. "The Virtues of Alasdair MacIntyre." *First Things*, October 1, 2007. https://www.firstthings.com/article/2007/10/the-virtues-of-alasdair-macintyre.
Heal, Felicity. *The Power of Gifts: Gift Exchange in Early Modern England*. Oxford: Oxford University Press, 2014.
Hegel, G. W. F. *Phenomenology of Spirit*. Trans. A. V. Miller. Oxford: Clarendon, 1977.
Herbert, Zbigniew. *The Collected Poems: 1956–1998*. New York: Harper Collins, 2007.
Hertzberg, Lars. "Gaita on Recognizing the Human." In *Ethics, Philosophy, and a Common Humanity*, ed. Christopher Cordner. London: Routledge, 2010.
Hertzberg, Lars. "On the Attitude of Trust." *Inquiry* 31 (1994): 307–22.
Hobbes, Thomas. *Leviathan*. Ed. Richard E. Flathman and David Johnston. New York: W. W. Norton, 1997.
Holland, R. F. "Good and Evil in Action." In *Against Empiricism: On Education, Epistemology, and Value*. Totowa, N.J: Barnes and Noble Books, 1980.
Homer. *The Iliad*. Trans. Robert Fagles. New York: Penguin, 1990.
Honan, Park. *Shakespeare: A Life*. Oxford: Oxford University Press, 1998.
Hooker, Richard. *Of the Laws of Ecclesiastical Polity*. Folger Library edition. Vol. 5, ed. W. Speed Hill. Cambridge, MA: Harvard University Press, 1977.
Horn, Patrick Rogers. *Gadamer and Wittgenstein on the Unity of Language: Reality and Discourse Without Metaphysics*. Aldershot: Ashgate, 2005.
Hunt, Maurice. "Qualifying the Good Steward of Shakespeare's *Timon of Athens*." *English Studies* 82, no. 6 (2001): 507–20.
Hunter, G. K. "Shakespeare's Last Tragic Heroes." In *Dramatic Identities and Cultural Traditions: Studies in Shakespeare and His Contemporaries—Critical Essays*. New York: Barnes & Noble, 1978.
Iczkovits, Yaniv. *Wittgenstein's Ethical Thought*. Basingstoke: Palgrave Macmillan, 2012.
Jackson, Ken. "'One Wish' or the Possibility of the Impossible: Derrida, the Gift, and God in *Timon of Athens*." *Shakespeare Quarterly* 52, no. 1 (2001): 34–66.
James, Heather. "A Modern Perspective: Coriolanus." Folger Shakespeare Library, accessed February 9, 2025. https://www.folger.edu/explore/shakespeares-works/coriolanus/coriolanus-a-modern-perspective/.
Johnson, Kelly S. *The Fear of Beggars: Stewardship and Poverty in Christian Ethics*. Grand Rapids, MI: Eerdmans, 2007.
Jones, Emrys. *Scenic Form in Shakespeare*. Oxford: Clarendon, 1971.
Jones, Norman. *God and the Moneylenders: Usury and the Law in Early Modern England*. Oxford: Blackwell, 1989.
Jowett, John. "Canon and Chronology." In *Thomas Middleton and Early Modern Textual Culture: A Companion to the Collected Works*, ed. Gary Taylor and John Lavagnino. Oxford: Clarendon, 2007.

Junker, William. "The Image of Both Theaters: Empire and Revelation in Shakespeare's *Antony and Cleopatra.*" *Shakespeare Quarterly* 66, no. 2. (2015): 167–87.

Kahn, Victoria. *Wayward Contracts: The Crisis of Political Obligation in England 1640–1674.* Princeton, NJ: Princeton University Press, 2004.

Kant, Immanuel. *Critique of the Power of Judgment.* Ed. Paul Guyer. Cambridge: Cambridge University Press, 2000.

Kenny, Anthony. *Wittgenstein.* London: Allen Lane, 2005.

Ker, James. *The Deaths of Seneca.* Oxford: Oxford University Press, 2009.

Kerrigan, John. *Shakespeare's Binding Language.* Oxford: Oxford University Press, 2016.

Knight, G. Wilson. *The Wheel of Fire: Interpretations of Shakespearean Tragedy.* London: Routledge, 1989.

Kottman, Paul. *Tragic Conditions in Shakespeare: Disinheriting the Globe.* Baltimore, MD: Johns Hopkins University Press, 2009.

Kottman, Paul. "What Is Shakespearean Tragedy?" In *The Oxford Handbook of Shakespearean Tragedy*, ed. Michael Neill and David Schalkwyck. Oxford: Oxford University Press, 2016.

Kraye, Jill. "Moral Philosophy." In *The Cambridge History of Renaissance Philosophy*, ed. C. B. Schmitt, Quentin Skinner, Eckhard Kessler, and Jill Kraye. Cambridge: Cambridge University Press, 2008.

Kronqvist, Camilla. "Our Struggles with Reality." In *Emotions and Understanding: Wittgensteinian Perspectives*, ed. Ylva Gustafsson, Camilla Kronqvist, and Michael McEachrane. Basingstoke: Palgrave Macmillan, 2009.

Kuzner, James. *Open Subjects: English Renaissance Republicans, Modern Selfhoods, and the Virtue of Vulnerability.* Edinburgh: Edinburgh University Press, 2011.

Kuzner, James. *Shakespeare as a Way of Life: Skeptical Practice and the Politics of Weakness.* New York: Fordham University Press, 2016.

Kyd, Thomas. *The Spanish Tragedy.* Ed. Clara Calvo and Jesus Tronch. London: Bloomsbury, 2013.

Lagerspetz, Olli. *Trust, Ethics, and Human Reason.* London: Bloomsbury, 2015.

Langland, William. *Piers Plowman: The B Version.* Eds. George Kane and E. Talbot Donaldson. London: Athlone Press, 1988, rev. ed.

Langland, William. *Piers Plowman: An Edition of the C-Text.* Ed. Derek Pearsall. York Medieval Texts, 2nd ser. Exeter: University of Exeter Press, 1994.

Laqueur, Thomas. *The Work of the Dead: A Cultural History of Mortal Remains.* Princeton, NJ: Princeton University Press, 2015.

Laugier, Sandra. "Introduction to the French Edition of *Must We Mean What We Say?*" *Critical Inquiry* 37, no. 4 (2011): 627–51.

Laugier, Sandra. "Voice as Form of Life and Life Form." *Nordic Wittgenstein Review* (2015): 63–81.

Laugier, Sandra. "What Matters: The Ethics and Aesthetics of Importance." In *Stanley Cavell on Aesthetic Understanding*, ed. Gary Hagberg. London: Palgrave Macmillan, 2018.

Laugier, Sandra. *Why We Need Ordinary Language Philosophy.* Trans. Daniela Ginsburg. Chicago: University of Chicago Press, 2013.

Laugier, Sandra. "Wittgenstein and Cavell: Anthropology, Skepticism, and Politics." In *The Claim to Community: Essays on Stanley Cavell and Political Philosophy*, ed. Andrew Norris. Stanford, CA: Stanford University Press, 2006.

Laugier, Sandra. *Wittgenstein: Le mythe de l'inexpressivité*. Paris: Vrin, 2010.
Lear, Jonathan. *Imagining the End: Mourning and Ethical Life*. Cambridge, MA: Harvard University Press, 2022.
Lear, Jonathan. *Radical Hope: Ethics in the Face of Cultural Devastation*. Cambridge, MA: Harvard University Press, 2008.
Leithart, Peter. *Gratitude: An Intellectual History*. Waco, TX: Baylor University Press, 2014.
Levi, Primo. *Survival in Auschwitz*. New York: Collier, 1993.
Lewis, Rhodri. *Hamlet and the Vision of Darkness*. Princeton, NJ: Princeton University Press, 2017.
Lofgren, Ingeborg. "Interpretative Skepticism: Stanley Cavell, New Criticism, and Literary Interpretation." PhD diss., Uppsala University, 2015.
Løgstrup, Knud Ejler. *The Ethical Demand*. Trans. Hans Fink. Notre Dame, IN: University of Notre Dame Press, 1997.
Long, Michael. *The Unnatural Scene: A Study in Shakespearean Tragedy*. London: Methuen, 1976.
Luckyj, Christina. "Volumnia's Silence." *Studies in English Literature, 1500–1900* 31, no. 2 (1991): 327–42.
Lupset, Thomas. *A Treatise of Charity*. London: Thomas Berthelet, 1533.
Lyne, Raphael. "The Shakespearean Grasp." *Cambridge Quarterly* 42, no. 1 (2013): 38–61.
Machiavelli, Niccolo. *The Discourses*. Trans. Leslie Walker. Ed. Bernard Crick. London: Penguin, 1983.
MacIntyre, Alasdair. *After Virtue: A Study in Moral Theory*. 2nd ed. Notre Dame, IN: University of Notre Dame Press, 1984.
MacIntyre, Alasdair. *Dependent Rational Animals: Why Human Beings Need the Virtues*. Chicago: Open Court, 1999.
Maitra, Ellorashree. "Toward an Ethical Polity: Service and the Tragic Community in *Timon of Athens*." *Renaissance Drama* 41, no.12 (2013): 173–98.
Mann, Michael. *On Wars*. New Haven, CT: Yale University Press, 2023.
Mann, Michael. *The Sources of Social Power*. 3 vols. Second ed. Cambridge: Cambridge University Press, 2012.
Marc'hadour, Germain, and Thomas M. C. Lawler. "Scripture in the Dialogue," in *The Yale Edition of the Complete Works of St. Thomas More*. Vol. 6, part II, ed. Thomas M. C. Lawler, Germain Marc'hadour, and Richard C. Marius. New Haven, CT: Yale University Press, 1981.
Margalit, Avishai. *On Betrayal*. Cambridge, MA: Harvard University Press, 2017.
Markell, Patchen. *Bound by Recognition*. Princeton, NJ: Princeton University Press, 2003.
Marshall, Peter. *Beliefs and the Dead in Reformation England*. Oxford: Oxford University Press, 2002.
Marx, Karl. *Capital*. Trans. Eden Paul and Cedar Paul. London: J. M. Dent, 1974.
Marx, Karl. "Economic and Philosophical Manuscripts of 1844." In *Collected Works*. Vol. 3. New York: International Press, 1976.
Matthewes, Charles T. *Evil and the Augustinian Tradition*. Cambridge: Cambridge University Press, 2001.
Mauss, Marcel. *The Gift*. Trans. and ed. Jane I. Guyer. Chicago: HAU, 2016.

Mayer, Roland. "Seneca *Redivivus*: Seneca in the Medieval and Renaissance World." In *The Cambridge Companion to Seneca*, ed. Shadi Bartsch and Alessandro Schiesaro. Cambridge: Cambridge University Press, 2015.
McDonald, Russ. *Shakespeare's Late Style*. Cambridge: Cambridge University Press, 2006.
McMyler, Benjamin. *Testimony, Trust, and Authority*. Oxford: Oxford University Press, 2011.
Mercer, Peter. *Hamlet and the Acting of Revenge*. Iowa City: University of Iowa Press, 1987.
Miller, Anthony. *Roman Triumphs and Early Modern English Culture*. Houndmills: Palgrave, 2001.
Milosz, Cseslaw. *New and Collected Poems, 1931–2001*. New York: Harper Collins, 2001.
Milton, John. *The Doctrine and Discipline of Divorce*. In *The Complete Poetry and Essential Prose of John Milton*. Ed. William Kerrigan, John Rumrich, and Stephen M. Fallon. New York: Modern Library, 2007.
Milton, John. *Paradise Lost*. In *The Complete Poetry and Essential Prose of John Milton*. Ed. *William Kerrigan, John Rumrich, and Stephen. M. Fallon*. New York: Modern Library, 2007.
Miola, Robert. *Shakespeare's Rome*. Cambridge: Cambridge University Press, 1983.
Moi, Toril. "A Phenomenology of Literary Criticism." In *Wittgenstein and Literary Studies*, ed. Robert Chodat and John Gibson. Cambridge: Cambridge University Press, 2021.
Moi, Toril. *Revolution of the Ordinary: Literary Studies After Wittgenstein, Austin, and Cavell*. Chicago: University of Chicago Press, 2017.
Moi, Toril. "'They Practice Their Trade in Different Worlds': Concepts in Poststructuralism and Ordinary Language Philosophy." *New Literary History* 40, no. 4 (2009): 801–24.
Moran, Richard. *The Exchange of Words: Speech, Testimony, and Intersubjectivity*. Oxford: Oxford University Press, 2018.
More, St. Thomas. "A Confutation of Tyndale's Answer." In *The Yale Edition of the Complete Works of St. Thomas More*. Vol. 8, part II, ed. Louis A. Schuster, Richard C. Marius, and James P. Lusardi. New Haven, CT: Yale University Press, 1973.
More, St. Thomas. "A Dialogue Concerning Heresies." In *The Yale Edition of the Complete Works of St. Thomas More*. Vol. 6, part I, ed. Thomas M. C. Lawler, Germain Marc'hadour, and Richard C. Marius. New Haven, CT: Yale University Press, 1981.
Mossman, Judith. *Wild Justice: A Study of Euripides' Hecuba*. Oxford: Clarendon, 1995.
Mullaney, Steven. *The Reformation of Emotion in the Age of Shakespeare*. Chicago: University of Chicago Press, 2015.
Munro, Lucy. "*Coriolanus* and the Little Eyases: The Boyhood of Shakespeare's Hero." In *Shakespeare and Childhood*, ed. Kate Chedgzoy, Suzanne Greenhalgh, and Robert Shaughnessy. Cambridge: Cambridge University Press, 2007.
Murdoch, Iris. "Against Dryness." In *Existentialists and Mystics: Writings on Philosophy and Literature*, ed. Peter Conradi. Harmondsworth: Penguin, 1997.

Murdoch, Iris. *Existentialists and Mystics: Writings on Philosophy and Literature*. Ed. Peter Conradi. Harmondsworth: Penguin, 1997.

Murdoch, Iris. "The Idea of Perfection." In *Existentialists and Mystics: Writings on Philosophy and Literature*, ed. Peter Conradi. Harmondsworth: Penguin, 1997.

Murdoch, Iris. *The Sovereignty of Good*. London: Routledge, 1970.

Narboux, Jean-Philippe. "Actions and Their Elaboration." In *Cavell's* Must We Mean What We Say? *at Fifty*, ed. Greg Chase, Juliet Floyd, and Sandra Laugier. Cambridge: Cambridge University Press, 2022.

Neill, Michael. *Issues of Death: Mortality and Identity in English Tragedy*. Oxford: Clarendon, 1999.

Neill, Michael, ed. *The Oxford Shakespeare: The Tragedy of* Antony and Cleopatra. Oxford: Oxford University Press, 1994.

Neill, Michael. "Servant Obedience and Master Sins: Shakespeare and the Bonds of Service." In *Putting History to the Question: Power, Politics, and Society in English Renaissance Drama*. New York: Columbia University Press, 2000.

Norris, Andrew. *Becoming Who We Are: Politics and Practical Philosophy in the Work of Stanley Cavell*. Oxford: Oxford University Press, 2017.

Norris, Andrew. "Skepticism and Critique in Arendt and Cavell." *Philosophy and Social Criticism* 44, no. 1 (2018): 81–99.

Noschka, Michael. "Thinking Hospitably with *Timon of Athens*: Toward an Ethics of Stewardship." In *Shakespeare and Hospitality: Ethics, Politics, and Exchange*, ed. David Goldstein and Julia Reinhard Lupton. London: Routledge, 2019.

Nussbaum, Martha. *Anger and Forgiveness: Resentment, Generosity, Justice*. Oxford: Oxford University Press, 2016.

Nussbaum, Martha. *The Fragility of Goodness: Luck and Ethics in Greek Tragedy and Philosophy*. Cambridge: Cambridge University Press, 1986.

Nuttall, A. D. *Timon of Athens*. Boston: Twayne, 1989.

Ornstein, Robert. "Love and Art in *Antony and Cleopatra*." In *Twentieth Century Interpretations of* Antony and Cleopatra. Englewood Cliffs, NJ: Prentice Hall, 1977.

Ovid. *Ovid: Metamorphosis: Books IX–XV*. Trans. Frank Justus Miller. Cambridge, MA: Harvard University Press, 1984.

Paster, Gail Kern. "'To Starve with Feeding': The City in *Coriolanus*." *Shakespeare Studies* 11 (1978): 123–44.

Peperzak, Adriaan. "Giving." In *The Enigma of the Gift and Sacrifice*, ed. Edith Wyschogrod, Jean-Joseph Goux, and Eric Boynton. New York: Fordham University Press, 2002.

Pfau, Thomas. *Minding the Modern: Human Agency, Intellectual Traditions, and Responsible Agency*. Notre Dame, IN: University of Notre Dame Press, 2013.

Pfau, Thomas, and Vivasvan Soni, eds. *Judgment and Action: Fragments Toward a History*. Evanston, IL: Northwestern University Press, 2018.

Pinches, Charles R. *Theology and Moral Action: After Theory in Christian Ethics*. Grand Rapids, MI: Eerdmans, 2002.

Pollard, Tanya. *Greek Tragic Women on Shakespearean Stages*. Oxford: Oxford University Press, 2017.

Putnam, Hilary. *The Collapse of the Fact/Value Dichotomy and Other Essays*. Cambridge: Harvard University Press, 2002.

Redfield, James M. *Nature and Culture in the* Iliad: *The Tragedy of Hector*. Chicago: University of Chicago Press, 1975.

Reid, Thomas. *Essays on the Active Powers of the Mind*. Ed. Knud Haakonssen and James A. Harris. Edinburgh: Edinburgh University Press, 2010.

Reynolds, L. D. *Texts and Transmission: A Survey of the Latin Classics*. Oxford: Oxford University Press, 1983.

Rhees, Rush. "Understanding What Is Said." In *Wittgenstein and the Possibility of Discourse*, ed. D. Z. Phillips. Cambridge: Cambridge University Press, 1998.

Rodowick, D. N. *An Education in Judgment: Hannah Arendt and the Humanities*. Chicago: University of Chicago Press, 2021.

Rossiter, A. P. *Angel with Horns and Other Shakespeare Lectures*. New York: Theater Arts, 1961.

Salskov, Salla Aldrin, Ondrej Beran, and Nora Hamalainen, eds. *Ethical Inquiries After Wittgenstein*. Cham: Springer, 2022.

Schalkwyk, David. *Shakespeare, Love and Language*. Cambridge: Cambridge University Press, 2018.

Schalkwyk, David. *Shakespeare, Love and Service*. Cambridge: Cambridge University Press, 2009.

Schalkwyk, David. "'Unpacking the Heart': Why It Is Impossible to Say 'I Love You' in Hamlet's Elsinore." In *Shakespeare's* Hamlet: *Philosophical Perspectives*, ed. Tzachi Zamir. Oxford: Oxford University Press, 2018.

Schein, Seth L. *The Mortal Hero: An Introduction to Homer's* Iliad. Berkeley: University of California Press, 1984.

Scheman, Naomi. "A Storied World: On Meeting and Being Met." In *Stanley Cavell and Literary Studies: Consequences of Skepticism*, ed. Richard Eldridge and Bernie Rhie. New York: Continuum, 2011.

Schleiner, Louise. "Latinized Greek Drama in Shakespeare's Writing of *Hamlet*." *Shakespeare Quarterly* 41, no. 1 (1991): 29–48.

Schulte, Joachim. "Did Wittgenstein Write on Shakespeare?" *Nordic Wittgenstein Review* 2 (2013): 7–32.

Schwartz, Regina. *Loving Charity, Living Shakespeare*. Oxford: Oxford University Press, 2016.

Segal, Charles. *The Theme of the Mutilation of the Corpse in the* Iliad. Mnemosyne Supplements 17. Leiden: Brill, 1971.

Seneca, Lucius Annaeus. *Anger, Mercy, Revenge*. Trans. Robert A. Kaster and Martha Nussbaum. Chicago: University of Chicago Press, 2010.

Seneca, Lucius Annaeus. *Moral and Political Essays*. Ed. John M. Cooper and J. F. Pocope. Cambridge: Cambridge University Press, 1995.

Seneca, Lucius Annaeus. *Seneca: Epistles 93–124*. Trans. Richard M. Gummere. Loeb Classical Library. Cambridge, MA: Harvard University Press, 1925.

Seneca, Lucius Annaeus. *Seneca: Hercules, Trojan Women, Phoenician Women, Medea, Phaedra*. Trans. and ed. John Finch. Cambridge, MA: Harvard University Press, 2002.

Seneca, Lucius Annaeus. *Seneca: Moral Essays*. Vol. 3, trans. John W. Basore. Cambridge, MA: Harvard University Press, 1953.

Seneca, Lucius Annaeus. *Seneca: On Benefits*. Trans. Miriam Griffin and Brad Inwood. Chicago: University of Chicago Press, 2011.

Sidney, Philip. *A Defence of Poetry*. Ed. J. A. V. Dorsten. Oxford: Oxford University Press, 1966.

Simmons, T. F., ed. *The Lay Folk's Mass Book*. Early English Text Society. Oxford: Oxford University Press, 1879.

Slack, Paul. *Poverty and Policy in Tudor and Stuart England*. London: Longman, 1988.

Smith, Bruce R. *Ancient Scripts and Modern Experience on the English Stage 1500–1700*. Princeton, NJ: Princeton University Press, 1988.

Sokolowski, Robert. *Moral Action*. Bloomington: Indiana University Press, 1985.

Soni, Vivasvan. "Introduction: The Crisis of Judgment." *Eighteenth Century: Theory and Interpretation* 51, no. 3 (2010): 261–88.

Stallworthy, Jon, ed. *The Poems of Wilfrid Owen*. New York: W. W. Norton, 1986.

Standish, Paul. "Democratic Participation in the Body Politic." *Educational Theory* 55 no. 4 (2005): 371–84.

Streete, Adrian. "The Politics of Ethical Presentism: Appropriation, Spirituality, and the Case of *Antony and Cleopatra*." *Textual Practice* 22 (2008): 405–31.

Tacitus, Cornelius. *Annals*. Vol. 15. Trans. A. J. Woodman. Indianapolis, IN: Hackett, 2004.

Tanner, Tony. *Prefaces to Shakespeare*. Cambridge, MA: Harvard University Press, 2010.

Taylor, Charles. "Cross-Purposes: The Liberal-Communitarian Debate." In *Philosophical Arguments*. Cambridge, MA: Harvard University Press, 1995.

Taylor, Charles. *The Explanation of Behaviour*. London: Routledge and Kegan Paul, 1980.

Taylor, Charles. "Iris Murdoch and Moral Philosophy." In *Iris Murdoch and the Search for Human Goodness*, ed. Maria Antonaccio and William Schweiker. Chicago: University of Chicago Press, 1996.

Taylor, Charles. *Philosophical Papers: Human Agency and Language*. Vol. 1. Cambridge: Cambridge University Press, 1985.

Taylor, Craig. *Moralism: A Study of a Vice*. Montreal: McGill-Queen's University Press, 2012.

Taylor, Gary, and Michael Warren, eds. *The Division of the Kingdom: Shakespeare's Two Versions of* King Lear. Oxford: Oxford University Press, 1983.

Tennenhouse, Len. "*Coriolanus*: History and the Crisis of Semantic Order." *Comparative Drama* 10 (1977): 328–46.

Viefhues-Bailey, Ludger. *Beyond the Philosopher's Fear: A Cavellian Reading of Gender, Origin and Religion in Modern Skepticism*. London: Routledge, 2007.

Virgil. *Eclogues, Georgics, Aeneid I–VI*. Loeb Classical Library, trans. H. Rushton Fairclough, rev. G. P. Goold. Cambridge, MA: Harvard University Press, 1999.

Virgil. *The Aeneid*. Trans. Robert Fagles. Hammondsworth: Penguin, 2006.

Walker, Jarrett. "Voiceless Bodies, Bodiless Voices: The Drama of Human Perception in *Coriolanus*." *Shakespeare Quarterly* 43 (1992): 170–85.

Wallace, John. "*Timon of Athens* and the Three Graces: Shakespeare's Senecan Study." *Modern Philology* 83, no. 4 (1986): 349–63.

Walsham, Alexandra. *Charitable Hatred: Tolerance and Intolerance in England 1500–1700*. Manchester: Manchester University Press, 2008.
Weil, Simone. *Gravity and Grace*. Trans. Emma Crawford and Mario von der Ruhr. London: Routledge, 1952.
Weil, Simone. "Human Personality." In *Simone Weil: An Anthology*, ed. Sian Miles. New York: Grove, 1986.
Weil, Simone. "The *Iliad* or the Poem of Force." Trans. and ed. James P. Holoka. New York: Peter Lang, 2006.
Weil, Simone. *The Need for Roots*. Trans. A. F. Wills. London: Routledge, 1978.
Weil, Simone, and Rachel Bespaloff. *War and the* Iliad. Trans. Mary McCarthy. New York: New York Review of Books, 2005.
Wells, Stanley, and Gary Taylor. *William Shakespeare: A Textual Companion*. New York: W. W. Norton, 1997.
Wetzel, James. "A Meditation on Hell." In *Parting Knowledge: Essays After Augustine*. Eugene, OR: Cascade, 2013.
Whittington, Leah. *Renaissance Suppliants: Poetry, Antiquity, Reconciliation*. Oxford: Oxford University Press, 2016.
Williams, Rowan. *Lost Icons: Reflections on Cultural Bereavement*. Edinburgh: T&T Clark, 2000.
Wilson, Thomas. *A Discourse on Usury*. New York: Harcourt Brace, 1925.
Winch, Peter. "*Eine Einstellung zur Seele*." In *Trying to Make Sense*. Oxford: Basil Blackwell, 1987.
Winch, Peter. "How Is Political Authority Possible?" *Philosophical Investigations* 25, no. 1 (2002): 20–32.
Winch, Peter. *The Idea of a Social Science and Its Relevance to Philosophy*. London: Routledge, 1958.
Winch, Peter. "Particularity and Morals." In *Trying to Make Sense*. Oxford: Basil Blackwell, 1987.
Winch, Peter. "Understanding a Primitive Society." In *Rationality: Key Concepts in the Social Sciences*. Ed. B. R. Wilson. Oxford: Blackwell, 1970.
Wittgenstein, Ludwig. *Culture and Value*. Trans. Peter Winch. Ed. G. H. von Wright. Chicago: University of Chicago Press, 1980.
Wittgenstein, Ludwig. *Culture and Value*. Rev. ed. Trans. Peter Winch. Ed. G. H. von Wright and H. Nyman. Rev. A. Pichler. Oxford: Blackwell, 1998.
Wittgenstein, Ludwig. *Lecture on Ethics*. Ed. Ermelinda Di Lascio, D. K. Levy, and Edoardo Zamuner. Oxford: Wiley-Blackwell, 2014.
Wittgenstein, Ludwig. *On Certainty*. Ed. G. E. M. Anscombe and G. H. Wright. New York: Harper & Row, 1969.
Wittgenstein, Ludwig. *Philosophical Investigations: The German Text, with an English Translation*. 4th ed. Trans. and ed. G. E. M. Anscombe, P. M. S. Hacker, and Joachim Schulte. Chichester: Wiley-Blackwell, 2009.
Wittgenstein, Ludwig. *Remarks on the Philosophy of Psychology*. Vol. 1, trans. G. E. M. Anscombe, ed. G. E. M. Anscombe and G. H. von Wright. Oxford: Basil Blackwell, 1980.
Wolf, Susan, and Christopher Grau, eds. *Understanding Love: Philosophy, Film, and Fiction*. Oxford: Oxford University Press, 2014.

Wolfe, Jessica. *Homer and the Question of Strife from Erasmus to Hobbes*. Toronto: University of Toronto Press, 2015.
Wood, Andy. *Faith, Hope, and Charity: English Neighbourhoods, 1500–1640*. Cambridge: Cambridge University Press, 2020.
Woodbridge, Linda. *Vagrancy, Homelessness, and English Renaissance Literature*. Chicago: University of Illinois Press, 2001.
Zalta, Edward N., and Uri Nodelman, eds. *The Stanford Encyclopedia of Philosophy*. https://plato.stanford.edu/. Stanford, CA: Stanford University.
Zamir, Tzachi. "Ethics and Shakespearean Tragedy." In *The Oxford Handbook of Shakespearean Tragedy*, ed. Michael Neill and David Schalkwyck. Oxford: Oxford University Press, 2016.
Zaret, David. *The Heavenly Contract: Ideology and Organization in Pre-revolutionary Puritanism*. Chicago: University of Chicago Press, 1985.
Zerilli, Linda. *A Democratic Theory of Judgment*. Chicago: University of Chicago Press, 2016.
Zimmerman, Susan. *The Early Modern Corpse and Shakespeare's Theater*. Edinburgh: Edinburgh University Press, 2005.

Index

Ab Urbe Condita (Livy), 131
Abel, Lionel, 40
Achilles, 22–25, 137, 139, 146
action, irreversibility of, 100
Actium, Battle of, 169, 176
Adelman, Janet, 151–152, 153, 224n80
Aeneid (Vergil), 22, 23, 24–25, 169
Aeschylus, 24–25
aesthetic judgment, 155–156
Affeldt, Steven G., 34, 35, 216n3, 217n4
"Against Dryness" (Murdoch), 109, 111
Agricola (Tacitus), 136
Akin, Todd, 98
Alcibiades (*Timon of Athens*), 88, 92–93, 197n8
Alexander, Nigel, 42
All's Well That Ends Well (Shakespeare), 178n7, 183n8
Améry, Jean, 58–59, 60
anger
  Aquinas on, 20
  grief and, 14–15, 20–21, 28–29
Annals (Tacitus), 172
Anscombe, Elizabeth, 102
Antony (*Antony and Cleopatra*), 157–161, 162–164, 166–170, 171, 172–175
Antony and Cleopatra (Shakespeare)
  chronology and, 216n2
  as critique of judgment, 4–5
  Hamlet and, 16
  Hunter on, 6
  inclusion of, 3
  judgment in, 149–152, 154, 157, 160
  modes of talking in, 158–161
  opening scene of, 148
  relationships in, 161–171
  suicide in, 171–173
  titles of wife and husband in, 161–162
  uncertainty in, 152
  world in, 158–159
Apologie for Poetry (Sidney), 26
Aquinas, Thomas, 20, 45–46, 87–88, 102

Arendt, Hannah, 5, 7, 49, 100, 130, 135, 150, 154, 191n20, 200n26, 209–210n30, 211n43
Aristotle, 20, 50, 77, 82
As You Like It (Shakespeare), 183n8
asking, act of, 121
Auden, W. H., 26
Augustine, 45, 65, 66, 106, 197n1, 211n38, 211n43
Augustus, 225n6
Austin, J. L., 9, 11, 28, 48–50, 51, 94–95, 132, 178n7, 197n3, 217n4
authority, speech acts and, 49–50

Backström, Joel, 191–192n25
Baier, Annette, 82
Barclay, John, 81, 197n1
Barton, Anne, 171
Beale, Simon Russell, 64
behaviorism, 209n24
Bennett, Edward, 115–116
Berger, John, 97, 143–144, 146, 177n5
Bernstein, Jay, 19, 32, 60, 204n59
Bespaloff, Rachel, 23–24, 139
betrayal, 82, 83–84
Bible citations
  1 Corinthians, 69
  Luke, 74
  Revelation, 84, 161, 173–174, 176
  Romans, 52
binding concepts, 3, 8
Biron (*Love's Labor's Lost*), 51–52
Blake, William, 52
bonds
  in *Coriolanus*, 73
  in *Cymbeline*, 72
  fragility of, 178n7
  in *King Lear*, 72, 73
  in *The Merchant of Venice*, 72
  speech acts and, 95
  in *Timon of Athens*, 70–71, 72–78

INDEX

in *Twelfth Night*, 71-72
in *The Winter's Tale*, 73
Bono, Barbara J., 152, 226n17
Book of Common Prayer, 19, 52
Bossy, John, 190n13
Boyd, Michael, 113-114
Braden, Gordon, 222n55, 231n71
Brockbank, Philip, 221n48
Brower, Reuben, 22, 222n54
Bullough, Geoffrey, 142, 163, 229n55
burial rites, 19
Burnaby, John, 66
Bushnell, Rebecca, 172

Caesar, 148, 159, 173, 175-176
Caius Martius Coriolanus, 120, 121-126, 128-130, 133-135, 136, 138-143
Calasso, Roberto, 20
Calderwood, James, 101-102
Cambridge Statute of Labourers (1388), 57
Camus, Albert, 171
Canovan, Margaret, 207n8
Cantor, Paul, 129
"Captivating Pictures" (Affeldt), 34
Carlisle, Claire, 230n61
Carroll, William, 194n54
Cascardi, Anthony, 48, 180n22
Caveat for Common Cursitors, A (Harman), 55-56
Cavell, Stanley
  Affeldt and, 34
  on asides, 190n8
  Austin and, 48, 50, 94, 95
  on being human, 117
  on convention, 220-221n39
  on *Coriolanus*, 142, 223n69
  on counting, 220n37
  on genre, 198n11
  on grief, 20
  humanity and, 97
  judgment and, 9, 150, 154, 155-157
  Kant and, 5
  on *King Lear*, 45, 47, 53, 54, 59
  language and, 6, 7
  moral argument and, 11
  on moral claims, 94
  on moralist, 225n4
  on outcast, 54
  private linguist and, 127-128, 129, 219n20

on promising, 201-202n42, 216n4
remarriage comedies and, 160-161
on Shakespeare as playwright, 10
speech acts and, 48-49, 50
on Wittgenstein, 132-133, 212n50, 217n4, 219n19
Chapman, George, 146, 186n49
charity, 45-46, 51-59
Churchill, Caryll, 182n42
Cicero, 148
Cinthio, Giraldi, 163
City of God (Augustine), 45
Claim of Reason, The (Cavell), 9, 34, 94, 127, 132, 156
Clark, Helen, 222n59
Clark, Max Stafford, 11
Claudius (*Hamlet*), 16-17, 18-19, 21, 29, 30, 31, 33, 42
Cleopatra (*Antony and Cleopatra*), 148-149, 157-159, 161-165, 166-168, 169-172, 173-176
Coles, Romand, 75
Comedy of Errors, The (Shakespeare), 183n8
Common Liar, The (Adelman), 151-152
Commons Petition Against Vagrants (1376), 57
Conant, James, 153, 157
conceptual amnesia, 109-110
conceptual loss, Diamond on, 177-178n5
Condell, Henry, 70
confession, 36
Confutation of Tyndale's Answer (More), 52
Contesting Tears (Cavell), 161
conversation, reciprocity and, 164-165
Cordelia (*King Lear*), 47, 50-51, 58, 60-66, 72
Cordner, Christopher, 225-226n8
Coriolanus (Shakespeare)
  Antony and Cleopatra and, 227n40
  asking in, 121-126
  bonds in, 73
  collectives in, 133-134
  dating of, 120
  De Beneficiis (Seneca) and, 78
  deathly force in, 208n17
  force in, 134-138
  Hamlet and, 16
  hand-holding in, 139-140, 141-143
  Hunter on, 6
  inclusion of, 3
  judgment and, 150

politics and, 130–131, 134–135
private linguist and, 4
reciprocity and, 139–140
supplication in, 138–139, 140–141, 144
tears and, 143–147
"voice" in, 130–134
warrior and, 136–137
covenantal theology, 72, 199n17
Cranmer, 52
Crassons, Kate, 56–57
criteria versus rules, 156–157
Critique of the Power of Judgment (Kant), 154–155
Culture and Value (Wittgenstein), 180–181n28
Cymbeline (Shakespeare), 6, 72, 120, 178n7

Danby, John, 150, 151, 152, 153, 154, 160
Daniel, Samuel, 163
Dante, 105
Dawson, Anthony B., 197–198n8
Day, William, 180–181n28
De Beneficiis (Seneca), 74–75, 78–82, 86–87
"deed," use of in *Macbeth*, 99
dehumanization, 99, 138
Dekker, Thomas, 56
Dench, Judi, 106
Derrida, Jacques, 81
"Dialectic of Perspective, The" (Conant), 153
Dialogue Against Heresies, 52
Diamond, Cora, 2, 5, 6, 7, 9, 19–20, 59, 67, 99, 109–110, 116, 178n6
Dickinson, Emily, 106
Dirisu, Sope, 144
Discourses on Livy (Machiavelli), 131
Doran, Gregory, 144, 145, 205n74, 223n65
Doran, Madeleine, 160
Doty, Mark, 214n76
Duffy, Eamon, 19

Eagleton, Terry, 95
Eichmann in Jerusalem (Arendt), 211n43
Eldridge, Richard, 157, 219n19
Eliot, George, 230n61
Erasmus, 26, 78
ethics, Wittgenstein on, 8–9
Eucharist, 203n51
Euripides, 26–27, 28, 29, 32

evil, conceptions of, 111
exile, linguistic, 5, 6, 8

fatalism, 40
fear, in *Macbeth*, 114
Fear of Beggars, The (Johnson), 55
Felski, Rita, 181n37
Fermor, Una Ellis, 197n8
Fiddes, Paul, 66
Findlay, Polly, 115
fine, puns on, 37–38
Fingarette, Herbert, 105
Fink, Hans, 203n56
1 Corinthians, 69
Fish, Stanley, 126, 217n4, 220–221n39
flattery, 47, 48
Flavius (*Timon of Athens*), 88–92
Forsberg, Niklas, 51, 67, 109–110, 210n34
Fortunate Man, A (Berger), 143–144
Friedlander, Eli, 44
Frost, Robert, 20
Fulvia (*Antony and Cleopatra*), 167–168

Gaita, Raimond, 9, 107, 108, 111–112, 179n21, 183–184n11, 207n12, 207n13, 224n75, 225n4
Galloway, Andrew, 88
Garnier, Robert, 163
Gaskill, Bill, 11
generosity, 75
gifts
    Derrida on, 81
    Seneca on, 79–81, 86–87
    slaves and, 86–87
    in *Timon of Athens*, 4, 89–90
gifts, obligations of, 74–75
Gloucester (*King Lear*), 53–54, 56, 59–60
Golding, Arthur, 78, 79
Good and Evil: An Absolute Conception (Gaita), 111
Goux, Jean-Joseph, 202n43
grace, 65
Graham, Kenneth, 47
gratitude, 80, 81, 87–88
Greenblatt, Stephen, 19
grief
    anger and, 14–15, 20–21, 28–29
    classical precedents for, 20–29
    in *Hamlet*, 3, 16–19, 20
    language related to, 14, 15
    revenge and, 25–26

254   INDEX

grievance, 14, 15, 20, 21, 22, 37
Griffin, Miriam, 78
Gross, Kenneth, 224n80

Hamlet (Shakespeare)
    action and, 109
    Aeneid and, 22
    anger in, 21
    Claudius's opening speech in,
        16–17, 19
    grief in, 3, 15–19, 20, 27–29, 36–37
    Hecuba and, 27–28
    inclusion of, 3
    last scenes of, 36–43
    speech as action in, 12–13, 33–36
    spying in, 30–31
    use of "truster" in, 204n61
Hare, David, 182n42
Harman, Thomas, 55–56
Heal, Felicity, 201n38
Hecuba, 23, 25, 26–29, 32
Hecuba (Euripides), 26–27, 28, 29
Hegel, George Wilhelm Friedrich, 19
Heminge, John, 70
Hertzberg, Lars, 112
Hobbesian psychology, 32–33
Holland, Peter, 140, 146
Holland, R. F., 207n13
Homer, 22–24, 186n49
Hooker, Richard, 17
hope, 96
Horace, 148, 176
Houston, Will, 223n65
How to Do Things with Words (Austin), 94
"human"
    scare quotes and, 97–98
    Shakespeare on, 99
"Human Abstract, The" (Blake), 52
human actions, 102, 108, 116
human agency, 200n26
Human Condition, The (Arendt), 100
"Human Personality" (Weil), 59
Hunter, G. K., 5–6
hyperbole, 160

Iliad (Homer), 22–24, 134, 136–138, 139,
    140, 146, 186n49
impropriety of action, 46
Inferno (Dante), 105
ingratitude, 80, 81–82
Intentions (Anscombe), 102

interpretative communities, 220n39
interpretative skepticism, 10
Inwood, Brad, 78

James, Heather, 223n72
Johnson, Kelly, 55
Johnson, Samuel, 164
Joint Stock Theatre Company, 11
Jones, Emrys, 229n53
Jowett, John, 197n6, 197–198n8, 198n9
judgment
    aesthetic, 155–156
    in *Antony and Cleopatra*, 149–152, 154,
        157, 160
    critique of, 4–5
    Kant on, 154–155
    moralized, 149
    subjectivity and, 154
Julius Caesar (Shakespeare), 70

Kahn, Victoria, 199n17
Kant, Immanuel, 4–5, 154–155,
    174, 175
Kerrigan, John, 198n12
King Jaspar (Robinson), 20
King Lear (Shakespeare)
    bonds in, 73
    chronology and, 216n2
    De Beneficiis (Seneca) and, 78
    failures of recognition in, 90
    Hamlet and, 16
    Hunter on, 5–6
    inclusion of, 3–4
    judgment and, 150
    language and, 3
    love in, 44–46, 47, 48, 51, 53–54,
        60–68
    outcasts and, 54–59
    speech acts in, 46–48
    torture and, 59–60
Klein, Karl, 205n74
Kornqvist, Camilla, 196n85
Kottman, Paul, 198n11, 198n12
Kyd, Thomas, 29, 35

Lady Macbeth, 106–109
Langland, William, 56–57
language
    agreements and, 7
    conceptual life and, 177–178n5
    grief and, 14, 15

INDEX   255

King Lear and, 3–4, 48
   ordinary language philosophy and, 11, 67, 155–156, 157, 181n32, 217n4
   private linguist and, 126–130, 132
   reality/representation and, 67–68
   Timon of Athens and, 4
   Wittgenstein and, 6, 9–10
   See also speech acts
Laugier, Sandra, 128, 132, 227n35
Lay Folk's Mass Book, The, 52
Lear, Johnathan, 202n46
Lectures on Ethics (Wittgenstein), 8
Levi, Primo, 105
Libation Bearers, The (Aeschylus), 24–25
Life of Caius Martius Coriolanus, The (Plutarch), 139–140
linguistic phenomenology, 50
Lipsius, Justus, 78
Livy, 131
Lodge, Thomas, 78
Lofgren, Ingeborg, 10, 181n37
logic of action, *Macbeth* and, 4
Løgstrup, Knud Ejler, 83
Long, Michael, 224n80
"Losing Your Concepts" (Diamond), 2, 109
love
   charity and, 51–54
   in *King Lear*, 44–46, 47, 48, 51, 53–54, 60–68
   Mitchell on, 1, 2
   Murdoch on, 3
"Love and Art in *Antony and Cleopatra*" (Ornstein), 162
Love's Labor's Lost (Shakespeare), 51–52
Luckyj, Christina, 223n73
Luke, 74
Lupset, Thomas, 53
Lyne, Raphael, 223n68

M. Antoine (Garnier), 230n60
Macbeth (Shakespeare)
   action and agency in, 100–106, 112–113
   chronology and, 216n2
   conceptual amnesia and, 109–110
   Duncan's murder in, 100
   Hamlet and, 16
   Hunter on, 6
   inclusion of, 3
   logic of action in, 4

   pity in, 117–118
   remorse in, 99, 106–109, 112–113, 116
Macduff (*Macbeth*), 113–116
Machiavelli, Niccolo, 131
MacIntyre, Alasdair, 102, 177n5, 203n56
Mann, Michael, 135
Margalit, Avishai, 83–84
Markell, Patchen, 182n45, 191n19
marriage, in *Antony and Cleopatra*, 161–165, 167
Marriage Question, The (Carlisle), 230n61
Marx, Karl, 70, 177n5
master-slave relations, 86–87
Matthewes, Charles, 106
Mauss, Marcel, 74, 81
McDonald, Russ, 227n40
McKellen, Ian, 211n44
Measure for Measure (Shakespeare), 150
Melanchthon, Philip, 26
Mendes, Sam, 58, 64
Menenius (*Coriolanus*), 124–125, 130, 137, 138, 139, 142
Mercer, Peter, 188n80
Merchant of Venice, The (Shakespeare), 72, 150
Metamorphoses (Ovid), 26, 28
Middleton, Thomas, 71
Milosz, Czeslaw, 117
Milton, John, 160, 211n42
Minding the Modern (Pfau), 109
Minton, Gretchen E., 197–198n8
Miola, Robert, 129
mistrust/distrust, 31–33
Mitchell, Joni, 1, 2
Moi, Toril, 10–11, 189–190n6
moral philosophy, evil and, 111
moral questions/claims, 9–10
Moran, Richard, 32
More, Thomas, 52–53
Mossman, Judith, 26
mourning
   ceremonies of, 17, 19–20
   in *Hamlet*, 16–18, 19
   Hecuba and, 26–27
   transformations in, 19
   See also grief
Much Ado About Nothing (Shakespeare), 183n8
Munro, Lucy, 224n80
Murdoch, Iris, 3, 9, 48, 53, 109, 111, 113, 177n5, 178n6

INDEX

Muret, Marc Antoine, 78
Must We Mean What We Say? (Cavell), 48, 156
Myth of Sisyphus, The (Camus), 171

naming actions, 105
Neill, Michael, 19, 164
Nicomachean Ethics (Aristotle), 20
Nunn, Trevor, 211n44
Nussbaum, Martha, 21, 28, 29
Nuttall, Anthony, 71–72

O per se O (Dekker), 56
Octavia, 162, 164, 174
Oedipus, 214n79
"On Mercy" (Seneca), 138
On Violence (Arendt), 135
"One More Day" (Milosz), 117
I Henry IV (Shakespeare), 14
Ophelia (*Hamlet*), 30–32, 34, 36, 38–39
ordinary language philosophy, 11, 67, 155–156, 157, 181n32, 217n4
Oresteia (Aeschylus), 24–25
Ornstein, Robert, 162
outcasts, 54–59
Ovid, 26, 28

Parker, Brian, 140
Paster, Gail Kern, 129
Pennington, Michael, 205n74
Peperzak, Adriaan, 202–203n50
Pericles (Shakespeare), 6, 178n7
perspective, 153–158
Pfau, Thomas, 109, 226n10
Philosophical Investigations (Wittgenstein), 6, 8, 32, 34, 107, 120, 126, 129, 143, 156
Piers Plowman (Langland), 56–57
Pinches, Charles R., 209n25
pity, 107, 117–118, 143
Plutarch
    Antony and Cleopatra and, 158, 161, 162, 163, 164, 168
    Coriolanus and, 124, 134–135, 139–140, 141–142, 145, 147
Pollard, Tanya, 26
Polonius (*Hamlet*), 26, 30–31, 32, 34, 36, 39
poor law legislation, 57
Poor Tom (*King Lear*), 55, 56, 58
Pope, Alexander, 190n7
Porter, Charlotte, 222n59
poverty, charity and, 54–59
Priam, 22–27, 39, 139

private linguist, 4, 120, 126–130, 132, 219n20
promises/promising, 32, 216n3
Pursuits of Happiness (Cavell), 160, 198n11

Rawls, John, 202n42, 214n74, 216n3
reality, difficulty of, 67
recognition, failures of, 90–91
reconciliation, 5–6
Reformation, 65
remarriage comedies, 160–161
remorse, in *Macbeth*, 99, 106–109, 112–113, 116
"Remorse" (Dickinson), 106
Revelation, 84, 161, 173–174, 176
revenge, 14–15, 20–22, 25–28, 29, 33, 36–37, 41, 188n80
Rhu, Lawrence, 225n2
Richard III (Shakespeare), 99
Robinson, Edwin Arlington, 20
Romans, 52
Romeo and Juliet (Shakespeare), 70
Romulus My Father (Gaita), 9
Rossiter, A. P., 220n33
Rowe, Nicholas, 65, 92
Royal Shakespeare Company, 113–114, 144
rules versus criteria, 156–157

Sassall, John, 143–144
satire, 71, 188n80
scare quotes, 97, 98
Schein, Seth L., 185n32
Schwartz, Regina, 77, 204n59
Searle, John, 217n4
self-deception, 104–105
self-knowledge, 157
Seneca, 26, 27, 74–75, 78–82, 84–85, 86–87, 138, 172
Settlement Acts (1662), 57
"Shakespeare's Last Tragic Heroes" (Hunter), 5–6
Shield of Achilles, The (Auden), 26
Sidney, Philip, 26
skepticism, 6–7, 10, 31, 95
Slack, Paul, 57
slaves, gifts and, 86–87
social contract theory, 204n59
Soni, Vivasvan, 152, 154, 226n10
Sovereignty of Good, The (Murdoch), 9
Spanish Tragedy, The (Kyd), 25–26
speech act theory, 126, 217n4

speech acts
    actors and, 11–13
    in *Coriolanus*, 120–121
    description of, 7
    in *Hamlet*, 16, 32, 33–34
    judgment and, 157
    in *King Lear*, 46–49, 50, 51
    trust and, 94–95
    See also language
stoicism, 172, 173
suicide, in *Antony and Cleopatra*, 171–173
Summa Theologica (Aquinas), 87, 102
suspicion, 31

Tacitus, 136, 172
talking, modes of, 158–161
Tanner, Tony, 24–25, 64, 101, 229n51
Taylor, Charles, 41, 164–165, 182n45
Taylor, Craig, 226n9
Taylor, Neil, 27
tears/crying, 143–147
telling, speech act of, 33–36
Tempest, The (Shakespeare), 6
testimony, idea of, 36
"Texts of Recovery" (Cavell), 20
thick relations, 83–84
Thompson, Ann, 27
"Three Ways of Spilling Ink" (Austin), 50
Timon of Athens (Shakespeare)
    bonds in, 72–73
    De Beneficiis (Seneca) and, 78
    despair and, 96
    gift and debt in, 4
    Hamlet and, 16
    human bonds and, 69–70
    Hunter on, 6
    inclusion of, 3
    language and, 4
    placement of in first folio, 70–71
    rhetoric of "all" in, 88–93
    Seneca and, 81–82
    servants in, 85–88
    trust and betrayal in, 82–84
torture, 58–60
Tractatus-Logico-Philosophicus
    (Wittgenstein), 158
Tragedie of Cleopatra, The (Daniel), 230n60
Tragic Conditions (Kottman), 198n12
Treatise on Human Acts, The (Aquinas), 209n24

Troades (Seneca), 26
Troilus and Cressida (Shakespeare), 70–71, 150
Trojan Women, The (Euripides), 26, 27
trust, 32–33, 60, 82–84, 95
Twelfth Night (Shakespeare), 71, 183n8
Tyndale, William, 52–53

unboundedness, *Coriolanus* and, 120
universal voice, 156
usury, 200n31

Vergil, 22, 23, 24–25, 37, 148, 176
Volumnia (*Coriolanus*), 125–126, 134–135, 136, 137–138, 139–143, 146, 224n78

Walker, Jarrett, 141
Wallace, John, 200n25
Weil, Simone, 23, 47, 59, 134, 136–138, 140
Wetzel, James, 195n76, 211n38
Whittington, Leah, 138, 185n33, 186n36
Wilders, John, 154
Williams, Rowan, 108–109, 212n51
Winch, Peter, 32, 67
Winter's Tale, The (Shakespeare), 6, 14, 73, 160, 175, 183n8
Wittgenstein, Ludwig
    Cavell and, 6, 157
    convention and, 178n7, 217n4
    ethics and, 8–9
    investigation of concepts and, 189n4
    language and, 10, 65–66
    on loss of concepts, 110
    on pity, 107, 118, 143
    private linguist and, 4, 120, 126–130, 132, 219n20
    on rules, 156
    speech acts and, 34
    on trust, 82
    trust and, 32
    working on oneself and, 2
    on world, 158
Wolfe, Jessica, 146
Woodbridge, Linda, 56
Woodvine, John, 205n74
working on oneself, 1–2
Wright, Georg Henrik von, 180n28

Zamir, Tzachi, 188n81

www.ingramcontent.com/pod-product-compliance
Lightning Source LLC
Chambersburg PA
CBHW031347230426
43670CB00006B/455